Glasgow Uncovered

Eighteen Walks through its Past, Present and Future

Colin M. Drysdale

Pictish Beast Publications

Text Copyright © 2024 Colin M. Drysdale

Imprint And Layout Copyright © 2025 Colin M. Drysdale/Pictish Beast Publications

All rights reserved. No part of this book shall be reproduced, stored in a retrieval system, or transmitted by any means, electronic, mechanical, photocopying, recording, or otherwise without permission from the author(s). Although every precaution has been taken in the preparation of this book, the publisher and the author(s) assume no responsibility for errors or omissions.

Paperback Edition ISBN 978-1-909832-89-3

Published by Pictish Beast Publications, Glasgow, UK

Printed in the United Kingdom

First Edition 2025

Also available as an electronic book

Background data for the maps provided in this book are © OpenStreetMap (www.openstreetmap.org/copyright) and were used under the Open Database Licence.

All photographs and other images included in this book (including the maps showing the routes and the points of interest for the individual walks) are @ Colin M. Drysdale.

Cover image © Colin M. Drysdale

Contents

Preface	iii
Introduction	1

Glasgow City Centre and the Clyde

1. Buchanan Street and St Enoch Square	7
2. Merchant City	24
3. Sauchiehall Street, Part I	38
4. City Centre West	51
5. Anderston and Argyle Street	69
6. Clyde Waterfront	88

West and North of Glasgow

7. Sauchiehall Street, Part II	103
8. West End, Part I	115
9. West End, Part II	130
10. Forth and Clyde Canal and Maryhill	146

East of Glasgow

11. High Street, Townhead and Old Glasgow	163
12. Alexandra Parade and Dennistoun	182
13. Bridgeton, the Calton and Glasgow Green	196

Southside of Glasgow

14. Hutchesontown, the Gorbals and Laurieston	217
15. Tradeston and Kingston	230
16. Govan	241
17. Queen's Park, Mount Florida, Crosshill and Govanhill	255
18. Pollokshields, Strathbungo and Shawlands	267

Additional Resources	280
Index	282

Preface

This book grew out of a social media account I started in 2020. This was during the COVID pandemic when travelling to my usual walking haunts outside the city was no longer possible. As a result, I started walking around the city itself, first in my local neighbourhood and then, when allowed, further afield. This took me to places I had either not visited in many years, or that I had never visited before, and I soon developed a new appreciation of many areas of the city which I had previously taken very much for granted. Being a keen photographer, I also started taking pictures of the city's buildings, sculptures, bridges and any anything else which caught my interest, and shared these online as *This Is My Glasgow*.

I had never really expected anyone else to be particularly interested in them, but I soon found there was a surprisingly wide audience for pictures of Glasgow, especially of its buildings and information about their history. This then led to me not just photographing buildings, but to learning more about the architects who designed them, the purposes for which they were built and their social history. From this, I developed a much deeper appreciation for a city where I had spent most of my life, but of which, I quickly realised, I had barely scratched the surface. In addition, I also found there was a thriving community of social media accounts dedicated to Glasgow's past and its built heritage. Through this, my interest in my home city deepened even further, and eventually led to the creation of this book. If you would like to follow any of these social media accounts (and I would heartily recommend doing so), there is a selection of the ones I personally find interesting in the Additional Resources section at the end of the book.

In *Glasgow Uncovered*, I aim to share a lot of the knowledge I have gained about Glasgow in the last few years, and to inspire others to learn more about a city which is full of beautiful buildings, stunning street art, surprising histories, strange tales and a breadth of architecture which has to be seen to be believed.

Introduction

This book contains eighteen walks which you can take around Glasgow to explore its past, present and future. As well as looking at the city's amazing and surprisingly diverse architecture, it also considers many aspects of the city's social history, its place in the world and how this has changed over time, alongside its current status and culture, and where it might go in the future. These walks cover a total of 74 kilometres (46 miles), and visit sites ranging from Iron Age earthworks through medieval buildings, Georgian mansions, Victorian factories, neo-Greek temples, the world's first sea-to-sea canal, a cemetery built on the remains of an extinct volcano, Glasgow style tenements, Gothic university buildings, modernist churches and many of the other features that help make Glasgow a truly unique to city live in and to visit. From these sites, you will learn about Glasgow's origins, how it developed over time, where its wealth came from, what industries drove its growth and how its fortunes have waxed and waned over the centuries.

The walks vary in length and difficulty, but all of them can be completed by anyone with a reasonable level of fitness. Where possible, routes have been selected to make them as accessible as possible, but as might be expected when exploring a city which was largely developed in the Georgian and Victorian Eras, there are some walks where steep hills and stairs cannot easily be avoided. Such potential issues are highlighted in the introduction to those walks. The location of the start and end points of each walk are provided in a number of formats which you can enter into any mapping app to help you find them. Maps of the routes for each walk are provided within this book.

The description for each walk starts with details of the start and end points, information about the nearest public transport links, its length and estimated duration, and information about what facilities are available along the route. It then provides a brief introduction to the general area it will cover, and maps showing the route which will be taken and the locations which will be visited. Finally, there is detailed information about each of thirty to sixty locations of interest which will be passed during the walk. Not every interesting building or structure you pass will be mentioned, and you will find some suggested resources at the end of the book to help you learn more about anything which catches your interest, but which is not covered in the accompanying text. In addition, Glasgow is a relatively dynamic city and things change on a regular basis. This means you may find that, even though the information was correct at the time of publication, certain features or buildings might not be quite as described in this book by the time you come to visit them, or may have disappeared completely.

What To Take With You When Doing These Walks

For each walk you should make sure you are wearing comfortable shoes which you can walk in for several hours. In addition, the weather in Glasgow can be rather changeable, so you cannot guarantee it will stay the same for the duration of any walk, even the shorter ones. As a result, it is advisable to take a rain jacket with you, as well as a sunhat and sunglasses. If the introduction to the walk states that refreshments are not readily available along the way, make sure you take a snack or two and something to drink. If you have them, it is also worth taking a pair of binoculars as many of Glasgow's buildings have details on them which are high above street level, but which are nonetheless interesting to examine in detail. Similarly, if you have one, it is always worth taking a camera so you can take photos of the buildings you see and anything else which sparks your interest. It is also advisable to take a small amount of cash with you as some areas have very few banks and it is not unusual for smaller shops to have a minimum spend limit for debit/credit cards. Finally, make sure that you take your copy of this book with you, so you can know where you are going and read about the different locations you will be visiting.

Respecting People's Privacy

The routes for the walks provided in this book are solely along public roads and pathways. However, many of the buildings you will pass are private buildings and a number of them are people's homes. As a result, please respect the privacy of the owners and users of the buildings you visit, both in terms of the places you go and the photographs you take. In particular, please do not venture off a given route into any areas marked as 'private', into fenced-off gardens, up or down steps towards the front doors of private buildings or into tenement closes. Similarly, do not take photographs directly into people's windows or of any private areas, and please be respectful of what you include in any pictures you take. In particular, do not take photos of school buildings when children are present or of religious buildings during services of religious observance.

Personal Safety

In general, Glasgow is a safe and friendly city, but as with any large city, you still need to keeps your wits about you. By far the greatest danger you will face is from traffic, so be careful when crossing roads and where possible, only cross at designated places, such pedestrian crossings. In addition, always look both ways before you step out, even if you are sure you have right of way, as bikes, cars and even buses can suddenly appear from quite unexpected directions. Similarly, when taking photos, be aware of your surroundings and make sure you do not step out into traffic while looking up distractedly at any buildings (although this is easier said than done!).

As you would anywhere, keep an eye on your personal possessions and do not leave them unattended at any time. If you get lost, it is generally acceptable to ask people for directions. Even if you only look slightly lost, you may find yourself being offered help even if you do not you actually need it. While visitors sometimes find this a little intimidating, this just the Glasgow way. However, be aware, that while most Glaswegians are more than willing to help someone who is lost, some are, on occasions, so keen to help that they will give you directions regardless of whether or not they actually know how to get to where you want to go.

Finally, Glasgow has a strong and passionate footballing tradition, and on some of the walks, you will pass between areas which are favoured by fans of different clubs. This means that if you are not familiar with Glasgow, it is best to avoid wearing football tops, strips or scarves while doing any of these walks. If you are familiar with Glasgow, you will know what you can and cannot get away with in different areas of the city, so please act accordingly.

General Location Of Each Walk

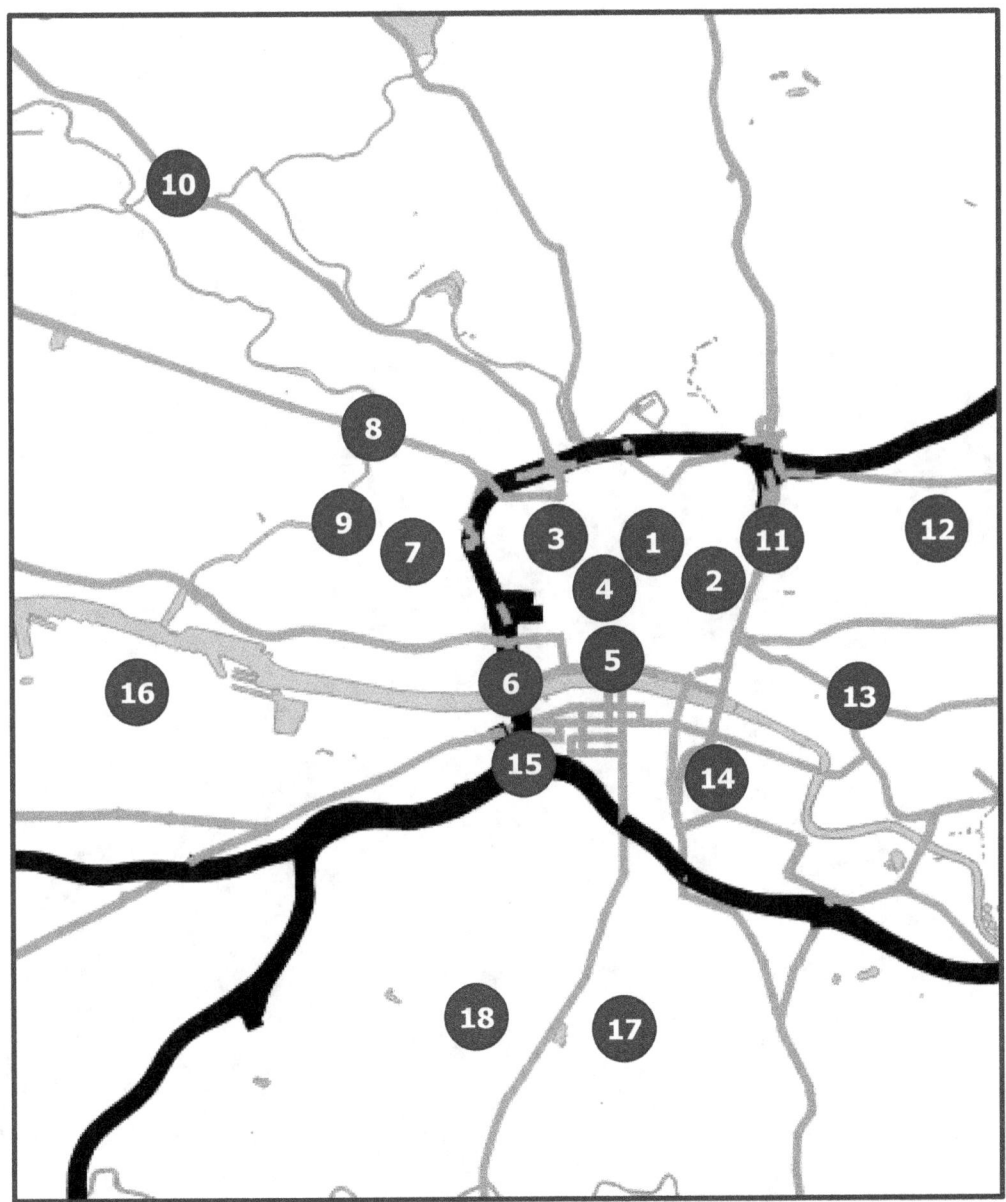

1. Buchana Street; **2.** Merchant City; **3.** Sauchiehall Street Part I; **4.** City Centre West; **5.** Anderston and Argyle Street; **6.** Clyde Waterfront; **7.** Sauchiehall Street Part II; **8.** West End Part I; **9.** West End Part II; **10.** The Forth and Clyde Canal and Maryhill; **11.** High Street, Townhead and Old Glasgow; **12.** Alexandra Parade and Dennistoun; **13.** Bridgeton, The Calton and Glasgow Green; **14.** Hutchesontown, The Gorbals and Laurieston; **15.** Tradeston and Kingston; **16.** Govan; **17.** Queen's Park, Mount Florida, Crosshill and Govanhill; **18.** Pollokshields, Strathbungo and Shawlands.

Glasgow City Centre and the Clyde

1. Buchanan Street and St Enoch Square

Start Point: Donald Dewer Statue, Buchanan Street, Glasgow (**Location:** Lat/Lon: 55.86400, -4.25286 ; What3Words: ///fund.precautions.radar; Plus Code: VP7W+JV2 Glasgow). **Nearest Public Transport:** Subway: Buchanan Street Station (2 mins); Train: Queen Street Station (5 mins); Bus: Buchanan Bus Station (5 mins).

End Point: St Enoch Square, Glasgow (**Location:** Lat/Lon: 55.85730, -4.25530; What3Words: ///fixed.again.deputy; Plus Code: VP4V+WVG Glasgow). **Nearest Public Transport:** Train: Central Station (5 mins); Subway: St Enoch Station (1 min); Bus: Argyle Street (1 min).

Distance: 1.6 kilometres/1 mile. **Time:** Allow 1 to 2 hours for this walk.
Level of Difficulty: Easy. This walk is on relatively flat, paved streets, many of which are pedestrianised.

Facilities: There are a number of shops, cafes, restaurants and bars where you can stop for refreshments along this route. Publicly accessible toilets are available in Buchanan Galleries Shopping Centre at the start of this walk, in Queen Street Station and in the St Enoch Shopping Centre at the end of it.

Introduction

This walk covers Buchanan Street and St Enoch Square (which marks the southern end of Buchanan Street) in the centre of Glasgow. While Buchanan Street is currently Glasgow's main upmarket shopping street, this is an area which has seen its fortunes grow and shrink many times over the years. Buchanan Street was created in the late 1700s and was named after Andrew Buchanan of Buchanan. A former Lord Provost of Glasgow, he was also a North American plantation owner and one of Glasgow's Tobacco Lords, who made their fortune with the aid of African slaves. It was Buchanan who, in 1766, purchased four acres of land which most considered to be too far west of the then centre of Glasgow (which was focussed around High Street further to the east) and used it to build a mansion on the plot now occupied by the House of Fraser at the south-western end of Buchanan Street. However, before he could develop the rest of the street itself, his fortunes were hit, in 1776, by the American War of Independence, and it was not until the 1780s that the development of Buchanan Street began in earnest.

By 1807, the first of what would become many grand buildings was constructed on the new street. This was St George's Church, and it remains a key part of the Buchanan Street streetscape to this day. Not only did Buchanan Street continue to develop throughout the nineteenth century, but so did areas further west, and Buchanan Street can be seen as the dividing line separating the older Merchant City area of Glasgow, which had been growing slowly since the city's inception and the newer, classical Georgian new town of Blythswood to its west, the creation of which was initiated around 1800.

Given its position between these two areas, Buchanan Street was well placed to become a new hub for the expanding city, and many large and imposing buildings were constructed along its length, housing businesses such as banks, theatres, newspapers, department stores and the Glasgow Stock Exchange. Although the businesses which occupy them have changed over the intervening years, many of these buildings still exist, and contribute to the unique and distinctive feel of a street which many would now consider to be the heart of Glasgow.

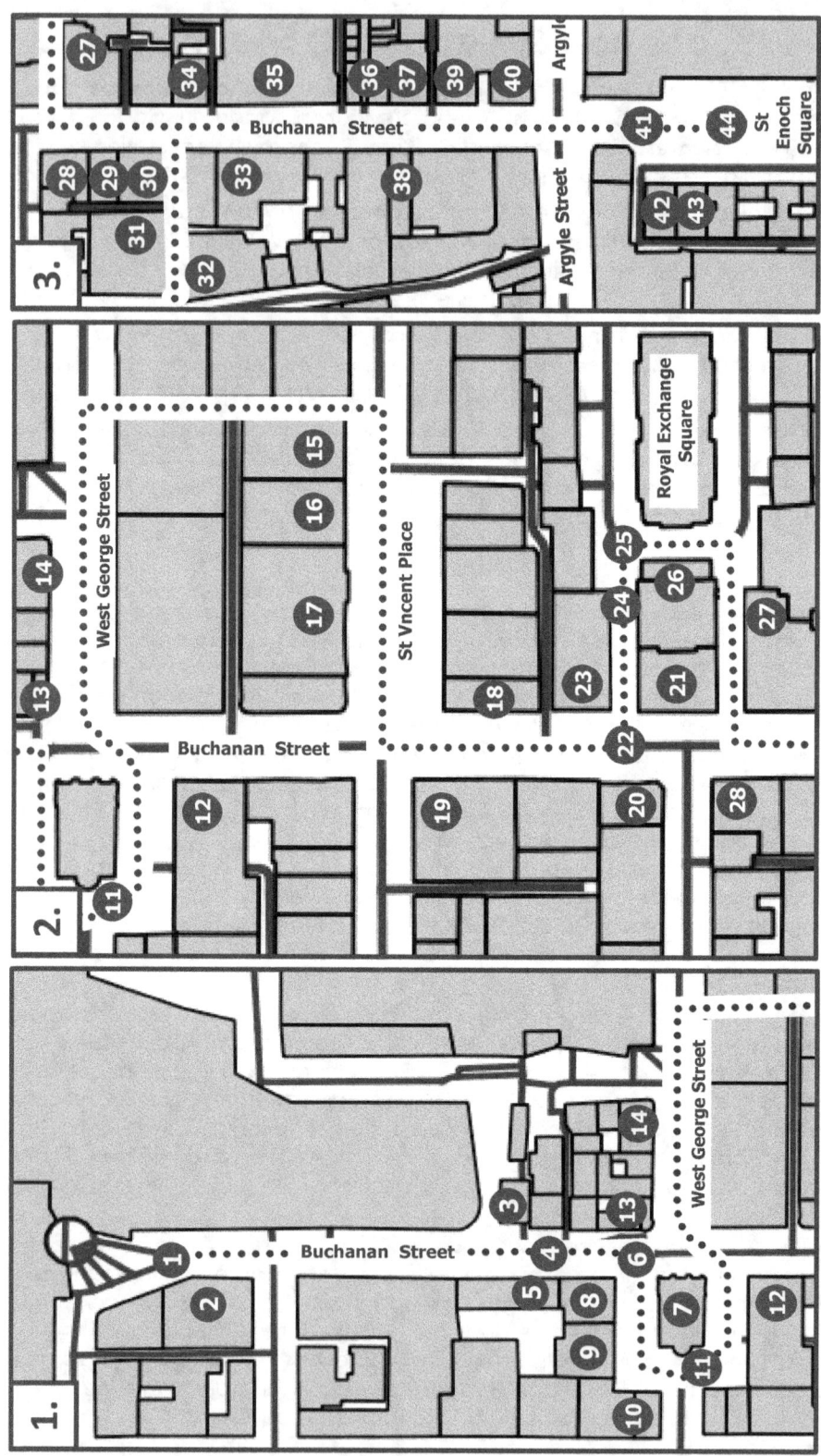

1. This walk starts at the statue of Donald Dewer at the northern end of Buchanan Street. Donald Dewer can be considered the father of devolution in Scotland and its first First Minister when the Scottish Parliament was re-established in 1999. He unexpectedly died the following year. This statue was created by Kenny Mackay and was erected in 2002.

2. On the west side of Buchanan Street just to the south of the Donald Dewer Statue is the former George Hotel. Designed by Neil Duff and built in 1907, it has a rather stylish facade with a recessed bow window around which the building pivots to follow a slight curve in the road. In its day, the George Hotel was one of the main hotels in central Glasgow and its proximity to the nearby railway stations meant it was popular with visiting actors and film stars, such as Stan Laurel, Cary Grant and Joan Crawford. By the 1990s, its former glory had faded away and it was empty apart from some otherwise homeless residents. However, the George Hotel did manage to find a second life as a film location, which included doubling for the London hotel room where Renton and his friends make their drug deal at the end of the film *Trainspotting*. By 2000, it was no longer a hotel and its interior was demolished to make way for retail spaces, leaving the facade as a reminder of its previous grandeur.

Kenny Mackay's statue of Donald Dewer, Buchanan Street, erected 2002.

3. Further down Buchanan Street on the left-hand side, at No. 166, is Dundas House. It was designed by John A. Campbell in a free style, and was built in 1898 for the British Workman's and General Assurance Company. At the time, this type of building was known as an 'elevator building', meaning it was constructed around a central lift shaft rather than stairs, a style imported from the USA. Although this allowed buildings to become taller, it also resulted in them preventing daylight from entering the rooms within the building itself and rooms in the surrounding buildings. The solution to this was to create light wells – open courtyards within the centre of buildings, or blocks of buildings, which were not only lined with windows, but also with white glazed bricks to reflect as much light as possible into them. If you go round the left-hand side of 166 Buchanan Street, you can see where the white bricks of its light well were exposed by the demolition of its neighbouring buildings.

4. In front of 166 Buchanan Street is the entrance to Buchanan Street Subway Station. Opened in 1896, Glasgow's Subway is the third-oldest underground railway system in the world, after the London Underground and the Budapest Metro System. It was also the first mass transit system to be known as a 'subway'. The Glasgow Subway consists of two tracks, each in their own tunnel, running in a 10.5-kilometre (approx. 6.5 miles) closed loop underneath the city's streets, with trains going in opposite directions on each one. This, along with the colour scheme introduced in the 1970s, has led to the system being nicknamed 'the Clockwork Orange'. The fact that the

whole system was underground would have caused a problem if the trains were powered by steam locomotives, as most trains were at the time it was built. Steam locomotives produced huge amounts of smoke, steam and dirt, and there would have been no way for it to escape from the tunnels. The solution to this problem was to situate a power plant containing stationary steam engines in the Tradeston area of the city, which pulled a pair of continuous cables though the tunnels. The trains were fitted with a system which allowed them to grip on to the cable and so be dragged through the tunnels. As a train approached a station, the cable was released allowing it to come to a stop. The cable-based system was used until the subway was converted to electricity in 1935, allowing more traditional train engines to replace the original cable-powered ones. At just over 500 metres (547 yards), the section between Buchanan Street Station and the next station, St Enoch (where this walk ends), is one of the shortest on the whole system and this has resulted in the creation of an extreme sport known as 'the Subway Challenge'. This involves getting off a train at Buchanan Street Station and racing it down Buchanan Street (the track passes directly beneath it) on a bike, in an attempt to reboard the same train at St Enoch Station, at its southern end.

5. Opposite 166 Buchanan Street is No. 179. This was originally home to the Athenaeum Theatre, and it is another of Buchanan Street's tall, skinny elevator buildings designed to make the most of the narrow plot on which it was built. It was designed by John James Burnet and John A. Campbell in an eclectic style, but with Renaissance details, and was constructed in 1891 specifically for training drama students. As such, it contained a theatre, a billiard room, a dining room and a gymnasium. While it is difficult to see from the street, it is topped by an octagonal cupola featuring relief sculptures based on those of the Tower of the Winds, built around 50 BCE in the agora (marketplace) in Athens.

Former Athenaeum Theatre, 176 Buchanan Street, built 1891.

6. Slightly further south down Buchanan Street is the entrance to a street which was originally St George's Place, but is now known as Nelson Mandela Place. In the 1980s, Nelson Mandela was viewed as a terrorist by the British Government (with several members of the then ruling political party calling for the imprisoned leader of the African National Congress to be hanged). In support of the South African anti-apartheid movement, Glasgow City Council not only gave Mandela the freedom of the city in 1981, the first city in the world to do so, but in 1986, they also decided to rename one of the city's streets after him. St George's Place was selected for this honour primarily on the basis that is was then home to the South African Consulate in Glasgow, meaning it would have to use an address containing the name of someone viewed by the South Africa's political establishment of the time as an enemy of the State. It was a small gesture, but also a typically Glaswegian one. After being released from prison in 1990, Nelson Mandela visited Glasgow in 1993 to belatedly receive the freedom of the city in person, and in his acceptance

speech he took the time to thank the people of Glasgow for their stand against apartheid.

7. Standing in the middle of Nelson Mandela Place is the magnificent St George's Tron Church. Topped by a wonderful and distinctive baroque steeple, it was designed by William Stark in 1807, making it one of the oldest buildings still standing on Buchanan Street.

8. Turn west into Nelson Mandela Place, and on its corner with Sauchiehall Street you will find an impressive red sandstone Edwardian baroque style building. This was originally built as the Liberal Club, but it later became the Royal Academy of Music and Drama. It was designed by Alexander N. Paterson and was constructed in 1908. It has a pair of particularly well-sculpted lion heads on the corbels on either side of its door.

Saint George's Tron Church, Nelson Mandela Place.

9. Next to the former Liberal Club is an equally impressive blonde sandstone building designed by John James Burnet and built in 1886. This was the home to the Glasgow Athenaeum, which had started in the Assembly Rooms on Ingram Street in 1847, with the inaugural address being given by Charles Dickens. It moved to this location in 1887, when its original home was demolished. The Athenaeum aimed to provide training not only in commercial skills, but also in philosophy, literature, languages and music. Unusually for the time, both men and women could be members and it was the first Ladies Club in the city. Its facade is decorated with a number of statues created by the famous architectural sculptor John Mossman. Across the top are statues of Mossman's fellow sculptor John Flaxman, the architect Charles Wren, the composer Henry Purcell and painter Joshua Reynolds. Below these to the left is a group of statues titled *Scientific Education*, which features the engineer James Watt beside a steam condenser and holding the governor mechanism he invented. On the right-hand side is a second grouping titled *Literary Education*, where an unidentified male is surrounded by books. Both of these figures are accompanied by a second younger figure, making them examples of the classic teacher-and-pupil sculptural pose which can be found in different forms on a number of buildings around Glasgow.

10. Beside the Athenaeum is the Royal Faculty of Procurators (a professional body for legal practitioners). Designed by Charles Wilson in a Venetian Renaissance style, it was built in 1854. Of particular note are the sculpted keystone heads representing distinguished members of the Scottish legal profession from previous ages. More information about these sculptures can be found in the description of the City Centre West walk.

11. Follow Nelson Mandela Place round to the south. Here, tucked in behind the rear of St George's Tron Church, is a bronze statue of a figure lying on a bench covered with a blanket. Created by Timothy Schmalz, this figure is known as the *Homeless Jesus* and is one of more than a hundred similar statues which have been erected around the world since the first one was installed outside Regis College in Toronto in 2013. The Glasgow version was unveiled in 2017 and was the first example in the UK. The idea of these statues is to raise awareness of homelessness, but they are not without controversy as some have suggested the money it cost to create them would have been better used actually helping homeless people. However, others claim that the awareness raised helps raise even more money for charities that help the homeless.

12. On the south side of Nelson Mandela Place, and wrapping round onto Buchanan Street, is the former Glasgow Stock Exchange. The building itself is a rather magnificent structure designed by John James Burnet (possibly inspired by the Royal Courts of Justice in London) and constructed in the 1870s. Although many Glaswegians will pass it without giving it a second look, visitors are often struck by its appearance, which is unsurprising as they might not expect to encounter such a beautiful Venetian Gothic style building in Scotland's largest city. However, Glasgow is such a mix of architectural styles that, on its streets, you can find at least one example (and often many more) of almost every major architectural movement from any point in the last 3,000 years. Along the Nelson Mandela Place and Buchanan Street facades of this building are a series of sculptures representing

Former Glasgow Stock Exchange, corner of Nelson Mandela Place and Buchanan Street.

different trades and realms of Glasgow's financial development, including engineering, mining and shipbuilding. Probably the most interesting one of these is the one depicting Science, because the sculptor chose to represent it using a female figure at a time when not only was science almost completely dominated by men, but women were still not permitted to study at Scottish universities (something which did not change until 1892). There is some debate as to whether this figure is simply a general allegorical representation, or whether it depicts a specific female scientist. If the latter, then one strong candidate is the mathematician and astronomer Mary Somerville, one of the first female members of the Royal Society, who died a few years before the Glasgow Stock Exchange building was constructed. Founded in 1844, the Glasgow Stock Exchange merged with the London Stock Exchange in 1973.

13. From the former Glasgow Stock Exchange, cross over Buchanan Street to its north-eastern corner with West George Street. Here, you will find the Tower Building. Designed by James Sellars and built around 1877, it is strongly reminiscent of the work of Alexander 'Greek' Thomson, and unusual in that the corner tower starts off octagonal, but gradually becomes circular by the time it reaches the top floor. Originally, this would have been crowned by a dome, but over the years, this has been lost. The carved nameplates for the building are still present and use a particularly distinctive and attractive font.

14. After viewing the Tower Building, head further east along the south side of West George Street until you are opposite No. 34. This is the Connall Building, which was built in the late 1890s for the iron merchant William Connall Jnr. Its design by James Thomson is classified as German Renaissance and it is thought to have been inspired by parts of Heidelberg Castle in modern-day Germany. The sculptures on this building are well worth examining in detail as they feature various aspects associated with Connall's business, including ships, trains and armaments. There is also a giant bee at the top of one facade, which is a Victorian emblem of industriousness, as well as portraits of both Connall and the building's architect, who can be seen on the western end of its West George Street facade. This was not unusual for James Thomson, and his likeness appears quite a number of the buildings he designed.

15. From the Connall Building, make a right turn a short distance further east along West George Street and head south down Anchor Lane. At its southern end, turn right onto St Vincent Place. Here you will find a number of interesting buildings. The first of these is the large white building which borders Anchor Lane itself – the Anchor Line Building, constructed in 1906 for the Henderson brothers of the Anchor Line Steamship Company. Designed in an Edwardian Renaissance style by James Miller, it is clad not with stone but with faïence, a type of ceramic tiling with a visual appearance similar to marble. Above the main door, and surrounded by putti (winged infants) riding sea monsters, is a sculpted head of Neptune, while to either side of this are masks of Mercury, the Roman god of financial gain, commerce and travellers, depicted wearing his typical winged helmet. These associations may explain why similar sculptures of Mercury appears so commonly on Glasgow's older commercial buildings.

Ornate entrance, Anchor Line Building, Saint Vincent Place.

16. Just to the west of the Anchor Line Building is the rather striking Dutch Renaissance style Citizen Building. Designed by Thomas Lennox Watson, it was constructed around 1885 as the offices of the *Evening Citizen*, one of Glasgow's most successful

newspapers of this time period, and you can still see the words 'Citizen Office' in the roundels on the right-hand side of the frieze between the ground and first floors. This building has two interesting claims to fame. Firstly, it was one of the first commercial buildings in Glasgow to be fully electrified, possibly due to a combination of the time it was constructed and its proximity to the Waterloo Street Power Station, which was opened in 1892. Secondly, and perhaps more importantly, it was the first building in the city to be made from red sandstone brought in to the city from the distant quarries of Ballochmyle and Locharbriggs. While there were earlier red sandstone buildings in Glasgow, mostly residential villas, these used more expensive locally sourced red sandstone. However, by the 1880s, the ever-spreading reach of the railways meant that, for the first time, it was relatively easy to move large quantities of stone greater distances, and in particular, to bring red sandstone, which was cheaper and particularly durable, from the quarries of Ayrshire and Dumfriesshire to Glasgow. This, in turn, led to a major change in the dominant colour of the city's buildings from the older blondes, yellows and greys of the sandstones of Giffnock and Bishopbriggs, to bright red. Improvements in transportation connections meant this red sandstone was not just transported to Glasgow, it was also shipped to the east coast of North America in large quantities and used for constructing buildings in New York and other east-coast cities, explaining why Glasgow is able to be used as a stand-in location when filming movie scenes set in these American cities. Red sandstone imported from Scotland was also used for the steps of the Statue of Liberty.

17. Neighbouring the Citizen Building is a large, white sandstone building. It was built in the 1870s, prior to the introduction of Ballochmyle and Locharbriggs red sandstone, and shows how different new buildings must have seemed compared with the older buildings which surrounded them when red sandstone starting being more widely used as a building material in the 1890s. This building was constructed as the headquarters of the Clydesdale Bank and was designed in Venetian Renaissance style by John Burnet Snr, the father of John James Burnet who designed many fine Glasgow buildings. It features sculptures by John Mossman and Charles Grassby, including the head of Father Clyde on a keystone on the right-hand end of the building. If you look closely at this sculpture, you can see some rather delightful little fish poking out of his long beard, while two more hold a ring over his head.

Sculpture of Father Clyde, former headquarters of Clydesdale Bank, Saint Vincent Place.

18. From the former Clydesdale Bank Building, head west along St Vincent Place until you reach Buchanan Street once more and then turn left and head south along it. On the corner of St Vincent Place and Buchanan Street is the imposing and ornate red sandstone St Vincent Chambers. Designed in a free style by John Baird and Alexander Thomson, it was built in 1902. The two highest points of the building are the gables on the left- and right-hand ends. The left one bears a carved cartouche with the initials W.B.C., which stands for William Blackburn Craig, a former drysalter turned wealthy property owner, for whom St Vincent Chambers was constructed. The one on the right bears a relief sculpture of a knight in full armour on horseback holding a broken tilting spear, which is the Craig Family crest. Below this is its motto, *Vive Deo et vives* (Live for God and you shall live). If you look closely at the left-hand side of the frieze between the first and ground floors, you can see the remains of a hand-painted sign which once read 'National Mutual of Australasia'.

Buchanan Street facade, 1902, free style Saint Vincent Chambers.

19. On the opposite side of Buchanan Street from St Vincent Chambers is the former National Bank Chambers, which is emblazoned on the beautifully carved banner above its main doorway. Designed by John M. Dick Peddie in a classical style with baroque detailing and built around 1900, it is typical of the grand banking and financial buildings constructed around this time. These contrast markedly with Glasgow's financial buildings of later periods, which are mainly to the west of Buchanan Street, many of which were built in a classical modern art deco style that would not seem out of place on the streets of New York or Chicago.

20. An even grander example of a late-nineteenth-century banking building can be found a short distance further south on the corner between Buchanan Street and Gordon Street. Now a restaurant, it was built in 1887 as a branch of the Commercial Bank of Scotland and was designed by Arthur G. Sydney Mitchell in a free Renaissance style. Of particular note is the five-storey octagonal corner tower featuring a dome with protruding dormer windows and topped by a lantern. It also features a number of interesting sculptures on both the Buchanan Street and the Gordon Street facades, as well as on the neighbouring (and slightly older) Gordon Street building, which was also part of the same bank. These include a roundel containing a camel, the coats of arms of various Scottish cities, putti minting coins and printing bank notes, and a series of stern-looking keystone heads.

21. Directly across Buchanan Street from the former Commercial Bank of Scotland is yet another imposing bank building which was designed by Charles Wilson in an Italian Renaissance palazzo style. Built in 1850 for the Royal Bank of Scotland, it is somewhat older than both the National Bank Chambers and the Commercial Bank of Scotland buildings. It may seem surprising that Glasgow could support quite so many major banks, but this reflects its growing level of affluence in the latter half of the nineteenth century and into the first decades of the twentieth century.

However, by the 1960s, the Royal Bank of Scotland had solidified its position as the major Scottish bank and had swallowed up these smaller competitors, a process that it would carry on doing until its disastrous takeover of the Dutch Bank ABN Ambro in the early 2000s, which destroyed its financial reputation and led to it being partially nationalised to avoid its failure during the banking and financial crises of 2007 and 2008.

22. To the left of the former Royal Bank building is one of Glasgow's few remaining police boxes and one of only four still in their original locations. While these are now most familiar from the British TV series *Doctor Who*, they were once a common sight on the streets of Glasgow and elsewhere. Although they could be used by patrolling policemen for a rest, their main function was to provide a direct line of communication with the local police station. While a key was required to enter them, there was also a hatch which could be opened by members of the public to access a phone to call both the police and the fire services.

23. Behind the police box, to the north of the Royal Bank building, is the Royal Insurance Company building. This was constructed in 1897 in a free Renaissance style from a design by the architects Thomson & Sandilands. While it is no longer used for its original purpose, it still has large bronze cartouches mounted on its walls identifying it as the home of this company.

Bronze cartouche, former office building of Royal Insurance Company.

24. Walk east along Royal Bank Place, which lies between the Royal Insurance Company building and the Royal Bank building. Before you get to the arch which leads on to Royal Exchange Square, look at the wall on the right-hand side. Here, there is a small relief sculpture commissioned by the Incorporation of Masons of Glasgow in 1998, titled *Medieval Masons at Work*, which shows the different tools and methods used by early stonemasons.

25. Pass through the arch at the east end of Royal Bank Place and you will find yourself in Royal Exchange Square which contains the grand former Royal Exchange building. Constructed in 1778, this building started life as the home of William Cunninghame of Lainshaw, but it was enlarged and expanded westward by David Hamilton in the 1820s to house the Royal Exchange. This is the part of the building which is visible as you enter Royal Exchange Square from Royal Bank Place. It now houses Glasgow's Gallery of Modern Art.

26. To the west of the Gallery of Modern Art is a building with a rather stunning facade modelled on an Ancient Greek Temple. This now forms the rear of the Royal Bank building on Buchanan Street, but it is actually the older part as it dates from 1827. The Buchanan Street section was added later to this older building. This building was designed by Archibald Elliot and is one of a surprising number of Glasgow buildings, including banks, municipal buildings, law courts and churches, with facades based on classical temples.

27. Pass through the arch to the south of the Royal Bank building and enter Exchange Place, which leads back to Buchanan Street. The stretch of buildings on the south side of this street were designed in a classical style by Robert Foote and were built around 1835. Of particular note is No. 11, which was formerly the home of the Rogano, one of Glasgow's oldest restaurants and a favourite haunt of actors, gangsters and rock stars. Amongst, others, Elizabeth Taylor, Mick Jagger and Davie Bowie were all known to have eaten there during visits to Glasgow. The Rogano started life in 1874 as the Bodega Spanish Wine Cellar, but it was bought in 1935 by Donald Grant, who oversaw its transformation into the art deco gem it is today. The new interior installed by Grant was based on the designs for the famous Cunard transatlantic liner the RMS *Queen Mary*, that was built at the John Brown's Shipyard in Clydebank in the same year. Local legend has it that the foremen from the shipyard would pay their bar bills with lengths of walnut and maple panelling intended for the liner itself, which were then used in the restaurant's transformation. Unfortunately, the Rogano is currently closed and at the time of writing it is unclear if and when it will reopen.

28. Continue along Exchange Place and once you reach Buchanan Street, turn left and head south to No. 95. Constructed in a classical style in 1828, with the later addition of an attic in 1884, this building is home to the Buchanan Street branch of the Willow Tea Rooms. Tea rooms were a Glasgow tradition which, in part, grew out of the Temperance Movement of the late 1800s and early 1900s, as they provided a welcoming and relatively inexpensive public space for people to meet, but which, unlike pubs and bars, did not serve alcohol. The undoubted queen of the Glasgow tea room was Catherine (or Kate) Cranston. Cranston opened her first tea room on Glasgow's Argyle Street in 1878, while her Buchanan Tea Room was opened a few years later in 1897. Located in the building next to Cranston's original Buchanan Tea Room, today's Willow Tea Room is actually modelled on the interior of her nearby Ingram Street tea room, designed in 1900 by the legendary Glasgow architect and designer Charles Rennie Mackintosh. This includes the Ladies Luncheon Room and the Chinese Room, known affectionately as the 'White Dining Room' and the 'Blue Room', respectively.

Flemish style 91 Buchanan Street, originally built as a tea room for Catherine Cranston.

29. Next door to the building which is currently home to the Willow Tea Room, at No. 91, is the original location occupied by Miss Cranston's Buchanan Tea Room. Designed by George Washington Browne in a Flemish style with François I detailing (King of France, 1494–1547). Constructed in 1896 using alternate bands of red and white, this is one of the most visually distinctive buildings on Buchanan Street. The original interiors of this tea room, designed by Mackintosh and George Walton, were removed during later renovations and have since been lost.

30. Further south at 85 Buchanan Street is the former British Overseas Airways Corporation, or BOAC, Building. The forerunner to British Airways, this building was constructed for BOAC in 1970, making it one of the newer buildings on Buchanan Street. Built in an unusual modernist style, it was designed by the renowned architects Gillespie, Kidd & Coia who were known for their mid-twentieth century architectural creations. Despite the obvious contrasts with the more traditional Edwardian, Victorian and even Georgian architectural styles of many of the other buildings on Buchanan Street, this building nonetheless still fits well into the general streetscape. In part, this is because its roofline is consistent with its neighbouring buildings.

Gillespie, Kidd & Coia's 1970s British Overseas Airways Corporation Building.

31. Running beside the BOAC building is Mitchell Lane. About halfway along this lane on the right-hand side is a small bar housed in a building called Gordon Chambers. This building was constructed in 1905, and in the 1990s it became home to Bar 10, whose interior was created by the celebrated design practice Ben Kelly Design. Kelly rose to prominence in the early 1980s due to his innovative work on the legendary Haçienda Nightclub in Manchester. Bar 10 was Glasgow's first Style Bar, and the interior referenced Glasgow's industrial past through its use of different materials mixed with primary colours. However, most of this original interior has been lost in more recent renovations.

32. At the western end of Mitchell Lane, on the right-hand side where it meets Mitchell Street, is the rear of the former Glasgow Herald building. The *Glasgow Herald* (now just called the *Herald*) is the city's main broadsheet newspaper, and this building was constructed in 1893 to act as an extension to their main building on Buchanan Street. It was designed in the Glasgow style by John Keppie and Charles Rennie Mackintosh, and it is one of the earliest buildings which Mackintosh had a major hand in designing. Of particular note is the large octagonal corner tower which rises high above the street. This structure was designed to hold a water tank for use in case the building, which would have held a large stockpile of papers for printing newspapers, caught fire. However, the finer details of the building, showing the flowing art nouveau inspired lines common to the Glasgow style created by Mackintosh and his contemporaries, are also worth taking the time to examine.

33. Return east along Mitchell Lane to Buchanan Street and walk a short distance south. Here at No. 69 is the front, and older, section of the Glasgow Herald Building. Designed by James Sellars, one of the key Glasgow architects of the generation before Mackintosh, it was built in 1879. It is rare to be able to contrast the architectural styles favoured by two consecutive generations on two sides of the same building, but in this case you can see how the classical style favoured by the likes of Sellars gave way to the sweeping lines of the art nouveau and Glasgow

style periods in a little over a decade. The sculptures on the top of the Buchanan Street facade of this building are William Caxton, the pioneering English publisher, and Johannes Gutenberg, the inventor of moveable type printing, which revolutionised the publishing industry in the fifteenth century.

34. Almost directly across from the former *Glasgow Herald* building is No. 60. Built of red sandstone, this is another of Buchanan Street's tall, skinny elevator buildings designed to fit onto a relatively narrow plot. It was created by Robert Thomson in the 1890s, making it contemporary with Mackintosh's Glasgow style extension to the Glasgow Herald Building on Mitchell Street. However, its style is markedly different and shows how not everyone was equally taken with the dramatic break from the past represented by the Art Nouveau Movement. It is, nonetheless, a magnificent building and a fine example of a free style commercial building. It was originally constructed for the rather wonderfully named North British Rubber Company. The use of the term 'North British' in its name is rather interesting as it seems that at the time of its creation many companies did not wish to be classified as 'Scottish', something which had not been nearly as much of an issue with earlier generations when the likes of the Royal Bank of Scotland were created.

35. On the same side of Buchanan Street as the former North British Rubber Company building, but on the next block further south is the Princes Square Shopping Centre. This building was formerly known as the Prince of Wales Building and was mostly constructed in 1854 from a design by John Baird. This building started life as a hotel before being converted into a business chambers, and then most recently, in the 1980s, into a shopping centre. One of its most distinctive features is the large art nouveau inspired peacock mounted on the roof. This was created by Alan Dawson as part of the renovations in 1987 which led to the creation of the current shopping centre.

36. Next to the Princes Square Building is Argyll Chambers. This elaborate Edwardian baroque building was designed by Colin Menzies and constructed in 1904. It also houses one of the entrances to Argyll Arcade, an enclosed, L-shaped covered area lined with shops, which connects Buchanan Street to Argyle Street. The arcade itself was designed by John Baird I and was modelled on the Parisian arcades of the late 1700s. The Argyll Arcade was built in 1827, making it the oldest indoor shopping arcade in Scotland.

37. To the south of Argyll Chambers at No. 20 Buchanan Street is the former Wylie Hill Department Store. The current building was constructed following a disastrous fire in 1888, and at one time it included a pond in the toy department for demonstrating model ships. The architect of the new

1904 Edwardian baroque style Argyll Chambers.

building was John Hutchison, under whom, at the time, Charles Rennie Mackintosh was serving an apprenticeship. Mackintosh's potential apparently shone through even then in the design of plaster column capitals, including ones on the ground and first floors which are still present to this day. The exterior of the building, which was created by Hutchison himself, is a more traditional Glasgow design and is based on an Italian Renaissance style.

38. On the opposite side of Buchanan Street from the former Wylie Department Store is a series of buildings now occupied by the House of Fraser department store. It was established in 1849 as a drapery business called Arthur and Fraser that specialised in silk, linens and woollens. James Arthur, the senior partner, concentrated on the wholesale side of the business, while Hugh Fraser focussed on the retail side out of a rented premises on the corner of Buchanan Street and Argyle Street. In 1865, the partnership was dissolved by mutual consent, with the business being continued by Fraser. Much of the current space occupied by Frasers on Buchanan Street started life as independent stores, which were later taken over or incorporated into House of Fraser. This included the current building at 21 Buchanan Street (on the left as you look at it), which was originally built in 1879 for MacDonald's Department Store, and the former warehouses of Wylie & Lochhead, at one time the largest cabinet-making business in Scotland, at 45 Buchanan Street (on the right). The former Wylie & Lochhead Building includes an elegant terracotta-fronted central section designed by James Sellars in 1884, which features an impressively sculpted pediment with the royal coat of arms of Scotland over a cartouche containing the Wylie & Lochhead monogram. Between these two buildings is another relatively slim and unassuming building which dates from the 1850s. This was originally the home of the wonderfully named Kemp's Shawl Emporium, which was established by David Kemp in 1832. Over the years, it gained a reputation for making the finest quality shawls and it soon expanded to become a more general clothing manufacturers, renowned for producing ladies clothes in the latest fashionable styles from London and Paris. Examples of Kemp's work can now be found in museum collections around the world.

39. Back on the east side of Buchanan Street are Nos. 12 and 16. Designed by James Thomson in the late 1880s in a simplified Venetian Renaissance style, No. 16 (the taller of the two buildings). It was originally built for the clothing wholesalers Brown, Smith & Company, who later employed Burnet, Boston & Carruthers to add a new upper section to it. No. 12 was built as a shop and warehouse for Matthew Pettigrew, who was one of the trustees of Hugh Fraser, the founder of what would later become Fraser's Department Store, who died in 1873.

40. On the eastern corner of Buchanan Street and Argyle Street stands a large and imposing art deco style building which was built in 1929 as a Burton's Department

Art deco former Burton's Department Store, corner of Buchanan Street and Argyle Street.

Store. Burton's was established in 1903 by Montague Burton. By the 1920s, the chain had more than 400 shops, as well as its own factories and mills. It also had its own in-house architectural team, led by Harry Wilson, to design its stores in a distinctive and impressive 'Modern Temples of Commerce' style. Many of the purpose-built Burton's stores had foundation stones placed at their entrance inscribed with the name of the member of the Burton family who laid it, and these are often all that remains to mark the location of where one of their shops once stood. However, the ones for this shop have either been removed or were never installed in the first place.

41. Buchanan Street ends at its junction with Argyle Street, but for this walk cross over Argyle Street and continue straight ahead into St Enoch Square. Saint Enoch, originally known as Thenava, was a Pictish princess who lived around AD 550. She was the daughter of King Lot (also spelt as Loth) of the Gododdin, after whom the Lothian region of eastern Scotland is named. She became pregnant out of wedlock by the young King Owain of North Rheged, now Galloway, and as a result, her father had her tied to a chariot and launched off Traprain Law, a hill to the south of Edinburgh. Miraculously, both she and her unborn child survived, but the Gododdin, fearing she was a witch, cast her adrift in a coracle in the Firth of Forth. Eventually, she made landfall in what is now Fife and was taken in by Saint Serf, who had established a religious community nearby. It was here Thenava gave birth to a son who would go on to become Saint Mungo, the founder of Glasgow cathedral and patron saint of the city. Today, St Enoch Square can be divided into two parts: the western part, which retains its traditional building; and the eastern part, where the St Enoch Station and Hotel once stood. In an act of architectural vandalism, this was demolished in the 1960s, and is now considered one of the city's greatest lost buildings. All that remains of the building is its clock, which is now housed in the 1970s Antonine Shopping Centre in the new town of Cumbernauld, to the east of Glasgow. It featured prominently in the Bill Forsyth's much-loved 1981 Scottish coming-of-age film *Gregory's Girl*. In the 1980s, the gap where the station and hotel once stood was replaced by the St Enoch Shopping Centre, a glass and metal building with very little architectural merit to it, which is, itself, now potentially facing demolished.

42. This tour focuses on the traditional buildings which remain on the west side of St Enoch Square, and on two of them in particular. The first of these buildings, immediately to your right as you enter the square from the north, is the beautiful Italianate style Teacher Building. Designed by James Boucher and constructed in 1875, it was built for

Italianate style, 1875 Teacher Building, St Enoch Square.

as the headquarters of the whisky-maker William Teacher & Sons. Born in 1811, Teacher started his career working in a small grocer's shop in the Anderston area of Glasgow, but after marrying the owner's daughter, he expanded the business into a chain of wine and spirit shops, and then 'dram' shops, where customers could drink high-quality whisky in a relatively refined atmosphere. Anyone who became unduly under the influence was ejected from the premises by one of the large Highlanders Teacher employed to serve the drinks. From here, Teacher moved into the wholesale whisky business and eventually into the production of blended (as opposed to malt) whiskies, such as Highland Cream, which went on to become a leading Scotch whisky brand. Despite the building no longer being associated with Teacher's whisky, it retains the large gold lettering proclaiming it to be the home of Teacher Scotch Whisky Distillers. However, the date above the door refers to the founding date of the Institute of Engineering and Technology, who owned the building until recently, rather than that of Teacher's, which was established in 1830.

43. Next to the Teacher Building is another similarly grand building, but one that is constructed in a very different style. This is a former branch of the National Bank of Scotland, which was constructed in 1906 and was designed by Alexander N. Patterson in a beaux-arts style. Of particular note are the sculptures on either side of the door by Phyllis Archibald, one of the few female sculptors to have their work grace Glasgow's many Victorian and Edwardian buildings. The sculptures are allegorical figures representing Prudence, Adventure, Exchange and Security; virtues seen as worthy of association with banking.

44. Underneath St Enoch Square is St Enoch Subway Station (the end point of the Buchanan Street Subway Challenge). It is currently accessed by two entrances covered with distinctive curved glass canopies which were installed in the 2010s. While they add a modern feel to the entrances, they are somewhat at odds with the traditional architecture of the square. However, they are of sufficiently low profile not to impinge too much on the surrounding buildings. In particular, they do not detract from the original St Enoch Subway Station building which remains standing in the centre of the square. Designed by James Miller and constructed in 1896, this building might be small, but it is a masterpiece of Glaswegian architecture. Its main features, like the pepper-pot turrets and crow-stepped gables, are typical of the Scottish baronial style, which had an influence not only on the Gothic revival architecture of the late 1700s and much of the 1800s, but also on the likes of Charles Rennie Mackintosh and his colleagues, who mixed its elements with the fluid lines of the European art nouveau movement to create the distinctive Glasgow style. However, it is also covered in a wealth of sculptural decorations, and features many masks of the Green Man, a figure of pre-Christian European beliefs, who represented the spirit of nature. Each

Small, but magnificent, Scottish baronial style former St Enoch Subway Station.

mask is unique and they can be found on every side of the building, but of particular note are the arch of six which surround the main entrance. Despite its unique beauty, this building could easily have been lost during redevelopments of the station below it towards the end of the 1970s, which involved digging a massive crater and constructing a concrete box to enclose the subterranean platforms. However, through a spectacular feat of engineering, the entire original building was relocated on to a pre-cast foundation supported on the station's new concrete pillars, resulting in the building being suspended in mid-air above the crater while the work on the station was carried out below. This allowed the building to survive the construction work and so remain at the heart of St Enoch Square for generations to come.

2. Merchant City

Start Point: Merchants House, George Square, Glasgow (**Location:** Lat/Lon: 55.86152, -4.25140; What3Words: ///edits.remove.cared; Plus Code: VP6X+JC5 Glasgow). **Nearest Public Transport:** Subway: Buchanan Street Station (5 mins); Train: Queen Street Station (1 min); Bus: George Square (1 min).

End Point: Glasgow City Chambers, George Square, Glasgow (**Location:** Lat/Lon: 55.86095, -4.24894; **What3Words:** ///traps.nights.garden; **Plus Code:** VQ62+9CF Glasgow). **Nearest Public Transport:** Subway: Buchanan Street Station (8 mins); Train: Queen Street Station (3 mins); Bus: George Square (1 min).

Distance: 2.7 kilometres/1.8 miles. **Time:** Allow 1.5 to 2.5 hours for this walk.
Level of Difficulty: Easy. This walk is on flat, paved streets. However, there are numerous road crossings.

Facilities: There are plenty of shops, cafes, restaurants and bars where you can stop for refreshments along this route. Publicly accessible toilets are available at Queen Street Railway Station close to the start and end of this walk, as well as in the Gallery of Modern Art on Queen Street itself.

Introduction

This walk visits many of the locations in a central part of Glasgow known as the Merchant City. While its current name was only introduced in the 1980s, the Merchant City is one of the oldest parts of Glasgow, and includes a number of its original medieval streets, such as Trongate. The development of this part of the city started around 1750 as Glasgow began its westward expansion, and it quickly became the favoured location for the houses and commercial buildings of Glasgow's Tobacco Lords. These were a group of Scottish merchants from the Georgian era who made much of their money from the 'triangular trade', where ships sailed from Britain to West Africa to trade textiles, rum and manufactured goods for slaves, who were then transported to the Americas and sold. The money was then used to purchase slave-produced products, such as tobacco and sugar, which were then taken back to Britain.

Some of the Tobacco Lords also expanded their business interests into owning slave plantations in the Americas to maximise their profits. They used the wealth generated from these activities to build grand houses and villas, construct churches, establish institutions and purchase lands and country estates in and around Glasgow. Many of the streets in the Merchant City are named after these Tobacco Lords, an issue which is now subject to some debate. While those running the city may have profited greatly from the slavery, it was by no means universally accepted within the city itself, particularly among the local Quaker community, the city's university professors and the working class, and by the 1800s, Glasgow had become one of the main centres of the anti-slavery movement in Britain. This led to anti-slavery activists, and former slaves, like Frederick Douglass, visiting the city as part of their campaigns to abolish slavery in the USA and around the world. In addition, it was to Glasgow that James McCune Smith, the first African American to hold a medical degree, came to study as he was unable to get a place at an American Institution due to his African ancestry.

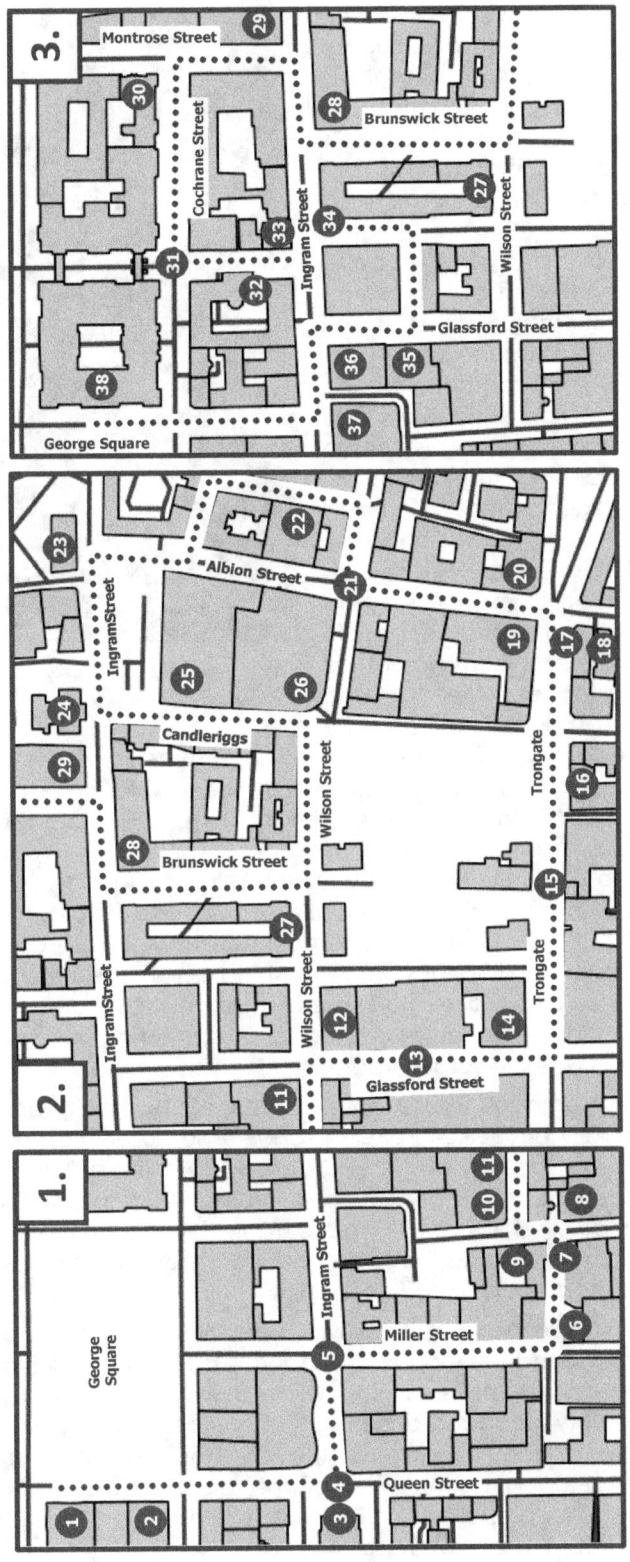

1. This walk starts at Merchants House on the north-west corner of George Square in central Glasgow. Glasgow's Merchants House was formed to represent the interests of the city's mercantile community, with its first written constitution being established in 1605. It was closely involved in the development of the city between the seventeenth and twentieth centuries. The original Merchants House (then known as the Merchants Hall) was constructed at the Bridgegate beside the Clyde, in 1659, but this building was demolished in 1818, and only its steeple now remains standing. From its original base on the Bridgegate, the Merchants House first moved to Hutcheson Street in the mid-1800s and then to its current location on George Square in the 1870s. This building was designed in 1874 by John Burnet to compliment the Italian Renaissance style of the neighbouring buildings designed by John T. Rochead and James Sellars. Originally, it was only three storeys high, but Burnet's son, John James Burnet, added a further two storeys and its distinctive corner dome in 1907. This dome is topped by a ship under full sail perched on top of a globe, the emblem of the Merchants House and a reminder of the importance of sea trade to Glasgow. It also echoes the ship on the top of the seventeenth-century steeple of the original Merchants House on the Bridgegate. However, until the early part of the 1800s, this international trade involved both sugar and tobacco from slave plantations in the West Indies and the Americas. The current Merchants House also features a series of imposing sculptures by James Young, including caryatids and atlantes around the entrances from George Square and the neighbouring West George Street.

Globe-and-ship finial, top of dome, Merchants' House, George Square.

2. To the south of Merchants House, on the corner of George Square and St Vincent Place, is a similarly grand Italian Renaissance style building. Designed by John T. Rochead and constructed at the end of the 1860s, this building established the style for the west side of George Square, and in particular the massive atlantes over its main entrance on St Vincent Place are mirrored in the atlantes and caryatids of the later Merchants House. It was originally built for the Bank of Scotland, with offices above its grand, ground-floor banking hall.

3. From George Square, head south down Queen Street to the eastern side of Royal Exchange Square and the Gallery of Modern Art (GoMA). Originally, this building was a much smaller mansion, and when it was constructed in 1778 for the eighteenth-century tobacco-and-sugar merchant William Cunninghame of Lainshaw, it was on the very edge of the city. However, as Glasgow's Georgian New Town developed to the west of the older medieval city, it was soon surrounded by other properties. In 1817, it was sold to the Royal Bank of Scotland, who then sold it, in 1827, to Glasgow's Royal Exchange, the forerunner of the

Glasgow Stock Market on nearby Buchanan Street. At this point, it was greatly altered and extended, with further extensions added in the 1880s, meaning that the original house, while still present, is pretty much hidden from view by these newer additions.

4. In front of the GoMA is probably the most famous statue in Glasgow. Created in 1844 by Baron Marochetti, it depicts the Duke of Wellington mounted on Copenhagen, the horse he rode during the Battle of Waterloo. However, the reason this statue is so famous has nothing to do with the subject or the sculptor. Instead, it is because it has become a tradition for people to climb the statue (usually late at night and while drunk) and place a plastic road cone on the duke's head. It is not certain when this tradition began, but it has certainly been going on since the early 1980s. In 2005, Glasgow City Council attempted to eliminate the practice, without success, and in 2013, they considered raising the height of the statue's plinth to make it more difficult to climb. However, after widespread opposition from the city's population, the council relented and the statue with a road cone in place has now become widely accepted as an unofficial symbol of the city. Different cones are often placed on the statue to denote different events and causes. This has included a golden cone to mark the London 2012 Olympics, a cone decorated in the EU colours as a protest against Brexit in 2020, and a blue and yellow cone in support of Ukraine in 2022. In 2011, the *Lonely Planet Travel Guide* included this statue and its cone in a list of the top-ten most bizarre monuments on earth.

Statue of Duke of Wellington, entrance to GoMA, with his now-traditional headgear.

5. From the Duke of Wellington statue, cross Queen Street at the traffic lights and walk a short distance east along Ingram Street to the junction with Miller Street. The building on the western side of this corner is an imposing French Renaissance style building designed by James Boucher and built in 1875. The one on the eastern side is designed in a similar manner and was built around the same time. At one point it was home to Miss Cranston's Lunch and Tea Rooms, which had an interior designed by Charles Rennie Mackintosh, the city's most famous architect. Most of this interior was removed in the 1970s and is now in storage as part of the collections of Glasgow Museums. However, some of it is on display in the Mackintosh exhibit in Kelvingrove Art Gallery and Museum. In addition, recreated versions of its Ladies Luncheon Room and its Chinese Room can be found in the Willow Tea Rooms on nearby Buchanan Street.

6. Turn right and head south down Miller Street. As you do, you will pass a number of grand buildings. However, nestled between these, at No. 42, is a much smaller and more unassuming one. Designed and built by John Craig in 1775, it has survived

relatively unchanged ever since and so is an important survivor from this period of the development of the Merchant City. In 1782, it was sold to the tobacco importer Robert Findlay of Easterhill, and as a result, it is now known as the Tobacco Merchant's House. It was restored in the 1990s by the Glasgow Building Preservation Trust and now serves as the offices for the Scottish Civic Trust.

7. To the left of 42 Miller Street is a narrow lane called Virginia Court, which takes you through to Virginia Street via a stone archway. The buildings surrounding this arch are known as the Virginia Buildings and date from around 1817. These are more remnants from the involvement of Glasgow merchants in the transatlantic tobacco trade, and were developed by Robert Findlay Jnr, the son of the tobacco importer who once owned 42 Miller Street. If you examine the doorways of Nos. 37 and 42, you will see a range of faded, hand-painted ghost signs, some of which are thought to date back to the 1820s, advertising the businesses which used to occupy the offices inside.

8. On the opposite side of Virginia Street, at No. 42, is a rather stunning Italian Renaissance style building designed by Robert G. Melvin and William Leiper, which dates from 1867. It was built for the Glasgow Gas Light Company. Pivotal to the development of gas lighting was the Ayrshire-born engineer William Murdoch who, while working in Cornwall in the 1790s, realised the gas released by heating coal dust could be ignited to create a bright artificial light. By 1817, the Glasgow Gas Light Company had been founded and the first gas-powered lights were lit on the city's streets in 1818. Although it was gradually replaced by electric lighting from the end of the 1800s onwards, gas light continued to be used in Glasgow street lights until 1971, when the last one was finally turned off.

Former Glasgow Gas Light Company Building, Virginia Street.

9. To the north of the Virginia Buildings, and on the same side of the street, is No. 51. Slightly older than its neighbours, this building is known as the Jacobean Corsetry due to the large gold ghost sign attached to its front for a corsetry business which occupied the premises between its establishment in 1946 and its closure in 2000.

10. Opposite the Jacobean Corsetry, on the corner of Virginia Street and Wilson Street, is the former Scottish Legal Life Assurance Society Building. Designed by Alexander Skirving in a Renaissance style and constructed in 1889, this is one of the earliest large commercial buildings made from red sandstone, a material which would go on to dominate the Glasgow construction industry for commercial, civic and residential buildings for the next thirty to forty years. This was also a time when the older classical styles favoured by the likes of Alexander 'Greek' Thomson were being replaced by newer art nouveau, Glasgow style and Edwardian baroque designs, and as such it is quite unusual to see classical pillars and pediments created from red sandstone.

11. A short distance to the east, on the corner between Wilson Street and Glassford Street, is the former Gordon Brothers Warehouse. Designed by Robertson and

Dobbie, it was built in 1908. While it is also constructed from red sandstone, its distinctive Glasgow style contrasts sharply with the more classical style of the Scottish Legal Life Assurance Society Building. However, unusually for a Glasgow style building, it features several 'Green Man' masks, as well as some lovingly carved dragons just below the monogram on the corner of the building.

12. Starting opposite the Gordon Brothers Warehouse, and continuing east along the south side of Wilson Street, are a series of 1930s red sandstone former warehouses, designed primarily by the architects Thomson, Sandilands & MacLeod. They reflect the next major evolution of Glasgow architecture after the explosion of art nouveau, Glasgow style and Edwardian baroque buildings between the 1890s and the 1920s. This style, known as 'modern classical', was the last to use red sandstone as a major building material, although for these buildings it is only used as cladding rather than as a structural material. This style can be thought of as blending art deco and classical features, and it was widely used in Glasgow for commercial and financial buildings in the 1920s and 1930s.

Modern classical style 1930s warehouse, Wilson Street.

13. From Wilson Street, turn right on to Glassford Street and head south towards Trongate. Glassford Street is named after John Glassford, a major player in the rise of Glasgow's fortunes towards the end of the 1700s. Probably the most prominent of the city's Tobacco Lords, his epitaph in the Ramshorn Cemetery, which will be visited later on this walk, states: 'He saw the sunrise and dawn of the tobacco trade from start to finish'. As well as owning ships, he also owned tobacco-producing slave plantations in the British colonies in North America, and much of his fortune was based on the products of slave labour. As such, there have been calls to consider renaming this street.

14. At the southern end of Glassford Street, on its corner with Trongate, is the stunningly beautiful former National Bank Building. While the castle-like style makes it seem much older, it actually dates from 1903. It was built on the site of Shawfield Mansion, which was constructed in 1712 and destroyed by fire in 1793. On the Argyle Street facade is a plaque which commemorates not just the site of this mansion, but also the fact that Charles Edward Stuart, better known as Bonnie Prince Charlie, stayed in it 1745. This was during the final Jacobite uprising which attempted to return the Stuart monarchs to the British throne. Among other things, this uprising featured the last battle on British soil (the Battle of Culloden, April 1746), the last Highland battle charge by men armed with swords, and the last siege of a castle in Britain (of Stirling Castle, February 1746). Yet, this was also during the lifetimes of both James Watt, who contributed greatly to the development of the steam engine, and Adam Smith, the creator of modern economics, all at a time when Glasgow was starting to move towards becoming the industrial powerhouse it would become by the end of the nineteenth century. As such, it marks a pivotal moment both in the development of Glasgow and of Scotland as a whole.

15. From its junction with Glassford Street, walk east along Trongate towards Glasgow Cross. Trongate is one of the original medieval streets which made up Glasgow. It is named after the Tron, an institution established by royal charter in 1489, charged with providing weights and measures to merchants and citizens wishing to bring goods into the city through the toll gate at the tolbooth, situated at the eastern end of the Trongate. Effectively, the Tron provided the standardised measurements used to determine how much duty needed to be paid to bring specific quantities of goods into the city. Under this royal charter, these duties were paid to the Bishop of Glasgow.

16. At 109 Trongate stands a rather grand-looking classical building, designed by Gildard & Macfarlane and built in 1857. As well as being a beautiful building, it is also home to the Britannia Panopticon, arguably the oldest surviving music hall in the world. Among other things, this was where Stan Laurel, who would go on to become half of the legendary comedy duo and early movie stars Laurel and Hardy, made his professional debut in 1905, when he was just fifteen. Much of the music hall remains in place and is well worth visiting if you have the time. It can be entered via New Wynd, although check in advance when it will be open as its hours are limited.

17. A short distance further east along Trongate is the Tron Steeple. Built in the 1630s, this is one of four ancient steeples visible from Glasgow Cross (the others being the Tolbooth Steeple, the Merchants' Steeple and the steeple of St Andrews in the Square), and it is all that remains of the original Tron Kirk. The Tudor arches at its base were opened up in 1855, and the decorated vaulted ceiling, which covers the pavement as it passes through these arches, adds an unexpected splash of colour to the street. The tower features square clock faces with a blue background and gold details – a fashion attributed to Henry VIII of England. Just below the clock face on the western side of the steeple is a kinetic sculpture of Saint Mungo installed by Sharmanka Kinetic Theatre (which can be found an 103 Trongate) in 2001. It was designed so that on the hour, the fish spins, the bird pecks and Saint Mungo raises his staff, but unfortunately, it no longer seems to function.

18. Behind the Tron Steeple is the former Tron Kirk. Built in 1793 to replace the original one (of which the Tron Steeple is all that remains), and much altered over time, this former church was converted into the Tron Theatre in 1981. On the corner of this building, where Trongate meets Chisholm Street, is a plaque which commemorates the men and women of the City of Glasgow Police. The City of Glasgow Police is the oldest police force in the UK, having been formed in 1779, some fifty years before the formation of London's Metropolitan Police, although it was not until 1800 that it became a permanent fixture in the city. Directly above this plaque is a statue of a cherub. This is one half of a two-part art installation by Kenny Hunter, with the other being an oversized skull set into a niche on the Parnie Street elevation of the Tron Theatre. Together, they refer to birth and death, with the theatre of life in between them.

Plaque commemorating men and women of City of Glasgow Police.

19. Directly to the north of the Tron Theatre, on the corner of Trongate and Albion Street, is a magnificent Scottish baronial style former warehouse designed by John T. Rochead and built in 1854 for the City of Glasgow Bank. Despite the modern shopfronts somewhat detracting from the architectural splendour above, it is nonetheless an impressive mix of crow-stepped gables and oriel windows, with a corner tower, equipped with stone cannons, looking out across the city's rooftops.

20. If you cross Trongate at the traffic lights at this junction and walk up Albion Street, on your right, you will pass a large red sandstone building. Designed by Thomson & Sandilands, and constructed in the early 1900s for the City Improvement Trust, it provided space for shops on the ground floor, particularly along Trongate, and offices above. A plaque on the Trongate facade of this building notes that it was built on the site of a workshop which, in 1769, was occupied by James Watt, one of Scotland's greatest engineers and inventors, whose improvements to the design of the steam engine helped advance the Industrial Revolution in Britain and across the world.

21. Further up Albion Street is its junction with Bell Street, which is marked by four rather grand buildings, each designed in a different style. These includes the city's former Fruit Market and Bazaar on the north-west corner and the former Cheese Market on the north-east corner. The Glasgow Police Museum, a small independent institution established by the Glasgow Police Heritage Society and devoted to telling the story of Britain's first police force, can be found in the building on the south-western corner of this junction.

22. Turn right on to Bell Street at this junction, and then a short distance later, turn left onto Walls Street. As you walk up Walls Street, you will pass the entrance to the former Cheese Market on your left-hand side.

23. At the northern end of Walls Street, turn left onto Blackfriars Street and then right onto Albion Street. Carry on north up Albion Street until you reach its junction with Ingram Street. On the opposite side of Ingram Street at this point is a large former warehouse built in 1875 in an Italianate style, which was converted into flats in 1988.

24. Turn left onto Ingram Street and follow it west to its junction with Candleriggs. At this point, on the north side of Ingram Street, you will see the Gothic style former St David's Parish Church, designed by Thomas Rickman and constructed in 1824. It is surrounded by Ramshorn Cemetery, which is one of Glasgow's oldest burial grounds and was in use between 1719 and 1915. As well as offering an oasis of calm within the city, this is also the last resting place of many of Glasgow's elite, including Tobacco Lords such as John Glassford (after whom Glassford Street is named), the natural philosopher John Anderson, nicknamed 'Jolly Jack Phosphorous', who founded Anderson's Institute (which ultimately became the University of Strathclyde), and William Logan, who founded the Logan and Johnston's Orphan Hospital. It also has associations with

Gothic style former Saint David's Parish Church, aka 'the Ramshorn'.

the infamous Madeleine Smith murder case, as her alleged victim, Pierre Emile L'Angelier, is buried here, and with body snatching, as the body of Janet McAllister, who was buried in Ramshorn Cemetery in 1813, was later found, along with four other bodies, in the nearby College Street Medical School. The fate of ending up on an anatomist's dissection table was greatly feared by many at this time, and there are still a number of iron cages around the burial plots in Ramshorn Cemetery which were designed to thwart the attempts of body snatchers to steal the recently interred. At one time, the cemetery was larger, and if you examine the pavement outside its current walls, you will see a flagstone which marks the burial place of the Foulis Brothers, who were not only the printers for the University of Glasgow, they also opened one of the city's first bookshops in 1741. In the pavement in front of the church itself, are the Ramshorn Engravings. Created by Kate Robinson, these images are linked to a variety of people and events associated with both the church and the wider city, including slavery, grave-robbing, scientific endeavours, the Cheapside Street disaster of 1960, where fourteen fire service and five salvage corps personnel died, and the conversion of the church into a theatre in the 1990s.

25. From the former church, cross the road at the traffic lights and head south down Candleriggs. This is another of Glasgow's more ancient streets, and its name most likely derives from a candle works which supplied nearby churches with candles. On the left-hand side of this street (as you walk south) is a large complex of buildings consisting of the former City Hall, Bazaar and Fruit Market. The first of these, at No. 104, is a rare example of a cast-iron building, including its facade, and it is one of the few such buildings remaining in the city. Further south, is the former City Hall. Started in 1839, this was the first hall built in Glasgow which was suitable for large gatherings and concerts. Over the years, it played host to the likes of Charles Dickens, Benjamin Disraeli and William Gladstone. However, it also hosted what would be considered more radical events, such as the visit to Glasgow in 1846 by the US anti-slavery campaigner, and former slave, Frederick Douglass. An audience of 1,500 turned up to hear him speak at the first meeting, and 2,500 at the second, with Douglass noting they were 'principally working people. Few learned or reverend gentlemen graced our platform – but the ladies of Glasgow united in rendering us aid'. There is also a plaque commemorating the life and activities of the 'Red Clydesider' and Socialist campaigner John Maclean, who also spoke frequently at City Hall.

26. Further south, on the corner with Bell Street, is the entrance to the former Fruit Market, marked by a sculpted finial consisting of a basket of fruit. At this point, it is worth venturing inside the building to see the elaborate and intricate cast-iron trussed roof which covered the marketplace itself.

27. From the old Fruit Market, head west along Wilson Street, which, as noted before, is lined with modern classical warehouses built in the 1930s. However, for this part of the walk, the main subject of interest is the old municipal buildings, which you will find on

Scenes from Walter Buchan's 1844 Trial by Jury *frieze, former Glasgow municipal buildings, Ingram Street.*

the right-hand side between Brunswick Street and Hutcheson Street. Designed by Clarke & Bell and constructed in the 1840s (with additions in the 1870s and 1890s), the neo-Greek facade facing Wilson Street is particularly impressive. These buildings originally served as the county buildings for Lanarkshire as well as for Glasgow, but once the new City Chambers were built on George Square in 1888, it was used solely as a court building. At the base of the Wilson Street facade is a sculpted frieze created by Walter Buchan in 1844 titled *Trial By Jury*, showing the different stages of such a trial and featuring people dressed in classical clothes.

28. Turn off Wilson Street and head north up Brunswick Street. On the right-hand side at the northern end of this street, and wrapping round on to Ingram Street, is a glorious Scottish baronial style building designed by Robert W. Billings and John Baird, and constructed in 1854. Originally, it had a cast-iron interior, but this has now been replaced by a modern development of residential flats. It was built for J. & W. Campbell & Company as a dry goods warehouse and, at the time it was constructed, it was viewed not only as one of the finest warehouses in Great Britain, but also as one of the finest Scottish baronial style buildings in the west of Scotland.

29. On reaching Ingram Street, turn right and then a short distance later, turn left onto Montrose Street. As you do so, you will pass a large free style former warehouse on the corner of these two streets. This was designed by John Thomson in 1898 and, like the earlier warehouse you just visited on Ingram Street, it was built for J. & W. Campbell & Company. When it was constructed, there was an underground passage beneath Ingram Street which connected these two buildings, but it is unlikely that this still exists.

30. Head north up Montrose Street to its junction with Cochrane Street. Here, on the right-hand side at No. 23, is an impressive, but unusual-looking building. Designed by Alexander B. McDonald in a Mannerist style and built in 1895, this is the former Sanitary Chambers. Above its entrance is a statue of Hygeia, the Greek goddess of health, who gives her name to the philosophy of hygiene, created by William Kellock Brown. At the time it was built, the Sanitary Chambers was a cutting-edge development aimed at improving Glasgow's public health. It contained not only the offices of the Sanitary Inspector and their staff, but also a vaccination department, including operating rooms and an isolation room, rooms for the Medical Officer of Health and a veterinary surgeon, and a chemical laboratory (in the corner tower). Particularly novel elements of its design were the inclusion of a bacteriological department and an exhibition room, where different types of sanitary appliances could be exhibited and tested by the Sanitary Inspector.

Former Sanitary Chambers, Montrose Street.

31. From Sanitary Chambers, head west along Cochrane Street to the corner with John Street. At this point, if you look north along John Street, you will see a pair of grand arches, featuring French Renaissance style detailing, which link the original Glasgow City Chambers, constructed to the west in 1888, with the extension built to the east in the 1910s and 1920s.

32. Turn south down John Street and head back towards Ingram Street. As you do so, on your right-hand side you will see a series of early to mid-nineteenth-century classical style buildings. These are now home to the Italian Centre, which opened in 1991, and was one of the first developments in the regeneration of the Merchant City area of Glasgow. It consists of series of residential flats and retail outlets centred around an internal courtyard, based on an Italian palazzo style, and it was designed by Page\Park architects to integrate sympathetically with the existing Georgian architecture. It also features a series of classical style sculptures along its rooftop, created by Alexander Stoddart as part of this redevelopment. Inspired by the work of famous Glasgow sculptors like the legendary John Mossman, they look as if they are made of bronze covered in centuries of verdigris, but they are actually glass-reinforced polymer. Stoddart was also the creator of the statue of Mercury on John Street itself outside the Italian Centre, which is actually made from bronze. Within the Italian Centre's central courtyard, there are also some interesting sculptures (called *Guardians*) created by Jack Sloan, and a rather beautiful piece by Shona Kinloch called *Thinking of Bella*.

33. Further south on the corner of John Street and Ingram Street is Hutchesons' Hospital. Designed by David Hamilton in a classical style, this building was constructed in 1802. However, it replaced an earlier building from the 1600s, which was originally created as a home for aged men. Hutchesons' Hospital was founded with money left by two Glasgow merchants, George and Thomas Hutcheson, who were born in the 1530s, to create a home for the elderly and a school for poor boys. The school is still operating today as Hutchesons' Grammar School in

Statues of Glasgow merchants, George and Thomas Hutcheson, former Hutchesons' Hospital.

the Southside area of Glasgow, although it is now a fee-paying school. There are statues of George and Thomas on the Ingram Street facade of the current building, which predate it by a considerable period of time, having been created around 1649 by James Colquhoun, making them the oldest figurative public statues in Glasgow. Both George and Thomas Hutcheson are buried in the Old Burial Ground of Glasgow Cathedral, and Thomas's tomb, designed in a Jacobean style, is still visible alongside its southern wall.

34. From the former Hutcheson Hospital, cross Ingram Street at the nearest traffic lights and head south along Hutcheson Street. Look back as you do so as this provides some of the best views of the hospital. About halfway down Hutcheson Street, opposite the junction with Garth Street, is one of the former Merchants House of Glasgow. Built in the 1840s and lined with Corinthian columns, this is part of the former municipal buildings, which you viewed earlier from Wilson Street. The Merchants House moved here from its original location on Bridgegate, but later moved to its current location on George Square, where this walk started. Outside the former Merchants House is a sculpture called *A Bouquet of Glasgow* created by Doug Cocker in 2005 to commemorate the 400th anniversary of the

reconstitution of the Trades House and the Merchants House. It consists of a woven basket containing ten tools representing different Glasgow trades and roles. They include a tailor's square, a dyer's tongs, a shoemaker's knife, a baker's paddle, a wright's chisel, a mason's dividers, a ship's mast and a bobbin (representing the role of merchants), and a mace and crozier as symbols of civic and ecclesiastical elements.

35. From the former Merchants House, head west along Garth Street. At its far end, on Glassford Street, is the grand classical facade and distinctive green dome of the Trades House of Glasgow. Originally designed by Robert Adam in 1791, it was later altered by David Hamilton in the 1830s, James Sellars in the 1880s, and John Keppie in the 1920s. The Trades House was created in 1605, when Glasgow's local Government was reformed. At this time, the city's electorate was divided into merchants, represented by Merchants House and craftsmen, represented by the Trades House, which was established to support Glasgow's craftsmen and provide training through the Trades Free School. Still in existence today, it is now primarily a charitable organisation.

36. Once you reach Glassford Street, turn right and head north back towards Ingram Street. At the junction with Ingram Street is the former Glasgow Savings Bank. Designed in an Italianate style by John Burnet, it was built in 1865. His son, John James Burnet, added the single-storey banking hall, which faces on to Ingram Street, in 1898. This is a beautiful building with some wonderfully ornate sculptures by George Frampton, including a figure of Saint Mungo over the Ingram Street entrance, and some very evocative crouching atlantes. There are also some fantastic examples of decorative ironwork and acid-etched glass on this building.

Crouching atlante on former Glasgow Savings Bank, Ingram Street.

37. To the west of the Glasgow Savings Bank building on Ingram Street is another former bank building, this time constructed for the Union Bank of Scotland. It was originally designed by David Hamilton in 1841 in a free Venetian mannerist style, but with additions by James Salmon Snr in 1853 and John Burnet in the 1870s. Its upper floors feature a series of allegorical figures by John Mossman representing Navigation and Commerce (holding a globe and sexton), Britannia (holding a trident), Wealth (holding a cornucopia), Justice (holding a sword and scales), Peace (holding an olive branch), Industry (holding a bobbin), Glasgow (holding the city's coat of arms and a key) and Mechanics and Agriculture (holding a sheaf of corn, a sickle and a wheel). Over the door are a series of shields inscribed with the names and founding dates of the six banks which merged to form the Union Bank in 1843. In the 1930s, this building was converted into the headquarters of Lanark County Council (formerly based in the municipal buildings further east along Ingram Street) and then into part of the Sheriff's Court and Justice of the Peace Court in 1964, which also occupied the same municipal buildings. It is now used as a private members club.

38. From the former Union Bank building, cross over Ingram Street at the traffic lights and follow South Frederick Street north to George Square. As you do so, look back towards the building you have just visited for the best views of Mossman's allegorical figures and to take in the building's full beauty. Once you emerge into George Square, where this walk ends, head towards Glasgow City Chambers which occupy its entire eastern side. Designed by William Young and constructed in the 1880s, this incredibly opulent building, both inside and out, was a major statement of the city's civic pride and its strength as a global industrial powerhouse. It is primarily Italianate in design, featuring Venetian and Roman references, and it is richly decorated with a variety of allegorical sculptures by a number of well-known sculptors. Although the interior is usually off-limits to visitors, it is generally accessible as part of Glasgow's Doors Open Day Festival, and if you have the opportunity to view it, it is well worth doing as much of it has to be seen to be believed. Directly above the main entrance is an allegorical frieze created by George Anderson Lawson. In the centre is the Glasgow coat of arms, surrounded by figures representing Glory, Victory, Hope, Faith, Truth and Charity. On the panel to the left are figures representing Astronomy, Geology, Chemistry and Medicine, while the panel on the right contains figures representing Architecture and Sculpture, Painting and Music. Above these figures, in the spandrels of the second-storey windows are sculptures by John Mossman representing the trades and industries of Glasgow. On the third storey are more allegorical figures, this time by John Rhind, representing Hygiene, Wisdom, Peace, Plenty, Harmony, Piety, History and Prosperity. Finally, at the top is the Jubilee pediment, again created by Lawson, which celebrates Queen Victoria's fiftieth year on the throne. The central figure is Queen Victoria, and she is surrounded by figures representing England, Scotland, Ireland and Wales, as well as the countries of the British Empire, including Canda, Australia and New Zealand (to her left) and Africa, India, and other eastern colonies (to her right). Standing on the pinnacle of the Jubilee Pediment is a figure often described as Glasgow's Statue of Liberty. However, the architect himself described this figure as representing Truth holding up the light of Liberty over the city, supported by the figures representing Riches and Honour. While at the City Chambers, it is worth looking at the bottom-right-hand corner of its George Square facade. Here, you will find a set of standards for imperial measures. This, along with two standards for longer measures set into the pavement of George Square itself, provided a way of standardising measurements, thus ensuring everyone in the city was using the same measurements, which was important for both industry and commerce. Similar standard measures were provided on public buildings

Grand entrance, Glasgow City Chambers, George Square.

throughout the British Empire, ensuring that something measured in feet and built in Glasgow was the same size as a similar item manufactured in Birmingham or London, or even on the other side of the world in Australia or New Zealand.

3. Sauchiehall Street, Part I

Start Point: The Donald Dewar Statue at the top of Buchanan Street, Glasgow (**Location:** Lat/Lon: 55.86400, -4.25286 ; What3Words: ///fund.precautions.radar; Plus Code: VP7W+JV2 Glasgow). **Nearest Public Transport:** Subway: Buchanan Street Station (2 mins); Train: Queen Street Station (5 mins); Bus: Buchanan Bus Station (5 mins).

End Point: Charing Cross Mansions, St George's Road, Glasgow (**Location:** Lat/Lon: 55.86637, -4.27063; What3Words: ///burst.games.dose; Plus Code: VP8H+GPX Glasgow). **Nearest Public Transport:** Train: Charing Cross Station (5 mins); Subway: Cowcaddens Station (15 mins); Bus: Sauchiehall Street (2 mins).

Distance: 1.6 kilometres/1 mile. **Time:** Allow 1.5 to 2.5 hours for this walk.
Level of Difficulty: Easy. This walk is on relatively flat, paved streets, many of which are pedestrianised.

Facilities: There are plenty of shops, cafes, restaurants and bars where you can stop for refreshments along this route. Publicly accessible toilets are available in Buchanan Galleries at the start of this walk, and in the Centre for Contemporary Arts towards the end of it.

Introduction

Sauchiehall Street stretches from the city centre to the West End, making it one of the longest in Glasgow. It is also one of the most famous and has long been a centre for entertainment, and many of the city's theatres, music halls and cinemas were built either on or near it. Its name derives from the Scots words for willow (sauchie) and a low marshy area or meadow (haugh), and it started life as a narrow, winding lane which led from the north end of Buchanan Street to Kelvingrove (which at that point was known as Clayslaps). As the city expanded westward, this lane was straightened and widened, first as far as Rose Street in 1807, then as far as Charing Cross in the 1860s, and eventually to its current junction with Argyle Street. This is the first of two walks along different sections of Sauchiehall Street, and covers the section between Buchanan Street and the M8 motorway at Charing Cross, all of which can be considered to fall within Glasgow city centre. As Sauchiehall Street developed throughout the nineteenth century, this section was first occupied by a series of villas, each set in their own gardens, and then by terraces of self-contained townhouses. These were followed by tenements, and by commercial premises as the street continued its development, gradually taking over from Argyle Street as the city's upmarket shopping street. Although many of the tenements and commercial buildings constructed towards the end of the 1800s still stand to this day, the villas are long gone. However, some of the original Georgian townhouses remain, hidden away behind the newer buildings which were constructed in what were previously their front gardens. With upmarket shopping came pubs and bars, and for those who wished to avoid the evils of alcohol, the ubiquitous Glasgow Tea Rooms, as well as theatres and other entertainment venues. Always keen to capitalise on the latest trends, when moving pictures were invented, a surprising number of its older buildings were turned into cinemas. Over the course of the twentieth century, Sauchiehall Street's former glory has faded somewhat. While it is still an important shopping street which has retained many of traditional buildings, its cinemas and theatres are largely gone, and several key buildings have been lost to fires. However, as always, there are plans to rejuvenate it, but these are yet to come to fruition.

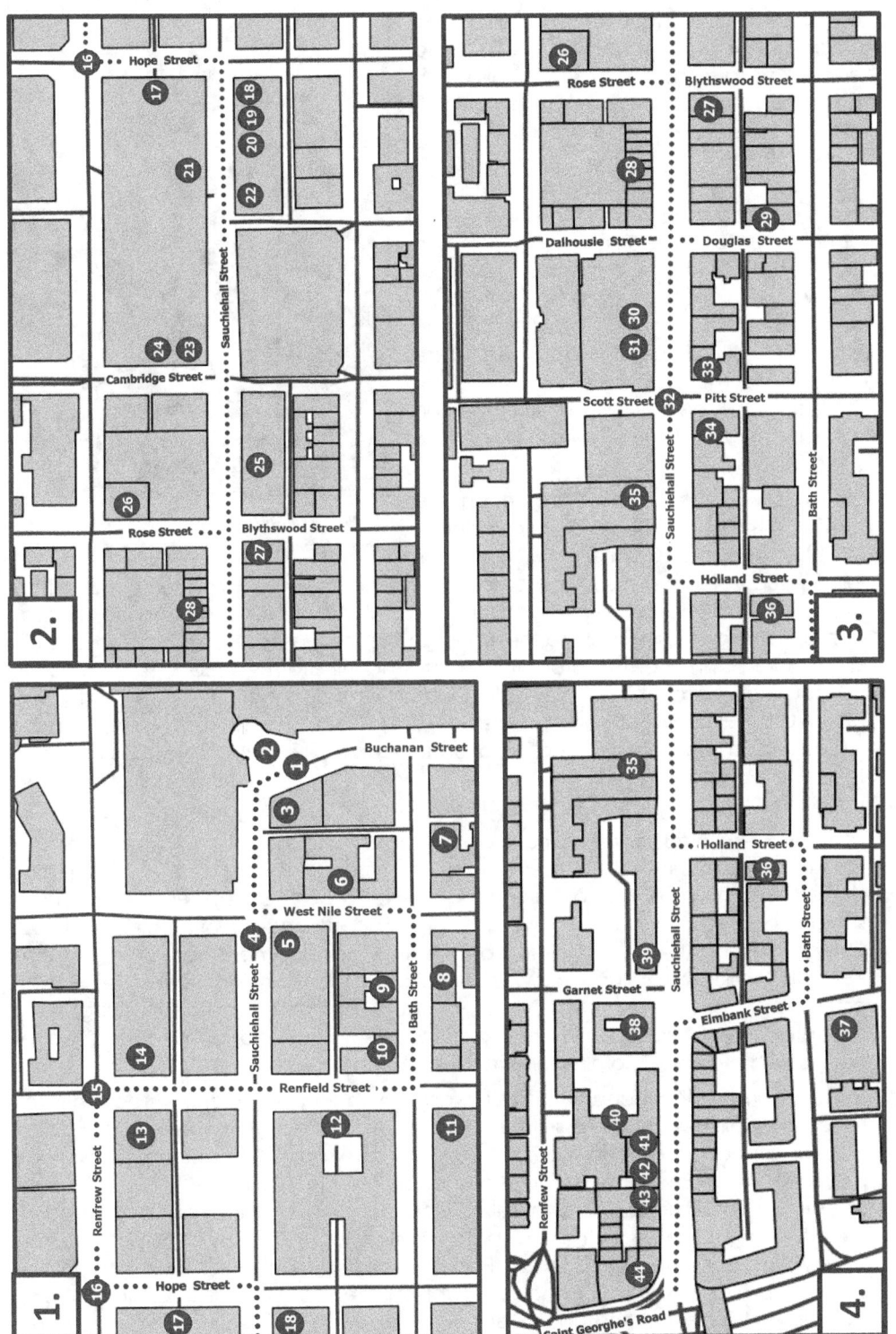

1. This walk starts at the Donald Dewer statue at the northern end of Buchanan Street, which was erected in 2002 to commemorate the life of the Glaswegian politician who served as Scotland's first First Minister when the Scottish Parliament was re-established in 1999 after a gap of almost 300 years. The Parliament had previously been disbanded in 1707, following the Act of Union, an event which was triggered, in part, by the failure of the Darien Scheme. This was Scotland's attempt at establishing an American colony in the Darien Gap, in what is now Panama, and its failure bankrupted much of the country. Dewer died quite suddenly and unexpectedly in 2000, at the age of sixty-three, while he was still in office.

Statue of Donald Dewer, Scotland's first First Minister.

2. Behind the Donald Dewer statue on the corner of Buchanan Street and Sauchiehall Street is the Royal Concert Hall. The steps leading up to it are a popular meeting and resting point, and on sunny days, they are often filled with people eating lunch, waiting to meet friends, taking a break from shopping or just watching the world go by. These steps also offer a great view down Buchanan Street and out to the hills and windfarms of Eaglesham Moor to the south of the city. The Royal Concert Hall was designed by Leslie Martin and opened in 1990. It was built as a replacement for St Andrew's Hall on Granville Street, just off the West End section of Sauchiehall Street, which was destroyed by fire in 1962.

3. On the opposite corner of Buchanan Street and Sauchiehall Street is the Cleland Testimonial Building. This tenement was designed by David and James Hamilton, and constructed in 1835 in memory of Dr James Cleland (1770–1840). Cleland started his working life as a cabinetmaker, but is best remembered as a public servant and statistician. He served as the Superintendent of Public Works for Glasgow during the pivotal period of the city's development between 1814 and 1834. Among other things, he was one of the main driving forces behind the creation of a public park at Glasgow Green. At the top of the building is the inscription 'The Cleland Testimonial' and the Cleland coat of arms, which features a hare with a hunting horn around its neck.

4. From its corner with Buchanan Street, walk west along Sauchiehall Street until you reach the point where it crosses West Nile Street. Ahead, you will see a red police box (or at least it was still there at the time of writing). The British police box is perhaps most famous for its appearance in *Dr Who* as the TARDIS, but it was invented by a Glasgow Fireman called Charles Eggar and they first appeared on the city's streets in 1891. In the days before radios and mobile phones, police boxes were a way for patrolling police officers to keep in touch with their local police station. Equipped with a phone, the light on the top was used to alert passing policemen to the fact that they were being called. Members of the public could also use the phone to contact both the police and the fire brigade in case of an

emergency. While police boxes are most often associated with the colour blue, red was the traditional colour for police boxes in Glasgow.

5. Also at the corner of West Nile Street and Sauchiehall Street is Empire House. Built in 1971, this is a prime example of the type of modern architecture that has blighted much of Glasgow. It sits on the site of the historic Glasgow Empire Theatre, which was demolished in 1963. The theatre was designed by the renowned theatre architect Frank Matcham for the Moss Empire theatre chain and first opened in 1897. Over the years, the Glasgow Empire played host to many famous names, including Laurel and Hardy, Tony Bennett, Frank Sinatra, Bob Hope and Judy Garland. Among performers, it was notorious for its rowdy audiences, and it was often referred to as 'the English Comics' graveyard' as the audience did not respond well to any act which failed to amuse them. This led one performer, Des O'Connor, to pretend to faint when the audience started to jeer so he would be dragged off stage rather being forced to continue.

6. From Empire House, head south down West Nile Street. On the left is Victoria Chambers. This red sandstone commercial building is a classic Glasgow design of the early 1900s, with bay windows to allow as much light in as possible. In comparison to many other Glasgow buildings, it has relatively few frills, but it has some ornate classically inspired relief sculptures around its doorway which are worth checking out.

7. A short distance further down West Nile Street is its junction with Bath Street, and looking left along Bath Street from this point, you can see Albert Chambers. Designed by Bruce & Hay in a free Renaissance style, this commercial building was constructed in 1901. It has a rather wonderful turret at its eastern corner and a beautifully carved art nouveau/Glasgow style street number above its entrance. As with many Glasgow buildings of this time, it originally contained a mix of warehouses, ground-floor shops and offices.

8. Turn right and head west along Bath Street. On the south side of the street is Central Halls, with its classical style entrance. Now used as a church, it started life as a Masonic hall.

9. Opposite the Central Halls at 38 Bath Street is the former Mechanics' Institute Building. Designed by James Salmon Snr in a classical style, it started life as a three-storey building in 1861. Two additional storeys were added by Arthur Hamilton around 1910, while a sixth storey was added in the 2000s. Mechanics' Institutes were found in many industrial cities around the world, and aimed to provide adult education to working men, particularly in technical subjects. The Glasgow Mechanics' Institute was founded in 1823 following a dispute between the mechanics' class and the managers at Anderson's Institute, and was the second one ever

Former Mechanics Institute, 38 Bath Street.

established (after the one in Liverpool, founded a few months earlier). It became the College of Science and Arts in 1881, and was absorbed into the Glasgow and West of Scotland Technical College in 1887.

10. Further west along Bath Street on the same side as the Mechanics' Institute, at No. 46, is Tara House which has a fine example of the Glasgow coat of arms over its main entrance, as well as carved panels featuring birds, bells and trees. Along with a fish, the fourth symbol on the city's coat of arms, these symbols can be found in many different forms on buildings across Glasgow.

11. At the corner between Bath Street and Renfield Street is the Refuge Assurance Building. Constructed in the 1930s, this building was designed by Stanley Birkett in the beaux-arts style and is a well-preserved example of a purpose-built office building from this period. The ground floor originally hosted a branch of the Bank of Scotland.

12. From this point, turn north onto Renfield Street and head back towards Sauchiehall Street. On the west side of Renfield Street is the 1960s British Home Stores (BHS) building. This was once the location of Renfield Street United Presbyterian Church, but it became one of Glasgow's magnificent lost buildings when it was demolished to make way for the current building.

13. When you reach Sauchiehall Street, cross it and carry on north along Renfield Street until you reach the Pavilion Theatre, one of Glasgow's oldest surviving theatres. It opened in 1904 as a music hall under the name The Pavilion Theatre of Varieties. The building was designed by Bertie Crewe as part of Thomas Barrasford's chain of British Music Halls. The outside of the building is in a French Renaissance style finished with glazed terracotta and features some wonderful relief sculptures, while the inside is considered 'Pure Louis XV' in style.

Beaux-arts style Refuge Assurance Building, Bath Street.

14. On the opposite side of Renfield Street at No. 126 (a site now occupied by a very modern cinema) once stood the legendary Apollo music venue. Originally Green's Playhouse, the Apollo opened in 1973 and featured a 'bouncy balcony', designed and built so it would move as the audience standing in it jumped up and down. Status Quo's first live album was recorded in this venue in October 1976, and Francis Rossi can be heard on it asking the audience to get the balcony moving. It also featured a 4.7 metre (15.5 feet) high stage, which was seen as a challenge for local concert-goers to try to climb on to. The Apollo closed in 1985, with the last performance being by the Style Council. The final song they played was a cover of Curtis Mayfield's 'Move On Up'. The venue was demolished in 1987 after a fire rendered it structurally unsafe, a surprisingly common end to historic Glasgow buildings (including at least four mentioned during this walk), leading to much local speculation whenever yet another one burns down as to why it happened.

15. From Renfield Street, the main walk turns left on to Renfrew Street. However, you can also carry on north up Renfield Street to the William Annan Fountain, on top of which sits a rather wonderfully sculpted unicorn. The fountain was presented to the City of Glasgow by William Annan of Port Dundas in 1915.

16. If you take this detour, return to Renfrew Street and follow it along to Hope Street, where you can take another optional detour up to the Theatre Royal and the impressive McConnell's Building with its art nouveau detailing, but for the main walk, turn left and walk south down Hope Street, back to Sauchiehall Street.

17. On the right-hand side of Hope Street, is the brutalist concrete Savoy Centre, built in the 1970s. Its main feature of interest is the nameplate set into the concrete in a classic 1970s style font.

18. On reaching Sauchiehall Street once more, turn right and head west. This section is home to a series of magnificent buildings in a wide range of architectural styles, although the modern shopfronts of many help to hide their magnificence. The first of these is Watt Brothers Department Store at 119 Sauchiehall Street, which extends back along Hope Street to Bath Street. The front part of the building was designed in a classical style by Alex S. Heathcote and was built in 1914, whereas the rear part (which can be seen by walking a short distance down Hope Street) was added later. This newer section was designed in an art deco style by Graham Henderson. The metal window casements and friezes were created by the Glasgow's MacFarlane & Co. foundry, then one of the leading producers of ornamental ironwork in the country. Watt Brothers Department Store survived until the 2000s, by which time it was the last family owned department store still operating in the city.

Bath Street elevation, former Watt Brothers Department Store.

19. Next to Watt Brothers Department Store at 133 Sauchiehall Street is the former Rhule Tea Room. Designed by James Carruthers and built in 1925, this is an excellent example of Glasgow's art deco tea room architecture, and contrasts with the earlier art nouveau/Glasgow style tea rooms created by the likes of Charles Rennie Mackintosh, an example of which can be found further west along Sauchiehall Street. Tea rooms were a Glasgow institution in the early part of the twentieth century and were much more than simple cafes. The Rhule Tea Room was a grand establishment with a shop, tea room, smoking room, luncheon room and function rooms spread over five storeys. It was referred to locally as the Unofficial Art Galleries of Glasgow as its walls were covered with an unrivalled collection of paintings by the Glasgow Boys, collected by James Craig, the tea room's owner.

20. Beside the former Rhule Tea Room, at 139 Sauchiehall Street, is a five-storey red sandstone commercial building. Built in 1904, it was designed in an Edwardian baroque style by John Keppie, who was also responsible for several other

impressive buildings on Sauchiehall Street. However, he is probably now best known not for his own work, but as being a mentor to Charles Rennie Mackintosh, one of Glasgow's most famous and influential architects.

21. On the opposite side of Sauchiehall Street is the Savoy Centre. Originally built in 1895 as a warehouse for the cabinetmakers Cumming & Smith, it was designed by Hugh and David Barclay in a free classical style. The sculptures along its facade are worth examining in detail, both because of their quality and because of the mix of symbolism they contain. Created by William Birnie Rhind, there are three groups of figures all holding objects associated in some way with commerce, trade or husbandry. These include a flail, a dove and a palm frond in the left-hand group, and a galleon, flaming torch, book, trumpet, mirror and a pair of dividers in the right-hand group. In the middle are two upright figures, one holding a sword and a shield, and the other holding a scroll and a dough paddle. Between these figures are other carvings, including a cockerel and a rising sun, both of which are common Masonic symbols. At a lower level, in the pediments above the first-floor windows, are a Scottish thistle, an English rose, an Irish shamrock and a group of three ostrich feathers tied together with a ribbon. This last one seems at odds with the other three, but represents 'Ich dien', the heraldic symbol of the Prince of Wales. Finally, at the very top of the building are relief masks of the ancient Greek goddess Athena and the Roman god Mercury. Although this facade was retained, the warehouse itself was later developed into the Picture House Cinema in 1910, as were a surprisingly large number of other warehouses on Sauchiehall Street around this time. In the 1970s, the building was once again redeveloped, this time into the Savoy Shopping Centre.

22. Across from the Savoy Centre is a building which currently houses a Waterstone's bookshop. This is another building which was originally built as a warehouse, but that was later converted into a cinema. In this case, it was called La Scala, which was designed by Duff & McKissack and opened in 1912. The cinema eventually closed in 1984, but the original entrance, flanked by pillars and topped by a large and beautiful art nouveau stained-glass window, has recently been restored.

23. Further west along Sauchiehall Street, on the corner with Cambridge Street, is an ornate free classical style commercial building. Built in 1902, it was designed by James Thomson, who designed a lot of the wildest-looking buildings constructed in Glasgow around this time. Thomson was well known for including his own portrait as a relief sculpture on many of the buildings he designed later in his career, and this one is no exception. If

Grand entrance, former La Scala cinema, Sauchiehall Street.

you walk round to the Cambridge Street facade and look to the left of the first column of bay windows, you can see his face, complete with his distinctive muttonchop facial hair, staring out from above a second-storey window.

24. While you are on Cambridge Street, it is worth checking out its neighbour at No. 18. Much more understated than Thomson's building, it is nonetheless a beautiful example of a Venetian style warehouse. At one point, it was used by William Thomson, better known as Lord Kelvin, one of the greatest scientists to have been educated in Glasgow.

25. Back on Sauchiehall Street, at No. 217, is the Glasgow style Willow Tea Room. Based on an older 1860s building, it was redesigned inside and out in 1903, by Charles Rennie Mackintosh and his wife, Margaret Macdonald, as a tea room for the legendary Glasgow businesswoman Catherine (Kate) Cranston. This building is often cited as the best of Mackintosh's tea rooms, and it was the only one where he designed the exterior as well as the interior. Cranston was the daughter of a tea merchant and a firm advocate of the Temperance Movement. This led her to establish a series of beautifully decorated art nouveau style tea rooms where people could meet and socialise in an alcohol-free environment. As part of this aim, she worked with Mackintosh for more than twenty years before she eventually sold her tea rooms in 1917.

26. A short distance further along Sauchiehall Street, west from the Willow Tea Room, is its junction with Rose Street and Blythswood Street, where the pedestrianised zone ends. To the right on Rose Street is the Glasgow Film Theatre, which remains a great example of an art deco style cinema.

27. On Sauchiehall Street itself, on the left-hand side of this junction, is one of Glasgow's monolithic modern classical style financial buildings which would not look out of place in New York or Chicago. Built for the Bank of Scotland in 1931, it was designed by John Keppie and Graham Henderson. It is interesting to compare this building to Keppie's Edwardian baroque warehouse at 139 Sauchiehall Street (No. 15 on this walk) to see just how much architectural styles in Glasgow changed over the first thirty years of the twentieth century.

1930s modern classical financial building.

28. On the other side of the junction is McLellan Galleries. Designed by James Smith and built in 1855, this was the first gallery for the McLellan Collection, named after the art collector Archibald McLellan (1795–1854). This collection was transferred to the Kelvingrove Art Gallery when it opened at the western end of Sauchiehall Street in 1901. The McLellan Galleries building was later altered by Frank Burnet and Boston in 1904, who added the distinctive dome on the corner and created the shopfronts. The bust of a young Queen Victoria over the main entrance is by John Mossman and was probably part of the original facade.

29. Further west along Sauchiehall Street is its junction with Douglas Street. A short distance to the south of this junction, at 121 Douglas Street, is the former City of Glasgow Friendly Society Building. It can be identified by a sculpture set into a recessed niche of John Stewart, the founder of the society, seated with his arm around a young boy, teaching him to read. This teacher-and-student composition is common in both classical and Victorian sculpture and can be seen on a variety of buildings associated with education, learning or social betterment around Glasgow. The City of Glasgow Friendly Society was founded in 1862 with the aim of allowing workers to provide each other with mutual aid should they become sick, or in old age. This was exceedingly important in the time before State pensions, the National Health Service and sickness benefits as it was often the only way working-class people could hope to remain financially solvent if, for any reason, they found themselves unable to work.

Statue of John Stewart, founded City of Glasgow Friendly Society in 1862.

30. Back on Sauchiehall Street, No. 302 was, at one time, the Women's Freedom League (WFL) Suffrage Centre. The WFL was founded in 1907 to campaign for votes for women, but it focussed more on civil disobedience rather than the more militant action associated with the Women's Social and Political Union (WSPU), which had a base at 141 Bath Street and was responsible for, among other things, the 1914 bombing of the Kibble Palace glasshouse in Glasgow's Botanic Gardens. From their centre on Sauchiehall Street, the WFL ran a tea room, sold newspapers and other literature, organised public meetings and held fundraising sales. Their presence here was relatively short-lived and they moved to St George's Road in 1912. The building itself has since been demolished and replaced with a much newer one.

31. Next to the location of former WFL Suffrage Centre is the O2 ABC music venue. Once home to the largest mirror ball in Europe, it was badly damaged by a fire in 2018. This fire also destroyed the neighbouring Glasgow School of Art, which was designed by a former student, Charles Rennie Mackintosh, and was often regarded as the city's most architecturally important building. This fire brought to an end almost 150 years of history for the ABC as an entertainment venue. It started life in 1875 as a venue called the Diorama, before becoming the Panorama (1878), Hubner's Ice Skating Palace (1885), Hengler's Circus (1904) and the Waldorf Palace Dance Hall (1927). It got its current art deco facade, which was designed by Charles J. McNair, when it was converted into a cinema in 1929. The ABC has an important place in Glasgow's cinema history as it was here, in 1896, that a film was first shown publicly in the city. This was when it was still an ice rink and was possible because, in 1888, it became one of the first buildings in Glasgow to be fitted with electricity. At the time of writing, the ABC is under threat of demolition and, despite

its social history and importance to the surrounding streetscape, it may well have been lost before this book is published.

32. To the west of the former ABC is Scott Street and if you look up at the lamp posts on this street as you pass, you will see sculptures of small birds sitting on the top of them. This is part of an art installation by Shona Kinloch called *Chookie Burdies*, which includes over 150 aluminium pigeons perched on top of street lights throughout the Garnethill area of Glasgow, which lies to the north of this section of Sauchiehall Street. *Chookie Burdies* was installed in 1993.

Shona Kinloch's Chookie Burdies *on top of lamp post, Garnethill.*

33. On the other side of Sauchiehall Street is a restaurant, currently called Antipasti, which features a traditional Edwardian shopfront, including rather wonderful curved glass windows on either side of the door. Many of the modern shopfronts along Sauchiehall Street greatly detract from the surrounding architecture, and older shopfronts like this one are a reminder that this was not always the case, nor does it need to be now.

34. Just across the Pitt Street junction with Sauchiehall Street is an imposing five-storey red sandstone commercial building. Constructed in 1903 as a furniture shop for the cabinetmakers and upholsterers James Simpson & Sons, this is another of the Sauchiehall Street buildings designed by John Keppie. This time it is in a Mannerist style, providing further evidence of the breadth of Keppie's abilities as an architect.

35. The next building of interest on Sauchiehall Street is Grecian Chambers at No. 350. Built in 1865, this terrace of commercial buildings was designed by Glasgow's other famous architect, Alexander 'Greek' Thomson. Many of the features of Grecian Chambers are typical of a 'Greek' Thomson building, including the roundels around the entrance, the Greek style inscribed friezes along the top and, in particular, the palmette or palm frond motifs. Interestingly, the same palmette motifs also appear on a number of nearby buildings, including a tenement on the southern side of the street and the neighbouring art deco ABC cinema, helping to provide a common thread to the local streetscape over more than fifty years of architectural change. Grecian Chambers is part of a series of buildings along this section of Sauchiehall Street, built in the front gardens of a row of six Georgian townhouses once known as Albany Place. Although the name Albany Place no longer appears on any maps, the townhouses themselves are still there, but have mostly been swallowed up by later developments. However, in some places they can still be seen and, in particular, if you go into the Centre for Contemporary Arts, which is housed in Grecian Chambers, you can see the front of one of these townhouses where it has been exposed in its atrium.

36. At the junction of Sauchiehall Street and Holland Street, turn left on to Holland Street. On the right-hand side just before you reach Bath Street is the Renfield St Stephen's Parish Church. If you look carefully at the corner of this building on Sauchiehall Lane, you will see one of Glasgow's many architectural sculptures,

which are somewhat hidden away and so easily missed by those who fail to look up as they explore the city. In this case, it is a rather beautifully carved griffin nestled into the eves. Once at Bath Street itself, turn right, where you can see the front of this church, which was designed by John T. Emmet and built around 1850. On either side of the door are two cast-iron boot scrapers. Boot scrapers were a ubiquitous piece of Glasgow street furniture in the Victorian and Edwardian periods when horses, and their dung, were a common sight on its streets, meaning boots had to be scraped clean before entering a building. However, these boot scrapers are unusually large and probably the largest ones in the city (although there is a pair at Pollok Country House in the Southside part of Glasgow which come close to rivalling them).

37. Further south down Bath Street, at its corner with Elmbank Street, is the Edwardian baroque King's Theatre. Commissioned by the theatre-owning company Howard and Wyndham Ltd, it was designed in 1904 by the renowned theatre architect Frank Matcham, who also designed the now-lost Glasgow Empire. Its interior is spectacular and one of the finest examples of a Matcham theatre in Scotland.

38. Turn north onto Elmbank Street and walk back towards Sauchiehall Street. As you do this, directly ahead you will see the Beresford, the gem in Glasgow's art deco crown. Designed by James Weddell and William Beresford Inglis, this eight-storey modernist building was originally constructed in 1937 as a hotel for visitors to the 1938 Empire Exhibition, held in Bellahouston Park, and it is often considered to be Glasgow's first skyscraper. Rather surprisingly, it played a small, but important, part in the global political landscape of the mid-twentieth century. This is because in 1939, it hosted the first public address by a then twenty-two year old John F. Kennedy, the future President of the United States of America. He had been sent by his father, the US Ambassador to the UK, to address the surviving passengers of the Clyde-built SS *Athenia*, the first British ship to be sunk by a U-boat after Britain declared war on Germany. Faced with an angry crowd, the young Kennedy remained composed and did his best to answer their questions and assuage their concerns.

39. Once back on Sauchiehall Street, look to the right of the Beresford. Here, at No. 450, stands a large commercial building constructed in a free Renaissance style in 1899, from a design by Watson and Mitchell. While the building itself is beautiful, perhaps its most interesting feature is a series of faded ghost signs just below the dome on the corner with Garnet Street and along the Sauchiehall Street facade, which says 'Grieve Limited'. This is a reference to William Robertson Grieve who owned a business which once occupied the building. Grieve was a member of the University of Glasgow Training Corps and was sent to the Western Front in 1917, where he was

Ghost sign, Grieve Limited, top of 1899 commercial building.

killed in action barely a month after his arrival. This sign remains as an unusual memorial to a life cut short by war.

40. Turn left and head south down Sauchiehall Street to the small lane between the Beresford and the neighbouring building to its south. If you walk up this lane and look to the left, you will see an old building with a large G2 painted on side. This is building forms part of the Garage Night Club, one of the largest night clubs in Scotland, but unknown to most of its customers, it is also one of the 'lost' Albany Place Georgian villas, which were built in 1812. It was originally occupied by a button manufacturer called James Deakin.

41. Head back to Sauchiehall Street and continue westward. On the northern side of the street, between Nos. 500 and 520, there is a row of three interesting buildings. The first of these (No. 500–516) is currently a casino, but started life in 1898 as a warehouse. However, it was soon redeveloped as Glasgow's first purpose-built cinema, opening in 1910 as the Charing Cross Electric Theatre. The cinema closed in 1926 and the building was later turned into a ballroom.

42. Next to this building is another of John Keppie's creations. Constructed in 1903 in an early Renaissance style, this four-storey building is currently home to the Royal Highland Fusiliers Regimental Museum, but it started life as a studio for T. & R. Annan & Sons, a photographer and fine-arts dealer. The two statues at the top of this building are derived from Michelangelo's Sistine Chapel.

Statues, Royal Highland Fusiliers Regimental Museum.

On the left is the Delphic Sibyl, a female prophet associated with early religious practices in Ancient Greece, while on the right is the Prophet Isaiah. The facade may have been designed by Charles Rennie Mackintosh, who had been made a partner two years previously, in the architectural firm Honeyman and Keppie, as his name appears on the working drawings of the building. This includes an earlier version of the facade featuring a third statue, the Libyan Sibyl, a prophetic priestess who also appears on the Sistine Chapel, something Mackintosh admired profoundly.

43. The final building in this row is 520 Sauchiehall Street. It was originally constructed in the 1890s as a piano showroom, known as the Ewing Galleries after the owner Thomas Alfred Ewing, with a roof-lit performance hall added later at the rear, along with a salon in a new storey above the original single storey at the front. In 1912, it was converted into a cinema called the Vitagraph, and continued as a cinema under various names until 1984. The statues on this building were created by James Alexander Ewing, Thomas Ewing's brother, and they include a winged female figure of Harmony on the apex. There also used to be a large bust of Beethoven above the rear entrance on Renfrew Street, but this has been removed for safety reasons, with the intention of it being replaced at some future date. Between the front and rear sections of this building is another of the Albany Place 'lost' villas, which was incorporated into this property as it was developed. It is no longer visible from the street, but parts of it can still be seen on aerial photographs.

44. Finally, at the Charing Cross section of Sauchiehall Street, where this walks ends, are two very grand red sandstone buildings. These are Albany Chambers on Sauchiehall Street itself and Charing Cross Mansions, which curves from Sauchiehall Street onto St George's Road and then Renfrew Street. Both were designed by John James Burnet in a French Renaissance style, with Charing Cross Mansions constructed in 1891 and Albany Chambers added later in 1896. Charing Cross Mansions is probably the grandest building on Sauchiehall Street, and some of the best views of it are either from the far side of St George's Road, or from the pedestrian bridge at the end of Renfrew Street. Of particular note is the sculpted nameplate and clock created by William Birnie Rhind. The clock, in particular, is a work of art. The dial is surrounded by signs of the zodiac, while just under this is a small mask of a bearded man. This is often thought to be a representation of Father Time, and may well be, but it also bears an uncanny resemblance to John James Burnet's father, the renowned classical architect John Burnet Snr. Below the clock itself are large sculpted female figures representing Spring (on the left, carrying a garland of flowers) and Autumn (on the right, carrying a sheaf of corn and a sickle). Above the clock are two more female figures representing Commerce (on the left, holding a dough paddle) and Industry (on the right, holding a hammer and cogs wheels).

John James Burnet's magnificent French Renaissance style Charing Cross Mansions.

4. City Centre West

Start Point: Royal Faculty of Procurators, West George Street, Glasgow (**Location:** Lat/Lon: 55.86216, -4.25488; What3Words: ///brains.tower.random; Plus Code: VP6W+V29 Glasgow). **Nearest Public Transport:** Subway: Buchanan Street Station (5 mins); Train: Queen Street Station (10 mins); Bus: West George Street (1 min).

End Point: The Clyde Navigation Trust Building, Robertson Street, Glasgow (**Location:** Lat/Lon: 55.85671, -4.26098; What3Words: ///feel.pack.flesh; Plus Code: VP4Q+MJJ Glasgow). **Nearest Public Transport:** Subway: St Enoch Station (10 mins); Train: Glasgow Central Station (10 mins); Bus: Argyle Street (5 mins).

Distance: 1.9 kilometres/1.2 mile. **Time:** Allow 1 to 2 hours for this walk.

Level of Difficulty: Easy. This walk is entirely on paved surfaces.

Facilities: There are shops, cafes, restaurants and bars available at fairly regular intervals along this walk. Publicly accessible toilets are available in the Buchanan Galleries near its start and at Central Station, which you pass close to around the middle of this walk.

Introduction

For the purpose of this walk, the City Centre West area of Glasgow is bounded by Buchanan Street in the east, Sauchiehall Street to the north, the M8 motorway in the west and the Clyde to the south. Its development started around 1800 when work began on the Blythswood New Town. Originally intended to be a western suburb on the edge of the city, by the end of the nineteenth century and into the start of the twentieth century, it had become the focus of Glasgow's rapidly growing financial district. This led to the area being filled with an eclectic mix of buildings constructed in a diversity of styles, ranging from classical Georgian through art nouveau and Edwardian baroque to art deco and modern classical, which is almost unmatched in any other city in Britain, and possibly the world. However, despite these many disparate architectural styles, the buildings nonetheless manage to come together to form a unified and unique streetscape. Much of this is the result of the choice of building materials (primarily blonde and red sandstone) and the wealth of wonderful, and sometimes rather weird, architectural sculptures which decorate them. These sculptures form a major element of this walk. In particular, as you follow this walk, you will see that similar sculptural elements appear repeatedly on very different styles of buildings from different eras of Glasgow's architecture, such as personifications of virtues the owners of buildings wished to be associated with, palmate or palm frond motifs, protruding ships' prows, lion heads, the Glasgow coat of arms (and different elements from it), Green Men, mythological and allegorical figures, and keystone masks. This helps not only to unite buildings constructed in very different architectural styles, but also to give them a uniquely Glaswegian feel.

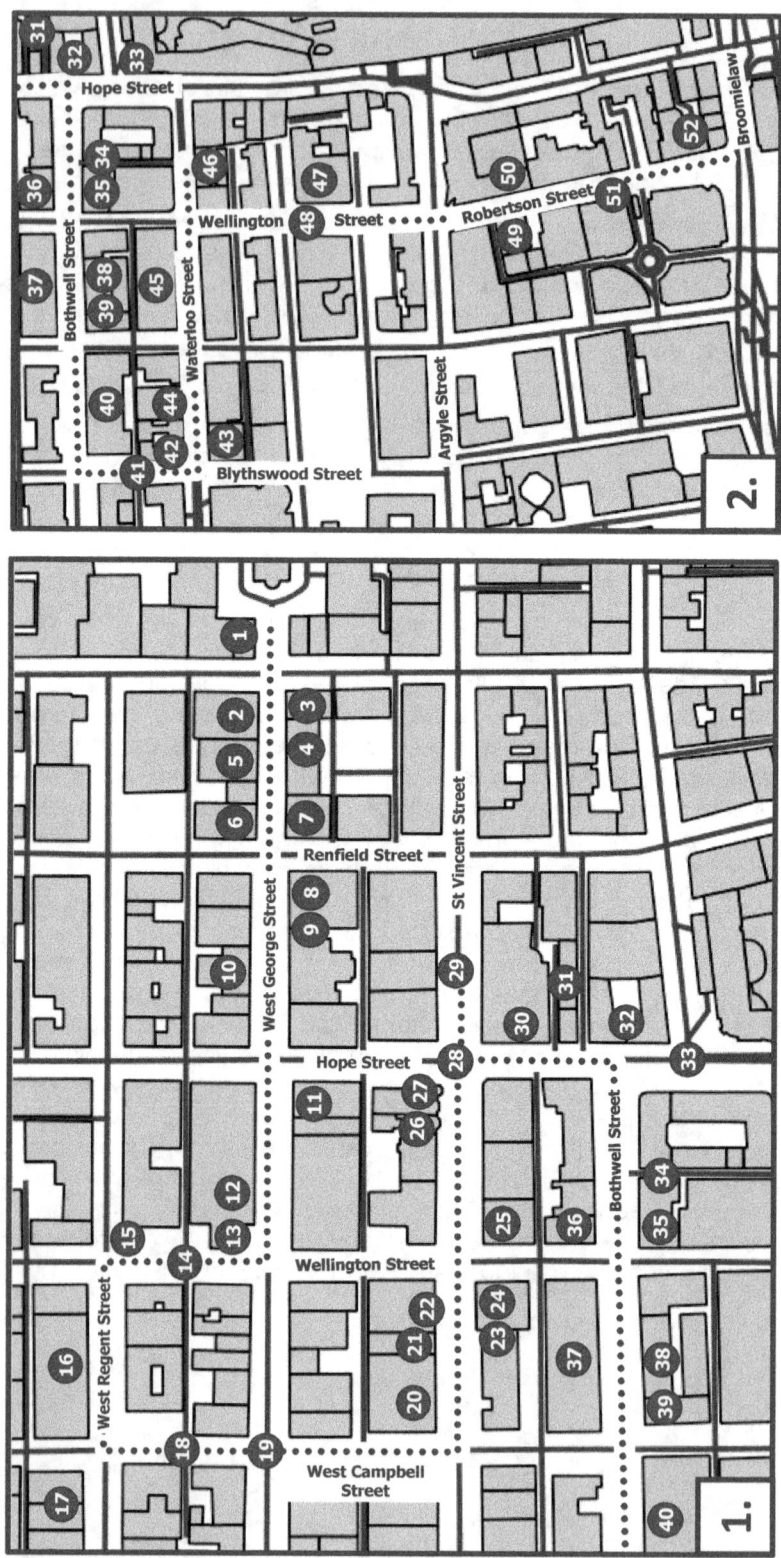

1. This walks starts at the Royal Faculty of Procurators on the corner of West George Street and West Nile Street. Designed by Charles Wilson in a Venetian Renaissance style, it was built in 1854. Of particular note on this building are the sculpted keystone heads representing 'the most distinguished Scottish law lords and lawyers' of previous ages. From right to left around the building these are: Lord Rutherford (1781–1854), Lord Cockburn (1779–1854), Lord Jeffrey (1773–1850; over the door on Nelson Mandela Place),

   Royal Faculty of Procurators, West George Street, decorative keystone heads in ground-floor arches.

   Lord Moncrieff (1776–1851), Professor John Miller (1735–1801), James Reddie (1733–1852), Duncan Forbes of Culloden (1685–1747), Lord Kames (1696–1782), Viscount Stair (1619–1695; over the door on West George Street), John Erskine of Carnock (1958–1792), Lord Blair of Avontoun (1741–1811), Baron Lord Brougham and Vaux (1778–1868), Earl of Mansfield (1705–1793) and Lord Erskine (1746–1817).

2. Just across West Nile Street from the Royal Faculty of Procurators is a rather stunning modern classical style building. While Glasgow is not usually associated with art deco architecture, this part of the city contains a fine series of modern classical buildings, most of which were constructed by financial institutions, whose design was strongly influenced by the architecture of New York and Chicago from the 1920s and 1930s. This particular building was constructed for the Commercial Bank of Scotland in 1930, from a design by James Miller, an architect who could turn his hand to many different styles and who was responsible for many of Glasgow's most distinctive buildings, including the Royal Infirmary, Central Station, the Anchor Line Building and Caledonian Mansions. This building is currently occupied by the Shilling Brewing Company, whose initials happen to match those of its original owner, meaning the monogram on the security gates at its front door, which are in a wonderful art deco font, remain relevant to its current occupant. This building is also unusual in having prismatic cellar lights set into the base of the walls to help bring light into its basement levels. Usually, such cellar lights are set into the pavement and not in the building itself. In addition, they had largely gone out of fashion by the time this building was constructed in 1930, with electric lighting replacing natural light.

3. At No. 91 West George Street, on the southern side of its junction with West Nile Street, is the former Royal Exchange Assurance Building. Constructed in 1911, this seven-storey building was designed by Frank Burnet and Boston in a style which seems to be a mix of art nouveau and art deco elements, representing the stylistic shift which was occurring in the decade it was built.

4. To the west of the former Royal Exchange Assurance Building, at No. 105 West George Street, is Fyfe Chambers. A more traditional style of building, it has an ornately decorated entrance and interesting relief sculptures in the corbels of its oriel windows, including some rather unusual representations of the Green Man shown in profile.

5. Directly opposite Fyfe Chambers is 100 West George Street. This is a relatively modern building which has been designed in a style which allows it to blend in with the older buildings that surround it. On the left side of the pediment over the door is a rather wonderfully sculpted cat, which many passing this building will miss. Designed by Callum Sinclair, it was added to the building during renovations in 1990, and appears to be reaching down to play with the stone ball supporting the pediment.

Modern sculpture of cat above door of 100 West George Street.

6. Further west along West George Street at No. 112 (on its corner with Renfield Street) is a Venetian Renaissance style building designed by David Bryce and originally built in the 1860s for the Junior Conservative Club. However, in the 1870s, it became the offices of the Scottish Widows Fund. The building was altered in 1958 to add a top floor and remove some of the original features, such as the upper-storey balconies and some of the distinctive keystone masks sculpted by Charles Grassby. While it is not officially attributed as such, the mask at the eastern-most end of the building appears to represent Father Clyde, the mythological embodiment of the river on which Glasgow's fortune was built. It features two fish on its headdress with rings in their mouths, as well as an anchor intertwined in its beard, and is similar in style to Grassby's known Father Clyde keystone mask on nearby 30 St Vincent Place. If they follow a similar theme, the remaining masks are most likely personifications of other rivers or places, and if you examine them closely, you can see they are adorned with a variety of decorations which could relate to other locations, such as Edinburgh/the Forth and Dublin/the Liffey.

7. On the south-eastern corner of the junction between West George Street and Renfield Street is the former Sun Life Building. Designed by William Leiper in a François I style and featuring sculptures by William Birnie Rhind, it was constructed in the late 1880s and early 1890s for the Sun, Fire and Life Insurance Company. The many financial companies which occupied this part of Glasgow around this time seemed to compete with each other to create the most impressive buildings to help signify their business prowess, creating some of Glasgow's most diverse and distinctive architecture. The sculptures on this building are a wonderful mix of mythological and allegorical images. They include a representation of the Persian god Mithras (above a ground-floor window at the western end of the West George Street facade), the signs of the zodiac (in the column capitals), the Sun, the planets and the gods of the solar system (Jupiter, Uranus, Mars, Venus, Mercury and Saturn – in various roundels between the floors), Apollo flanked by reclining figures representing Day and Night (on the pediment on the Renfield Street facade), and the symbols of the three kingdoms of the UK (the Lion Rampant for Scotland, the three lions passant for England and the harp for Ireland, all flanked by winged figures on the corner tower). Presiding over all of these, in front of the dome at the very top of the corner towner is Aurora, the goddess of the dawn, standing on a

chariot, or biga, being pulled by two horses as she chases the fleeing night across the sky.

8. On the south-western corner of the same junction is the Pearl Assurance Building, built in 1896 and designed by James Thomson in a free classical style. There is often an easy way to tell when a building was designed by James Thomson later in his career: there will be a relief sculpture of his head somewhere on it! In this case, it can be found prominently displayed on the keystone above the building's entrance on West George Street.

Mask of architect James Thomson, by sculptor James Young, 1896 Pearl Assurance Building.

9. To the west of the Pearl Assurance Building, at 45 West George Street, is the General Life Assurance Company Building. This rather skinny building, designed by Robert Alexander Bryden and constructed around 1900, features, among other things, corbels just above the ground-floor windows decorated with masks of Green Man-type creatures.

10. On the opposite side of West George Street, between Nos. 138 and 154, is a row of three classical style buildings. The outer two buildings in this group were designed by the same John Thomson as the Pearl Assurance Building, but were constructed much earlier in his career (c.1860 for the right-hand one, and c. 1878 for the left-hand one) when he was still working in partnership with John Baird. At this time, his style was more classical and restrained, and he had yet to start putting his own face on the buildings he designed. The central building is the grandest of the three. Originally constructed as the New Club in 1879, it was designed in a French classical style by James Sellars, one of Glasgow's greatest unsung architects. Sellars reportedly visited every major private members club in London prior to designing this building, in order to make it as modern and as luxurious as possible. The building was refurbished extensively in 1979, resulting in much of its internal decoration and external ironwork being lost. Somewhat ironically, at this time it was also renamed Sellars House after its architect, whose work the refurbishments partially destroyed. However, its facade still features sculptures by William Mossman, particularly around the entrance, where there are reclining figures of Summer (holding a scythe and stalks of corn) and Autumn (holding grapes and a pitcher) on either side of the head of a male figure wearing a winged helmet. In addition, it features some wonderful oval-shaped oeil-de-boeuf windows on its ground floor.

11. Back on the southern side of West George Street, on its corner with Hope Street, is No. 169. This red sandstone commercial building is an example of one of Glasgow's mini-skyscrapers, which started appearing around 1900, driven in part by the influence of the architecture of American cities like New York and Chicago on Glasgow's architects, but also by the development of construction methods and elevator technology. Designed by John A. Campbell and constructed in 1902, this building is much more restrained than many of the others built in this part of Glasgow, but it still features a tower topped by a bellcast dome. Unusually, this is not situated on the corner itself, but rather one bay away from it along West

George Street. The base of this tower is decorated with winged female figures topping decorative corbels between the windows of the second and third floors. The Hope Street elevation is slightly more ornate, particularly the decorations over the main entrance, which features two putti supporting a shield surrounded by two rather regal-looking lions. There is also a blindfolded mask over the West George Street entrance, which may be a representation of Justice, suggesting the building might have been intended to be used as a law chambers. However, there is no evidence to support or refute this assumption.

12. A short distance further west on the northern side of West George Street, at No. 190, is Ocean Chambers. This is a beautiful red sandstone building designed in a free classical style by Robert A. Bryden and constructed in 1899 for the Ocean Accident & Guarantee Corporation. At the time it was described as 'the latest contribution to the list of palatial insurance buildings' in Glasgow. While not easily visible from the street, it has a distinctive bellcast dome topped by a golden ball-shaped finial. Just below this, on a central pediment above its third-floor window, are the figures of the Greek god Poseidon and his wife Amphitrite (the one holding a golden trident). These sculptures have been criticised as badly carved, while the building itself has been considered ugly and vulgar by some. However, it is, in truth, a rather attractive building, especially in comparison to the newer buildings to its left and on the other side of the street. In particular, it has some wonderful sculptural work above the door, which features a lighthouse flanked by Glasgow's only known pair of architectural walruses, although it is questionable as to whether the sculptor had ever seen a real walrus before carving them, as their bodies seem more otter-like than walrus.

Free classical style Ocean Chambers, 100 West George Street.

13. Next to Ocean Chambers, at the junction with Wellington Street, is a classical style house (now converted into offices). It was built around 1830 as part of the development of Glasgow's Georgian New Town centred around Blythswood Hill (topped by what is now Blythswood Square), which formed part of a major westward expansion of the city from about 1800 onwards. Although a good deal of this Georgian New Town development remains, it is largely overshadowed by the later, and grander, Victorian and Edwardian buildings, and is rarely mentioned in discussions of Glasgow's architecture.

14. Turn right and head north up Wellington Street. A short distance up this street is West Regent Lane. If you look east down this lane, you can make out a small portion of the rear of Ocean Chambers which is covered in white glazed bricks. This is what is known as a light well, a feature relatively common on older Glasgow buildings. A light well was an open area, usually in the middle or to the rear of the building, lined with glazed bricks to reflect as much natural light as possible into the windows of the internal offices within a building.

15. Further north up Wellington Street, on the corner with West Regent Street, is a plot which was once the site of an A-listed classical Georgian-Era house. It was heavily remodelled by Alexander 'Greek' Thomson in the 1870s, to allow him to use it as the offices of his architectural practice. However, in the early 2000s, despite protests from many heritage groups, the building was demolished to be replaced by the bland modern building which now stands on this corner.

16. From its junction with Wellington Street, head west along West Regent Street. At this point, the north side of West Regent Street is still lined primarily with Georgian-Era houses and commercial buildings constructed in the 1830s. This gives a flavour of how the Blythswood New Town would have looked when it was first developed, with its wide streets and three-storey, classical style, blonde sandstone buildings. These would have contrasted sharply with the much narrower crowded streets of the city centre to the east of Buchanan Street, which at that time would have still been lined with medieval buildings, overcrowded eighteenth-century tenements, workshops and the warehouses of the city's merchants.

17. At the corner with West Campbell Street is a pair of red sandstone buildings which contrasts markedly with the Georgian architecture further east on West Regent Street. These are Sovereign House, which was built in the 1890s for the Institute for Adult Deaf and Dumb, and the former John Ross Memorial Church for the Deaf, built around 1929. Designed by Robert Duncan, the more ornate of the two buildings is the Institute, with its pepper-pot towers and a relief sculpture over its door of Jesus healing a deaf man. The former church, designed by Norman A. Dick, is the plainer of the two, but features some wonderful sculptures by Archibald Dawson around the door, including mice, frogs, lizards and dragons, as well as the *Agnus Dei* (the lamb of God)

1890s Sovereign House, West Regent Street.

directly over the entrance. This building is now home to Keppie Design, which has its origins in the firm set up in 1854 by the architect John Honeyman. In 1889, Honeyman took on John Keppie as a partner (after the death of John Sellars in whose practice Keppie had previously worked), to create Honeyman and Keppie. It was this firm where Charles Rennie Mackintosh served as a draughtsman and assistant before he too became a partner in 1904.

18. From Sovereign House, head south down West Campbell Street. If you look left down West Regent Lane as you pass it, you can see part of another light well lined with white glazed bricks, as well as the outline of a small building on the exposed red-brick gable. Such 'ghost' buildings are often all that is left to remind us of structures which have long since been demolished yet remain visible for many decades after the building itself is gone.

19. When you reach the junction with West George Street, there is a great view looking down Blythswood Hill to the 1807 St George's Tron Church on Nelson Mandela Place, close to where this walk started. In the foreground of this view are a series of 1830s Georgian houses built as part of the Blythswood New Town development, while further down the street are the grander Victorian and Edwardian buildings constructed for Glasgow's booming financial industry of the late 1800s and early 1900s, and which were viewed earlier in this walk.

20. Carry on south down West Campbell Street, and then turn left at its junction with St Vincent Street. Here, and best viewed from the southern side of the street, is an imposing building constructed for the North British and Mercantile Insurance Company. At the time this company was formed, the term 'North British' was used by a number of Scottish businesses to signify their geographic origins, something which seems rather anachronistic today. The building itself was constructed in the late 1920s and was the last major project designed by John James Burnet. The building features an impressive entrance topped by a central figure of Saint Andrew standing on the prow of a boat, while below him are the crouching figures of a seafarer and his wife.

Decorative capital, entrance to former North British and Mercantile Building, with hidden message in its sails.

Once you have viewed it from across the street, cross carefully to the other side so you can examine the details around the entrance in close up. In particular, the capitals on the columns on either side of the door are ornately sculpted ships. If you look closely at the one on the right-hand side, you will see the letters IOU on its sail (with the I formed by the mast of the ship). This unusual inscription is a message from Archibald Dawson, the sculptor engaged by Burnet, as a permanent reminder that he was never paid for his work on this building, in part because of Burnet's own financial issues, resulting from a series of problem with the building's construction. This means the monogram should probably be read as UOI (as it was Dawson who was owed the money) rather than the more usual IOU. This was the start of almost a decade of financial problems for Dawson, and in 1936, his business was taken over by his former apprentice Jack Mortimer in lieu of debts. This led to another interesting element of this building. If you examine the sculpture of the seafarer's wife, you will see she has a 1930s hairstyle. This is because these statues, although they were always part of the original plan, were only added in 1953. Created by Mortimer's firm (Mortimer, Willison & Graham), they are based on Dawson and his wife, as a tribute to Mortimer's one-time mentor.

21. Next door to the North British and Mercantile Building, at 190 St Vincent Street, is a much smaller and very different style of building. Designed by Frank Burnet of Burnet and Boston in an English Renaissance style, it was constructed in 1897. Although made of red sandstone, it is almost black in colour due to more than a century of dirt and grime accumulating on the stonework. Until the 1970s, this was the colour of most of Glasgow's older buildings, regardless of whether they were built with red or blonde sandstone. However, starting in the 1980s, a comprehensive cleaning plan has revealed these buildings' true colours, making the city a much brighter and more attractive place to live and work. At the top of this building is a statue of Justice, suggesting it was originally constructed as offices for a legal firm, but it is not known if this was, in fact, the case. If it was not, the choice of Justice for the only statue of this building would seem rather unusual.

English Renaissance style 190 Saint Vincent Street.

22. A short distance further west on the north side of Vincent Street (the same side as Nos. 200 and 190, which you have just viewed) is a large oval-shaped post box. This is an example of a double post box, which had separate slots for posting first- and second-class mail. If you examine its left-hand side, you will see it has the distinctive VR cipher of Queen Victoria, indicating it was installed prior to her death in 1901.

23. On the opposite side of St Vincent Street is No. 149. This is another of James Miller's American-inspired modern classical mini-skyscrapers, of which there are a number in this part of Glasgow. Constructed in 1931, it sits remarkably comfortably among the other older buildings in many different styles, which can be found in this part of Glasgow. From the mid-1800s onwards, Glasgow's economy was sufficiently buoyant to be able to support a surprising number of architects, and many of those who worked in this city remained there for most of their working lives. As a result, they were not only intimately familiar with the city, but also with the buildings of their contemporaries and those designed by the architects who came before them. As a result, even when working in very different styles, they were able to produce buildings which not only had a local Glasgow feel to them, but which also managed to complement each other. This is one of the major problems facing Glasgow today. Many of its buildings now seem to be designed by architects with little or no knowledge of the city, its buildings or its history, and as a result, all that is being constructed are rather generic-looking structures of a type which could be found in many cities around the world rather than being distinctly Glaswegian, much to the detriment of Glasgow's many different streetscapes.

24. A good example of the blending of different styles can be found by comparing 149 St Vincent Street with its neighbour at No. 147. Built in 1904, No. 147 was designed in a free classical style by William Hunter McNab. Despite the almost thirty years which separate these two buildings, they nonetheless complement each other to the point where they could have been designed by a single architect to be two parts of the same building.

25. On the other side of the junction with Wellington Street is another modern classical building. Constructed in 1931, it was designed by Frank Burnet and Boston. These were the same architects who, a little over thirty years earlier, designed the English Renaissance style building at 190 St Vincent Street that you recently viewed. This shows how architectural styles evolved quite dramatically within Glasgow in a very short period of time. Rather than looking to the older buildings of Britain and Europe for inspiration, as they had done in earlier generations, by the 1920s and 1930s, architects were instead looking to the growing cities of the east coast of America. Yet, despite this change, there is still a feeling of continuity between the two buildings, especially in the choice of red sandstone for their facades. This building also has some rather beautiful art deco details in the shape of its golden-winged eagle-head door handles and the relief sculptures of griffins carved in pink granite on the pillars at the base of its steps.

26. A short distance further east on St Vincent Street is No. 144, or as it is better known, 'the Hatrack'. Many people's favourite Glasgow building, it was designed by James Salmon Jnr around 1900, and is one of the gems of the city's art nouveau architecture. It gets its nickname from the ornate, multipronged metalwork which sits on its top, which is best viewed from the opposite side of the street. This building also features some fantastic sculptural work by Francis Derwent Wood, including a magnificent screaming goat's head on the keystone over the entrance. Above this is also a wonderful piece of curved decorative stained glass.

Ornate, multipronged finial, 144 Saint Vincent Street, better known as 'the Hatrack'.

27. Next to the Hatrack, at No. 142, is the former Royal Bank Chambers. Another Burnet and Boston building, it was designed in a late Victorian Renaissance style and was constructed in 1899. Again, while this building is in a very different style from others on this street, it nonetheless complements them, especially through the use of red sandstone, which helps tie different styles of buildings into a relatively seamless, but eclectic, streetscape, which is almost instantly recognisable as Glasgow. This contrasts sharply with the rather soulless modern, glass-fronted building immediately to the north of the Hatrack.

28. As well as the former Royal Bank Chambers, the junction between St Vincent Street and Hope Street is marked by three other impressive buildings, all constructed in very different styles. On the north-east corner is a classical style commercial building designed by James Thomson, which was built in 1876 for the glass and china merchant Dr J. MacDougall. On the south-west corner is the free Renaissance style Norwich Union Chambers, built for the Norwich Union in 1897. Designed by Robert Hutchison, it features some wonderful roaring lions on the keystones of its ground-floor corner arches. The final building on this junction, on its south-east corner, is the most impressive. Again designed by James Thomson, but some thirty years after his

classical style building opposite it, this building is an example of a stunning and elaborate early German Renaissance style. Constructed for the Liverpool and London and Globe Insurance Company, it is decorated with a series of allegorical sculptures and animal figures, including Glasgow's very own 'Liver birds', which are usually synonymous with Liverpool. As with many of James Thomson's later buildings featuring sculptures by James Young, it features a mask of Thomson himself, which you can have a bit of fun trying to find (as you have already seen what he looks like from his portrait on the keystone of the Pearl Assurance Building, visited earlier on this walk.

29. From this junction, walk along the stretch of St Vincent Street between Hope Street and Renfield Street. This section of St Vincent Street, largely (but not completely) unmarred by intrusive modern buildings, is lined with a range of magnificent buildings by some of Glasgow's most notable architects, including John Burnet Snr, John James Burnet's father (No. 117), Frank Southorn (No. 107), James Thomson (Nos. 121, 101 and 136), John Campbell (No. 126), and James Miller (No. 110). Constructed between 1870 and 1925, mostly for financial institutions, in a variety of different styles, these buildings again show how the city's architects working over many decades managed to create an eclectic streetscape, which, although it borrows styles from across the world and the centuries, still manages to work in a uniquely Glasgow way. As a result, from an architectural perspective, this is one of the best-preserved and most important stretches of streetscape in the city centre.

30. Return to the junction with Hope Street and head south along it. This will allow you to view the Hope Street facade of the Liverpool and London and Globe Building, which is just as spectacularly over-the-top as its St Vincent Street facade. Next to it, at No. 108, is the Scottish Temperance League Building. Built in 1894, it was designed in a Dutch Renaissance style by William Forrest Salmon (the son of James Salmon Snr, and father of James Salmon Jnr, who designed the Hatrack building and who, alongside J. Gaff Gillespie, helped with the design this building). It is decorated with sculptures by Richard Ferris, including allegorical statues of Faith (on the right holding a torch), Fortitude (on the left holding a vase) and Temperance (on the top). This building is inscribed with the dates 1844 and 1894, marking the first fifty years of the league's campaign against the evils of alcohol.

1894 Scottish Temperance League, Hope Street.

31. Directly behind the Temperance League Building is the former Daily Record Building. Constructed in the early 1900s, it was designed by Charles Rennie Mackintosh, one of the greatest architects and designers Glasgow has ever produced. To see this building, turn left on to Renfield Lane, just to the south of the Temperance League Building. The Daily Record Building is a short distance along it on the left-hand side, and can be identified by its art nouveau detailing, and the use of blue and white glazed bricks to decorate its upper floors. Such glazed bricks were traditionally used in Glasgow to line light wells to help bring natural light into the centre of buildings, but here Mackintosh has turned the tradition on its head and used them as highlights on the main facade of the building.

32. Return to Hope Street, cross to its western side and then walk the short distance south to its junction with Bothwell Street. From here, look back across to Hope Street to the Standard Building. Another of James Thomson's creations, it was built in 1899 in a free classical style with additional storeys being added in 1909. Constructed for the Standard Life Insurance Company, it features a number of sculptures by James Young. The most impressive of these is the figure of Atlas supporting the world on his shoulders at the very top of the building. This seems to be one of the few buildings designed later in Thomson's career which does not have his likeness featured somewhere on its facades.

33. The view south along Hope Street from this junction has changed little in well over a hundred years, and is dominated by the clock tower of the Central Hotel at Central Station, which was built in the 1880s when Central Station was first constructed.

View south down Hope Street to Central Station.

34. Head west along Bothwell Street. As you pass Waterloo Lane, a narrow, partially cobbled street leading off to the south, look down it and you will see that the left-hand side is lined with metal plates. These served two purposes: the upright part protected the kerb from damage by cartwheels hitting off them, while the flat section provided a smooth area, which made it much easier for horses to pull carts up the otherwise cobbled lane. Known as 'tramways', these are more usually made of smooth stone and predate the metal tramlines which used to run along many Glasgow streets when trams were a major form of transport in the city. In fact, the word 'tram' originates from an old Scottish word for a mining cart, and the term 'tramway' comes from the stone-lined tracks on which these used to run.

35. West of Waterloo Lane, at 25 Bothwell Street, is a large red sandstone building. Constructed in 1889, this Renaissance style building was designed by Robert Ewan for the merchants and shipowners James and Alexander Allan. Each of the two entrances are ornately decorated with sculptures, including plants, birds and keystone masks.

36. On the northern side of Bothwell Street at No. 30 is another of James Miller's American-inspired modern classical financial buildings. Constructed for the Commercial Bank of Scotland in 1934, its facade is dominated by two-storey high Corinthian columns, with Vitruvian scrolling along its roofline. Between these are a series of relief sculptures by Gilbert Bayes, which represent (starting on the right and wrapping around the building on to Wellington Street) Commerce, Industry, Prudence, Contentment, Wisdom and Justice. These subjects were chosen as they were deemed to be the six qualities of man in modern society. Above the entrance is a winged orb containing the bank's monogram (CBS).

37. Just across Wellington Street, covering the whole block on the northern side of Bothwell Street between Wellington Street and West Campbell Street, are the former buildings of the Central Thread Agency. Designed by Hugh and David Barclay, they consist of three free Renaissance style buildings constructed between 1891 and 1901. This is one of the few examples where all the buildings in a single block in central Glasgow were designed by the same architects. The buildings themselves are stunning and feature sculptures by McGilvrey and Ferris. In addition, over the entrance to the western-most building (the last to be built), is a wonderful carved wooden insert featuring an oval art nouveau stained glass window decorated with Mackintosh-inspired roses.

38. On the opposite side of Bothwell Street is the quite different, but equally stunning Mercantile Chambers. It was originally owned by the Mercantile Chambers Company Limited, which was formed specifically in 1897 to construct this building. Designed by James Salmon Jnr, this art nouveau/Glasgow style building features some impressive sculpture work by Francis Derwent Wood, James Young, and McGilvray and Ferris. This includes a sculpture of Mercury above the main entrance, as well as allegorical figures representing Prosperity, Prudence, Industry and Fortune. Along the ground floor, is a series of minor sculptures including some wonderfully evocative grotesque heads on the keystone of the arches, and various creatures, both real and mythological, on the intervening pillars them. Finally,

Decorative sculpture, Mercantile Chambers, Bothwell Street.

between the lower floors is a series of sculpted ribbons inscribed with the words 'Trees Grow, Birds Fly, Fish Swim, Bells Ring'. This appears to be a parody of a popular rhyme about the symbols on the coat of arms of Glasgow (all associated with the city's patron saint, Saint Mungo), which goes 'This is the bird that never flew, this is the tree that never grew, this is the bell that never rang, this is the fish which never swam'. This building was purchased from the Mercantile Chambers Company by Scottish Oils Limited in 1924, to be used as its headquarters. Scottish Oils Limited was established by the Anglo-Persian Oil Company (which later became British Petroleum) in 1919, by amalgamating five Scottish shale oil companies, an event which can be thought of as marking the beginning of the Scottish oil industry.

39. Beside the Mercantile Chambers, at 75 Bothwell Street, is a smaller, but still ornate, red sandstone building. Built around 1890, the pediment over its entrance features an impressive carving of the prow of a ship surrounded by writhing sea serpents and the head of a bearded male wearing a turban on its keystone. On the spandrels on one side of the door is an olive bow, representing peace, and on the other is an oak branch, indicating knowledge, This was once home to the *Glasgow Weekly Mail*, a penny weekly newspaper, which published, among other things, much of the work of Marion (Mirren) Bernstein, a Glasgow-based poet, whose work, unusually for the time, highlighted issues facing women and the need for women's rights in the 1870s.

40. On the next block to the west on Bothwell Street is the flamboyant Scottish Legal Life Assurance Society Building, which is possibly the pinnacle of Glasgow's financial architecture. Designed in 1927 by Edward G. Wylie in a modern classical style, it occupies the entire block between West Campbell Street and Blythswood Street. Like other nearby financial buildings, it features sculptures created by Archibald Dawson, signifying the virtues the building's owners wished to be associated with. In this case, these are Industry, Prudence, Thrift and Courage. Unusually for a Glasgow building, it also features some wonderful decorative enamel work, the most accessible part of which can be found over the entrance to No. 81 at its eastern end.

Relief sculptures, Scottish Legal Life Assurance Society Building, Bothwell Street.

41. From Bothwell Street, turn south down Blythswood Street. This street forms a dividing line between the area closer to the city centre, where older buildings have been preserved, and the area to the west, which was largely demolished as part of the Anderston Comprehensive Development Area in the 1960s to make way for a series of modern structures, such as the M8 motorway, the Kingston Bridge and the modernist concrete megastructure, the Anderston Centre. As a result, on the east side this road, is the western facade of the Scottish Legal Life Assurance Society, while to the west, the area is dominated by nondescript modern buildings with little character, no local flavour and no elements tying them together into a single unified streetscape. This trend of replacing traditional buildings with modern, generic-looking ones continues to this day and such buildings are encroaching ever further towards the city centre. In doing so, they are gradually destroying the distinctive and unique feel of this part of Glasgow.

42. Turn left at the junction between Blythswood Street and Waterloo Street. Here on the north-east corner of this junction is a modern classical style building currently known as Fortune House. It is notable for its Greek detailing, particularly around the doorway, which would not look out of place on an Alexander 'Greek' Thomson building from the 1850s. However, this particular building was built some seventy-five years later in 1925. It was designed by James Thomson, but not the same James Thomson who was in the habit of adding his own image to his buildings, or indeed, the earlier James Thomson, who worked as an architect and engineer in Glasgow between the 1850s and 1880s, and who designed the former Govan Poorhouse on Govan Road. The existence of multiple architects with similar, or the same, names (such as the three James Thomsons, the two James Salmons, and John and John James Burnet) does make understanding Glasgow's architecture a little more complicated than it might otherwise be. This building on the corner of Blythswood Street and Waterloo Street was formerly known as Metro-Vickers House, after the British electrical engineering company Metropolitan-Vickers, which had its

Glasgow offices here. Along the roofline is a series of sculptures representing persistence (a ram), wisdom (an owl) and bravery (a lion). These were carved by Phyllis M. Bone, one of the few female sculptors to have her work featured on a Glasgow building. Born in 1894, Bone was the first female member of the Royal Scottish Academy. Known particularly for her animal sculptures, in 1924 she created the lion and the unicorn, and some other sculptural details, for the Scottish National War Memorial in Edinburgh.

43. Opposite Fortune House is a larger modern classical office building designed by Alexander McInnes Gardner and constructed in the late 1920s. It features dark, polished granite cladding on its ground floor with art deco style features running along it and on the top corners of an otherwise relatively plain facade.

44. A short distance further east at 64 Waterloo Street is Distillers' House, one of Glasgow's most distinctive buildings. Designed by James Chalmers in a free classical style, it was constructed in 1898 for the whisky producers Wright & Greigs. Its most notable feature is its polygonal corner tower topped with stone cannons, but it also features sculptures created by Richard Ferris based on Sir Water Scott's narrative poem *The Lady of the Lake*. On the main facade are Roderick Dhu (wearing a kilt) and James Fitz-James, the would-be suitors of the eponymous lady, Ellen Douglas, who herself appears on the corner of the building. This choice of subject matter for the sculptures of this building was probably due to Roderick Dhu's Highland Whisky, the most popular product produced by Wright & Greigs.

Distinctive tower, former Distillers' House, Waterloo Street.

45. The northern side of next block to the east is occupied by a single large blonde sandstone building. Designed in a classical style by William Thomas Oldrieve, it was built in 1903 as the Waterloo Street Post Office Building. Of particular note are the sculpted lion heads which decorate its facade. Along with palmate or palm-frond motifs, such lion heads are one of the sculptural details which feature on many traditional Glasgow buildings constructed in many different styles, ranging from classical Victorian, through art nouveau and Edwardian baroque to art deco and modern classical, and help tie such diverse buildings into a single unified streetscape.

46. Further east, at 19 Waterloo Street, is Waterloo Chambers. Constructed in 1899, it is a free classical commercial building designed by John James Burnet. While much of Burnet's early work, such as Charing Cross Mansions, was inspired by his time spent studying in Paris, his later work was strongly influenced by a visit he made to America in 1896, and Waterloo Chambers was one of the first American-inspired 'elevator' buildings he designed on his return to Glasgow. At present, the pub on the ground floor is called Roderick Dhu, named after the same character who appears on the facade of Distillers' House just a short distance further west on the same street.

47. Head back to the junction between Waterloo Street and Wellington Street, and turn south down Wellington Street. On the left-hand side at No. 50 is Baltic Chambers. Designed by Duncan McNaughtan in a free classical style and constructed in 1897, it features a pair of wonderful corner towers topped by ornate cupolas. Between these, at the very top of the building is an aedicula (or a small shrine), which features Solomonic or barley sugar columns, with a putto just below it. The lower floors of the facade are richly decorated with intricate sculptural work by William Vickers, including the prows of ships in the pediments of the outer two doorways, and various creatures on the pillars of the windows along the ground floor. Above the central main entrance is a stone nameplate bearing the words Baltic Chambers in an art nouveau style font under a row of three stained-glass windows, featuring art nouveau designs.

1897 free classical style Baltic Chambers, 50 Wellington Street.

48. Set into the edge of the road on the opposite side of Wellington Street from the northern end of Baltic Chambers is a distinctive oblong metal plate with the letters 'H.P.' on it (with what looks like an O between them). This is an access cover for the Glasgow's public hydraulic power system, which sent high-pressure water from its pumping station on High Street, through more than 48 kilometres (30 miles) of pipes under Glasgow's streets, to provide power to machinery in workshops across the city. Now largely forgotten, when this system was established it was seen as the power source of the future, and meant that small workshops did not need to have their own expensive hydraulic power systems. However, it was soon superseded by electricity, which could be used just as easily to power industrial machinery.

49. Carry on south down Wellington Street and cross over Argyle Street to Robertson Street. At 73 Robertson Street is a rather wonderful Glasgow style office building designed by John Archibald Campbell, and constructed in 1901 for the carting contractors Robert Buchanan and Company. Surrounded by modern buildings, this building has been sadly neglected for many years and is at great risk of being lost.

50. On the opposite side of Robertson Street, at No. 60, is a red sandstone building constructed for William Macleod & Company, metal merchants and founders' factors, in 1902 (but dated 1905) from a design by Steel and Balfour. While much of the original building has been demolished, to allow a newer building to be constructed on the same plot, its facade has been retained and renovated, allowing it to survive among the newer developments which now surround it.

51. A short distance further south along Robertson Street, you will find the word 'Bootes' set into the edge of the pavement. Close to this are a number of small steel and glass markers laid out in the shape of the celestial constellation of the same name. This is part of a street art project which has inset a number of different stars and constellations into the streets of this area of Glasgow. Boötes is one of a number of constellations used since ancient times for navigation, and is mentioned by Homer

in his epic poem *The Odyssey* for just this purpose. This makes it an appropriate subject to decorate the streets of a part of Glasgow which was once dominated by warehouses containing goods to be shipped to and from places across the world. It is not clear exactly who the constellation Boötes represents, but in one version of Greek mythology, it is Philomenus, son of Demeter, the goddess of the harvest and sister of Zeus.

52. The final stop on this walk is the Clyde Navigation Trust Building which is on the corner of Robertson Street and the Broomielaw. Designed by John James Burnet, this building was constructed in two phases. The first phase, built in the 1880s, is the northern section on Robertson Street, while the second, built in the early 1900s, wraps round onto the Broomielaw. Other planned phases, originally intended to go further north along Robertson Street and east along the Broomielaw, were never constructed, leaving the building looking oddly asymmetric and truncated, especially at the Broomielaw end. The building is largely in the beaux-arts style favoured by Burnet in the earlier part of his career, and features a series of impressive sculptures. Those in the first phase were created by John Mossman, whereas those in the second were created by Albert Hemstock Hodge.

Sculpted prow of boat, beaux-arts style, Clyde Navigation Trust, Robertson Street.

Between the ground-floor arches on Robertson Street are two protruding ship's prows. This is another feature common to many Glasgow buildings, and is another element which helps tie buildings designed in very different styles together, However, these are the largest, and most finely sculpted examples to be found on any building in the city. Above these at the top of the building is a large pediment which features Father Clyde in the centre surrounded by figures representing the eastern and western hemispheres bringing their merchandise to Glasgow. Above this, at the apex of the pediment, is Poseidon standing on the bow of a small boat being pulled by two seahorses. Beneath this boat rises Triton, a half-man, half-fish sea god who was Poseidon's son. To the left and right of this pediment are the figures of two great Scottish engineers, Thomas Telford (on the left) and James Watt (on the right). Further south, there is a similar figure of Henry Bell, another Scottish engineer who is less well known, but who played an important role in the development of steam-powered shipping. Surrounding the dome at the top of the corner section of this building are two groups of figures, The first is Demeter (the goddess of the harvest and mother of Philomenus, who the constellation Boötes is thought to represent), leading a bull. The second is Amphitrite, the wife of Poseidon and mother of Triton, riding a pair of seahorses. Built for the Clyde Navigation Trust, which was responsible for ensuring that the Clyde became, and remained, navigable as far east as Glasgow, and for developing its infrastructure, this building was clearly intended to proclaim

Glasgow's status and wealth to the world. In addition, with the original phase constructed at the same time as the City Chambers on George Square, it may also have been intended to show that the Clyde Navigation Trust played just as important role in the economy of Glasgow as the Glasgow Corporation (as the Council was known at that point). Interestingly, Burnet also unsuccessfully entered the 1880 competition to design the new City Chambers, and may well have borrowed elements from this rejected submission for the rival Clyde Navigation Trust Building. If this is the case, this would mean there are three versions of the City Chambers in Glasgow: the Winning design in George Square, and versions of rejected designs in the Clyde Navigation Trust Building and on the other side of the river, in the shape of the Scottish Cooperative Wholesale Society Building on Morrison Street.

5. Anderston and Argyle Street

Start Point: The Charles Rennie Mackintosh statue on Argyle Street, Glasgow (**Location:** Lat/Lon: 55.86299, -4.27831; What3Words: ///slurs.smiled.stamp; Plus Code: VP7C+5MV Glasgow). **Nearest Public Transport:** Subway: Kelvinhall Station (30 mins); Train: Exhibition Centre (10 mins); Bus: St Vincent Street (1 min).

End Point: The Junction of Argyle Street and Trongate, Glasgow (**Location:** Lat/Lon: 55.85752, -4.24939; What3Words: ///adopt.scarcely.vouch; Plus Code: VQ52+265 Glasgow). **Nearest Public Transport:** Subway: St Enoch Station (10 mins); Train: Argyle Street Station (5 mins); Bus: Trongate (5 mins).

Distance: 3.5 kilometres/2.2 miles. **Time:** Allow 1.5 to 2.5 hours for this walk.
Level of Difficulty: Easy. This walk is entirely on paved surfaces.

Facilities: There are shops, cafes, restaurants and bars available at fairly regular intervals along this walk. Publicly accessible toilets are available in Central Station about halfway along this walk, and in the St Enoch Shopping Centre which is to the south of Argyle Street towards its end.

Introduction

Lying along the northern side of the Clyde to the west of the city centre, Anderston started life in the early eighteenth century as a small weaving village established on lands which had been given to the Bishop of Glasgow by King James II in 1450. By 1824, it had grown into small town with a population of around 10,000 people. It was also around this time that the work of deepening the Clyde started to allow ships, for the first time, to sail into the heart of the city, and Anderston found itself well positioned to make the most of the new opportunities which arose from this development. This included shipbuilding, iron founding, tool manufacturing, grain stores, whisky bonds and timber yards. By the time Anderston was incorporated into Glasgow in 1846, it was growing rapidly in size and, by the start of the 1900s, it was a densely populated area filled with workshops and closely packed tenements. Despite this rapid growth, it maintained the feel of a large village with its own distinct local identity within the wider city. This all changed after World War II, when the *Bruce Report* led to the creation of the Anderston Comprehensive Development Area. The result was the almost total destruction of the local area in a bid to make way for more modern housing and to allow the creation of large-scale infrastructure projects, such as the Anderston Centre, the M8 and the Kingston Bridge. The effect was dramatic, and between 1951 and 1971, the population of Anderston dropped from 31,902 to just 9,235, as residents were moved from the area to new housing developments on the edges of the city, such as Drumchapel, Easterhouse and Knightswood, and out of Glasgow entirely to new towns such as Cumbernauld and East Kilbride. This is now seen by many as having largely been an unmitigated failure, and it is only in the last few years, since work began to reverse some of the worst mistakes of the Anderston Comprehensive Development Area, that this area has started to return to a semblance of its former glory.

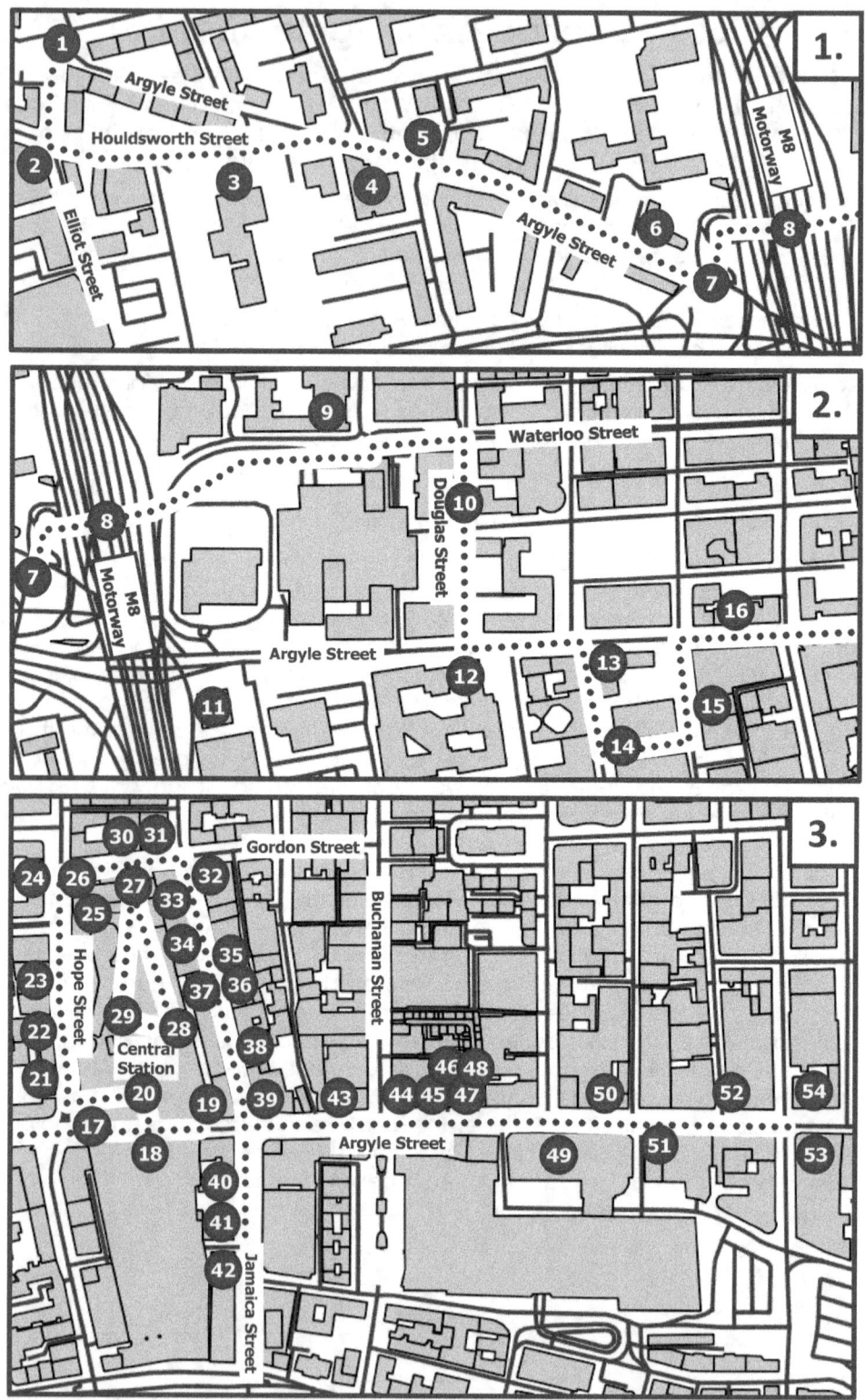

1. This walk starts at the statue of Charles Rennie Mackintosh on Argyle Street, close to its junction with St Vincent Street and Elliot Street. Installed in 2018 to mark the completion of a new development of affordable housing, this is the world's first public sculpture of Glasgow's most famous architect and designer. One of the originators of the distinctive and acclaimed Glasgow style at the end of the nineteenth century, Mackintosh had (and still has) an influence which reached well beyond his native city. The statue, created by Andy Scott, shows Mackintosh sitting on one of his characteristic tall-backed chairs, and staring west along Argyle Street. The new housing development which surrounds it allowed the reopening of a section of Argyle Street between this junction and Houldsworth Street a short distance to the south-east, which had been closed off since the 1960s, reuniting what had, until then, been two disjointed parts. This means that at 3.4 km (2 miles) in length, Argyle Street can once again lay claim to being the longest street not only in Glasgow, but in the whole of the UK. However, Argyle Street's claim to this title is hotly contested by residents of the East End of Glasgow, who assert that the title should go to Duke Street, which is marginally shorter. The crux of this argument all depends on whether or not Argyle Street is considered to be continuous at the point where it meets North Street below the M8 motorway. As you will pass this junction during this walk, you can judge for yourself which point of view you think is correct.

Andy Scott's 2018 statue of Charles Rennie Mackintosh, Anderston.

2. From the Charles Rennie Mackintosh statue, head south along Elliot Street to its corner with Houldsworth Street. Here, among the newer buildings, are a collection of old industrial buildings, which are some of the few remaining reminders of Anderston's industrial past. Starting around the 1850s, Anderston rapidly developed into an industrial suburb serving the shipyards, engine buildings and engineering companies based along the nearby Clyde. The attractive, if rather run down, polychromatic brick building on the corner of this junction dates from 1870, and was home to the saw and files manufacturers Cook & Son Limited, and ghost signs bearing the company's name still remain on the building's facades. Next to it on Elliot Street are the buildings of the Anderston Brass Foundry (the red-brick building with the large semicircular window over its main entrance), and the Cranston Iron Foundry (the surprisingly modern-looking building with the tall rounded windows), both of which also date from the 1870s. There are few similar groups of mid-Victorian industrial architecture left in Glasgow, and they give a hint at how Anderston as a whole would have looked at this important stage of its development.

3. From its junction with Elliot Street, turn left on to Houldsworth Street (named after Henry Houldsworth, who became the first Provost of Anderston in 1824) and head east towards Argyle Street. As you do so, on the right-hand side, you will pass

Anderston Primary School. At one time, this was home to the Glasgow West Fire Station. Constructed in 1859, this fire station was designed with an engine room and stables on the ground floor, and housing for the officers and men above. Originally, a rather magnificent building, by the 1920s it was described as an ancient monument and a disgrace to the city, owing to the difficulties in adapting it to suit the newer, motorised appliances which had, by then, replaced the previous generation of horse-drawn fire engines. However, it was not until 1970 that it was finally closed and replaced by a new fire station further to the west on Kelvinhaugh Street. It was also around this time that the Kingston Bridge was constructed to carry the new M8 motorway over the Clyde. As you will see, it passed dangerously close to the school which then served the children of Anderston on Washington Street, resulting in the need for a new school to be constructed elsewhere. As the old fire station was no longer in use, it was demolished, and Anderston Primary School was built in its place.

4. Further east, where Houldsworth Street terminates at its junction with Argyle Street, is the distinctive, verdigris-covered, pyramid-shaped roof of the former Anderston Kelvingrove Parish Church. Designed by Honeyman, Jack & Robertson, it was built in the late 1960s as part of a comprehensive redevelopment of the Anderston area. Anderston was one of twenty-nine areas in Glasgow covered by plans to modernise the city. However, only half of these were ever enacted. In Anderston, this involved the relocation of many of the residents and the demolition of almost all the existing buildings along this section of Argyle Steet, so they could be replaced by an inner-city housing estate consisting of high-density

Verdigris-covered, pyramid-shaped roof, 1960s Anderston Kelvingrove Parish Church.

housing. Work began on this plan in 1961, but it was poorly thought out, and did not take into account the negative effect that the construction of the nearby motorway would have on the local community. Specifically, it created a barrier to the easy movement of people in and out of the area, leaving the western half of Anderston as an isolated enclave, which is almost always detrimental and something urban planners now work hard to avoid creating. However, in recent years, a great deal of work has been carried out to correct the mistakes of the 1960s, including the demolition of much of the high-density housing, replacing it with modern versions of the tenements which would once have lined its streets, as well as improving its connectivity to the surrounding areas. As a result, Anderston is once again starting to thrive. However, Anderston Pyramid, as it is now called, remains as a monument to these plans and still forms an important focus for the local community.

5. Just beyond the Anderston Pyramid, on the opposite side of Argyle Street, surrounded by the latest generation of buildings, is the former Anderston branch of the Glasgow Savings Bank. One of the few tenement buildings to survive the orgy of destruction initiated by the Anderston Comprehensive Development Area, it is also one of the city's architectural hidden gems. Designed by James Salmon Jnr and John Gaff Gillespie, with sculptures by Albert Hodge, it was built in 1899. Its details demonstrate the beauty and novelty of the Glasgow Style Movement led by Charles Rennie Mackintosh. Like Mackintosh, both Salmon and Gillespie studied at the Glasgow School of Art, and Gillespie was a joint winner of the 1889 Glasgow Institute of Architects prize alongside Mackintosh himself. While not as well-known as they should be, Salmon and Gillespie were among the best proponents of the Glasgow style, and this building is one of their finest surviving works in this style.

Glasgow style former Anderston branch, Glasgow Savings Bank.

6. Further east along Argyle Street is another, even older, tenement which also survived the work of the city planners in the 1960s. Situated at No. 654, this classical style blonde sandstone tenement was built in 1869 and features a number of sculptures, including a relief sculpture of a greyhound surrounded by the words '*Fulget virtus intaminata*'. This is the crest of Clan Belshes and the motto translates as 'virtue shines unstained'. Below this are the Masonic symbols of the divider and the square. However, there is no obvious explanation of why either of these are present on this particular building.

7. From No. 654, it is only a short distance to the point where Argyle Street meets North Street and is crossed by the M8 motorway. Here, on the right, are three metal silhouette statues, each of a famous resident of Glasgow selected by the local community. From left to right these are the climber, author and broadcaster Tom Weir (1914–2006), the trade union activist, politician and journalist Jimmy Reid (1932–2010), and the engineer and inventor James Watt (1736–1819). The empty plot directly behind these statues was formerly home to the Victorian Music Hall, which opened in 1899. It later became a cine-variety theatre called the Gaity Theatre, before becoming a full-time cinema in 1935. However, it still hosted live acts, including a concert by the Beatles in 1963. It closed in 1965 and was demolished shortly afterwards to make way for an on-ramp to the Kingston Bridge, and nothing has occupied the site since.

8. Directly to the east of these statues are more on-ramps for the Kingston Bridge, which carries the M8 motorway high over the Clyde. This was built on top of what was once Anderston Cross, which marked the location of the original weaving village from which the local area grew. Not only did these developments in the 1960s destroy what was once the heart of Anderston, they also divided it into two parts, and there was no easy way for local residents to cross from one part to the

other. Originally, a pedestrian bridge had been planned at this point, and it was even partially built, but for decades it remained unfinished. One of Glasgow's infamous 'Bridges to Nowhere', it simply ended some 12 metres (40 feet) above the ground. However, in 2013, more than forty years after its construction was started, it was finally completed, once again allowing pedestrian access between the two sections of Anderston without having to cross busy roads. For this walk, head to the base of this bridge, to the left of the point where the M8 passes over Argyle Street and use it to cross over the motorway. When you reach the centre of the bridge, take the time to stop and look around. Among the newer buildings to the north, you can see Peter P. Pugin's 1898 Gothic style St Partick's church, while to the south, you can see the red sandstone edifice of the former Washington Street School, designed by Henry E. Clifford and constructed in 1889, nestled almost directly below one of the on-ramps of the Kingston Bridge. Despite the long history of Anderston, almost every other building you can see was built post-1960, and it is only from this vantage point that you can appreciate quite how much of a scar the motorway created through this part of Glasgow. In addition, if you look below the bridge, there are nineteen lanes of traffic, ten on top and nine below, highlighting quite how much of a barrier the M8 forms to the free and easy movement of people around the city. While there are pedestrian bridges over it, such as this one, it is worth considering quite how high and exposed these often are, and when gale-force winter winds are whipping freezing rain across them on a dark winter's night, they are hardly the most pedestrian-friendly way to get from one side of the motorway to the other.

9. The eastern end of this pedestrian bridge descends down onto Waterloo Street. At this point on the north side of Waterloo Street is Telephone House. This is a former telephone exchange, and its architecture is typical of the many exchanges built across Glasgow during this period of rapid expansion of the telephone network. Built in 1937, it was one of the first public buildings in the city to bear the royal cipher of King George VI, who ascended to the throne on the abdication of his brother, King Edward VIII, in December 1936.

10. From Waterloo Street, head south down Douglas Street to return to Argyle Street. This will take you past, and indeed through, some of the remaining parts of the Anderston Centre. Designed by Richard Seifert, it was one of the UK's earliest examples of the megastructure style of urban renewal which was popular around this time. However, while it opened in 1972, it was never actually completed (as, among other things, it was meant to be connected to the western section of Anderston by the now-completed Bridge to Nowhere, which you just crossed). Built in a brutalist style, primarily using concrete, it was once voted No. 54 in a list of the 100 best modern Scottish buildings. However, by the 1980s, Seifert's dream had turned sour, with its many walkways proving difficult to police, resulting in crime running rampant.

Brutalist Anderston Centre, designed by Richard Seifert and opened in 1972.

By the 1990s, it was partially derelict and several parts of it have since been demolished. Those that remain stand as a reminder of the mistakes of 1960s' and 1970s' town planning. Yet, at the moment, Glasgow seems destined to repeat many of the same mistakes all over again, as traditional buildings are currently being demolished at an alarming rate to make way for high-rise buildings and megastructures, which are likely to fall foul of many of the same issues as their predecessors did some fifty years earlier.

11. Once you reach Argyle Street, look to the right. In the distance, with the now-abandoned former Washington Street School below it, is the M8 motorway as it rises to cross the Clyde via the Kingston Bridge. To its left, and closer to your current location, is a tall, pale building which started life as a cotton store in the 1840s, and was later converted into the Anderston Rice Mill. This is one of the few industrial buildings which

Former Washington Street School, with access ramp for Kingston Bridge.

remains standing in this part of Anderston. Between it and the Clyde is a large area of mostly derelict land which has yet to recover from the devastation inflicted on the local area by the Anderston Comprehensive Development Area project.

12. Directly across from the southern end of Douglas Street is a large, yellow-brick building called Kentigern House. Constructed in the 1980s, and named after the city's patron saint (who is known both as Saint Mungo and Saint Kentigern), it is used primarily as a UK Government building, but its existence is a link to the destruction of one of Glasgow's greatest lost buildings. In 1977, the UK Government announced it would be moving 6,000 Ministry of Defence jobs to the city. St Enoch Station in central Glasgow had closed a few years before, and the site where it stood was earmarked for the location of the new building where these jobs would be based. In preparation, the station and the adjoining hotel, which was, and still is, viewed by many as one of Glasgow's greatest architectural masterpieces, similar in style to St Pancras Station in London, were demolished. However, before construction on the new building began, the UK Government scaled back its plans to include only 1,400 jobs and it was decided this site on Argyle Street would be more suitable for this smaller contingent and Kentigern House was built instead. So, as it turned out, the St Enoch Station and Hotel buildings were demolished for no discernible benefit to the city.

13. From Kentigern House, head east to the junction with Blythswood Street. Using the traffic lights at this junction, cross over to the southern side of Argyle Street. Here, on the corner of Argyle Street and James Watt Street, which leads off to the south, is a classical style tenement constructed around 1858 for the grain-store keeper J. Kennedy. The ground floor of this building is now home to a bar and restaurant, which appears to have a ghost sign along its facade which reads 'the Duke of Argyle Street Umbrella Merchants, Glasgow'. However, there appears to be no trace of a business of this name ever having existed, let alone one having occupied this location. Glasgow, however, does have at least one interesting umbrella connection as the first umbrellas manufactured in Britain were made in the city in

1786 by one John Gardiner, although his design was rather heavy and cumbersome and never really catch on.

14. Turn south down James Watt Street and then turn left into Atlantic Square by passing through one of the arches in the retained facade of a tall classical style warehouse opposite No. 59. This was originally part of a grain and general store built in 1863 for Thomas Mann. The rest of the building was demolished in 1995 to make way for a new series of developments between James Watt Street and York Street, which run parallel to it.

15. At the eastern end of Atlantic Square, you will emerge onto York Street. As you do so, on the far side of the road, you will see a red sandstone building. Constructed in 1901, and designed in a free Renaissance style by Neil C. Duff, it was originally occupied by the Carsewell Fishing Gut Company. This building features some impressive sculptural details, including a skilfully-carved Glasgow coat of arms, topped by a bust of Saint Mungo. Directly above this is a rather wonderful griffin, while an imperious-looking lion sits at either end of its first floor. This building also has some beautifully constructed sash windows with curved edges designed to fit into the curves of the building's arches and pediments – a design flourish which is rarely found in other similar buildings. If you look up and down York Street, you will see this is the only traditional sandstone building to have been retained on it, while the rest have been replaced by much newer ones. Even then, it is only the facade which has been kept, with a new building having been constructed behind it.

Lion sculpture, facade of former Carsewell Fishing Gut Company, York Street.

16. Head north up York Street to its junction with Argyle Street. On the opposite side of the road is one of the few blocks in this part of Argyle Street to retain all of its older buildings, and it gives you an idea of how Argyle Street would once have looked. Fixed into the stonework of these buildings are tram rosettes, which are all that remains of the overhead electrical wires that powered the trams which once ran along the middle of the street, carrying passengers to and from the city. At the western end of this block is an Italian Renaissance style building designed by James Thomson and constructed in 1892 for the Clydesdale Bank. Beside this is a free classical style hotel which is thought to have been designed by Alex Petrie and was built in 1897. Finally, at the eastern end of the block is a Renaissance style commercial building designed by Frank Burnet and Boston, and constructed in 1896. The name of the pub on its ground floor, the Waterloo, actually predates the building itself as it was the name of a previous pub which was demolished to make way for this new building.

17. If you look east along Argyle Street from this point, you will see an ornate cast-iron structure stretching across it. This is part of the concourse of Glasgow's Central Station and is the next stop on this walk. Glasgow Central is now the city's largest station, primarily serving trains coming in from south of the city, such as the Clyde coast, once the destination of choice for many Glaswegians on their days off, especially during the summer months. Many who made this journey would take the last train back to the city much poorer and much worse for wear, but having made the most of their excursion – a journey immortalised in the Billy Connolly song 'Glasgow Central'. However, Central Station was not always the city's largest station. In the 1840s, the main terminus for trains coming in from the south was at Bridge Street, on the southern side of the Clyde, where passengers alighted before travelling across Glasgow Bridge (now more commonly referred to as the Jamaica Street Bridge) into the city itself. The main reason for this was due to objections by the Clyde Navigation Trust to the construction of any bridges further downstream, which might interfere with the ability of ships to reach the docks of the Broomielaw, which lay a short distance further west. However, with Glasgow's population rising, a solution needed to be found. The first of these came from the Glasgow and South Western Railway Company, which built St Enoch Station in the city centre and accessed it from the south by way of the City of Glasgow Union Bridge, the first railway bridge across the Clyde. As it was well upstream of the city's docks, it created no hinderance to the movement of ships on the Clyde. Caledonian Railway, which still operated out of Bridge Street was keen to remain competitive and finally in 1873, it was given permission to build a new station, originally called Gordon Street Station, but now known as Central Station, on the north bank of the Clyde, and construct a bridge to extend the line which previously terminated at Bridge Street into the heart of the growing city. Central Station proved very popular, and between 1899 and 1905, it was greatly expanded. A key part of Central Station is the cast-iron viaduct which carries its platforms and the railway lines over Argyle Street, which, along with much of the rest of the station that will be visited on this walk, was designed by the architect James Miller and the engineer Donald Mathieson. This viaduct provided a relatively large area which was sheltered from Glasgow's inclement weather and it quickly became a popular meeting place for people who had been forced to move from the Highlands of Scotland to Glasgow to find work, earning it the nickname of 'the Hielanman's Umbrella'. This tradition reached its height in the 1920s and 1930s, but died out during World War II, when the blackout meant the lights under the bridge were no longer lit.

18. While one tradition of meeting to socialise under the Central Station Viaduct died out at the end of the 1930s, another one began in 1991, when a new bar, arts and entertainment venue opened in the vaulted tunnels under the southern end of Central Station. Called the Arches, it occupied some 7,800 m² (84,000 ft²) and was accessed from the south side of Argyle Street underneath the station's viaduct. Run by a not-for-profit organisation, it grew to become one of Europe's leading cultural venues funded primarily by revenue generated from

Sign for former Arches nightclub, under southern end of Central Station.

commercial nightclub events. These clubbing events soon became famous not only in Glasgow, but throughout the world. Such was their legendary status, they were name-checked in Arab Strap's 1996 single 'The First Big Weekend', and in 2007 the Arches was voted the twelfth-best club in the world. Unfortunately, due to licensing issues, the club nights were forced to end in April 2015, and shortly afterwards, the entire venue closed due to the resulting loss of income. The venue is now occupied by a food market called Platform, but the Arches remains one of Glasgow's most missed former venues.

19. Carry on all the way under the Central Station Viaduct to its eastern side, where there is a building with an unusual and distinctive art nouveau style facade. This was created by James H. Craigie in 1908, but the history of the building goes back much further. The area on which Glasgow Central was built in the late 1800s was previously the site of the village of Grahamston, founded by James Graham in 1709. As with many other villages close to Glasgow, such as Anderston, it greatly benefitted from the industrial developments along the Clyde, and Grahamston soon grew into a bustling centre of commerce, well positioned between the docks of the Broomielaw and Glasgow itself. It addition, it stood at one of the western-most crossings of the Clyde, making it an important stopping point for traffic travelling north and south, as well as east and west. At its peak, Grahamston had a population of around 2,000 people and around 300 businesses. However, its enviable position also sealed its fate, and despite objections from the local population, it was largely demolished to allow the construction of Glasgow Central Station in the 1870s and its expansion in the early 1900s, with a number of its roads, such as Alston Street, disappearing completely beneath the station's foundations. Largely forgotten, the building which now houses the Grant Arms, which may date from the early 1800s, is one of only two that remain from this lost Glasgow village.

Grant Arms, from lost village of Grahamston.

20. Cross to the north side of Argyle Street at the nearest traffic lights and then return west under the Central Station Viaduct. When you reach it, turn left into the Argyle Street entrance of the station. Here, at the top of the stairs leading down to the low-level platforms, is a small plaque that marks the site of Grahamston's Alston Theatre, which once stood on the now-vanished Alston Street. Built in 1764, the Alston was one of the earliest theatres established in the Glasgow area. It benefitted greatly from being just beyond the then-boundary of the city (which ran down Union Street, a short distance to its east). This meant it did not fall under the purview of the city itself, or its ban on theatrical performances, which originated with the Reformation and lasted until 1752. Many objected to the Alston on moral and religious grounds, and on its opening night a large crowd disrupted its debut performance by setting fire to the stage and ransacking the rest of the building. However, the theatre recovered and survived for another sixteen years until it was gutted by fire in 1780, which may or may not have been suspicious in origin. Certainly, during attempts to extinguish the fire, local magistrates were heard telling

firemen to use their hoses to 'save ither folk's hooses an' let the Deil's [or Devil's] hoose burn'.

21. From the Alston Theatre plaque, turn left and head out of Central Station via the nearby Hope Street exit. Almost immediately across from this exit is a distinctive four-storey commercial building topped with attic dormer windows. Built around 1875, it was among the first buildings constructed around the new station after the destruction of Grahamston. Its ground floor is home to the Solid Rock Cafe, which was established in 1987, and is Glasgow's oldest rock bar.

22. Further north, at 46 Hope Street, is Atlantic Chambers. Designed by John James Burnet in an ornate free style, it was built in 1899. Its entrance is topped with a nameplate carved in a beautiful art nouveau font surrounded by figures of Columbia (holding a shield decorated with stars and stripes, representing the United States of America) on the left, and Britannia (representing Britain) on the right created by McGilvray and Ferris. Above this is a relief sculpture of a ship under full sail topped by a winged figure. At seven storeys high, it was tall for a Glasgow building of its time, and it has an internal steel frame reminiscent of the elevator buildings constructed in Chicago around this time. When it first opened, it was noted as having been fitted with all the latest improvements, including a passenger elevator and electrical lighting throughout.

Art nouveau nameplate, John James Burnet's 1899 Atlantic Chambers, 46 Hope Street.

23. A few doors further north from Atlantic Chambers, at No. 67, is another ornate building dating from 1899. Designed by Robert Thomson in a free classical style, it was originally built for J. M. Smith and Company as the offices and printing works for the *Glasgow Evening News*. This was a local newspaper which was, at one time, edited by Neil Munro, and his stories about the adventures of crew of the *Vital Spark*, a Clyde puffer, were first published within its pages. Again, this building features some fine sculptural elements, including putti reading a book in front of a printing press surrounded by a pair of rather wonderful art nouveau style owls, presumably signifying the wisdom of the printed word. Higher up on the building are two mirror-image seated female figures, but they seem to be purely decorative rather than representing anything in particular. The large arch at the centre of the building's facade served originally as the cart entrance through which the newspapers printed here would have passed on their way to be distributed around the city.

24. On the next block to the north, between Hope Street's junctions with Waterloo Street and Bothwell Street, stand the former offices of Caledonian Railways, the company responsible for the construction of Central Station. Designed by the firm of Peddie & Kinnear, and built in 1876, this was originally intended to be the station hotel, with the railway offices being housed in the station itself. However, shortly after it was completed, a decision was made to swap the use of the two buildings

over. However, this led to an office building with an unusual internal configuration clearly designed for a different purpose.

25. On the corner of Gordon Street and Hope Street, opposite the former Caledonian Railways offices, is the Central Hotel. Built in 1883 to a design by Robert Rowand Anderson, and extended in the early 1900s by James Miller, this impressive building was, at one time, Glasgow's most prestigious hotel, with the likes of Winston Churchill, Gene Kelly, Frank Sinatra, Laurel and Hardy and John F. Kennedy all staying there when they visited the city. It was also the site of the world's first long-distance transmission of a television picture by John Logie Baird on 24 May 1927. The signal was transmitted by telephone line over 700 kilometres (approx. 440 miles) from Glasgow to London. Just over a month earlier, Herbert Ives of Bell Laboratories had transmitted a picture, again by telephone wire, some 300 km (approx. 200 miles) from Washington DC to New York, but using a different technology to that developed by Baird.

26. Outside the entrance to the Central Hotel is a statue by Kenny Hunter called *Citizen Firefighter*. It is a memorial to all firefighters past and present, especially those who have died in the line of duty. First unveiled in 2001, just a few months before the terrorist attacks on the Twin Towers of the World Trade Centre, in New York, in September of that year, it became a focal point for people in Glasgow to pay tribute to those who died on that day, including the 343 members of the New York Fire Department who lost their lives trying to save others. In October 2001, two hundred members of the Scottish Fire Brigade gathered at this statue to pay tribute to the loss of their New York colleagues.

Kenny Hunter's 2001 Citizen Firefighter, *outside Central Hotel.*

27. For the next part of this walk, enter Central Station through its main gates on Gordon Street. These gates are a fine example of the metalworker's craft, and feature large roundels decorated with intricate wrought-iron scrollwork. The station itself is covered by a glass roof supported by steelwork created by the Motherwell Bridge and Engineering Company. Below this, to the west of the entrance, are a series of timber station offices and shops, which have a rather wonderful art nouveau feel to their detailing. Hanging over the main concourse is a clock, which like many station clocks was (and still is) a popular meeting place for young couples, especially on Friday and Saturday nights.

28. As well as being a terminal for trains for those travelling to and from Glasgow for work and pleasure, Central Station has, in the past, also played an important role as a departure point for hundreds of thousands of men and women from all over Scotland, who headed off to fight in World Wars I and II, many of whom would never see their native land again. Their departure is remembered on a small, but poignant plaque on the far left-hand side of the station's concourse. Surrounding it are plaques commemorating many of the recipients of the Victoria Cross, Britian's

highest medal for military valour, who were from Glasgow and the west of Scotland. There is also a war memorial at the Gordon Street entrance dedicated to the workers from the Caledonian Railway who died in World War I, and a collection box for the Royal Hospital for Sick Children at Yorkhill, made from a 38-centimetre/15-inch Howitzer shell casing made by William Beardmore and Company during World War I. This is currently situated underneath the clock which hangs above the station concourse. It is also worth remembering that Central Station was not only a departure point for the living; it was also the returning point for the dead, with many servicemen killed in action being repatriated to their families via its platforms. Indeed, in World War I, an area beneath the station was used as a makeshift morgue, where many of the city's women had to walk through rows of bodies to identify their loved ones before they could be taken away for burial.

29. On the western side of the station concourse is the *Beacon of Hope*, a statue created by Steuart Padwick, which was installed here during the COP26 meeting held in Glasgow in November 2021. It is one of three related artworks installed across the city (the other two being in the Rottenrow Gardens and at Cunningar Loop), as monuments to the creation of a better future.

30. Return to Gordon Street through the main entrance of Central Station. Almost directly opposite, at No. 76, is the Grosvenor Building, which, if you look at it closely, has quite different designs for its lower and upper floors. This is because the first four floors, which were built in 1864, and were designed in a distinctive classical style by Alexander 'Greek' Thomson. In contrast, the top two floors and the attic were designed in a more elaborate, but still complimentary, Edwardian baroque style by James H. Craigie, and were added around 1905.

31. Turn right and head east along Gordon Street to its junction with Renfield Street (leading north) and Union Street (leading south). On the north-western corner of this junction is a former warehouse for John Black & Son which was built in 1858 and designed by Boucher & Cousland. This is a stunning building, topped, as it is, with a series of beautiful sculptures by William Birnie Rhind, added during alterations carried out by John James Burnet in the 1890s for R. W. Forsyth, a chain of department stores founded in Glasgow in 1872. The main sculpture features Eos, the goddess of the dawn, riding a quadriga (a chariot pulled by four horses) and bringing light to the new day. Above this are two female figures representing Summer (semi-naked and standing on the left) and Winter (clutching a shawl tightly around her and standing on the right). On the pillars on either side of these figures are putti holding

Eos, Goddess of the Dawn, former Forsyth Department Store.

shields, one decorated with a lion, representing Africa, and one decorated with an elephant, representing India. Further down, on the keystones above the arched first-floor windows, are some rather glorious grotesque masks, possibly based on the Green Man. Below these same windows are some other wonderful little flourishes in the form of a row of small iron flag holders, each tipped with the head of a lion.

Finally, if you look at the first-floor windows themselves, the ones closest to the corner feature an acid-etched F for Forsyth's, while the western-most one features a picture of Eos on her quadriga, mirroring the building's main statue.

32. On the opposite corner of this junction is the distinctive Ca' d'Oro Building. Designed by John Honeyman in a Venetian Renaissance style, it was built in 1872 as a furniture warehouse for F. & J. Smith. Inspired by the Ca' d'Oro in Venice, its ground-floor facade is made of stone, while the facade of its upper storeys are made of cast iron. The building was badly damaged by a fire in 1987, but while the interior was lost, and has since been replaced by an atrium surrounded by shops, its distinctive facades survived and have been refurbished. Glasgow's traditional buildings seem rather prone to catching fire, something which leads to a great deal of speculation among the residents of the city, but this building demonstrates that with a bit of effort and willingness, fire-damaged buildings do not need to be knocked down, but can be saved and brought back into use.

Decorative stonework, spandrels of Venetian Renaissance style Ca' d'Oro.

33. From Gordon Street, turn south onto Union Street. The first building on the western side of the street was built in the 1850s, and so predates Central Station. It was designed by James Brown and built in a classical style for Orr and Sons. Given that it is west of Union Street (which, at one time, marked the border between Glasgow and the lost village of Grahamston), it is unclear why this is not considered to be a survivor from this village.

34. The next building to the south is Caledonian Chambers. This is an Imposing Edwardian classical building designed by James Miller, with sculptures by Albert Hodge, which was constructed in 1903 for the Caledonian Railway to serve as, among other things, railway offices.

35. Across Union Street from Caledonian Chambers is Alexander 'Greek' Thomson's Egyptian Halls. Built in the 1870s for James Robertson, this was among the last major building projects undertaken by Thomson before his death in 1875. Described as one of Glasgow's finest buildings, it has sadly lain empty, neglected and screened by scaffolding for many years, and is often cited as a prime example of the problems associated with preserving the building heritage of the city, particularly the problem of absentee landlords and multiple untraceable owners. Its name, Egyptian Halls, is a bit of a misnomer as its style is more Grecian than Egyptian, but it may have originated with London's 1812 Egyptian Hall, designed by Peter Frederick Robinson.

36. Immediately to the south of the Egyptian Halls is another fine classical style building. Designed by James Thomson (who was no relation to Alexander Thomson), it was built in 1880. However, the ground floor was altered by Andrew Balfour in 1924, to serve as a branch of the National Bank of Scotland, and this explains the more art deco style nature to the classical features of this part of the building, especially around the outermost doorways.

37. Opposite the former branch of the National Bank of Scotland is a relatively plain building which now houses a hotel. Its main feature of interest is that, along with the Grant Arms, visited earlier in the walk, it is considered one of only two buildings from the lost village of Grahamston to survive the construction of Central Station.

38. Back on the eastern side of Union Street, at No. 36, is an art deco style building which was designed by White and Galloway and constructed around 1930. It was originally built for R.A. Peacock and Son as the Georgic Restaurant. Despite its name, it was in fact one of Glasgow's world-renowned tea rooms, which provided an alcohol-free environment for people to meet and socialise. It featured a smoke room, a tea room, a restaurant and a reception room. Rather unusually, the kitchen was positioned at the top of the building on its fourth floor.

39. At the southern end of Union Street is its junction with Argyle Street. In the past, this junction was known as Boots Corner after the branch of Boots the Chemist situated there. As it had a large clock outside it, it was another popular place for people to meet. In particular, young men and women from across Glasgow, who had met each other while dancing on a Friday night, would often arrange to meet here again on the Saturday. However, so many of these prospective dates were broken that it earned the meeting spot the alternative nickname of 'Dizzy Corner', after the phrase 'getting a dizzy', which was Glaswegian slang for being stood up (possibly originating as a shortening of the word 'disappointment'). Such was the notoriety of the spot that parents would often advise their children to 'never meet a lumber at Dizzy Corner' (a lumber being Glaswegian slang for a date).

Glasgow's legendary 'Dizzy Corner'.

40. From Dizzy Corner, cross over Argyle Street and head south down Jamaica Street. Here on the western side at No. 20 is a classical building dating from the 1860s, which originally served as a warehouse. However, like many warehouses, in the 1910s its lower floors were converted into a cinema designed by William B. White. Called the Grand Central Cinema, it seated 750 people. However, this closed in 1966, and while it was reopened as a smaller specialist cinema seating just 365 people, and showing the types of films that were not readily available to rent from your local video-hire shop, it closed for good in 1992. In 1987, the basement of this building became home to the Sub Club, another legendary Glasgow nightspot and the longest-running underground dance club in the world.

41. To the south of the former Grand Central Cinema on Jamaica Street, at its junction with Midland Steet, is the beautiful and impressive former Gardner's Furniture Warehouse. Designed by the architect John Baird and the iron founder R. McConnel, it is another of Glasgow's surprising number of Venetian style warehouse buildings. Constructed in 1855, and employing materials and methods used to build the Crystal Palace in London in 1851, it was the first commercial building in the UK to feature a cast-iron facade. It also contains the oldest elevator in Britain. Made by the Otis Elevator Company, founded in 1853 by Elisha Otis, the

inventor of the safety elevator, it was imported from the United States and installed in 1857. Rather unexpectedly, the original elevator is still in use to this day.

42. On the opposite corner of the junction, between Midland Street and Jamaica Street, is a fine example of a free classical style building with an art nouveau style pub on its ground floor. Designed by George Bell, it was built in 1897 for the wine and spirit merchant turned publican Philip MacSorley. When it was opened, MacSorley's quickly gained a reputation for its fast service and its American-style cocktail bar. It also featured a snack and oyster bar, electric lights and what were described as the most up-to-date toilets in Glasgow.

43. Return north along Jamaica Street and turn right on to Argyle Street. A short distance to the east, just beyond the junction with Mitchell Street, is a massive free classical style former warehouse designed by the wonderfully named Horatio K. Bromhead and built in 1903. On its ground floor, it features two of the largest atlantes in Glasgow (possibly only rivalled in size by the atlantes on the facade of the former St Andrew's Halls on Granville Street in the West End). Carved into the edifice above these statues are the names Stewart and MacDonald, leading generations of Glasgow children to believe these are the names of the two stone giants guarding the building's entrance. Rather less romantically, this actually refers to the name of the clothing wholesalers and retailers for whom the building was constructed.

44. On the eastern corner of the junction, between Buchanan Street and Argyle Street, stands a large and imposing art deco style former Burton's Department Store. It was designed by Burton's own in-house architectural team, led by Harry Wilson, in their distinctive and impressive 'Modern Temples of Commerce' style, and was constructed in 1929.

45. Further east, at No. 110, is one of the oldest buildings still standing on Argyle Street. Constructed in the eighteenth century, this tenement building was where Catherine Cranston, who would go on to dominate the Glasgow tea room scene, opened her first tea room in 1878. Known as the Crown Luncheon Room, it was expanded in 1898 to fill the whole building. This expansion included its remodelling by David Barclay and the creation of a tea room, a luncheon room and a games room for her customers, as well as a central store for her other tea rooms across the city.

Monogram of intertwined Cs, rear of Catherine Cranston's Crown Luncheon Room, Argyle Street.

One addition made to the building at this time was a door piece with intertwined Cs (for Catherine Cranston) on the rear elevation, where parts of the original eighteenth-century tenement are still visible. This monogram bears a striking resemblance to the logo of Coco Chanel invented in the 1920s, and it is quite possible that Chanel, who was a regular visitor to Scotland, was inspired by Catherine Cranston's monogram. At one time, the Crown Luncheon Room featured interior decorations by George Watson, with details by Charles Rennie Mackintosh, but these have largely been destroyed during more recent renovations.

46. The former Cranston tea room also contains an arched entrance leading to Sloans, one of Glasgow's oldest restaurants. Sloans started life in 1797 as a coffee house in Morrisons Court, which lies just to the north of Argyle Street, and at one time it was the arrival and departure point for stage coaches travelling to and from Edinburgh. It came into existence in its current from when it was bought by David Sloan around 1900, who turned it into an opulent venue complete with cocktail bar, lounge bar and grand ballroom. This remodelling was carried out by Charles H. Robinson and featured art nouveau detailing, including timberwork, plasterwork, acid-etched glass and tiling, much of which remains in place to this day.

47. To the east of Catherine Cranston's first tea toom is a rather wonderful tenement constructed around the latter half of the nineteenth century. Its upper floors retain many of its original classical style details and, unusually for Glasgow, its ground floor retains a relatively traditional shopfront which does not detract from the rest of the building's architecture. There is a growing concern in Glasgow that modern shopfronts all too often overpower the traditional architecture above them and that, as a result, they are having a detrimental impact on the city's streetscapes. Although work has been carried out to address these concerns in areas such as Govan, where grants have been provided to shop owners to reinstate the original scale, proportion and details of their shopfronts, this is still an issue in many other parts of the city.

48. At 100 Argyle Street is the southern entrance to Argyll Arcade. Designed by John Baird and built in 1827, this is Scotland's oldest indoor shopping arcade, and indeed the oldest covered shopping mall in Europe. Modelled on the late-eighteenth-century arcades of Paris, it has a striking cast-iron hammerbeam roof supporting a glass ceiling to provide the feel of a street without being exposed to the Glasgow weather. Argyll Arcade is now primarily home to Glasgow's jewellery district, but to the left of this entrance is a doorway leading to Sloans. This doorway is decorated with some rather stunning art nouveau tiles which were added during the 1900 remodelling by Charles H. Robinson.

Art nouveau decorative tiles, entrance to Sloans Bar and Restaurant, Argyll Arcade.

49. East of the entrance to Argyll Arcade and on the opposite side of Argyle Street is the former Lewis's Department Store, which was built in 1932 in a classical art deco style designed by Gerald de Courcy Fraser, with later additions by Clarke, Bell & J.H. Craigie. In 1988, this building was incorporated into the St Enoch Centre, the bulk of which sits to its rear on the site of the former St Enoch Station and Hotel, and which is now being considered for demolition after a lifespan of less than forty years. This contrasts sharply with Glasgow's many older buildings which have survived for a century or two, and have been adapted for a number of different uses throughout their lifetimes.

50. Directly across from the eastern end of the former Lewis's building, at No. 50 Argyle Street, is an imposing red sandstone building constructed in an American-derived style with an eclectic mix of Mannerist and Glasgow style details. Erected in 1905, this eight-storey office building was designed by John A. Campbell for the trustees of Mrs Mary Goodson, with the ground floor formerly being occupied by a branch of the Bank of Scotland. For many years, this building was greatly underused before becoming vacant and slipping into dereliction in the early 2010s. It was threatened with demolition in 2015 and has been concealed behind scaffolding since at least 2018. By the start of the 2020s, it seemed that the threat of demolition had been dropped, but the building remains vacant and deteriorating. The fact that such a major and impressive listed building on one of Glasgow's main shopping streets has remained empty and unloved for so long again highlights the complex issues associated with maintaining the city's built heritage. This includes issues associated with multiple ownership, absentee landlords, unidentifiable owners and the provision of adequate levels of funding.

51. A short distance further east at 63 Argyle Street is the magnificent Buck's Head Building. Designed by Alexander 'Greek' Thomson, it was constructed in 1863. It is often stated that the name of the building comes from John Mossman's sculpture of a male deer which crowns the corner of the building facing Argyle Street. However, this building was constructed on the site of a grand eighteenth-century Georgian mansion built by John Murdoch of Rosebank, a merchant and Provost of Glasgow, around 1750. When Murdoch died in 1776, the mansion was sold and by 1788, it had come into the ownership of Colin McFarlane and was home to the Buck's Head Tavern. As well as providing accommodation (which is why it later became known as the Buck's Head Hotel), it was also a stopping point for stage coaches. As a result, it is this older name which seems to have inspired the addition of the statue to 'Greek' Thomson's 1860s' building, rather than the statue having been the inspiration for its name. This version of events is also more consistent with Thomson's architectural style, as very few of his designs include sculptures of animals (or indeed sculptures of any kind).

Alexander 'Greek' Thomson's 1863 Buck's Head Building, 63 Argyle Street.

52. At the corner of Argyle Street and Virginia Street stands a rather unremarkable mid-twentieth century concrete building. However, on its side, facing Virginia Street a short distance from Argyle Street, is a plaque erected by the Scottish Burns Club commemorating the fact that Robert Burns, Scotland's national poet, lodged at the Black Bull Inn, which formerly occupied this site, when he visited Glasgow in both 1787 and 1788.

53. Further east is the point where Argyle Street ends and Trongate, one of Glasgow's original medieval streets, begins. On the southern side of this junction is a large red sandstone building designed by Frank Burnet and Boston and constructed in the 1920s. While the building itself is relatively plain, it features an impressive set of sculptures over its entrance at 177 Trongate, with the largest figures representing Neptune and Ceres, but also including a number of much smaller figures, including one of Mercury. Given the date of construction, these are among the last great architectural statues created to adorn a Glasgow building. By the end of the 1920s, with the move into modern classicalism, the preference had shifted away from the use of statues towards using relief sculptures to decorate the city's buildings, ending a fashion which had dominated the city's commercial and civic architecture since the 1880s.

54. The final building on this walk is the Renaissance style former bank building on the opposite corner of the Argyle Street–Trongate junction. Built for the National Bank of Scotland in 1903, it was designed by Thomas P. Marwick. This building stands on the site of Shawfield Mansion, another grand Georgian mansion once owned by the tobacco merchant John Glassford, and which was destroyed by a fire in 1793. Probably the most famous visitor to Shawfield Mansion was Charles Edward Stuart, better known as Bonnie Prince Charlie, who stayed there when passing through Glasgow following his retreat from England in December 1745, while his troops camped on the nearby Glasgow Green. Bonnie Prince Charlie and his troops departed Glasgow in January 1746, and just a few months later, on 16 April, his attempt to reclaim his father's throne came to a bloody end at the Battle of Culloden, the last pitched battle fought on British soil. The aftermath of Culloden had a devastating and long-lasting effect on the lives of the Highland clans which had supported Bonnie Price Charlie's cause, and in the decades that followed, lands were confiscated and many Highlanders were driven from their ancestral homes by aristocratic landlords in order to make way for more profitable sheep – a series of events now known collectively as the Highland Clearances. While large numbers of these Highlanders emigrated to North America and to British colonies there and elsewhere, others moved to Glasgow, where they became an integral part of the city's industrial expansion during the nineteenth century, leading it to become known as the industrial workshop of the British Empire and its second greatest city.

Former National Bank of Scotland building, Argyle Street.

6. Clyde Waterfront

Start Point: The McLennan Arch, Glasgow Green (**Location:** Lat/Lon: 55.85339, -4.24590 ; What3Words: ///frogs.stored.penny; Plus Code: VQ33+9J5 Glasgow). **Nearest Public Transport:** Subway: St Enoch Station (15 mins); Train: Argyle Street Station (10 mins); Bus: Trongate (5 mins).

End Point: The Riverside Museum, Pointhouse Road (**Location:** Lat/Lon: 55.86500, -4.30807; What3Words: ///logic.encounter.scarf; Plus Code: VM8R+2Q3 Glasgow). **Nearest Public Transport:** Train: Patrick Station (15 mins); Subway: Partick Station (15 mins); Bus: Partick Bus Station (15 mins).

Distance: 6.5 kilometres/4 miles. **Time:** Allow 2.5 to 4.5 hours for this walk.
Level of Difficulty: Moderate. Although this walk is primarily on flat, paved streets, it is relatively long.

Facilities: There are few places where you can stop refreshments during this walk, so make sure that you bring a drink and some snacks with you. There is, however, a cafe at the Riverside Museum at the end of it. Likewise, there are no publicly accessible toilets along this route until you reach the Riverside Museum.

Introduction

This walk follows the banks of the Clyde from the point where the river becomes tidal at Glasgow Green to Partick, which started out as separate burgh, but which was incorporated into the city in 1912 as it expanded westward. Glasgow's history and development is very much tied to the Clyde and this walk includes a number of aspects of this history, including shipbuilding, international trade and Glasgow's involvement in slavery. Much of the landscape you will see was created and/or controlled by the River Improvement Trust and its successor, the Clyde Navigation Trust. Until the end of the eighteenth century, much of the Clyde between Glasgow and Dumbarton, some 20 kilometres (12 miles) to its west, was a shallow estuary which could be waded across at low tide. This meant that ships could not sail directly into the city, and instead, they were loaded and unloaded in the distant Port Glasgow. In the 1760s, discussions began on how to how to solve this problem, and by the end of that decade, there were several proposals regarding how to make the Clyde navigable as far east as Glasgow, including by engineers such as John Golborne and James Watt. Work to implement these and other solutions was initiated in the 1770s and led to the creation of the River Improvement Trust in 1809. This was superseded in 1858 by the formation of the Clyde Navigation Trust which brought together the city fathers, shipbuilders, merchants and industrialists to develop and manage the Clyde, and in many ways its power rivalled that of the other major institutions that played an important role in Glasgow's development up until the mid-twentieth century. These included the Merchants House (established to represent the city's merchants), the Trades House (that looked after the interests city's craftsmen and manufacturers) and Glasgow Corporation, which ran the city itself.

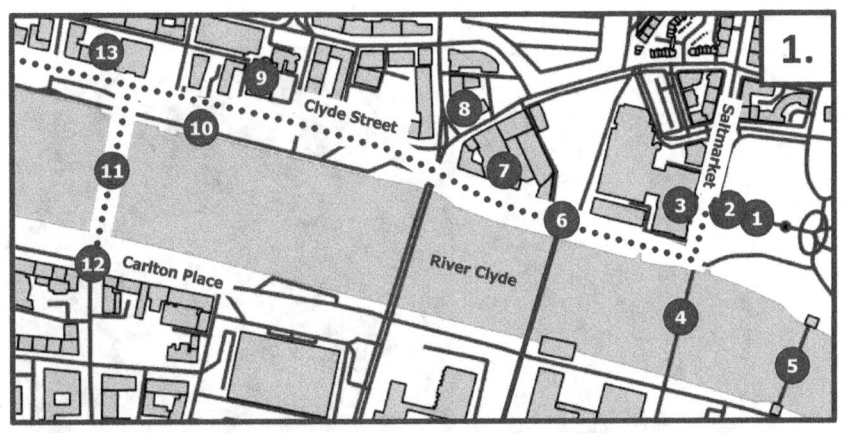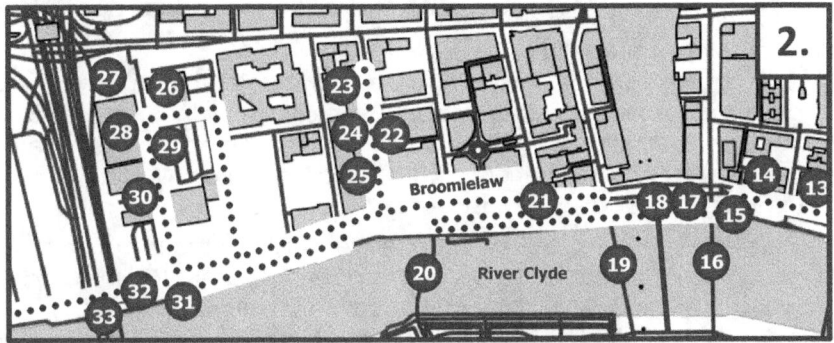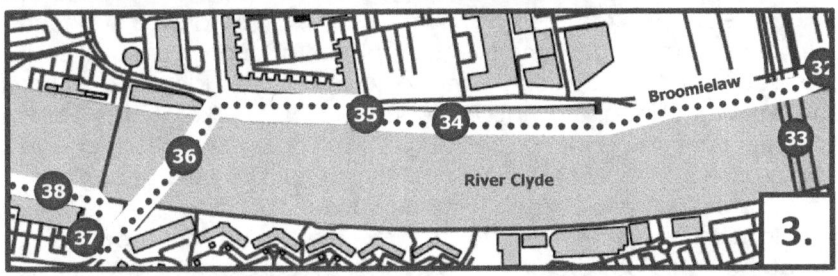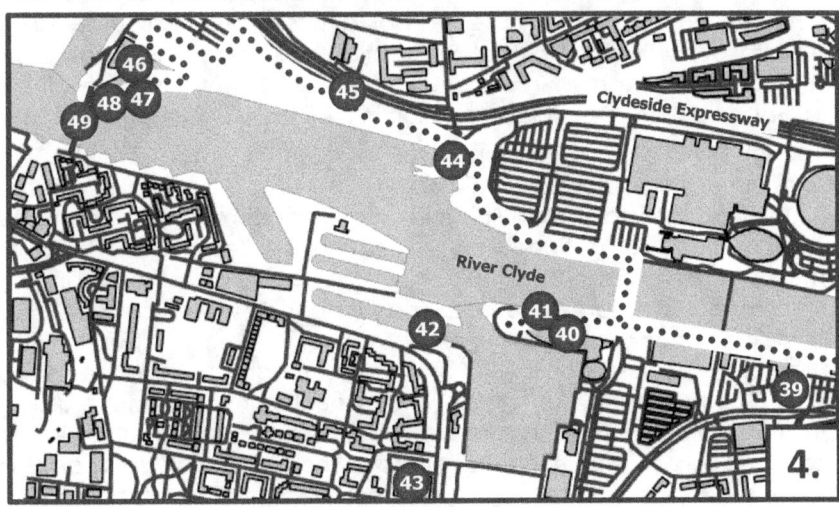

1. This walk starts at the McLennan Arch. Although it currently marks the western entrance to Glasgow Green, the largest open area in the city centre, it was only moved to this location in 1991. The arch originally formed part of the entrance to the old Assembly Rooms on Ingram Street, which were designed by Robert and James Adam and were built in 1792. When they were demolished in the 1890s, a number of fragments from it were salvaged and reconstructed as a stand-alone structure on Monteith Row, to the north of Glasgow Green. It was at this time that it gained its current name from Bailie James McLennan, who presented it to the citizens of the city in 1893. In 1922, the arch was moved again, this time further west to the entrance to the park on Greendyke Street, at the southern end of Charlotte Street, before finally being moved to its current location almost seventy years later.

McLennan Arch, western edge of Glasgow Green.

2. Set into the flagstones immediately to the west of the arch is a marker which is engraved with the name Jocelyn Gate, and notes that until 1865, this area was the location of public executions. Originally, executions were carried out at Howgate, close to Glasgow Cathedral, at Gallowgate, near Glasgow Cross, and at the Tolbooth at Glasgow Cross itself. However, in 1814, a new jail was built further south on Saltmarket and this became the main place for public executions. The exact location seems unclear, but it is unlikely to be at the point identified by this marker. Instead, the actual location of public executions is more likely to have been to the right of the Justiciary Buildings on Saltmarket, in an area now called Jocelyn Square. Either way, it is commonly accepted that the scaffold for public hangings was built facing towards Glasgow Green, and specifically facing towards the large obelisk erected in 1806 as a monument to Admiral Lord Nelson, who had died the year before at the Battle of Trafalgar. This led to the local expression 'You'll die facing the monument', meaning that a person would mostly likely end up being hanged for their nefarious activities. No public executions were held in Glasgow after 1865, and instead they were held in private, first at Duke Street Prison and then, after 1928, at Barlinnie Prison. The final execution in the city took place there in 1960.

3. From the Jocelyn Gate marker stone, walk towards Saltmarket, which is the road that forms the western boundary of Glasgow Green. On the other side of Saltmarket is the Justiciary Building. This building, with its distinctive neoclassical style and columned portico, was designed by the Scottish architect William Stark and was built in 1814 to replace the older Justiciary buildings of the Tolbooth on Trongate. Of particular note is the large Greek portico supported by Doric columns which was one of the earliest and, at the time, largest such structure to be built in Britain. This is also one of the earliest examples of a hexastyle (meaning supported by six pillars) portico in Glasgow, but it was a style which would, from then on, be used across the city for civic buildings, banks and even churches, until the move towards art nouveau and baroque architecture replaced the fashion for classical designs at the end of the nineteenth century. It is rumoured that there was an underground

tunnel linking this court building with the site of public executions in Jail Square, through which condemned prisoners would be transported to meet their fate, but there appears to be no evidence to support its existence.

4. Walk south along the western edge of Glasgow Green and onto the bridge over the Clyde at its southern end. This

Medallions of Queen Victoria and Prince Albert, Albert Bridge.

is the Albert Bridge, named after Queen Victoria's consort and it was built in 1868 to replace an earlier bridge dating from 1829. It was designed by Bell and Miller, and it is the only substantial wrought-iron arched bridge in Scotland. Instead of being cast in moulds using liquid metal (like the aptly named cast iron), wrought iron is heated and beaten into shape, making its production much more labour-intensive. However, it also produces iron products which are less brittle and more resistant to fatigue. There are bronze medallions of Queen Victoria and Prince Albert in profile set into the northernmost and the southernmost piers of the bridge, on the sides which face towards the water, meaning they will look at each other across the Clyde for as long as the bridge remains standing.

5. When on the Albert Bridge, look upstream over its eastern parapet. Here, you will see the Glasgow Green tidal weir and pipe bridge. The purpose of this weir is to control the tidal flow of water up the Clyde, thus maintaining a steady river level above it. This means that the weir now marks the end of the River Clyde and the start of the Clyde Estuary, which in itself is an offshoot of the North Atlantic Ocean. However, remarkably few Glaswegians are aware of this fact or that, as a result, to the west of the weir, the Clyde varies in depth by up to 5 metres (16 feet) every few hours as the tide goes in and out. The first weir was built here in 1852, which coincided with the final phases of the century-long project to deepen the Clyde and make it navigable by large sea-going vessels as far east as Glasgow City Centre, but the current one, designed by Alexander B. McDonald, was not built until 1896. This consists of a series of sluice gates which can be raised and lowered as needed to control the water flow across it. Two bridges were added to the weir at the end of the 1940s to carry a service pipe across the river.

6. Return to the north bank of the Clyde and cross Saltmarket at the traffic lights before heading west along Clyde Street until you reach the next bridge. This is the City of Glasgow Union Bridge, and it marks the site of Glasgow's oldest railway bridge across the Clyde. Built in 1864, this bridge allowed trains coming from the south to reach the now-demolished St Enoch Station, which at the time was the main station for the city, rather than having to terminate on the southern bank of the Clyde. The current Union Bridge was built in 1898, and features elaborately decorated red sandstone turrets. However, it does not just cross the Clyde, but carries on as a pair of brick-built arched viaducts which stretch out for an unexpectedly lengthy distance across the city to its north and south.

7. On the western side of the Union Bridge is a large stone building known as the Briggait. Originally, this was the site of the Merchants Guild Hall. Built in the seventeenth century, it was the base from which the city's merchants despatched their ships to return months later heavy with cargo such as sugar and tobacco, bringing much wealth to them and to the city. However, these products came primarily from the slave plantations of North America and the West Indies, meaning that much of this wealth was derived from the suffering of others. The only part of the Merchants Hall which remains is the Merchants Steeple, topped by a ship, and in the 1870s, current building was constructed around it to house the city's fish market. Designed by Clarke & Bell, one of its most notable features is the magnificent pair of hippocampi or winged seahorses on the balustrade above the entrance, which face each other across a bust of a young Queen Victoria.

Hippocampus on the Briggait, with 17th-century Merchants' Steeple in background.

8. From the Briggait, carry on west along Clyde Street and cross the road at the north end of Victoria Bridge. As you do so, look to your right. Here, occupying a narrow strip of land between Stockwell Street and Bridgegate, is a fine example of a Glasgow style red sandstone tenement. The Glasgow style is best described as European art nouveau mixed with Scottish baronial elements, creating a sensuous and ornate style which is unique to the city. While the most famous proponent of the Glasgow style was Charles Rennie Mackintosh, this particular tenement, built in 1905, was designed by Alexander B. McDonald, one of the most underappreciated heroes of Glasgow's architecture.

9. A short distance beyond Victoria Bridge on the north side of Clyde Street is St Andrew's Metropolitan Cathedral. Designed by James Gillespie Graham in a neo-perpendicular style, this church was built in 1814, and raised to the status of a cathedral in 1889. It is the largest Roman Catholic church in Glasgow.

10. In front of the Metropolitan Cathedral, between Clyde Street and the Clyde itself, is a set of stone steps. At one point, these steps provided seating for the Clyde Bandstand which was directly in front of them. There was also space for a small cafe nearby, and further on, a public toilet. However, since the 1980s, the bandstand and the other facilities have been lost, leaving the area with a rather abandoned feel to it. Despite this, or maybe because of it, the section of the Clyde Walkway has long been a place where various alternative communities meet and hang out, including Mods in the 1960s and Punks in the 1980s. There is still a counterculture air to the area to this day, with the concrete walls now providing a legal space for street art. Although the quality varies, at times there are some very impressive murals painted on them.

11. Rising above this part of the Clyde Walkway is the South Portland Street Suspension Bridge, which provides a pedestrian connection between the north and south banks of the Clyde. The current bridge was built in 1851 to replace an earlier timber footbridge and was designed by Alexander Kirkland. The bridge consists of pylons shaped liked classical triumphal arches supporting a single span of 126 metres (414 feet), and when it was first opened there was a toll of half a penny to cross it. To access the bridge itself, climb up the steps in front of the former bandstand, or walk up one of the ramps which lie beneath either end of the structure.

12. For the next part of this walk, cross the South Portland Suspension Bridge to Carlton Place, a largely unaltered Georgian Street, making it pretty much unique within Glasgow. It was created as the showpiece for John Laurie's development of a high-class residential area on the southern banks of the Clyde. It consists primarily of two ranges of classical townhouses designed by Peter Nicholson. The western range was built in the 1810s, while the eastern range was built a few years earlier, in around 1802. The most impressive of these townhouses is Laurieston House, which is the centrepiece of the eastern range and, at one time, it was the home of John Laurie himself and his brother David. Laurieston House has been described as being the last of Glasgow's great merchant houses to have survived largely unaltered, and its internal plasterwork makes it one of the most ornate Georgian townhouses left in the UK. This plasterwork, possibly inspired by the excavations at Pompeii and Herculaneum, is in the Greek revival style, and is believed to be the work of Francisco Bernasconi, who had been brought to Britain by King George III to decorate Windsor Castle. Despite its impressive internal decoration and its importance as a rare surviving representative of the Georgian period in Glasgow, Laurieston House is boarded up, and is in a very poor, rather neglected state of repair, as is Carlton Place as a whole. This is a particular shame not just because of its architectural importance, but also because, if it was developed properly, it has the potential to be a major tourist attraction.

Georgian Era Laurieston House, Carlton Place.

13. From Carlton Place, return to the north bank of the Clyde via the South Portland Suspension Bridge. As you do so, you will see a collection of three buildings ahead of you which together illustrate three different phases in Glasgow's development. The eastern-most of the three buildings is a rather generic-looking modern seventeen-storey hotel building, which dwarfs the surrounding architecture and has no local flare whatsoever. Immediately to its left, is the seven-storey Riverside House, designed by Eric A. Sutherland in an Edwardian free style and built using red sandstone in 1907. The western-most of this group is a three-storey classically designed Victorian building constructed around 1860. You can imagine that when the central building was constructed at the start of the twentieth century, its height relative to the neighbouring older Victorian building, the choice of red, rather than blonde sandstone as the building material, and its architectural style might have been subjected to the same level of debate and disparaging remarks as the construction of the modern hotel was when it was built at the beginning of the twenty-first century. However, it seems unlikely that in a hundred years' time, if it is even still standing, the right-hand building will ever be looked on with anything close to the kind of fondness that its neighbours inspire today.

14. A short distance further west on Clyde Street is the former Custom House. Designed by John Taylor in a Greek revival style, it was built in 1840, when the work to create a navigable channel through the previously shallow estuary of the Upper Clyde was close to completion, and large ships were able to sail right into the heart of the city, rather than having to be unloaded in Port Glasgow some 30 kilometres (20 miles) to the west. This building is topped by the royal coat of arms of Scotland supported by a lion on one side and a unicorn, Scotland's national animal, on the other.

15. Walk back down to the banks of the Clyde using the steps in front of the former Custom House. Here, you will find *La Pasionaria*, a distinctive statue of woman with clenched fists raised above her head. Erected in 1979, this is a statue of Dolores Ibárruri, a communist heroine of the Spanish Civil War. She is believed to have inspired the character Pilar in Hemmingway's *For Whom The Bell Tolls*. Created by Arthur Dooley, the statue is a memorial to 2,100 British members of the International Brigade, who travelled to Spain between 1936 and 1939 to fight Fascism, 534 of whom died, including 65 from Glasgow. It bears the inscription 'Better to die on your feet than live forever on your knees'. Excluding Queen Victoria, this is one of only three statues of real women in Glasgow. The other two are statues to Mary Barbour and Isabella Elder, both of which are in Govan.

La Pasionaria, *Clyde Street.*

16. From the statue of Dolores Ibárruri, continue downstream along the Clyde Walkway and pass under Glasgow Bridge at the bottom of Jamaica Street. Also known as Jamaica Street Bridge, it was designed by Blyth & Westland, and was built in the 1890s. It is similar in design to an earlier bridge constructed by Thomas Telford, which it replaced, but features a wider roadway. This bridge provides an important link between the north and south of Glasgow, and in the days before the first railway bridge was constructed across the Clyde, it was across this bridge that passengers travelled, on foot or by carriage, to get from the rail terminus at Bridge Street Station in Laurieston to the centre of the city.

17. Between the Glasgow Bridge and the railway bridge which now lies to its west is another Spanish Civil War memorial. Unveiled in 2019, this one is dedicated to the merchant seamen and members of the Royal Navy who broke Franco's blockade of Republican Spanish ports, of whom at least forty-three died in action. Unlike the International Brigade, which is relatively well known, thanks in part to the writings of Ernest Hemmingway, fewer people know about the Blockade Runners and the role they played in fighting the forces of Fascism in Spain. The memorial is inscribed with the words: '"I had a ship," the Captain said, "a ship that sailed for Spain, and when I get another ship, I'll sail there once again."'

18. Passing almost directly above the Blockade Runners memorial is the current railway bridge, which carries trains into Glasgow's Central Station. However, this replaced the earlier Caledonian Railway Bridge, which was built in the 1870s, and allowed trains travelling up from the south to cross directly into the centre of Glasgow for the first time, rather than having to terminate at Bridge Street Railway Station on the south side of the Clyde, or take a detour to the east to cross it using the City of Glasgow Union Bridge further upstream. The large stone piers of this original bridge remain and are still visible, rising out of the water to the east of the current bridge. Two of these piers carry inscriptions by the artist Ian Hamilton Finlay, written in both English and Ancient Greek, that consist of a quote from Plato's *Republic* which read: 'All greatness stands firm in the storm. All great things are perilous, and it is true, as the proverb says, that beautiful things are hard'. The current bridge was built alongside the first in 1905, as part of the expansion of Central Station, and first bridge remained in use until the 1960s, when it was finally demolished.

19. From Glasgow Central Railway Bridge walk down the small flight of stairs which takes you down and under the King George V Bridge that links Oswald Street coming down from the north with Commerce Street coming up from the south. Designed by Thomas Somers, it was built in the 1920s. The memorial stone for this bridge was laid by King George himself on 12 July 1927.

20. Once you have passed under the King George V Bridge, carry on west beside the Clyde until you reach the pedestrian Tradeston Bridge. Built in 2009, it was designed by Dissing+Weitling to provide a link between Anderston, on the north side of the Clyde, and the areas of Kingston and Tradeston to the south. A distinctive bridge, the route it takes across the river is curved rather than straight, giving rise to its nickname of 'the Squiggly Bridge'. Such is the popularity of this nickname that few Glaswegians will refer to it as anything else, and many do not even know its official name.

Tradeston Bridge, better known as the Squiggly Bridge.

21. From the Squiggly Bridge, walk up to the street which runs alongside the north side of the Clyde. This is the Broomielaw, a name which is derived from the Scots word 'law', meaning a grassy slope, and 'broom', a distinctive flowering bush common throughout Scotland. This was the location of Glasgow's first harbour, which was built in 1688. However, despite being tidal, the Clyde was relatively shallow at this point, and only small vessels could reach this harbour. As international trade increased, and ships grew bigger, Glasgow found itself in the awkward position of having to unload ships far downstream, on the coast of the outer Clyde Estuary, at a place which became known as Port Glasgow, and then transport all goods up to the city by cart. This led to a scheme in the late 1700s to deepen the Clyde to allow ships to sail right into the city itself. Among other things, this involved creating what is known as the Lang Dyke, a large wall along the centre of the Clyde near Dumbarton, to constrain the width of the river, thus increasing its speed and allowing the water to scour out a deeper channel. By 1775, the channel created by these efforts was sufficiently deep to allow large ships to sail right up to the Broomielaw and unload their cargo there. However, work to further increase the

navigability of the Clyde carried on well into the nineteenth century and led to the creation of the Clyde Navigation Trust in 1858. By the 1880s, the Trust had built itself a large and imposing headquarters at the eastern end of the Broomielaw. Designed by John James Burnet in a beaux-arts style, it features a series of very fine sculptures by Albert Hodge. The best place to view this building is from the south side of the Broomielaw, opposite the end of Robertson Street. However, once you have viewed it from a distance, cross over the Broomielaw at the traffic lights at the bottom end of Oswald Street, and walk back to the Robertson Street junction. This will allow you to have a better view of the facade which stretches up Robertson Street, and particularly the statues which adorn it (and which are described in detail at the end of the City Centre West Walk).

22. From the Clyde Navigation Trust Building, walk along the north side of the Broomielaw and then turn north up James Watt Street. On James Watt Street, keep to the right-hand side and look for a small inscription in the pavement which says 'Polaris'. Part of a street art installation, this marks a point where, on a clear night, you can stand and see Polaris, the Pole Star, above the northern skyline of the city.

23. Further north on James Watt Street, at No. 69, is the facade of a warehouse built in 1855. This is one of the few remaining remnants of the warehouses which once dominated this part of Glasgow. At the very top is a pediment featuring a barrel, an anchor and a packing crate, which are presumably references to its former function as a grain warehouse for Harvie & McGavin, who operated the nearby Anderston Grain Mill. Only the facade of this building remains, and behind it, a new one containing residential flats has been constructed.

Polaris art installation on pavement, James Watt Street.

24. Return south along James Watt Street, and at No. 37 you will find another former warehouse which was built in 1855 for Messers Connal and Company to store tobacco. While it was built after the end of slavery in the British colonies, it is a reminder of Glasgow's links with the tobacco trade. Slavery continued in the United States of America until 1865, so this warehouse may still have handled materials produced by the labour of slaves.

25. Immediately to the south of the former tobacco warehouse is an empty plot, in front of which is a memorial to the twenty-two people who died in a fire in the building which once stood there. It was being used as a furniture factory when the fire broke out in July 1968, but it had previously been a bonded whisky warehouse and still had the bars on its windows from this previous use (just as its neighbour still does to this day). This meant those trapped inside could not easily get out. However, it might still have been possible for them to escape had the doors to the fire exit not been locked from the inside. It took seventy firemen to bring the fire under control and specialist cutting gear to get through the steel doors and allow

them to enter the building. Only four of the twenty-six people who had been inside at the time of the fire survived. This was one of a number of major fires in Glasgow in the period after World War II which led to substantial improvements in fire safety across the country, including banning bars on factory windows, greater controls on the storage of foam plastics and other highly flammable materials which give off toxic fumes when they burned, more frequent inspections of factories with a high fire risk, and the introduction of certificates to ensure they had safe and suitable means of escape.

26. Return to the Broomielaw and head west along it until you reach McAlpine Street. Walk up this street, and at its northern end, turn left onto Balaclava Street. Here you will find the former Anderston Rice Mill. Consisting of three separate buildings, two mills and an office block, they were built between 1844 and 1865 using a polychromatic brick design common to Glasgow industrial buildings of the time.

27. At the end of Balaclava Street is Washington Street, and up to the right is the former Washington Street School. Designed by Henry E. Clifford and built in 1889, this was the main public school for the Anderston area of Glasgow. It later served as the home for Anderston Primary School until the Kingston Bridge was built in the 1970s, to carry the M8 motorway cross the Clyde. At this point the school moved to a new location and its former home, which now has an on-ramp passing within a few metres of its upper floors, has since been allowed fall into disrepair.

28. To the south of the former Washington Street School is a large Renaissance style building. Designed by Alexander Gardner in 1897, with additions by Henry Clifford in 1907, it was constructed as a bonded warehouse, where whisky could be stored without paying duty on it. At one time, it was home to James Buchanan & Company, which was formed by a Canadian of Scots descent in 1884, and which had a number of distinguished customers, including the House of Commons Members Bar, Queen Victoria and her sons, the Prince of Wales and the Duke of York. When it was built, it was said to be the largest bonded warehouse in the world. This building is now called the Pentagon Centre and has found a second life as offices.

Former bonded whisky warehouse, once largest such warehouse in the world.

29. Just across from the former bonded warehouse at 43 Washington Street is another building associated with the Scotch whisky industry. Designed by Archibald Stodart in a seventeenth-century Scottish style, it was built in 1893 for Robert Brown & Sons, a whisky exporter, and a wine and cognac importer. While primarily used as a warehouse, it also served as an office with a tasting room for clients on the upper floor.

30. Further south, on the western side of Washington Street is the remains of the former Crown Flour Mills, and its name can just be made out as a ghost sign on what is left of the facade. This mill was originally built in 1862 for John Ure and Son, and much of it was demolished in the 1970s to make way for the Kingston Bridge.

31. From the bottom end of Washington Street, turn left and walk back along the Broomielaw to the junction with Brown Street. At this point, use the traffic lights to cross to the southern side of the road so you can return to the walkway along the banks of the Clyde. When you reach it, turn right and carry on downstream. Moored alongside the walkway at this point is an old ship which has been converted into a restaurant and music venue. This vessel started its life transporting people and vehicles across the Clyde much further to the west, between Renfrew and Yoker. This ferry route has been in operation since at least the 1790s, and possibly as early as the 1300s, and continued until 2025, when it was finally replaced new swing bridge. The ferry moored at the Broomielaw was one of the last vehicle vessels to ply this route before it changed to become a pedestrian-only route in 1984.

32. Opposite the old Renfrew Ferry, on a concrete divider between the walkway and the road, are two memorials to those who died in the Cheapside Street Fire, one erected by the Scottish Fire Service, and one created by the children from two nearby primary schools. On 28 March 1960, a fire broke out in a bonded warehouse on Cheapside Street, owned by Arbuckle, Smith and Company, and which contained over 1 million gallons of whisky and some 30,000 gallons of rum. Within minutes, the first firefighters and members of the Glasgow Salvage Corps were on the scene, but as the fire spread to the neighbouring buildings, and as the temperatures increased, it caused the whisky and rum to vaporise. This created an extremely dangerous phenomenon called a BLEVE (Boiling Liquid Expanding Vapour Explosion). The BLEVE blew out an 18-metre (60-foot) high wall, killing 14 firefighters and 5 members of the Salvage Corps. Now burning well out of control, the fire continued to rage, creating a glow visible across the city. At its peak, there were 450 fire personnel fighting it, and it took a week before it was finally extinguished. The dead were carried first to Ramshorn Church in the Merchant City before being taking to the Necropolis, the cemetery to the east of Glasgow Cathedral, for burial. This remains the worst peacetime fire services disaster in British history.

Memorial created by children of Anderston and St Partick's Primary Schools to mark 50th anniversary of Cheapside Street fire.

33. Between these memorials and Cheapside Street itself is the Kingston Bridge. This is a large concrete bridge designed by William Fairhurst, and built in the 1960s to carry ten lanes of the M8 motorway from one side of the Clyde to the other. Its northern end was built where Anderston Cross, once the heart of this former weaving village, stood until it was demolished to make way for the bridge. The southern end was built on the former Kingston Dock, the first enclosed dock in Glasgow, which was filled in during its construction. The bridge was originally designed to handle 120,000 vehicles a day, but by the 1990s, the volume of traffic using it, combined with the weight of vehicles, was causing it to crumble, and it had to be substantially

strengthened. This created a problem as there was no way that the bridge itself could be closed without bringing traffic to a standstill across much of Glasgow. As a result, while the bridge was still in use, its main deck was jacked up and new supporting piers were constructed underneath before it was lowered back into place. Such was the complexity of this process that it took almost ten years to complete. It also earned a Guinness World Record for being the biggest ever bridge lift. As well as being a major traffic route across the Clyde, the pillars of the bridge are also rumoured to the final resting place of one Archibald McGeachie, thought to have been the getaway driver for a still-unsolved bank robbery which took place in Williamwood, near Glasgow, in 1969. However, there is little evidence to support this claim.

34. From the Kingston Bridge, carry on downstream along the Clyde Walkway. As you do so, another bridge will soon come into view. Built in 2006, this was the new first bridge constructed across the Clyde in Glasgow since the Kingston Bridge was opened in 1970, and it was intended to help relieve some of the traffic pressure on the older bridge. Designed by the Halcrow Group, due to its distinctive shape, its official name is the Clyde Arc. However, due to the unusual angle at which it crosses from one bank to another, to almost everyone in Glasgow it is simply known as 'the Squinty Bridge'.

Clyde Arc, more commonly known as the Squinty Bridge.

35. Further west at Lancefield Quay, there is a small area projecting out into the Clyde which provides a perfect spot for photographing the Squinty Bridge, and on a calm day, from here you can see it reflected in the water, forming an almost complete oval. At this point on the Clyde Walkway, there are also some pieces of large industrial-looking machinery attached to a small platform set into the pavement. This was an access ramp for one of the Clyde's rather unusual elevator ferries. These were small vessels fitted with moveable decks which sat high above the water, allowing cars and other vehicles to drive onto them from the quayside. The exact height of the deck could be adjusted up and down to account for the state of the tide, and the machinery you can still see on the quayside was used to lower the access ramp into place, to allow the vehicles to drive on and off. You can see a second similar ramp and its associated machinery almost directly opposite this point on the far side of the Clyde.

36. Once you reach the Squinty Bridge, cross the road at the traffic lights at its northern end and then walk along the pavement on its western side. This will allow you to look down the Clyde and see the Finnieston Crane and the modern, unique-looking buildings of the Scottish Events Campus on the right, and those of BBC Scotland and the Glasgow Science Centre on the left.

37. At the southern end of the bridge is a circular building constructed from red brick. This is the South Rotunda, which was designed by Simpson and Williams, and was built in the 1890s as part of the Glasgow Harbour Tunnel. At this time, Glasgow was

still a major port, with ships passing regularly between the docks of the upper Clyde and the open sea. As a result, it was felt it would not be possible to build a bridge to cross it at this point, so instead, a set of three tunnels – one for pedestrians and two for vehicles – were dug beneath the Clyde. The South Rotunda, along with the North Rotunda on the far bank, served as the access points, allowing people and vehicles to descend the 22 metres (72 feet) into the tunnels below. The tunnels closed to vehicles in 1940, and all the metalwork for the lifts was removed to help with the war effort, while the pedestrian tunnel stayed in use until 1980. The descent by lift into the tunnel was described by one writer in 1932 as involving 'a bewildering medley of wheels and cables', whereas walking through the tunnels was described as having 'a certain beauty', due to the flickering light of the electric lamps. Adding to this atmosphere were spectacular stalactites hanging from the roof, formed by water oozing through from the Clyde above.

38. From the southern end of the Squinty Bridge, turn right down to the walkway along the south bank of the Clyde and head west once more. As you do, there are great views across to the far side and up to the West End of the city. In the foreground, you can see the Northern Rotunda, which was formerly the northern entrance to the Glasgow Harbour Tunnel, the spaceship-like Hydro Arena, one of Glasgow's premier entertainment venues, the Finnieston Crane and the Armadillo, another entertainment venue. In the distance, you can see the Italianate towers of the former Trinity College, as well as the white tower of the former Park Church, the tall, thin spire of St Jude's Congregational Church, the golden dome of the Sikh Gurdwara Singh Sabha and Gothic tower of the University of Glasgow. Of all the structures you can see from here, possibly the most iconic is the Finnieston Crane. More correctly called 'Stobcross Crane Number 7', this massive Titan crane was built in the 1920s by Cowans Sheldon and Company Limited to load steam locomotives, built in the North British Locomotive Company factory in Springburn, into the holds of ships, so they could be sent all over the world. However, it was also used to lower boilers into newly launched ships which had been constructed in the nearby shipyards. At 53 metres (175 feet) tall, it is the largest of the four massive Titan cranes which remain on the Clyde, and when it was in full working order, it was capable of lifting up to 159 tonnes (175 tons).

Finnieston Crane rising above the Armadillo on the left and the Hydro Arena on the right.

39. A short distance to the west of the Finnieston Crane, but on the southern side of the Clyde, is a red-brick and sandstone building. This is the former Prince's Dock Hydraulic Power Station, which was designed in a mix of Italian and Romanesque styles by Burnet, Son & Campbell, and built in 1894. It originally had a 52-metre (172-foot) chimney decorated with relief sculptures based on those on the ancient Tower of the Winds in Athens, but it was cut down to just 16 metres (55 feet) in 1927. However, the sculpted friezes showing the personifications of the winds have been retained, and can be viewed by walking round to the Govan Road side of the

building. This hydraulic power station was constructed for the Clyde Navigation Trust to power travelling cranes on the Prince's Dock. Opened in 1895, and containing 35 acres of water, the Prince's Dock was once the largest dock on the upper Clyde. However, it closed in the 1970s, and in the 1980s was filled in and used as the site of the 1988 Glasgow Garden Festival, which is often credited with kickstarting the regeneration of Glasgow as a post-industrial city.

Chimney of former Prince's Dock Hydraulic Power Station.

40. Return to the southern bank of the Clyde and continue further west until you reach the Glasgow Science Centre complex, which was built on the remains of the former Prince's Dock. Consisting of an IMAX Cinema, the Science Mall and the Glasgow Tower, it was first opened in 2001, and has since become one of the most popular paid-for visitor attractions in Scotland. The Glasgow Tower, designed by Richard Horden to be the tallest freely rotating tower in the world, is 127 metres (417 feet) in height, making it the tallest structure in Glasgow – a title previously held by the University of Glasgow tower since 1887. As long as it is not too windy, in summer months, visitors can take a lift to the top of this tower and are rewarded with some amazing views across the west of the city and out to the hills which surround it.

41. The wharf in front of Glasgow Science Centre is the docking point for the PS *Waverley*, the world's last sea-going passenger-carrying paddle steamer. Built by A. & J. Inglis of Glasgow, it was constructed to replace a previous ship of the same name which had been sunk in 1940, while helping to evacuate British troops from Dunkirk at the start of World War II. She operated as a commercial vessel until 1973 when she was bought by the Paddle Steamer Preservation Society, and now offers excursions up and down the Clyde, as well as trips around the Western Isles of Scotland, and even as far afield as London.

42. At the far end of the walkway, to the west of Glasgow Tower, you can look across the entrance to what is left of the Prince's Dock to the gates of the Govan Graving Docks. Built between 1869 and 1893, these docks were constructed for the Clyde Navigation Trust at a time when the shipyards of the Clyde led the way in building the most advanced and innovative ships in the world. When they were built, they contained the deepest dry docks in Britain, capable of handling the largest ships. However, they closed in 1988 and have lain pretty much abandoned ever since.

43. To the left of the entrance of the Govan Graving Docks is a large, ornate building. This is the former Govan Town Hall. Built at the end of the 1800s, it was designed in a beaux-arts style by Thomson & Sandilands. At the time, Govan was still an independent burgh and this town hall was meant to be its answer to Glasgow's then recently completed City Chambers. However, in 1912, Govan was swallowed up by its larger neighbour and became part of the newly enlarged city of Glasgow. Govan had long been an independent centre of commerce, industry and religion, and its old parish church contains a carved sarcophagus and hogback stones dating back to the Viking Era. In many ways, it could easily have been Govan

which grew to be the dominant centre of population in the west of Scotland, rather than Glasgow. However, Glasgow seems to have offered an easier crossing point for the Clyde for those travelling between north and south, and this may have been enough to tip things in its favour.

Former Queen's Dock Hydraulic Pumping Station, with Glasgow Tower in background.

44. Walk back east along the banks of the Clyde, cross it using the Millennium Bridge beside the Science Centre complex, and then head west along its northern side. From here, you have good views back across to the Science Centre, Glasgow Tower and the entrance to the Govan Graving Docks. Further west, you will find the former Queen's Dock Hydraulic Pumping Station, with its distinctive Italianate campanile style accumulator tower. This power station was, at one time, used to power the cranes of the Queen's Dock, as well as the 11-ton swing bridge at its entrance. Constructed by the Clyde Navigation Trust in the 1870s, the Queen's Dock, named after Queen Victoria, was once one of the busiest docks in Glasgow. However, a decline in usage led to its closure in 1969. In 1985, It was filled in and the newly reclaimed land was used to build the Scottish Events Campus, containing the Scottish Exhibition Centre, the Armadillo (which was originally called the Clyde Auditorium, but became so widely known by its local nickname, that its operators gave in and changed it), and the Hydro Arena. Some of the materials used to fill in the Queen's Dock came from the former St Enoch Station and Hotel in central Glasgow, viewed by many as one of the city's greatest lost buildings. The former pumping station is now the home to the Clydeside Distillery, one of Scotland's first dedicated single-malt whisky distillery built in more than a century. You can see its distinctive copper stills through the windows on the western side of the building.

45. From the former Queen's Dock pumping station, carry on westward along the walkway. As you do so, if you look to your right, you will see a raised railway line, with arches underneath. These arches are home to a series of street art murals which are regularly updated. If you wish to get a closer look at them, you can cross the footbridge by the pumping station and walk along the far side of the road. You can then return to the main route for this walk through the pedestrian underpass which runs alongside the River Kelvin.

46. The next stop on this walk is Glasgow's iconic Riverside Museum. Designed by Zaha Hadid, its distinctive shape represents three waves joined together to form a single structure. Opened in 2011, it is now home to the impressive collection of the Glasgow Museum of Transport, and is well worth visiting.

47. Walk around the eastern end of the museum and on its southern side, you will find a viewing point where you can look east along the Clyde towards the new buildings which have been constructed along its banks, including the Science Centre, the Glasgow Tower and the buildings of the Scottish Events Campus. This view makes it a favourite spot for taking sunrise and sunset pictures of the modern Glasgow skyline.

48. Just west of this viewing point is the Tall Ship Glenlee. The Glenlee was built as a cargo ship in Port Glasgow in 1896 for the Glasgow shipping company Archibald Sterling and Company Limited. However, she ended her days as a training ship for the Spanish navy. Destined to be scrapped, she was rescued in 1993 by the Clyde Maritime Trust and returned to Glasgow where she has since been restored and now serves as a museum and tourist attraction.

Tall ship, the Glenlee, *moored alongside Riverside Museum, seen from Partick–Govan Pedestrian Bridge.*

49. This walk ends at the new 115-metre-long (377 feet) pedestrian suspension bridge across the Clyde, which connects Partick on the north side to Govan on the south. Opened in August 2024, it re-established a link between these two formerly independent burghs which was lost in the 1960s when the final ferry services across this part of the Clyde ceased. At the time of writing, there is no official name for this bridge, but due to its 28.5-metre (93.5-feet) tall tower, it seems most likely that its nickname will become 'the Pointy Bridge', to go with the Squiggly and Squinty Bridges further upstream. This bridge is designed to swing open in the middle to allow ships, such as the *Waverley*, to still be able to access the areas of the Clyde further upstream.

West and North of Glasgow

7. Sauchiehall Street, Part II

Start Point: The main entrance to the Mitchell Library on North Street (**Location:** Lat/Lon: 55.86510, -4.27157 ; What3Words: ///test.lobby.areas; Plus Code: VP8H+29V Glasgow). **Nearest Public Transport:** Subway: Cowcaddens Subway Station (15 mins); Train: Charing Cross Station (7 mins); Bus: St Vincent Street or Sauchiehall Street (5 mins).

End Point: The main entrance to Kelvingrove Museum (**Location:** Lat/Lon: 55.86886, -4.28985; What3Words: ///bags.noon.period; Plus Code: VP96+G3R Glasgow). **Nearest Public Transport:** Train: Partick Station (20 mins); Subway: Kelvin Hall Subway Station (10 mins); Bus: Argyle Street (3 mins).

Distance: 2.6 kilometres/1.6 mile. **Time:** Allow 2 to 3 hours for this walk.
Level of Difficulty: Easy. This walk is on relatively flat, paved streets.

Facilities: There are plenty of shops, cafes, restaurants and bars where you can stop for refreshments along this route. Publicly accessible toilets are available in the Mitchell Library at the start of this walk, and in Kelvingrove Art Gallery and Museum at the end of it.

Introduction

This is the second of two walks based around Sauchiehall Street, which runs between the city centre and Glasgow's West End. A brief introduction to the history of this street can be found in the introduction to the first walk, which covered the eastern section between Buchanan Street and the M8 at Charing Cross. This walk will focus on the western section, which stretches from the M8 motorway to its junction with Argyle Street. Just like the city-centre section of Sauchiehall Street, historically this has been an important area for entertainment and recreation activities, but since the 1870s when the University of Glasgow moved to the West End, it has played an important role in education. There is also a long residential history, and along the route of this walk you will pass Georgian townhouses and Victorian tenements, as well as a number of impressive civic and university buildings.

1. The starting point for this walk is the magnificent Mitchell Library Building on North Street. As well as being the centre for the Glasgow public library system, it is also the largest public reference library in Europe. The Mitchell Library was originally established in 1877, with a bequest from the wealthy tobacco-producer Stephen Mitchell, who made his money working for Stephen Mitchell and Sons, established in 1723 by his great-grandfather (a Linlithgow resident also called Stephen Mitchell). This means that much of his wealth originated within the slave plantations of the Caribbean and the American South. The original Mitchell Library Building was on Ingram Street in the Merchant City, but it moved to this purpose-built building in 1911. The 1911 building was designed by William B. White in an Edwardian baroque style and with its verdigris-covered dome, it is one of the most distinctive buildings of the Glasgow skyline. Seated in front of the portico above the main door is the figure of Wisdom, created by Johan Keller, while on top of the dome is the figure of Literature, created by Thomas John Clapperton. The latter figure is sometimes referred to, especially by children, as 'Mrs Mitchell', and it is one of a number of similar figures topping public library buildings across the city. Unfortunately, views of the Mitchell Library are somewhat marred by the presence of the M8 motorway which runs along a large trench directly in front of it, making it difficult to appreciate its full architectural majesty.

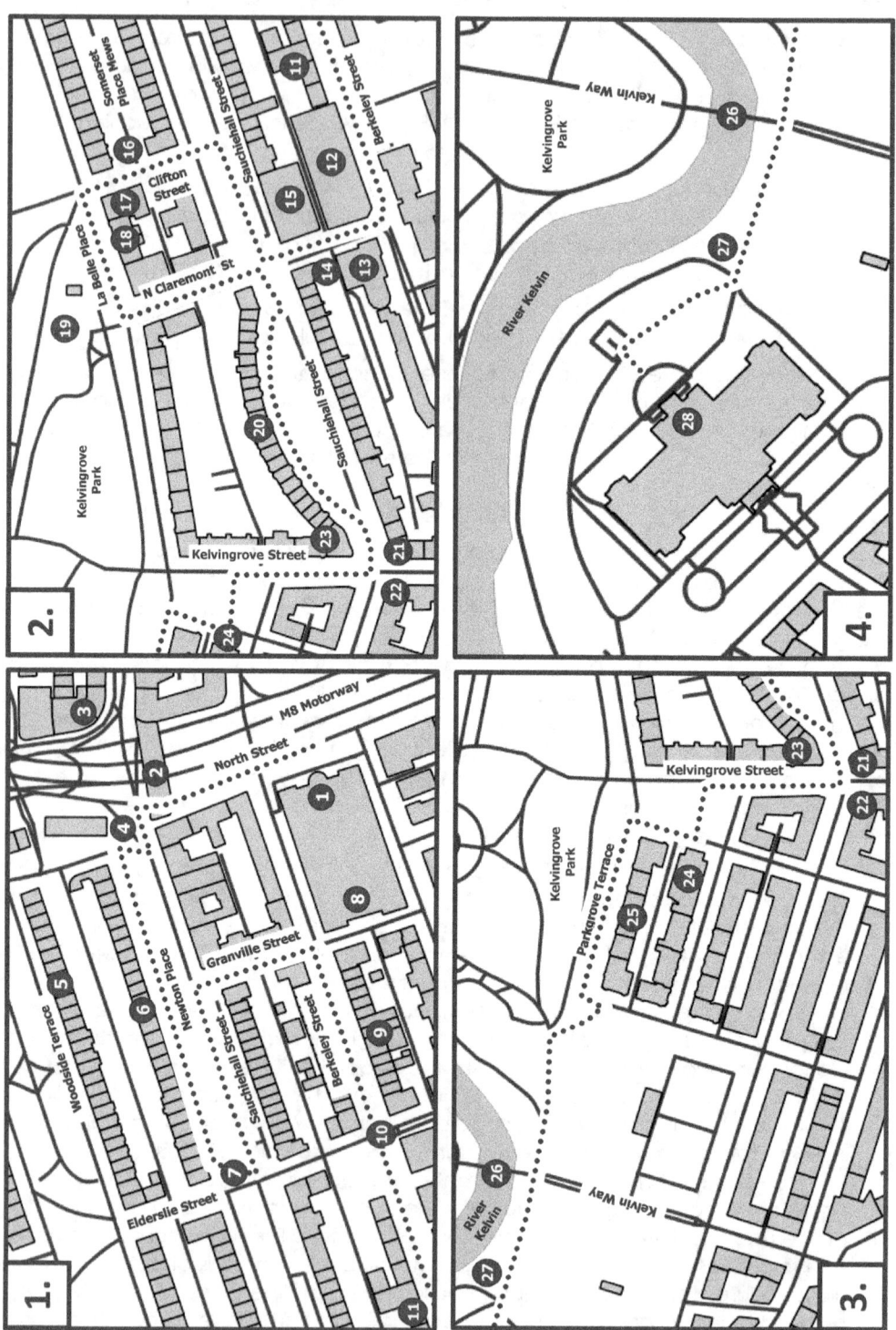

2. From the Mitchell Library, turn right and walk north along North Street towards Charing Cross. Just before you get there, you will pass one end of a large concrete structure which appears at odds with much of the surrounding architecture. Built in the 1970s, along with the M8 motorway, this was always intended to act as the base for a building development. However, for years it remained an empty and unfinished concrete plinth joined to nothing but air, making it one of Glasgow's infamous Bridges to Nowhere. These were features built as part of the motorway's development, but which, for various reasons, were never completed or connected to anything else. An office development was finally constructed on this particular Bridge to Nowhere in the 1990s, but it remains an architectural monstrosity, which contrasts sharply with the older architecture that surrounds it.

3. On the other side of this former Bridge to Nowhere is Sauchiehall Street. If you look to your right when you reach it, you will see the magnificent Charing Cross Mansions. Designed by John James Burnet and built in 1891, this is one of the grandest of the Edwardian residential developments in the west of Glasgow, and it gives an idea of what this area looked like before the M8 was driven through the middle of it. There is growing pressure to cover this section of the M8 and create a city square, both to allow easier access between the West End and the city centre, and to provide an atmosphere which is more in keeping with neighbouring buildings.

4. Cross over Sauchiehall Street using the pedestrian lights at its junction with North Street. Directly ahead of you, you will find a large red sandstone water fountain and clock. Designed by Clarke & Bell and erected in 1896, it is dedicated to the memory of Charles Cameron. Cameron was a doctor, newspaper editor and Liberal politician who was, among other things, responsible for abolishing imprisonment for debt in Scotland, conferring municipal franchise on women, reforming Scottish licensing laws and the wonderfully named Inebriates Acts, which allowed non-criminals convicted of repeated public drunkenness to be incarcerated in an Inebriates Reformatory. Given this, it is perhaps not surprising that Cameron was also one of Glasgow's foremost Temperance Movement campaigners, which may explain the choice of a public drinking fountain as his memorial. This is because many in the Temperance Movement believed that the provision of free access to clean water made abstinence from beer easier as beer was drunk by many simply because it was considered safer. Given this, it is somewhat ironic that the Cameron Memorial Fountain has, over time, developed a noticeable lean and as a result it has been nicknamed 'the Tipsy Fountain'. There is an urban myth that the lean developed due to the construction of the nearby M8 motorway, but as the lean was first noted as far back as 1926, well before the motorway was built, this is simply not true.

1896 Charles Cameron Memorial Drinking Fountain, Sauchiehall Street.

5. At this point, the main walk continues west into Newton Place. However, if you wish, you can take a detour up Woodside Crescent and along to 17 Woodside Place. Here, you will find the house where Joseph Lister lived and worked while serving as the Regis Professor of Surgery at the University of Glasgow between 1860 and 1869. It was during this time that Lister developed the concept and application of antiseptic surgery using carbolic acid, paving the way for what has come one of the main principles of modern medicine. There is a plaque on his former residence marking this time and work in Glasgow. If you make this detour, return back along Woodside Place and down Woodside Crescent to Newton Place to rejoin the main route for this walk.

6. On Newton Place, which was originally known as Caledonia Place, you will find a terrace of well-preserved late Georgian townhouses. While Glasgow is most famous for its Victorian and Edwardian architecture, there is a surprising amount of Georgian architecture still be the found in the city. Built in 1837, right at the end of the Georgian period, the Newton Place townhouses were designed by George Smith. As well

Terrace of classical style Georgian townhouses, Newton Place.

as the buildings themselves, there are a series of ornamental cast-iron lamp stands along this street. Although they have now been converted to electricity, these lamps were originally gas-powered. Gas lighting was invented by a Scotsman, William Murdoch, in 1792, and by 1818, it was rolled out to the streets of Glasgow. Gas lamps, such as the ones on Newton Place, ran on city gas, which was created by burning coal inside a closed container, to create a volatile mixture of methane, hydrogen and other flammable gases. Glasgow's first gasworks was sited in the Townhead area of the city but, as demand increased, other gasworks were built. The remains of several can still be seen on the outskirts of the city, most notably Temple Gasworks in the west and Provan Gasworks in the east, and their massive gas storage units (also known as gasometers) are an indicator for many returning to Glasgow by road that they are almost home. However, the use of gas for lighting did not last, and by 1893, the first electric lights were installed in Glasgow. The last gas-powered street lamps in Glasgow were turned off for the final time in 1971. If you look closely at some of the gas lamps on Newton Place, you can still see the tap which would have been turned on each night by one of Glasgow's army of lamplighters, or 'leeries', to allow the gas to flow up to the mantle where it would then be lit. In the morning, the lamplighter would return and turn the gas off to extinguish the flame. Coal gas, often referred to as town gas, was also used for domestic lighting, and it was not unknown for teenagers and alcoholics to bubble the gas through milk to create an intoxicating and mildly hallucinogenic, but potentially lethal, purple mixture known locally as 'electric soup', This practice died out when North Sea gas replaced coal gas in the 1970s, as its different composition meant it did not lend itself to the creation of this intoxicating substance.

7. At the western end of Newton Place, it is worth stopping to examine the railings which run along Sauchiehall Street and up Elderslie Street. On these, you will see a metal cutout of a bird perched on the outline of a boat. This is the logo of the Allied

Irish Bank. Based on a carving on a ninth-century Celtic cross at Killary Church, near Lobinstown, in Ireland, it depicts Noah's Ark as a Celtic longship, with a dove perched on the top of its mast.

8. After leaving Newton Place, cross Sauchiehall Street at the pedestrian lights and then return east along it to Granville Street. Once there, turn right, and walk down to its junction with Berkeley Street. Across the road from here you will see a grand neo-Greek style building adorned with many sculptures. This currently forms the rear portion of the Mitchell Library complex, but it was originally part of a separate building called St Andrew's Halls. Built in the 1870s, the Halls were the creation of three of the relatively unsung heroes of Glasgow's architecture: the architect James Sellars and sculptors John and William Mossman. Built by a private company to meet the demand for a large hall in the rapidly expanding West End of the city, the building contained a series of concert halls, including the Grand Hall, which could accommodate 4,500 people for events such as musicals, concerts and music hall acts, as well as civic and religious meetings, and a 22 × 15 metre (72 × 50 ft) ballroom. The Halls were bought by the Corporation of the City of Glasgow (a forerunner of the current Glasgow City Council) in 1889 and survived until 1962, when the building was gutted by fire. Only the Granville Street facade could be saved and in the 1970s this was remodelled and incorporated into the neighbouring Mitchell Library. There are four main sculpture groups on the facade which represent (from left to right): Literature (consisting of a central figure of Homer, the ancient Greek poet who composed *The Odyssey* and is dressed in a toga, with Shakespeare seated on the left and Dante on the right); the Visual Arts (consisting of the central figure of Michelangelo flanked by Leonard da Vinci on the left and Raphael on the right); the Ancient Arts (consisting of the central figure of the Greek goddess Athena between two male figures representing sculpture and architecture); and Music (consisting of the Greek god Apollo in the middle playing a lyre, or a *kithara*, accompanied by two female muses, possibly Erato on the left and Polyhymnia on the right). Along the top of the building are two sets of caryatids (female figures that function as pillars), which carry a variety of items emblematic of the arts, such as a lyre, an artist's palette and a pair of dividers. Between one group of caryatids are the names of various composers, such as Bach, Handel and Mozart, while between the other are the names of artists, like Michelangelo, as well Newton, a scientist, and Watt, an engineer. Around the entrance are two large atlantes or Atlas figures (possibly the largest in Glasgow), the male equivalent of caryatids. Although only a small part of the original building was saved, it shows what can be done to retain older buildings, even after such a serious fire.

Caryatids, facade of former St Andrew's Halls, now part of Mitchell Library.

9. After viewing the facade of the old St Andrew's Halls, return to Berkeley Street and head west along it. At 73 Berkeley Street you will find the Ottoman Coffeehouse. Built as a townhouse around 1855, this building was formerly home to the Glasgow Society of Musicians. This society was formed in 1884 in MacLean's Hotel, at 250 St Vincent Street, to run a range of events including concerts, lectures and dinners, as well as a benevolent fund. Initially, its meetings took place at a variety of locations around Glasgow, including St Andrew's Halls. However, in 1905, the society purchased 73 Berkeley Street, where it erected a concert room at the rear for its events and musical activities. The society was wound up in the 1990s and the Ottoman Coffeehouse took over the building in 2015, but you can still see the name of the society on the custom-made door of its former home, where it surrounds a circular acid-etched window decorated with a lyre. If you have time, it is worth stopping for some refreshments here so you can see the interior, which retains many of the features first installed by its previous inhabitants.

Insignia of Glasgow Society of Musicians, door of 73 Berkeley Street.

10. From 73 Berkeley Street, continue west to the junction with Elderslie Street. If you look north up Elderslie Street, in the distance you can see a series of towers. The one on the left is the Gothic tower of the former Park Parish Church, which was designed in 1858 by John T. Rochead in a West-of-England perpendicular style. In 1968, the church was dismantled, leaving only the tower still standing, to be replaced by a building constructed as an office for Bank of Scotland using reinforced concrete, which to this day contrasts markedly with the beauty of the surrounding Victorian architecture. To the right of the Park Church Tower are the Italianate towers of Trinity College, built in 1856 as one of three colleges for the then newly formed Free Church of Scotland. It was designed by Charles Wilson, who also designed much of the rest of the surrounding Park District. The college left this building in 1976 and moved to neighbouring Gilmore Hill, which is home to the University of Glasgow, but its Italianate main tower remains a key landmark in the West End of Glasgow.

11. Carry on along Berkeley Street to the red-brick building at No. 135, which is constructed in a markedly different style from the surrounding Victorian tenements. This is a late-nineteenth-century military drill hall and by 1914, it was home to the 1st City of Glasgow Battery, 3rd Lowland Brigade, of the Royal Field Artillery. Drill halls such as this were created for use by volunteers to expand the number of trained soldiers, and there are a surprising number of them around Glasgow, including four which remain standing in the West End alone. It seems that they were often designed by one of the volunteers who was based there (presumably one who had some architectural experience in their day job), which might explain why their architectural style is often at odds with other nearby buildings. Between the 1960s and the 2010s, it served as a Gurdwara for the Sikh community in the west of the city.

12. To the west of the former drill hall lies the unmistakable Gurdwara Singh Sabha. Built from pink sandstone and topped with a golden dome, it took six years to construct and was finally opened in 2016. Much of the building materials, including all the

facing stones, were designed and made in India before being shipped to Glasgow in fifty shipping containers. It is built on the site of the former Glasgow Eye Infirmary's accommodation block, which burned down in 1971.

13. Next to the Gurdwara Singh Sabha, at the junction between Berkeley Street and Claremont Street, is the former Trinity Congregational Church. Designed in a late Gothic style by John Honeyman, who would later employ a young Charles Rennie Mackintosh, this church was built in 1864. In 1979, it became home to the Scottish National Orchestra (SNO), which had been looking for a new permanent home since its former home of St Andrew's Hall burned down in 1962. At this time, it was renamed the Sir Henry Wood Hall after one of the UK's most famous conductors. In 2015, the SNO moved to a new home in the Glasgow Royal Concert Hall on the corner of Buchanan Street and Sauchiehall Street, and the building returned to ecclesiastical use as the Tron Kelvingrove Church. If you look closely at the stonework above the smaller of the two doors on Claremont Street, you will see a small, but rather cute and beautifully sculpted, dragon. Similar depictions of dragons can be found on many of Glasgow's Gothic style churches, but like this one they are often quite difficult to find, suggesting they may have been added by the stonemasons working on the building rather than being part of the architect's original design.

14. Just beyond the former Trinity Congregational Church on Claremont Street is a lane leading off to the left. If you look up at the gable end of the building to the north of the entrance to this lane, there is stone inscribed with the text 'Glasgow Botanic Gardens Instituted 1817'. For those familiar with Glasgow, this may seem rather confusing as the Glasgow Botanic Gardens can be found at the northern end of Byres Road, which is about 1.5 kilometres (1 mile) from this spot. However, the Botanic Gardens only moved to their current location in 1842 and originally, they occupied an 8-acre site here in the Sandyford area of the city. The gardens were founded in 1817 by Thomas Hopkirk and James Jeffray, and were

Plaque commemorating original location of Glasgow Botanic Gardens, Sandyford.

originally run by the Royal Botanic Institution of Glasgow in order to provide supplies to the nearby University of Glasgow. Jeffray was Professor of Botany at the university for fifty-eight years, making him one of the longest-serving professors in Scottish history. Rather unusually, he was also Professor of Anatomy, and it was in this role that he took part in a public experiment, in 1819, on the body of a recently executed murderer by the name of Matthew Clydesdale. This involved using a Galvanic battery (a new invention at the time) to pass electric currents through the dead man's corpse, causing it to twitch and move, much to the amazement and shock of the assembled crowd. Over time, these events have grown in retelling to become an urban legend, whereby the deceased criminal was accidentally resurrected by the electrical currents coursing through his body, causing him to stand up, only to be killed once again by a scalpel-wielding Jeffray. However, a scientific account, written shortly after the experiment was conducted, failed to mention any such sensational details.

15. Continue north along Claremont Street to its junction with Sauchiehall Street. Cross Sauchiehall Street using the pedestrian lights at this point and then turn right to head east. On the other side of the road is a three-storey building with an golden art deco ghost sign bearing the words 'Glasgow Eye Infirmary'. The eye infirmary was founded by Dr G. C. Montieth and Dr William Mackenzie in 1824, and was originally located in the city centre near Glasgow Cross. In 1874, it moved into these buildings in the West End of the city, where a 100-bed accommodation block was also built. In 1971, this accommodation block burned down and the in-patient accommodation was moved to the then newly built Gartnavel General Hospital further to the west. The rest of the eye infirmary followed in 1998. However, the building itself remains in use as part of the Glasgow's National Health Service, which makes it one of the oldest NHS buildings still in use in the city.

16. On reaching the next junction, turn north onto Clifton Street. About halfway up Clifton Street on the right-hand side is Somerset Place Mews. As the name suggests, this once housed the stables for the townhouses which face on to Somerset Place to the south and Clairmont Gardens to the north. It was here that the owners would keep their horses and carriages, which were the main mode of transport for those who could afford to live in such grand accommodation at the time they were built, in the 1850s, as well as providing accommodation for the grooms and stable hands. Many of these former stables have since been adapted for other purposes. The one nearest Clifton Street, which is part of 12 Clairmont Gardens, has been completely replaced by a new brick building with a distinctive double-arched front. Erected in 1898, it originally housed a billiard room on the upper floor, and a laundry and coal store on the lower floor. It was designed by the architectural firm Honeyman and Keppie, who, at the time, employed a young draughtsman by the name of Charles Rennie Mackintosh, whose duties included creating the plans for this building. Mackintosh, who would go on to become one of Glasgow's most famous architects, may also have contributed to the design of its interior.

17. On the opposite side of Clifton Street from the entrance to Somerset Place Mews is a grand building which was originally constructed as the Queen's Halls Assembly Rooms. Designed by Charles Wilson in 1857, it features some beautiful sculptural work by John Mossman both on its Clifton Street and La Belle Place facades. Of particular note is the sculpted frieze along the top of these facades, which tells the story of the progress of humanity from barbarism to enlightenment, and the development of the arts, including music, painting, sculpture and architecture. The Queen's Rooms were erected by the merchant David Bell of Blackhall as a venue for concerts, theatrical performance, arts exhibitions, lectures and other public events. It is now the Om Hindu Mandir, and the doors on La Belle Place are richly carved with Hindu symbolism, which does not look remotely out of place on such a grand building. On either side of the door are some original cast-iron lamp stands created by the Shotts Ironworks to the east of Glasgow. This foundry specialised in the production

Former Queen's Hall Assembly Rooms, corner of Clifton Street and La Belle Place.

of decorative ironwork, and beneath the many layers of thick, black paint on these lamp stands, you can just make out their many intricate details, including dolphin heads, seahorses with intertwined tails and, higher up, the prows of boats with figureheads consisting of strange, mermaid-like creatures with double tails.

18. Next to the former Queen's Rooms on La Belle Place is a pair of rather ornate Italianate style tenement buildings. These were also designed by Charles Wilson for David Bell and was built at the same time as the neighbouring Assembly Rooms. If you look at the relief sculpture in the arch above the ground-floor bay window at the left-hand side of these buildings, you will see it consists of a winged bell over the intertwined initials D.B. These presumably refer to David Bell, and it is not uncommon for Glasgow buildings to feature such monograms of the person who commissioned them.

19. On the other side of La Belle Place is Kelvingrove Park, a large urban park which, for more than 150 years, has provided a relatively peaceful green space for the residents of the West End of Glasgow. As you walk west along La Belle Place, you can look across Kelvingrove where, through the trees, you can just about make out the impressive townhouses of the Park District set on the hill high above it, and also the grand Gothic buildings of the University of Glasgow on the neighbouring hill.

20. At the junction between La Belle Place and North Claremont Street, turn south and walk back towards Sauchiehall Street. Once you reach the traffic lights on Sauchiehall Street, turn right and head into Royal Crescent. This is another of Glasgow's grand Georgian terraces built in the 1830s and 1840s. It was designed by Alexander Taylor and the terminal pavilion on the corner of North Claremont Street and Sauchiehall Street is a particularly fine example of neoclassical architecture. As you walk along Royal Crescent, keep an eye out for boot scrapers at the entrances of these townhouses. Although only a few are left, these

Cast-iron boot scraper outside townhouse, Royal Crescent.

would once have been found outside almost every building in Georgian and Victorian Glasgow. Given the ubiquity of horses as a means of transport around the city's streets at this time, the roads were, unsurprisingly, littered with horse manure and caked in mud. Boot scrapers allowed householders and visitors alike to clean their boots before entering a building and so avoid tracking any muck from the street inside. The boot scrapers of Glasgow come in many different designs, with grander houses having ornate free-standing cast-iron ones on either side of their entrances, while on less grand tenement buildings, they consisted of a simple metal bar across a small alcove near the communal entrance from the street.

21. When you emerge onto Sauchiehall Street at the western end of Royal Crescent, cross it using the traffic lights and head towards the restaurant on the corner with Kelvingrove Street, currently called Mother India. Set into the pavement outside this restaurant, you will find a series of cellar lights. These were designed to allow light into the coal cellars and storage areas in the buildings' basements. Two different types of cellar lights can be seen here. The most obvious are the prismatic cellar

lights patented by the Hayward Brothers in 1885. These consist of a metal grid holding small, square semi-prisms which help gather as much light as possible, and bend it so that it reaches into even the darkest recesses of the basements below. Up against the wall of the building itself is an older style of cellar light, and rather than containing semi-prisms, they have larger glass tiles which, despite being larger, are much less effective at bringing light into the basement area below. Such cellar lights were once a common feature of Glasgow's streets, but with the advent of electric lighting, there was not as much need for them and many have been sealed up or removed over the years (especially in the last couple of decades). As a result, there are now few in as good and complete condition on the city's streets as the ones outside Mother India.

22. Across Kelvingrove Street (on the same side of Sauchiehall Street) from Mother India is another of Charles Wilson's grand classical buildings. However, this one is a tenement rather than a townhouse, and like many of the surrounding buildings, it was constructed in the 1850s as part of the westward expansion of the city.

23. Cross Sauchiehall Street again using the traffic lights and head north up Kelvingrove Street. As you do so, you will have a good view of the western terminal pavilion of Royal Crescent. This has an imposing curved front on the corner and is an example of what is known locally as a 'gushet building'. This is a building constructed at a junction where two roads meet at an angle of less than 90 degrees, creating a narrow strip of land known in Scotland as a 'gushet'. Gushet buildings are a key part of Glasgow's architecture and can be found at road junctions across the city. Comparisons are often made with the world's most famous gushet building, the Flatiron Building in New York. However, many of the ones in Glasgow, such as this one, are much older than their better-known American counterpart, suggesting that Glasgow's gushet buildings may have inspired the design of one of New York's most iconic buildings.

24. Further north on Kelvingrove Street, is a small open area called Kelvingrove Square. This leads up to one of the main entrances to Kelvingrove Park, but for this walk, turn left towards the large and unmissable Greek temple style building which looks onto the square from its western side. Built as the Finnieston Church in 1879, one of the most impressive features of this building is the roof lantern on its tower. It is modelled on the Choragic Monument of Lysicrates, near the Acropolis in Athens, which was built in 335 BCE. This is another of the buildings designed by James Sellars who, as can be seen from this church, was heavily influenced by Alexander 'Greek' Thomson. One of

James Sellar's 1879 Greek temple inspired former Finnieston Church, Kelvingrove Square.

the reasons he is not as well-known as other Glasgow architects is the fact that he died relatively young, at the age of just forty-five, after contracting blood poisoning from an injury caused by a nail piercing his boot when he was on a site visit.

However, in some ways Sellars can be considered the link between the older classical style of Glasgow architecture typified by 'Greek' Thomson and the art nouveau style which would come to replace it by the end of the nineteenth century. This is because Sellars worked in partnership with John Keppie, who would later go on to become the mentor of Charles Rennie Mackintosh.

25. From the former Finnieston Church, head north towards the gates of Kelvingrove Park, but before you reach them, turn left and walk west along Parkgrove Terrace. About halfway along this street is the Sikorski Polish Club. Established in 1954, it is named after General Władysław Sikorski, the Polish Prime Minister in exile and Commander-in-Chief of Polish Armed Forces during World War II. Fixed to the outside of this building are three memorial plaques: one for the Smolensk Disaster of 2010; one for the loss of the ORP *Orkan* in 1943, which was sunk by a German U-boat in 1943; and one for the Katyn massacre in 1940, when up to 22,000 Polish military officers and other prisoners of war were killed by the Soviet Union. There is another important Polish memorial in Clydebank to the west of Glasgow, dedicated to the crew of the ORP *Piorun*, a Clyde-build Polish destroyer which was docked at the John Brown Shipyard during the Clydebank Blitz of March 1941. Despite the shipyard being a potential target for German bombers, the crew remained at their posts and used the destroyer's guns to help defend the town. Shortly after this, the *Piorun* was involved in the sinking of the *Bismarck*, a key moment in World War II.

26. At the western end of Parkgrove Terrace, head through the small gate into Kelvingrove Park and walk towards Kelvin Way, which divides the park into two parts. Immediately to the right on Kelvin Way is the Kelvin Way Bridge over Glasgow's second river, the Kelvin. This bridge was built around 1919 from a design by Alexander B. McDonald (another of the unsung heroes of Glasgow's architecture), and features four impressive groups of bronze sculptures by Paul Montford. They represent Philosophy and Inspiration (on the north-west corner of the bridge, closest to the University of Glasgow), War and Peace (on the south-west corner)

Part of the bomb-damaged Kelvin Way Bridge balustrade still lying in the river beneath it.

Navigation and Shipbuilding (on the south-east corner), and Commerce and Industry (on the north-east corner). As with many other parts of Glasgow, this bridge was severely damaged by a German bomb during the Clydebank Blitz in March 1941, causing its ornate balustrade, featuring pink granite pillars, and two of the sculpture groups to fall into the river below. The bridge's parapet was repaired during the war using simple blocks of red sandstone, and the statues were eventually retrieved from the river in 1949. At this time, they were repaired and reinstalled on the bridge. These repairs included replacing arms lost by several of the statues. The original arms remained in the Kelvin until they were rediscovered in 1995. Somewhat ironically, one of these recovered arms belonged to the statue representing War. By this time, the replacement arms had weathered enough to blend in with the original statues, it was decided not to replace them. If you look over the bridge's western parapet, as long as the water level is low enough, you can still see the remains of the original balustrade, including one of the elegant pink granite pillars lying where it has been for more than seventy years, half-buried in the gravel at the northern edge of the river.

27. After viewing the Kelvin Way Bridge, head into the grounds the Kelvingrove Art Gallery and Museum. However, before you get to the museum itself, you will pass a sculpture of a small ship. This is the *Vital Spark* by George Wyllie. The *Vital Spark*, a fictional boat in Neil Munro's *Para Handy* books, was a Clyde puffer, a type of small coal-fired cargo vessel built mostly on the Forth and Clyde Canal, which was the workhorse of the west coast of Scotland, moving goods between coastal towns and the many islands between the 1850s and the 1930s.

George Wyllie's sculpture of Neil Munro's Clyde puffer, Vital Spark.

28. Finally, head towards the Kelvingrove Art Gallery. Once you reach it, you will find yourself looking up at its grand front entrance. This is a magnificent free classical red sandstone building and is one of the most impressive gems of Glasgow's architecture. It was designed by John W. Simpson and Edmund J. Milner Allen, and was completed in 1901. Local legend has it that the building was originally meant to face south onto Argyle Street, and that when the architect (it is never specified which one) realised that it had been built back-to-front, he leapt to his death from one of the towers. Despite this being a good story, there is absolutely no truth to it and it was always intended that the art gallery would face towards the equally grand Gilbert Scott Building of the University of Glasgow, on the other side of the River Kelvin. Incorporated into the main entrance is a bronze statue depicting Saint Mungo as the Patron of the Arts and Music created by George Frampton. Frampton also created the relief sculpture of the *Industries of Glasgow at the Court of Mercury*, which is over the arch at the top of the steps to the left of the Saint Mungo statue. Around the outside of the building are a number of allegorical sculptures by George Frampton, W. Birnie Rhind, E.G. Bramwell, A. Shannon, F. Derwent Wood, A. Falkner and Johan Keller, who created the statue of Wisdom over the entrance to the Mitchell Library where this walk started. These statues represent the personification of subjects associated with the museum and include Literature, Commerce, Music, Architecture, Painting, Sculpture, Religion and Science. Inside, you will find a world-class collection of artwork, including Salvador Dali's *Christ of Saint John on the Cross*, which is frequently voted as one of Scotland's favourite paintings. However, for many Glaswegians, the art gallery is just as fondly remembered as a place to spend wet childhood days playing hide-and-seek among the Egyptian mummies, dinosaur skeletons, stuffed elephants, suits of armour and the works of many famous artists. If hide-and-seek is not your cup of tea, you can simply explore the galleries, stop in the cafe for a bit of cake, or listen to a free recital on the magnificent Kelvingrove pipe organ, which is played every day at 1 p.m. (Monday to Saturday) or 3 p.m. (Sundays).

8. West End, Part I

Start Point: The north end of Byres Road near its Junction with Great Western Road, Glasgow, **(Location:** Lat/Lon: 55.87774, -4.29054 ; What3Words: ///monkey.potato.cloak; Plus Code: VPH5+3QW Glasgow). **Nearest Public Transport:** Subway: Hillhead Station (5 mins); Train: Partick Station (45 mins); Bus: Great Western Road (1 min).

End Point: The Stewart Memorial Fountain, Kelvingrove Park, Glasgow (**Location:** Lat/Lon: 55.86796, -4.28387; What3Words: ///hours.heads.drops; Plus Code: VP98+5FJ Glasgow). **Nearest Public Transport:** Subway: Kelvinhall Station (15 mins); Train: Exhibition Centre Station (20 mins); Bus: Sauchiehall Street (5 mins).

Distance: 4.2 kilometres/2.6 miles. **Time:** Allow 2.5 to 3.5 hours for this walk.

Level of Difficulty: Moderate. This walk contains a number of steep hills, steps and areas away from paved pathways. Although there are alternatives without steps, the main route for this walk is not suitable for wheelchairs or baby buggies

Facilities: There are a number of shops, cafes, bars and restaurants on Byres Road near the start of this route, and on Great Western Road around the halfway point. There is also a range of cafes, bars and restaurants around Kelvingrove Park which are within easy walking distance of the endpoint. Publicly accessible toilets are available in the Botanic Gardens at the start of this route, and on Kelvin Way near its end.

Introduction

There is much debate as to exactly where the borders of the West End of Glasgow lie. However, most people would agree it is centred around three areas: Byres Road, Kelvingrove Park and the Gilmorehill Campus of the University of Glasgow. The West End is home to a large number of interesting features, some obvious and some very much hidden away and, as a result, the walk through this area has been divided into two parts in order to keep each one to a manageable length. However, if you wish, you could do them one after another. There are plenty of cafes, bars and restaurants along the routes of these two walks if you wish to stop and take your time while you complete them. The first of these two walks concentrates on the northern section of the West End, between the Glasgow Botanic Gardens and Kelvingrove Park, and also takes in the River Kelvin, Great Western Road and the Park District.

1. This walk starts at the junction between Byres Road and Great Western Road opposite the former Kelvinside Parish Church, which was designed by John James Stevenson in an Italianate Gothic style and was built in 1862. Like many former churches in Glasgow, it has had to find a new use in order to survive, and in this case, it has been converted into a bar-restaurant and entertainment venue called Òran Mór. Òran Mór opened in 2004, and internally, it features decorations by the Glasgow writer and artist Alasdair Gray, who died in 2019. This includes a rather stunning mural in its auditorium. Òran Mór is also the birthplace of *A Play, a Pie and a Pint*, a highly successful lunchtime theatre experience. which aims to put on a new one-hour, single-act play each week, often by new or emerging writers. This was established by David MacLennan in 2004, and has now spread around the world as a way to bring theatre to a wider audience.

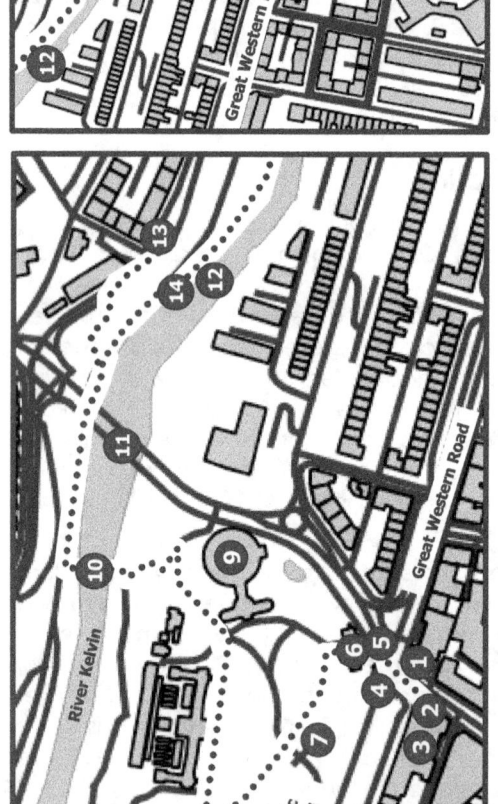
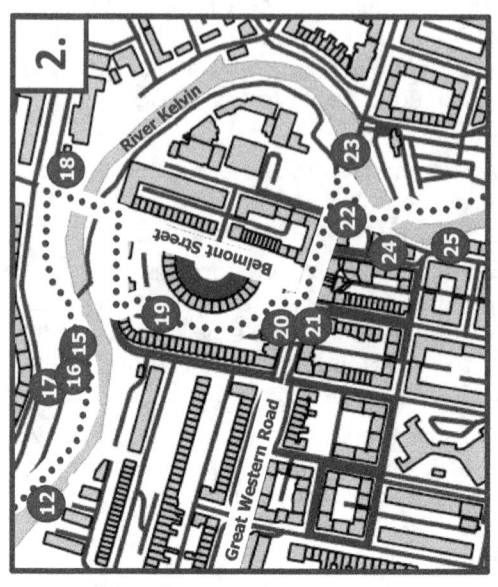
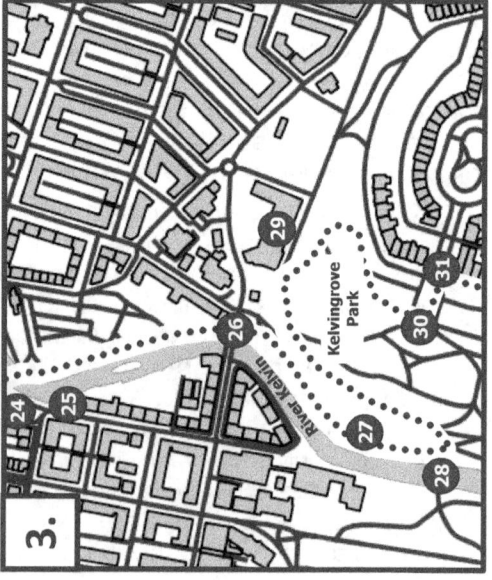
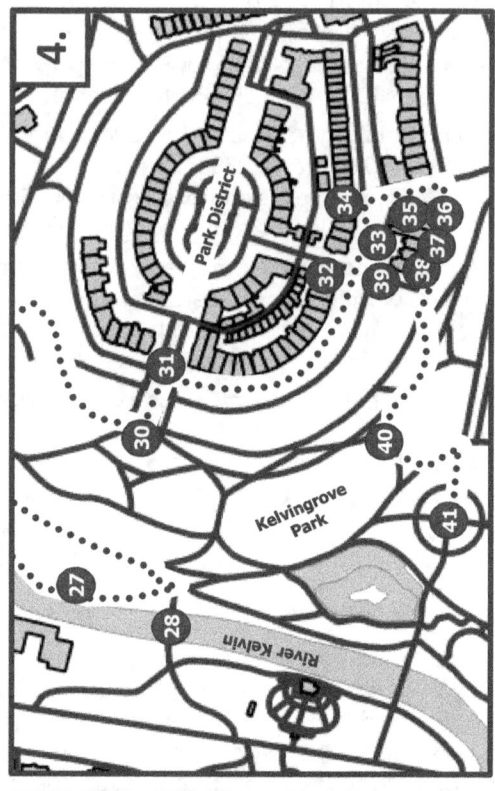

2. On the other side of Byres Road, and running west parallel to Great Western Road, is Grosvenor Terrace. Built in 1855, it was designed by John T. Rochead and consists of a series of classically inspired symmetrical townhouses. At the time it was built, Rochead described Grosvenor Terrace as 'the finest range of buildings in Great Britain'. In the 1930s, the first two houses in this terrace were converted into the Grosvenor Hotel. This hotel was later expanded under the ownership of the Glasgow hotelier Reo Stakis, but in 1978 it was destroyed by a massive fire which engulfed the entire eastern portion of the terrace. This took place during a strike by firefighters and so it was instead attended by military personnel. Local legend has it that when they realised that the fire could not be stopped, the soldiers liberated large amounts of alcohol from Reo Stakis's personal wine cellar, which was later used to stock the officers' mess at their nearby base. After the fire, the lost sections were rebuilt using glass-reinforced concrete to recreate the original facade. While you cannot tell simply by looking at them, you can easily identify which sections were rebuilt in this way by knocking on them, as the concrete sections ring hollow rather than returning the expected dull thud of solid stone. This makes this one of the best examples of an important Glasgow building which was reconstructed after being severely damaged by fire, rather than being demolished, as many have been, or left standing as an empty, ruined shell, like others, and it shows what can be done to preserve the city's architecture if the will is there.

3. Just in front of Grosvenor Terrace, on Byres Road itself, stands a large, rusted cast-iron box, with a smaller box mounted on top of it. If you inspect it, you will see it is decorated with the Glasgow coat of arms and the letters GCT (these letters are only visible on the road side of the box, so you need to be very careful while viewing them). This stands for the Glasgow Corporation Tramways and signifies that this is a Lucy box (named after the Lucy Foundry in Oxford where they were first made) which once provided power to the parts of the Glasgow Tram and Trolleybus network which ran up Byres Road and along Great Western Road. The small box on top contained a telephone which could be used by the driver or the conductor to communicate with their depot. Introduced in 1872, Glasgow trams were originally horse-drawn, but in 1898, the first tests of electric trams were carried out. These were deemed so successful that by 1902 electric trams had replaced all the older horse-drawn ones. At one time, the Glasgow Corporation Tramways was the largest urban tramway system in Europe, with over 1,000 trams travelling along routes totalling a 160 kilometres (100 miles) in length. By the time it closed in 1962, it was the last of the original tram networks still operating in Britian. Once a common feature on Glasgow's streets, only a very small number of these Glasgow City Tramways Lucy boxes remain in place, but you can still see the tram 'rosettes', which served as attachment points for the electrical system used to power the trams, on many of Glasgow's older buildings.

Glasgow Corporation Tramways Lucy Box, Byres Road.

4. Cross Great Western Road using the traffic lights, and on its northern side, you will find the entrance to the Glasgow Botanic Gardens. Before you enter it, there are two features worth checking out. To the left of the entrance is the Botanic Gardens police box. Designed by Gilbert Mackenzie Trench in 1928, this police box is made of reinforced concrete and was installed around 1935 as a way for patrolling policemen and members of the public to be able to contact the nearest police station. This is one of only a handful of such police boxes in Glasgow still in their original locations.

5. To the right of the entrance to the Botanic Gardens is the base of an old gas lamp inscribed with the words 'Glasgow Corporation Lighting Department 1902' in a rather wonderful art nouveau script. This is one of the few reminders of the days when Glasgow streets were lit by gas rather than by electricity.

6. The Botanic Gardens themselves are entered via an ornate gateway. Its wrought-iron gates, featuring the Glasgow coat of arms, were designed by the Glasgow City architect Alexander B. McDonald, and were installed in 1894. McDonald also designed the two lodges just inside the gates which were built in the same year. One of them features a rather wonderful relief sculpture of the city's coat of arms, and the second a date plaque with the year 1894 on it. The Botanic Gardens themselves are much older than these gates. They were first created in 1817 on a site in Sandyford, to the south of what is now the University of Glasgow's Gilmorehill campus, and they only moved to their current location in 1842. It is a popular spot for locals to hang out (on the benches on sunny days and in the glasshouses on rainy ones), and as a result, is a great place to indulge in a spot of people-watching. However, it also has a number of interesting features which are well worth exploring.

1902 Glasgow Corporation Lighting Department gas lamp base.

7. On entering the Botanic Gardens take the path which leads off to the left just beyond the two lodges. A short distance along this path, on the left-hand side, is an area fenced off with green metal fencing. This is the remains of the former Botanic Gardens Railway Station. This station was opened in 1896 as part of a railway line built by the Caledonian Railway Company which ran from the city centre under much of the West End and out to Kelvinside. It was initially closed in 1917, but reopened a few years later only to be closed for good in 1939. In 1970, the station building, which once stood above the platforms, was destroyed by fire. Since then, the station and its underground tunnels have proved popular with urban explorers, organisers of illegal raves and film-makers, with it being used as a location for at least one *Batman* film. The tunnels are now sealed off with heavy security gates making it difficult to enter without permission. However, if you approach the fence, you can look down on to the long-abandoned platforms. Here you will also find one of a number of plaques installed around Glasgow by an anonymous organisation calling itself the Glasgow Information and Kultural Identity

Taskforce – or Glaikit for short (a Scots word meaning foolish or silly). Their plaques feature stories from Glasgow's past which, while amusing, are completely untrue. If you carry on along the path until you get to a junction you can turn to the left, where there is another spot to view the remains of the station.

8. From the former Botanic Gardens Station, walk up the curving path on its northern side (the same side as the garden's glasshouses) until you come to a junction. Take the left-hand path, and then turn left at the next junction a short distance further up the hill. Here, to the right of the entrance to the herb garden is a small tree with a stone standing in front of it with the words 'Diospyros kaki Nagasaki Glasgow' carved into it (the inscription can be difficult to see and is often obscured by the plants growing in front of it). This the offspring of a kaki tree (also called a persimmon) which somehow survived the atomic bomb dropped on Nagasaki in Japan on 9 August 1945. Known as a Hibakujumoku, or survivor tree, its seeds have been grown into saplings and sent around the world as symbols of peace. The Glasgow one was bought to the city in 2002 by Gerry Loose, the then poet-in-residence at the Botanic Gardens and planted here. Unfortunately, the original one was stolen and was never seen again. Luckily, Gerry had been given two saplings and the second one was grown in a secret location until it was large enough to be planted out to replace the original one.

9. From the Nagasaki Peace Tree, turn around and head east on the main pathway. This will take you down to the large and ornate glasshouse close to the garden's entrance. This is the Kibble Palace. Covering 2,137 square metres (2,556 square yards), this Victorian glasshouse was designed in the 1860s by the architects James Boucher and James Cousland for the house of John Kibble at Coulport on Loch Long. Made

Kibble Palace glasshouse, Glasgow's Botanic Gardens.

from components cast at the Saracen Foundry in the Possilpark area of Glasgow, it was later taken apart and transported by sea to Glasgow before being rebuilt at its current location in 1873. As well as being a popular subject for Glasgow's photographers, who like to capture its glass domes glowing in the light of the rising or setting sun, it is also home to a collection of tropical and subtropical plants, and a number of impressive sculptures by the likes of Antonio Rossetti, Scipione Tadolini and George Henry Paulin.

10. From the front of Kibble Palace, follow the path that curves round its northern side. When you reach the toilets beside the Queen Maragret Drive gates, turn left and follow the small path which leads down a set of steep steps to the River Kelvin. At the bottom of these steps is an impressive cast-iron footbridge crossing the river. This is the Humpback Bridge, built in 1908 by Orr, Watt and Company from Motherwell to provide access to the Botanic Gardens from the north bank of the Kelvin. On the far side, is the Kelvin Walkway, which is popular with dog-walkers, cyclists and runners, as well as those just wanting to stretch their legs in a space which feels far away from the bustling city which surrounds it. It is also a great place for spotting wildlife, including mergansers (a species of colourful fish-eating duck), dippers, kingfishers and even the occasional otter.

11. From the Humpback Bridge itself, you can see the next bridge downstream. This is a road bridge which carries Queen Margaret Drive high above the Kelvin, and so provides an important connection between the communities north of the Kelvin to the West End, and from there to the city centre. Designed by Thomas Somers, the Queen Margaret Drive Bridge was built in the 1920s using reinforced concrete faced with red sandstone and topped by a red granite parapet. After viewing the bridge from a distance, cross to the north bank of the Kelvin, turn right and follow the Kelvin Walkway under one of the bridge's arches. From this viewpoint, you can get a much better idea of quite how much of a barrier the River Kelvin is to easy movement between its northern and southern sides. For many years, the development of the north bank was limited by the lack of an easy connection between the two. However, this was solved using a variety of different engineering and architectural solutions, of which the Queen Maragret Drive Bridge is only the most recent.

12. Walk under the Queen Maragret Drive Bridge and when you emerge on the other side, take the small path which branches off to the left and heads up a steep hill. When you reach the road at the top of this path, turn right and walk towards the large stone wall. From the parapet at the base of this wall, you can look down and across the River Kelvin. Here you will see some old stone piers and also a similar platform on the far side of the river. This is the remains of the original Queen Margaret Bridge, which was built in 1870 to connect the lands north of the Kelvin, known as North Kelvinside, with Great Western Road and so open it up for development. It was replaced by the newer Queen Margaret Drive Bridge in the 1920s and was finally demolished in the 1970s.

13. Turn around to face the retaining wall behind you. Immediately to its left is a flight of stone steps known as the Sixty Steps. These, and the associated retaining wall, were designed by Alexander 'Greek' Thomson in the 1870s to provide access to the Queen Margaret Bridge. They were the last of Greek Thomson's creations, and even though they are intended to be purely functional, they still retain many of the features associated with Greek Thomson's architecture. In particular, there are a number of seemingly closed-off windows, and even a false classical style doorway (to the right of the remains of the original Queen Margaret Bridge) set into the lower levels of retaining wall in an attempt to give it the appearance of great age even when it was first built. It is not unknown for local parents to tell their children that this is a fairy portal and that if they press their ears against it and listen very carefully, they will be able to hear the fairies working away inside.

Alexander 'Greek' Thomson's Sixty Steps.

14. Return back the way you came and descend once more down to the Kelvin Walkway. When you reach the river, follow it downstream. Just before you get to the remains of the original Queen Margaret Bridge, you will see a small wooden bridge off to your right which leads over a small stream. Cross this bridge, and immediately ahead you will see a weir which has been built across the full width of the river. This weir was constructed around the middle of nineteenth century to provide a head of water to feed a water mill positioned further downstream. The small stream you just crossed is actually a lade (a man-made channel) for this mill, and takes water from above the weir and carries it down to the mill. At the far end of the weir is a concrete structure known as a fish-ladder, which was installed to make it easier migratory fish, such as salmon, to travel upstream.

15. Walk along the bank between the river and the lade (an area which once served as a hidden garden for the miller's family, where chickens roamed and vegetables were grown), and you will soon reach the remains of the mill itself. Known as the Woodside Flint Mill, these include the remains of a large kiln, the foundations of various mill buildings and the channel which used to house the wheel powered by the water passing down the lade. There are also three large millstones, but these were transported here after the mill was shut from a different one further upstream. While there had been a mill on this site since at least the mid-seventeenth century, the current one was built in 1846. It finally closed in the 1950s, ending some 300 years of milling on this site.

16. Within the remains of the old flint mill is another rather amusing plaque. To find it, stand with your back towards the millstones and walk towards the path, which lies just beyond the mill's ruins. On reaching it, turn left and look for the remains of a small building between the path and mill's lade. Attached to a fence at the back of this ruined building is a brass plaque which claims to mark the location of the Glasgow Sherbet Municipal Works and tells the story of an explosion, caused by a young apprentice dropping a bottle of pineappleade, which destroyed it in 1906. None of this it true, and the creator of the plaque remains unknown, but it is part of a long Glaswegian tradition of telling tall tales which persists to this day.

Plaque telling fictional story of explosion in Glasgow sherbet factory.

17. The Sherbet Municipal Works plaque is just one of a number of alternative creative expressions to be found along this stretch of the River Kelvin. On the wall on the other side of the path from the plaque are two relief sculptures, one of the head of a wild man, which may be a depiction of the Green Man from pagan mythology, and one of a small lighthouse-like structure on the top of a rock. Created in the 1980s, these have been part of the wall ever since. More recently, this wall has become home to the Glasgow Penguins, a series of art installations displayed in the drainage niches of the wall featuring small penguins doing all sorts of different activities. Again, the artist behind them remains anonymous, and the number of

them comes and goes, but they provide great pleasure to passing children and adults alike.

18. Turn and follow the pathway back towards the river and a metal pedestrian bridge which allows people to cross to its far side. From here, you can see another tall stone bridge a short distance further downstream and rising above this, is a distinctive red sandstone church, topped by a crown-like steeple. This is was originally built as the Nathanial Stevenson Memorial Free Church, but it is now known as Kelvinbridge Parish Church. It was designed by John James Stevenson in a Scottish Gothic style and built in 1898. To take a closer look at the church, rather than following the Kelvin Walkway across the footbridge, take the road which leads up the hill to the left. At the top of this hill, there is a concrete staircase on the right-hand side which allows you to climb up to Belmont Street, from where you can see the church more clearly.

19. From the Kelvinbridge Parish Church, head south along Belmont Street. Once across the Belmont Street Bridge, turn right onto La Crosse Terrace. As you walk along this road, keep an eye out for a small path leading off between the buildings to the left. Take this path and you will come to a narrow cobbled street called Belmont Lane, where you will find a sizeable, brick-built structure. This is an old coach house where the carriages and horses for the grand townhouses which surround it would once have been kept. This is one

Old brick-built coach house behind grand stone buildings of West End.

example of a surprising number of old stables and servants' quarters which still remain hidden away from the view of the main streets in the back lanes of Glasgow.

20. Carry on south along Belmont Lane until you come to Great Western Road. This is one of the main thoroughfares leading from the centre of Glasgow, through the West End and out of the city towards Loch Lomond, and eventually to the mountainous Highlands of Scotland. To the right of the point where you emerged onto Great Western Road is an art deco style building which has clearly seen better days. Built around 1930, it had two shops on its ground floor, owned by James Campbell and Walter Hubbard, with a tea room with a separate smoking room above them. However, these businesses are long gone, and the ground floor is now occupied by a bar and the upper floor by a separate night club. In the 1980s and 1990s, this was home to a legendary Glasgow night spot, complete with stuffed camel. Officially called Cleopatra's, it was more commonly referred to as 'Clatty Pats'. It is hard to find anyone who was a student at the nearby University of Glasgow at the time who did not, at one point or another, stumble drunkenly out of the club and stagger home to their, or someone else's, nearby lodgings. This is all rather ironic, considering that tea rooms of the type which originally occupied the building were created to provide a space where people could socialise without the inebriating effects of alcohol.

21. Directly across from the building that was once home to Clatty Pats is a much grander and much older building. Topped by a tall clock, this is the former Cooper's Building. Designed by Robert Duncan in a flamboyant French Renaissance style in 1886, this was originally home to Cooper & Co., an upmarket chain of grocery stores founded in 1871. By 1895, Cooper's had 31 branches throughout Scotland and England, and employed more than 2,000 people. It built its reputation on innovation and quality, and it was one of the first chains of shops to have both electric lighting and telephones. In the 1950s, the company was taken over by Fine Fare, which ran some of Britain's earliest supermarkets, and continued to operate until the 1980s when most of its stores closed.

22. Turn left and walk east along Great Western Road. After a short distance, on the opposite side of the road, you will see a magnificently ornate red sandstone building. This is Caledonian Mansions. It was built in 1897 in the Glasgow style from a design by James Miller. As the name suggests, the Glasgow style was uniquely Glaswegian and evolved from a mix of the older Arts and Crafts Movement, the newer European art nouveau movement and the Scottish baronial Gothic revival style, and this is one of the best, and best-loved, examples of a Glasgow style building in the world. It was originally built for the Caledonian Railways, and their monogram can be found on the eastern end of the building. While it might not seem like it from the Great Western Road side, it was in fact built directly above the old Kelvin Bridge Railway Station. To see this, cross Great Western Road at the nearest traffic lights and walk down the small cobbled lane, called Caledonian Crescent, which is just to the east of the building. Here, you can peek over the wall to your right and look down on the long-abandoned railway platforms. You can also the see the tunnel (now sealed off) which once carried the line beneath the West End of Glasgow to the Botanic Gardens Railway Station you viewed earlier on this walk. Kelvin Bridge Station closed to passengers in 1952, and to freight twelve years later, with the station building itself destroyed by fire in 1968.

Ornate Glasgow style Caledonian Mansions seen from Kelvin Bridge.

23. From Caledonian Mansions, look for the flight of stairs which leads off Caledonian Crescent beside the bridge which carries Great Western Road over the River Kelvin. Take these stairs back down to the Kelvin Walkway. Once you reach it, turn right and walk past the bar on your right to a short, but broad low-lying bridge. This bridge once carried the railway line from Kelvinbridge Station across the Kelvin and onwards towards the centre of Glasgow. While on the bridge, look upstream towards the much grander Great Western Road Bridge. Built in 1891 to replace an earlier bridge (the remains of which can still been seen underneath it), it was designed by Bell and Miller, and was made from cast iron by William Arrol.

24. Turn and look over the downstream side of the bridge and across to the what is now the northern side of the river. Here you will see a large polychromatic brick building. Although not widely associated with Glasgow, such polychromatic brickwork was commonly used for the construction of industrial and commercial buildings up until the 1870s. In this case, this is a former warehouse which, among other things, was once a bonded warehouse for Red Hackle Whisky. Describing itself as 'Scotland's best whisky', Red Hackle was established in 1920 by Charles Hepburn and Herbert Ross, two former Scottish soldiers. The whisky's name came from the distinctive red feather worn by the members of the Black Watch Regiment, with whom Hepburn had served in World War I. While not clearly visible from the banks of the Kelvin, this building retains a faded hand-painted advertisement for Red Hackle Whisky on its gable end.

25. Downstream of the former Red Hackle warehouse, on the same side of the river, is a tall, narrow house which is overshadowed by the neighbouring tenement. This is Janesfield, one of the oldest surviving villas in the Hillhead area of Glasgow. Originally one of three neighbouring houses called Kelvin Cottage (which later became Janesfield), Kelvinside Cottage and Rose Cottage, it was built around 1840 in the cottage orné (or decorative cottage) style created as part of the Romantic Movement of the late eighteenth and early nineteenth centuries. This is one of a very small number of houses built in this style to survive not just in Glasgow, but in the whole of Scotland. While the view of Janesfield is often obscured by trees, if you approach the fence along the edge of the river, you can see it more clearly. Although it is possible to climb over the fence and down the retaining wall to get a better view, it is not advisable to do this, especially when the river is in spate.

Janesfield, one of oldest surviving villas in Hillhead.

26. After viewing Janesfield Cottage, carry on along the pathway as it follows the River Kelvin downstream. You will soon come to the bridge which carries Eldon Street over the river. This bridge, which is made of cast iron, was designed by Forman and McColl and was built in 1895. At one time, it would also have crossed over the railway line running from Kelvin Bridge Station towards the centre of Glasgow. If you walk up the ramp which takes the footpath under this bridge, you can still see the entrance to the tunnel which carried this railway line under Kelvingrove Park. This line closed in 1964, but for many years it was still possible to enter this tunnel and walk beneath the park and emerge close to what is now the Exhibition Centre Station, in Finnieston. In December 1994, while in spate, the River Kelvin broke through its retaining wall just north of the tunnel entrance, allowing much of the river to flow into it. The surging waters travelled along the path of the old railway line before flooding Exhibition Centre Station, and from there they carried on across what was then a carpark and into the River Clyde. Soon after this, the tunnel entrance was sealed off and blocked with a large pile of gravel to stop such an event ever happening again.

27. Follow the path under Eldon Street Bridge, and you will emerge into Kelvingrove Park. Designed by Joseph Paxton and created in 1852, this is the largest public park in the West End of Glasgow and is a very popular spot, especially on sunny summer days. It has also been home to three large-scale exhibitions which were intended to present Glasgow to the world. These were the International Exhibition of Science Art and Industry in 1888, the Glasgow International Exhibition in 1901, and the Scottish Exhibition of National History, Art and Industry in 1911. Only a few traces of these events remain within the park, but if you follow the path along the river, making sure to keep right when it forks, you will eventually come to a small clusters of stones and, a short distance further on, a second stone set into the ground close to the edge of the path with the inscription 'An Clachan 1911' (which is Scots Gaelic for a village). This marks the location of a model Highland village, consisting of traditional Highland black houses and but-and-ben cottages, created for the 1911 exhibition and inhabited for its duration by Gaelic speakers from the Highlands of Scotland. Other features from these exhibitions also survive in Glasgow, and these include the Sunlight Cottages, created for the 1901 exhibition and still located in Kelvingrove Park, the Doulton Fountain, created for the 1888 exhibition and which is now outside the People's Palace on Glasgow Green, and the Saracen Fountain, created for the 1901 Exhibition, which is now in Alexandra Park in the East End of the city.

Stone marking site of model Highland village built for 1911 Scottish Exhibition of National History, Art and Industry.

27. From the Clachan Stone carry on along the path and up the slope to the eastern end of Prince of Wales Bridge. This stone bridge was built in 1894 and is decorated with ornate cast-iron lamp brackets. At its western end is a bust of the Scottish philosopher Thomas Carlyle, who was a leading writer of the Victorian Era and had a profound influence on its art, literature and philosophy. However, his reputation has been somewhat tarnished over the years by how others have interpreted his views. At the eastern end of the bridge is another statue – the Highland Light Infantry Memorial. Sculpted by William Birnie Rhind, it was created in 1906 as a memorial to those members of this regiment who died in the South African War between 1899 and 1902.

28. Turn left at the Highland Light Infantry Memorial and head up the hill. At the next junction, ahead you will see a gate and two paths that curve back and head further up the hill. Take the wider of these paths and follow it up towards the top of the park. If you look to your left as you do so, you will see a large red sandstone building with ornate decorations around its doorways and above its ground-floor windows. Designed by Walter Robert Watson and built in 1913, this is the former Glasgow and West of Scotland College of Domestic Science. It was formed in 1908 by the merger of the West of Scotland Cookery School and the Glasgow Cookery School. Nicknamed 'the Dough School', it was the birthplace of the world-famous *Glasgow Cook Book*. Put together by the college's staff, it started life as a textbook

for their students, but it quickly earned a reputation for dependable and economic advice. As a result, it soon took on a life of its own both across Scotland and around the world and is still in print to this day.

29. As you reach the hill at the top of Kelvingrove Park, you will be met with views west across the park to the main buildings of the University of Glasgow, complete with its distinctive Gothic tower, on the neighbouring Gilmore Hill, and the towers and spires of the world-famous Kelvingrove Art Gallery and Museum to the south. With its westward-facing views, this is a popular spot to watch the sunset on summer evenings. It is also home to the Lord Roberts Memorial. Unveiled in 1916, this is a replica of a monument in Calcutta to Field Marshal Earl Roberts who died in 1914 while visiting troops in France. It features an inscription of a speech which Lord Roberts made in Glasgow in 1913. While this is undoubtedly a superb work of art, especially the sculpture of War on the eastern side of its pediment, the scenes it depicts and the glorification of the British Empire sit quite uncomfortably among the much more multicultural and cosmopolitan twenty-first-century city of Glasgow. Nonetheless, it remains a distinctive and important landmark within Kelvingrove Park.

Sculpture of War, Lord Roberts Memorial.

30. From the Lord Roberts Memorial, head east out of the park gates and turn right along Park Terrace. This is an area known as the Park District, and it was developed in the 1850s, with many of the buildings, including the grand townhouses along Park Terrace, designed by Charles Wilson. With views across Kelvingrove Park, these buildings were constructed as homes for wealthy industrialists, merchants and professionals, but by the 1950s, they were no longer popular as houses and most had been turned into offices. By the 1970s and 1980s, the area had a distinctly rundown and shabby feel to it, with many of the houses occupied by bedsits, and even a student hall of residence. However, the area has since undergone a major revival, and almost all of the buildings have been converted, once more, into highly desirable residences.

31. At the eastern end of Park Terrace is its junction with Park Street South. Here you will see the gable end of another block of grand townhouses on the left-hand side, just before the point where Park Street South meets Park Circus. If you examine it closely, you will see that high up on this wall there is an inscription which reads 'James Boucher Architect, James Steel Senor Plasterer, R. McCord Builder'. This is a nice example of those involved in creating a building leaving their mark on it. While not usually as obvious, this is much more common than you might think.

32. To the east of this junction is Woodlands Terrace, and to its south is a small grassy area. At first, this may seem like a private garden, but if you examine the piers supporting the iron fence on its far side, you will notice several have chimney pots on them. This is because this grassy area forms the roofs of a series of stables and servants' quarters for the townhouses further down the slope. They were buried in

the slope so that they would not spoil the view of those who lived on Woodside Terrace itself.

33. At the far end of this grassy area, there is a small set of stone steps. If you look at the townhouses opposite these steps, you will find some fine examples of the ornate metalwork which was typically used to decorate the outside of Victorian buildings in Glasgow. Many of these railings were removed during World War II in a drive to provide iron to make weapons, although it is debatable whether any weapons were ever actually produced from such recycled materials. However, in a few cases, the metalwork remained in place, such as these here, allowing you to see the level of detail they often included. In this case, the railings are decorated with winged figures, as well as urns with griffin-shaped handles. The angels have been aligned in such a way as to face the Italianate tower of Trinity at the end of the street, which was a training college for the Free Church of Scotland.

34. Descend the stone steps at the eastern end of the grassy area and look along the small cobbled lane behind the townhouses at their base. Here, on the left-hand side, you can see servants' quarters hidden under the grassy area you viewed previously from Woodlands Terrace. These are now private houses, so please respect the privacy of those who live in them and do not go down the lane itself to get a closer look.

Former servants' quarters for Park Gardens townhouses, marked by chimneys hidden in pillars of cast-iron fence.

35. Carry on south down the hill, turn right at the next junction and walk along Park Gardens. Just west of this corner is a red post box with the monogram VR on it. This is the royal cipher of Queen Victoria, indicating it was installed sometime between the start of the postal service in 1851 and the death of Queen Victoria in 1901. All British post boxes are marked in this way, with the cipher of the monarch who was on the throne when they were installed. The only exception to this are those installed in Scotland during the reign of the recently deceased Queen Elizabeth II. This is because she was the *first* Queen Elizabeth in Scotland, and when the first post boxes bearing the cipher EIIR were initially installed in Scotland, they were attacked in a variety of ways, including at least one which was blown up using dynamite. These events were known as the Pillar Box Wars and only came to an end when post boxes in Scotland bearing the EIIR cipher were removed and replaced with ones bearing only the Royal Crown of Scotland. This practice continued for the rest of her reign.

36. Further west is 5 Park Gardens. This was once the home of Archibald Young, the Professor of Surgery at the nearby University of Glasgow, and when Albert Einstein visited Glasgow in 1933 to receive an honorary degree from the university, he stayed here. There is a great photo available online of Einstein and Young smoking on the steps of this house as it seems that even being the most famous scientist in the world was not enough to earn Einstein the right to smoke his pipe indoors.

37. Next door, at No. 6, is the one-time home of the Scottish Football Association, and there is still a mosaic set into the top step at the entrance with the SFA's logo on it. Again, please respect the privacy of those who live in this property and view this from a distance rather than climbing the steps for a closer look.

38. Just west of No. 6 are the Park Garden Steps. These were designed by Charles Wilson, the same architect who designed much of the surrounding Park District, and built in 1853. Although they were constructed to allow people to move easily between Park District and Argyle Street (as the nearer Sauchiehall Street was little more than a winding path at the time these steps were built), and to provide access to Kelvingrove Park, they have since become a popular spot for the fitter members of the West End community, who can often be found running up them, in scenes reminiscent of the 1980s' movie *Rocky*.

39. Enter the gates of Kelvingrove Park at the bottom end of the Park Garden Steps. Here, you will find three paths. The main one goes up the hill to the Lord Roberts Memorial, while the one on the left, leads down to La Belle Place. For this walk, take the middle path, which leads down the hill to a statue of a big female cat holding a peacock in her mouth, while her cubs look up at her from below. Described as either a lioness or a tigress, depending on the source, this statue was donated to the city in the 1860s by John S. Kennedy, who left his native Glasgow to make a new life in New York. It was created by Augustus Nicholas Cain from a design by R. Bonheur, and is one of three identical statues found around the world. The other two are in the courtyard of Central Park Zoo in New York, and the Jardin des Tuileries in Paris.

Kennedy statue of big cat and her cubs, by Augustus Nicholas Cain, donated to Glasgow in 1860s.

40. From the Kennedy statue, take the path which leads south further down the hill. This will lead you to the Stewart Memorial Fountain where this walk ends. One of the most intricate and best-loved fountains in Glasgow, it was built in 1872 to commemorate the completion of the Glasgow Corporation Water Works. This project sought, for the first time, to provide the city with clean drinking water. In an incredible feat of Victorian engineering, a series of underground tunnels and aqueducts were created to carry water from Loch Katrine, a body of water some 65 kilometres (40 miles) away in the hills of the Trossachs to the north of Glasgow down to the city itself, powered by nothing more than gravity. Started in 1855, it was completed in 1860, and is still the basis of Glasgow's water supply to this day. While he was Lord Provost of the city, Robert Stewart, to whom the fountain is dedicated, was a major driving force behind this project. The fountain itself was designed by James Sellars, one of Glasgow's most prominent architects of the time, with sculptures by John Mossman, and bronze work by H. Pringle & Co. The design of the fountain itself is based around Walter Scott's narrative poem *The Lady of the Lake*, a love story set in the landscapes around Loch Katrine and the Trossachs. The figure at the top of the fountain, which was originally gilded, is Ellen Douglas, the eponymous heroine of this tale. Around the outer edge of the fountain are a set of four identical cherubs or putti, cast by the Cruikshank and Company Foundry in

Denny. If you keep your eyes open, you will see this same cherub on a number of other fountains around Glasgow, such as outside Alexandra Park and at Govan Cross. This reuse of statues or individual elements of larger pieces was by no means uncommon in the Victorian era, and you will often find yourself face to face with the same sculpture in quite different, and sometimes rather unexpected, locations. For example, the very same cherub from Kelvingrove Park looks out over Tobermory Harbour from an old fountain on the Isle of Mull.

9. West End, Part II

Start Point: The Stewart Memorial Fountain, Kelvingrove Park, Glasgow (**Location:** Lat/Lon: 55.86796, -4.28387; What3Words: ///hours.heads.drops; Plus Code: VP98+5FJ Glasgow). **Nearest Public Transport:** Subway: Kelvinhall Station (15 mins); Train: Exhibition Centre Station (20 mins); Bus: Sauchiehall Street (5 mins).

End Point: Kelvingrove Art Gallery and Museum, Dumbarton Road, Glasgow (**Location:** Lat/Lon: 55.86817, -4.29179; What3Words: ///scales.album.deed; Plus Code: VP95+779 Glasgow). **Nearest Public Transport:** Subway: Kelvinhall Station (8 mins); Train: Partick Station (20 mins); Bus: Argyle Street (1 min).

Distance: 5.3 kilometres/3.3 miles. **Time:** Allow 2 to 3 hours for this walk.

Level of Difficulty: Moderate. This walk contains a number of steep hills and sections with steps. Although there are alternatives without steps, the main route for this walk is not suitable for wheelchairs or baby buggies.

Facilities: There are plenty of shops, cafes, restaurants and bars where you can stop for refreshments along this route, especially in the areas around Byres Road. Publicly accessible toilets are available beside the bandstand on Kelvin Way, in the main building of the University of Glasgow, in the Kelvin Hall and in the Kelvingrove Art Gallery and Museum at the end of this walk.

Introduction

This is the second of the two walks around the West End of Glasgow, and it concentrates on the southern section which is centred on the University of Glasgow's Gilmorehill Campus, but includes parts of Kelvingrove Park, Hillhead, Byres Road and Dumbarton Road, before finishing at Kelvingrove Art Gallery and Museum. This area was developed primarily between the early the 1820s and the 1920s, and features a wide range of architectural styles, from Georgian villas, through Victorian townhouses to Edwardian tenement buildings, each marking a different period in the area's development. However, it is dominated by two major features, Kelvingrove Park, which was created in the 1850s and is where this walk starts, and the University of Glasgow's Gilmorehill Campus, which was created in the 1870s, and which will be visited several times during it.

1. This walk starts at the Steward Memorial Fountain in Kelvingrove Park. Dating from 1872, this magnificent fountain was designed by James Sellars and features sculptures by John Mossman. You can find a full description of it at the end of the West End, Part I walk. As you look west from this fountain, you will see the Gothic tower of the University of Glasgow on a hill looking down on Kelvingrove Park. After wending its way around the West End, this walk will eventually take you to the base of this tower, where you can look out across the park, before descending into it once more to reach its end at the Argyle Street entrance to Kelvingrove Art Gallery and Museum. Among other things, this area inspired a rather moving poem by Thomas Lyle, published in the 1830s, called 'Kelvin Grove'. It is about a pair young lovers walking along the banks of the River Kelvin as one of them prepares to head off to war, uncertain if he will ever return to the place and the woman he loves. This was later paired with an earlier tune and turned into a well-known and rather haunting folk song of the same name.

1.
Kelvin Way
River Kelvin
Kelvingrove Park
1
2
3
4
5
6
7
8
9
10
11
12

3.
Kelvingrove Park
River Kelvin
Dumbarton Road
33
36
37
38
39
40
41
42
43
44
45
46
47
48
49
50
51

2.
Saltoun Street
Byres Road
Great George Street
Byres Road
University Avenue
13
14
15
16
17
18
19
20
21
22
23
24
25
26
27
28
29
30
31
32
33
34
35
36

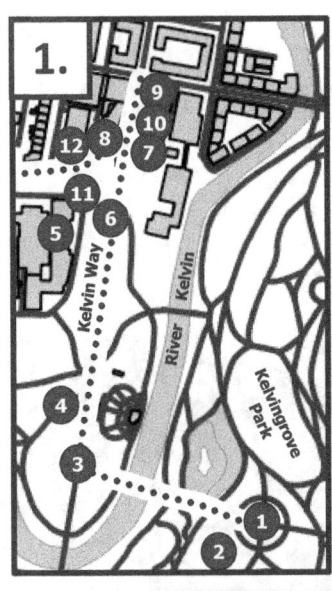

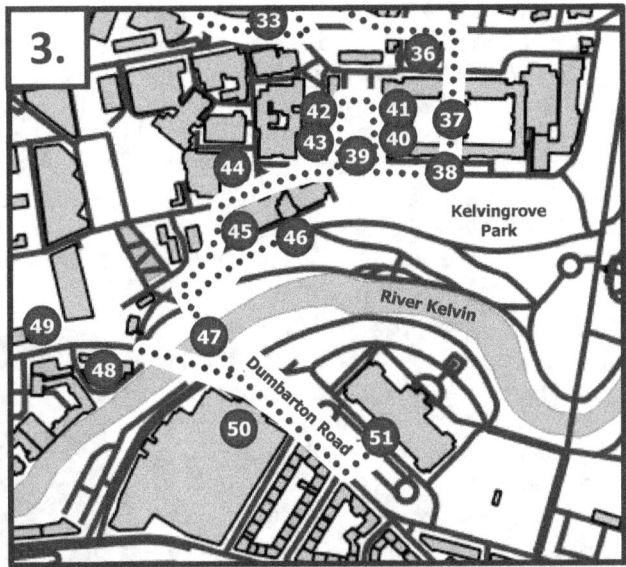

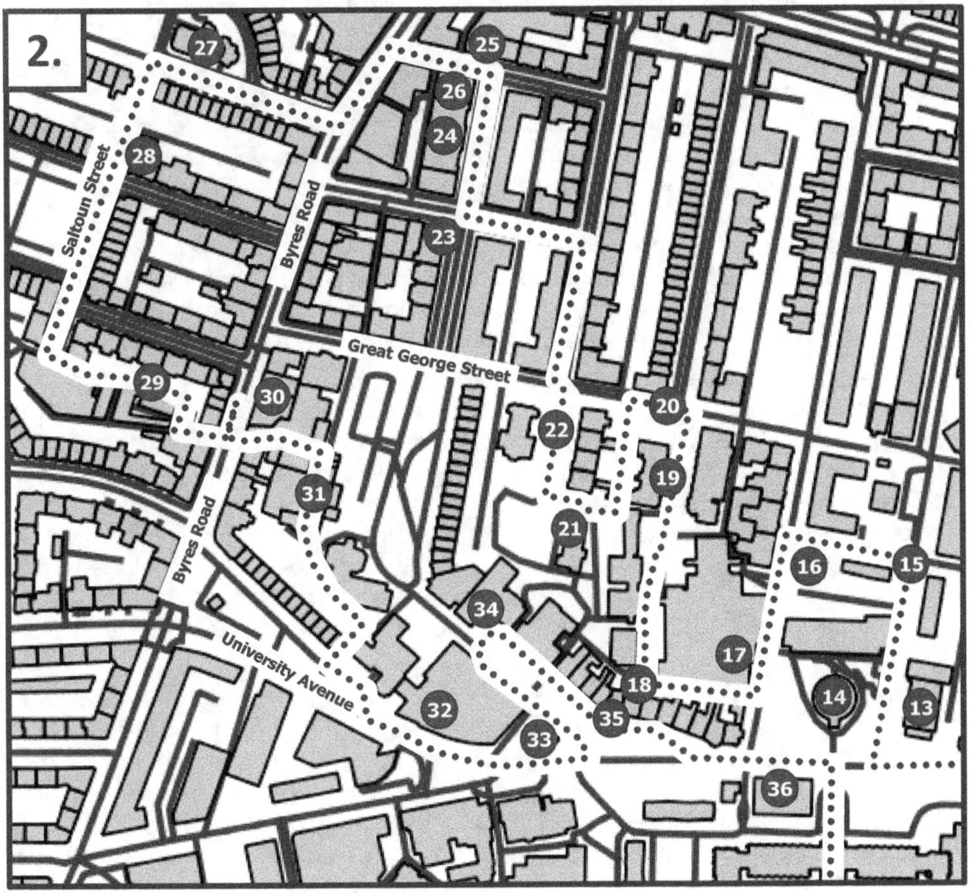

2. From the Steward Memorial Fountain, head west down the hill towards the River Kelvin, after which the park is named. As you do so, you will see a small hill covered in trees and bushes to your left. In the 1970s, this was the location of the legendary Kelvin Wheelies Skatepark. This was one of the first public skateboarding parks in Scotland. and was where the first Scottish National Skate Competition was held in 1978. It consisted of a side-by-side slalom run, a half-pipe, a clover bowl, a snake run and a free style area. Unfortunately, by the 1980s, skateboarding was starting to drop in popularity and much of it was demolished or filled in. The last part of this original skatepark was replaced by the much smaller existing one in 2005. However, within the trees and bushes, the remains of various parts of the original skatepark can still be found.

3. Carry on west to the point where a small pedestrian bridge crosses over the River Kelvin and then head up towards Kelvin Way. Built in the 1910s, this road divides the park into two sections, and was previously a busy thoroughfare. However, during the COVID-19 pandemic, it was closed to traffic and it has remained so ever since, creating a pleasant tree-lined pedestrian avenue. When you reach Kelvin Way turn right and head north along it. As you do so, on your right-hand side you will see Kelvingrove Bandstand and Amphitheatre. This bandstand was built by the Glasgow Public Parks Department in 1924, and it is one of the few Edwardian public bandstands left in Glasgow. By the 1990s, it was in a very poor state of repair and rarely used, leading to it being officially shut in 1999. However, in the run-up to the Glasgow Commonwealth Games in 2014, it was restored and is now once more used regularly for concerts and other similar events.

Tree-lined Kelvin Way, West End.

4. On the opposite side of Kelvin Way to the bandstand, and directly below the University of Glasgow campus, are statues of two of the university's most renowned professors. These are William Thomson, more commonly known as Lord Kelvin, and, further west, Joseph Lister. Thomson was Professor of Natural Philosophy at the university between 1846 and 1899 and is most famous for his work on the concept of absolute zero, the coldest possible temperature in the universe. His statue was created by Archibald McFarlane Shannan in 1913. Meanwhile, Lister pioneered the concept of antiseptic surgery while working as a professor at the University of Glasgow between 1860 and 1869. His statue was created by George Henry Paulin and unveiled in 1924.

5. Carry on north along Kelvin Way, and just before its end, through the trees to the west, you can see a large Scottish baronial building with an octagonal turret in the middle of its facade. This is the James Watt Building. Constructed to house the Engineering Department, it is named after another famous former employee of the University of Glasgow, the engineer and inventor James Watt, who was first employed as a mathematical instrument maker when he was still in his teens. He later went on to greatly improve the efficiency of steam engines by adding a separate condenser, an idea which supposedly occurred to him while walking on Glasgow Green in the East End of the city in May 1765.

6. Between Kelvin Way and the James Watt Building is the Suffrage Oak. This tree was planted in 1918 by Louisa Lumsden on behalf of a number of organisations which had campaigned for the right for women to be able to vote. It commemorates the passing of the Representation of the People Act of that year which, among other things, extended voting rights to women aged over thirty who occupied property with a rateable value of £5 or more. However, it would be another decade before women's voting rights finally became equal to men's. In 2015, this tree was voted as Scotland's Tree of the Year after being nominated by the Glasgow Women's Library. Although it was badly damaged by Storm Ophelia in 2019, it is still going strong more than a hundred years after it was planted.

Suffrage Oak, planted 1918 to mark extension of voting rights to some women.

7. From the Suffrage Oak, carry on north along Kelvin Way until you reach its junction with University Avenue. To the right of this junction is a large former church. Designed by James Sellars in a Normandy Gothic style and constructed in 1878, this imposing building was originally the Anderston Free Church. Initially, the plans included a tall, slender tower, but for some reason, this was never built. Like many other buildings in this part of the West End, it has now been incorporated into the University of Glasgow's Gilmorehill Campus. As you pass it, it is worth examining the carvings around the doorway which include a pair of rather cute dragons, one at either end of the arch surrounding the door.

8. Across the road from the former Anderston Free Church is the Glasgow University Union, the older of the two student unions at the University of Glasgow. It originally occupied what is now the John McIntyre Building (which you will visit later in this walk) further up University Avenue, but it moved to its current location at the end of the 1920s. The building was designed by Alan McNaughton in an imposing free baronial style, with a pair of prominent towers flanking the entrance. Traditionally, this was the men's union, and it was the last student union in the UK to have single-sex membership, something which only ended in 1980. In part, this only happened when the Queen Margaret Union, which had traditionally only admitted women, voted to extend membership to men in 1979. Originally, attempts were made to join the separate men's and women's unions together, but this was voted down, and the University of Glasgow maintains the presence of these two distinct institutions, each with its own unique ethos and membership, to this day.

9. Turn right and walk along University Avenue until you reach its junction with Gibson Street. Cross University Avenue at the traffic lights at this junction, and then look back at the church which stands on the corner of these two streets. This is the former Hillhead Congregational Church, which was designed by Hugh Barclay in a French Gothic style and was constructed in 1889. It is now part of the University of Glasgow, and is called the Sir Charles Wilson Building, not after the architect who designed many of the grand buildings around the West End of Glasgow, but the Scottish political scientist of the same name, who became the Principal of the University in 1961.

10. Beside the Sir Charles Wilson Building is a rather impressive tenement. Built in 1901, it is unusual for two reasons. Firstly, by the start of the twentieth century, almost all Glasgow tenements were being constructed from red sandstone brought in from quarries in Ayrshire and Dumfries, yet this tenement was built with the blonde sandstone more typical of older Glasgow buildings. Secondly, while most tenements in Glasgow are four storeys high, this one has five storeys. Both of these characteristics may have been driven by its location, with blonde sandstone being chosen to allow it to blend in more readily with the surrounding older buildings, and the five storeys being allowed due to its position between two relatively tall churches.

11. Follow University Avenue as it curves round to the west. On its southern side, just after this corner, is one of the main entrances into the older section of the university campus. The building beside this entrance is called Pearce Lodge. Despite its appearance, it was only built in the late 1800s, when the university was developing its new Gilmorehill Campus here in the West End of Glasgow. However, it incorporates a seventeenth-century arch and two stone panels from the Old College on High Street, in central Glasgow, where the university was located for the first 420 years of its existence.

12. Opposite Pearce Lodge on the northern side of University Avenue is the 1960s brutalist Rankine Building, which is adorned with a cubist stainless-steel sculpture by Lucy Baird. This was designed and installed in 1990 to mark the 150th anniversary of the establishment of the Regis Chair of Engineering and Mechanics at the University of Glasgow.

13. Further west on University Avenue is a monumental Greek revival style building. This is Wellington Church and it is one of a surprising number of Glasgow churches based on ancient Greek temples. However, it is also one of the few still used for its original ecclesiastical purpose. It was built in the 1880s and was designed by Thomas Lennox Watson.

Thomas Lennox Watson's monumental Wellington Church, University Avenue.

14. To the west of Wellington Church is Southpark Avenue, and on the opposite side of this is another building with an equally monumental entrance, albeit in a very different style. This is the art deco McMillan Reading Room, which was built in the 1930s. Designed by Thomas Harold Hughes and David S.R. Waugh, it won the RIBA Bronze Medal for the best building in Scotland 1936 to 1949. At this point, it is worth reflecting on the range of architectural styles which can be found on this very short stretch of University Avenue, something which continues along much of the rest of its length. However, despite the very different styles involved, the buildings do, somehow, hold together as a single complete streetscape, with none of them seeming too out of place with the rest.

15. The route for this walk now turns onto Southpark Avenue and carries on to its junction with Gibson Street. On the far side of Gibson Street are two very different styles of buildings representing two different periods of the development of the Hillhead area of Glasgow. On the west side of Southpark Avenue is Southpark House. Built around 1850, this was the last of the grand villas constructed in Hillhead before the density of development increased and construction turned to the building of terraces of townhouses, and then tenements. Southpark House is unusual in that it is actually a double villa which was built for William Govan Snr and William Govan Jnr, the father-and-son team behind the muslin manufacturers William Govan & Son. On the opposite side of Southpark Avenue is a row of rather beautiful 1860s townhouses of the type which replaced the individual villas that had previously dominated this area. While Southpark House is now part of the University of Glasgow, these townhouses are part of the neighbouring Hillhead High School.

South Park House, last grand villa built in Hillhead.

16. Turn west and follow Gibson Street up the hill to its junction with Hillhead Street. Immediately to the south of this junction is Florentine House. Built in 1828, some forty years before the university, which now surrounds it, moved to its current location, this was one of the first villas to be constructed in Hillhead. As it is now owned by the university, this makes it one of the oldest buildings on its Gilmorehill Campus.

17. From Florentine House, follow the short pedestrianised section of Hillhead Street southwards down the hill towards University Avenue. About halfway down this stretch, on your right-hand side, you will see what appears to be a roughcast pastiche of a traditional Glasgow tenement with its front door floating in mid-air. This is, in fact, a new wrapper for the reconstructed interior of a flat shared by Charles Rennie Mackintosh and his wife Margaret Macdonald, on nearby Southpark Avenue, between 1906 and 1914. The building itself was demolished as part of the expansion of the university in the 1970s. Although the outside is nothing much to look at, the inside is well worth visiting, and can be accessed through the Hunterian Art Gallery, slightly further north up Hillhead Street. While the art gallery is free to visit (and contains some stunning pictures by the Glasgow Boys, the Scottish Colourists and Mackintosh, as well as the American artist Whistler), there is an admission charge for visiting the Mackintosh House.

18. Branching off Hillhead Street to the south of the Mackintosh House is University Gardens Lane. This takes you along behind the grand townhouses of University Gardens (which will be visited later in this walk), where their servants' quarters and coach houses were once located. Although it is quite hard to find, one of these buildings has the words 'Tak Tent o' Time' carved into an arched gable above a window. This is a common inscription associated with Scottish sundials, and if you look above it, you will see a square space where the sundial would once have been positioned. These words come from an old Scots proverb, 'Tak' tent o' time ere time be tint', which means 'take care of time while it lasts', and is a reminder that time is both precious and limited, and so should not be wasted. This may seem

quite poetic, but as something sited on an old servants' quarters, it takes on more authoritarian overtones.

19. Opposite the building with this inscription is a small alley leading off to the right. This appears to be a dead end, but there is a set of metal steps at its far end. Climb these steps to reach Bute Gardens. Walk north along it until you come to a short run of two-storey, red sandstone townhouses on its left-hand side. These simple, but elegant houses were designed by John Nisbet in the Glasgow style (a mix of art nouveau and Scottish baronial styles unique to Glasgow), and were built in 1907. They feature some rather fine and unique stained glass and metalwork on their doors.

20. At the northern end of Bute Gardens is its junction with Great George Street, which is marked on the far side by a red pillar box. This is one of the few pillar boxes in Glasgow (and indeed in the whole of Britain) to feature the cipher of King Edward VIII, who ascended to the British throne following the death of his father, George V, in January 1936. However, he abdicated in December of the same year over his wish to marry Wallace Simpson, a twice-divorced American citizen. As British post boxes traditionally feature the cipher of the monarch who was on the throne at the time they were made, only a very limited number of post boxes bear his cipher.

21. Head west down the hill of Great George Street until you find a narrow lane leading off to the left behind the townhouses of Bute Gardens. Walk along this path and pass through the metal gate at its far end. Ahead of you and to the right, is Lilybank House. Lilybank House was originally built in 1850, but a

Rare Edward VIII post box, top of Great George Street.

south wing was added by Alexander 'Greek' Thomson in the 1860s. Interestingly, a north wing was added later by the architectural firm Honeyman, Keppie and Mackintosh, so making it one of the few buildings in Glasgow to have links to both of the city's most famous architects.

22. Walk down the right-hand side of Lilybank House, and follow the narrow pathway leading to the north. From here, you will emerge on to Lilybank Terrace, which has a row of imposing blonde Victorian townhouses on one side, and a red sandstone church on the other. Ahead, and on the far side of Great George Street, are a series of red sandstone tenements typical of the later development of the Hillhead area. At the end of Lilybank Terrace, cross over Great George Street and then head north along Kersland Street (which is slightly offset to the south of Lilybank Terrace). This will take you past several blocks of these tenements.

23. At the first junction on Kersland Street, turn left and walk west down Cresswell Street. This will take you down to Cranworth Street. Here, stands the former Hillhead Baptist Church. Built in 1883, this is another of the Greek revival style churches designed by Thomas Lennox Watson (who also designed Wellington Church which you visited earlier). Unfortunately, it is currently empty and has had its roof removed by developers who wish to demolish it, despite protests from the local community and its B-Listed status. As a result, whether this rather magnificent building will survive very much hangs in the balance.

24. Turn right and head north along Cranworth Street until you reach the Western Baths Club. This stunning building was designed by William Clarke and Graham Bell in a mix of Byzantine and Gothic styles, and was constructed in 1876. It is one of the earliest surviving examples of a private members swimming baths in Scotland, and it opened shortly after the nearby Arlington Baths, which was the first such facility in Britain. Initially, there was segregation between men and women, with mixed bathing only introduced in 1965.

Western Baths, designed by Clarke & Bell, built 1876.

25. Continue north along Cranworth Street until you reach its junction with Vinicombe Street. Here, you will find the former Botanic Gardens Garage. With its distinctive white and green faïence facade and Italian Romanesque style arches, it was designed by David V. Wyllie and was built in 1906, right at the dawn of the era of the motor car. This makes it one of the earliest examples of a public motor garage, and few of a similar age survive in Glasgow or elsewhere.

26. On the opposite side of Vinicombe Street is a low, white building which currently houses a bar, but which started its life as one of Glasgow's earliest suburban cinemas. It was originally designed by Brand and Lithgow using Hennebique ferro cement, which was an early form of reinforced concrete. It opened as the Hillhead Picture House in 1913, with a seating capacity of 630 in the auditorium and a further 133 in a small balcony. Early films were made from cellulose nitrate, which was highly flammable, and cinema fires were not uncommon. This resulted in the Cinematograph Act of 1910, which required film projectors to be separated physically from the auditorium to help protect the audience from the risk of fire, and the Hillhead Picture House was one of the first cinemas in Scotland built under this new rule. The risk of fire was also the main driving force behind the choice of concrete as a building material, as it aided with fireproofing, and even the screen itself was made from this material. The building was later modified by James McKissack in 1931, presumably to add the facilities required for showing movies with sound, and by Burnet and Boston in 1940 to alter the seating capacity. It closed as a cinema in 1992 and was later converted into a restaurant.

27. Carry on to the junction where Vinicombe Street meets Byres Road. Turn left and walk south along Byres Road until you come to a set of pedestrian traffic lights. Cross the road at these lights and then head west up Observatory Road (also known as Loudon Terrace). This will take you to the imposing Belmont and Hillhead Parish Church. Designed by James Sellars in a French Gothic style inspired by the Sainte Chapelle in Paris, this rather stunning church, which is quite unlike any other in Glasgow, was built in in the 1870s. The main entrance is off Saltoun Street and features a magnificent rose window.

28. Turn left onto Saltoun Street and walk southwards along it. Here, you will find yourself in a relatively leafy neighbourhood filled with fine tenements and grand townhouses. Of particular interest is the tenement block at 33–35 Saltoun Street. Designed by Adam and Short, and constructed in 1897, it features a central column of square bay windows with a large circular corner tower at either end. Although this general design of tenement is relatively common in the West End of Glasgow, this particular building has now become much more familiar than most as it was the subject of Avril Paton's 1993 painting *Windows in the West*. When she painted this picture, Paton lived in a top-floor flat on the opposite side of the street. One January evening, a heavy blizzard began. This, combined with the light streaming from the windows, made for a near-perfect composition, and so one of Glasgow's favourite contemporary paintings was born. While copies of the this painting adorn the walls of many tenement flats throughout the city, the original is on display in the Kelvingrove Art Gallery and Museum, where this walk ends.

29. Carry on along Saltoun Street until you reach Ruthven Lane, which can be found at its southernmost end. At this point, turn left and walk along the cobbled back alley, past a mix of restaurants, independent shops and small businesses. As you arrive towards its eastern end, look up at the rear wall of the tenement building to your left, where there is a relief sculpture of a cat set into the stonework. This is the Ruthven Lane Cat, and its presence here is a bit of a mystery as there is no clear explanation as to where it came from, or why it was set into this particular wall.

30. At the eastern end of Ruthven Lane, turn left onto Byres Road and walk north along it until you reach a set of pedestrian lights. Opposite this point is a low two-storey building which is home to the oldest bar on the street. It is thought that there has been a tavern on this site since the seventeenth century, when this part of Glasgow was still primarily countryside. Indeed, the name Byres Road may have originated from the fact that it was here that the Bishop of Glasgow kept a herd of cows (with 'byre' being a Scots word for a cattle shed). However, this area was also on the main route along which cattle were driven from the West Highlands of Scotland to provide meat to those living in the growing city, and this may explain the presence of a tavern in the local vicinity. The current pub, which dates from the eighteenth century and is rumoured to have been visited by King Charles II, was initially named the Curlers Tavern, after a large pond where curling matches took place in winter months. The pond has long since disappeared, but the history of this location is remembered to this day in the pub's name, which is currently the Curlers Rest.

31. Cross Byres Road at the traffic lights near the Curlers Rest, and walk a short distance south to where a cobbled lane leads off to your left. This is Ashton Lane. Turn into it, and then at the T-junction, turn right. At this point, you will find yourself in an old-fashioned street lined with low buildings which seems far from the hustle and bustle of nearby Byres Road, both in space and in time. This lane is home to a number of cafes, bars, restaurants and the Grosvenor,

Former Barr & Stroud Building, Ashton Lane, West End.

Glasgow's oldest cinema and its last surviving example of the type of small, suburban cinema which was once common across the city. On the corner beside this cinema is a polychromatic brick building which was constructed in the 1890s. This was once home to Barr & Stroud, a pioneering optical engineering firm started in 1895 by the University of Glasgow professor, Archibald Barr, and his former colleague at Yorkshire College (now the University of Leeds), William Stroud. This company went on to become a major employer in Glasgow and an important supplier of high-quality optical equipment to the British Armed Forces.

32. Continue along Aston Lane towards the large modern building at its eastern end. Just before you reach it, turn right and a short distance further on, you will find yourself back on University Avenue. Turn left and walk east up the hill until you reach the James McCune Smith Learning Hub. This building, completed in 2021, is named after the first African American to earn a degree in medicine, which was bestowed on him by the University of Glasgow in 1837. It may seem odd that an American had to travel to Scotland in order to be able to study for a medical degree, but at that time, even though he had the required qualifications, no American Institution would admit him. It is still unclear precisely why he came to Glasgow, rather than London or even Liverpool, where he first landed in the UK, but the city had a strong anti-slavery movement, particularly among its workers, the local Quaker community and a number of the university's professors, and this may have made it an attractive destination for him.

33. Carry on east along University Avenue and the next buildings you will reach are Nos. 11 and 13 University Gardens. These are an attractive pair of townhouses designed by John James Burnet and built in 1882. As well as being impressive buildings, No. 11 is also recognised as the birthplace of the word 'isotope'. This came about during a dinner party held by the father-in-law of the radiochemist Frederick Soddy, winner of the Nobel Prize for Chemistry in 1921. At this dinner party, which is given a variety of dates between 1909 and 1912, Soddy was discussing the recently discovered idea that the same element could come in different variations with different atomic masses. His cousin, the physician Margaret Todd (who was also a the dinner, and who was one of the first women to qualify as a doctor from the Edinburgh School of Medicine for Women), suggested he use the term 'isotope', meaning 'at the same place' in Greek, to refer to such variants. This suggestion was based on the fact, that despite the differences in their atomic masses, different isotopes of the same element occupy the same place on the periodic table. Soddy liked this term enough to use it in a 1913 paper in the scientific journal *Nature*, and from there it passed into common usage. Although there is a plaque on No. 11 to commemorate the birth of this word, it wrongly attributes its origins to Soddy rather than Todd.

11 University Gardens, where the word 'isotope' was first used..

34. Turn left onto University Gardens and walk along it to the point where it curves round and doubles-back on itself. The large concrete 1960s building on this corner is home to the Queen Margaret Union, the rival to the Glasgow University Union visited earlier on this walk. While not as architecturally grand, the QMU, as it is more commonly known, more than makes up for this as the home to the more alternative side of student life, and is particularly well known for the music events it hosts, with the likes of Queen, the Smiths, Nirvana, the Pogues, the Ramones, Coldplay and Franz Ferdinand all having played here over the years.

35. Continue along University Gardens and as you head back towards University Avenue, you will pass another series of townhouses. Most of these were designed in a Renaissance style by John James Burnet and were built between 1883 and 1896. However, No. 12 was added later in 1900 and was designed by John Gaff Gillespie in the Glasgow style. Many of these buildings have interesting little features on them, such as stained glass in the doors, boot scrapers and other ornamentations. In particular, 2 University Gardens features heraldic symbols associated with the four nations of the University of Glasgow. The 'nations' were a way of dividing up students at Scotland's three oldest universities (St Andrews, Glasgow and Aberdeen). At the University of Glasgow, the four nations were Glottiana, Rothesay, Transforthana and Loudoniana. Students were assigned to nations depending on where they came from, with these nations referring approximately to Clydeside, Lothian, Rothsay and students from anywhere else.

Symbols of four nations of Glasgow University.

36. Cross University Avenue at the pedestrian lights near the eastern end of University Gardens. Next to these lights is the John McIntyre Building. Constructed in 1886, and designed in a collegiate Gothic style by John James Burnet, this was originally home to the University's student union, and you will also find the symbols for the university's four nations carved into the stone above its main door. This building is reputed to have been where the last duel fought in Scotland took place in 1899, between Robert Henderson Begg and Carlo La Torre, after a dispute over who should be the next rector of the university got out of hand. However, there is a great deal of doubt as to whether this event ever actually took place or whether the only contemporary description of it, published in the *Glasgow University Magazine*, was purely satirical in nature.

37. From the John McIntyre Building, walk through the university's main gates, to its east, and head towards the main university buildings. Designed by George Gilbert Scott in a mix of Gothic and Scottish baronial styles, these were built in 1867 when the university moved from its original home on High Street to the West End of the city. Pass through either of the entrances and follow in the footsteps of more than 150 years' worth of students as you climb up the heavily worn stone stairs to the two quadrangles in the centre of the building. These are separated by an undercroft,

which is more commonly referred to as 'the cloisters' (the main difference being that an undercroft has a building above it, while cloisters do not). From within the quadrangles, you can view the many turrets, chimneys and towers of these buildings, including the impressive main tower. At 85 metres (278 feet) in height, for many years this was the tallest structure in Glasgow, and it was only recently surpassed by Glasgow Tower, which was built in 2001 and is 127 metres (416 feet) tall. In 1938, there was briefly another building taller than the University of Glasgow Tower, the 91-metre (298-feet) Tait Tower in Bellahouston Park, but this was built for the Empire Exhibition and was taken down the following year. Within these buildings, you can also find the Hunterian Museum, which is free to visit and houses a fine and varied collection, including tools and experiments belonging to Lord Kelvin and an unrivalled collection of relics from the Antonine Wall, which was built

Undercroft of main buildings of Glasgow University, more commonly referred to as 'the cloisters'.

by the Romans between the Firth of Clyde and the Firth of Forth in AD 142 and for a short period served as the northern edge of the Roman Empire. However, after around twenty years it was abandoned and the Romans retreated to the previously constructed Hadrian's Wall, which roughly follows the line of the modern border between England and Scotland.

38. Once you have looked around the quadrangles and the undercroft of the main building, head out through one of the doors which leads from the quadrangles to the southern side of this building. From the base of the flagpole which stands here, you can get fine views across Glasgow, especially at sunset, including down to the Kelvin Hall and the Kelvingrove Art Gallery and Museum, which lie below the university. Further off, you can also see the Finnieston Crane (one of the last four Titan cranes left on the Clyde), the Glasgow Tower and the buildings of the Scottish Events Campus (although in summer when the trees of Kelvingrove Park are covered with leaves, you may have to move around a bit to see these different buildings). It is also worth looking back towards the main building itself. If you are lucky, you might spot a peregrine falcon perched on its tower as they regularly nest in a box installed close to the top.

39. From the southern side of the main building, head down to the Principal's Lodge, which lies immediately to its west. This was also designed by George Gilbert Scott and was built around the same time as the main university building. However, unlike the main university building, it was designed in a Netherlandish style, but with sixteenth-century Scottish details.

40. Take the narrow road which leads north between the main building and the Principal's Lodge and you will come to an old set of stone steps leading up to your right. This is the famous Lion and Unicorn Staircase, named after the two statues which decorate it. Dating from 1690, it was originally part of the University of Glasgow's Old College campus on High Street, but it was moved to the Gilmorehill Campus in the 1860s. It was then moved again to its current location when the University Chapel was built in 1929. However, this required some substantial re-engineering as originally the staircase turned 90 degrees to the right, but now it turns to the left instead.

Unicorn on Glasgow University's 17th-century Lion and Unicorn Staircase.

41. Just to the north of the Lion and Unicorn Staircase is the University of Glasgow Chapel. Built in the 1920s, it stands as a memorial to those members of the university community killed in World War I. It was designed by John James Burnet, and features some impressive sculptures by Archibald Dawson. This includes a range of animals hiding within the smaller corbels, the bird, fish, bell and tree symbols from the Glasgow coat of arms, tradesmen, such as a bricklayer and an architect, and saints, such as Saint George fighting a dragon. There is also an art deco style sculpture of a stylised pelican feeding her young, which is a representation of Jesus caring for his followers.

42. Turn your back on the Memorial Chapel and you will find yourself looking west across Professors' Square. The houses which line two sides of this square were originally built as accommodation for twelve of the university's professors, but they are now primarily occupied by various academic departments. However, other than that, it probably looks pretty much the same now as it did when it was first built in the 1860s. No. 8 is currently occupied by the School of Law, and outside its door is a plaque commemorating Madge Easton Anderson, the first woman to practise law in the UK and who graduated from the University of Glasgow in 1919. This was only possible after the passing of the Sex Disqualification (Removal) Act in 1919, which allowed women, for the first time, to become solicitors, barristers, chartered accountants and vets.

43. The most notable person to have lived in Professors' Square inhabited the house at No. 11 (marked with a blue plaque). Between 1870 and 1899, this was the home of William Thomson, now more commonly known as Lord Kelvin. Thomson, whose statue on you visited on Kelvin Way towards the start of this walk, became Professor of Natural Philosophy at the university in 1846 and continued in this post until 1899. During this time he worked on a range of important areas, but is now most widely associated with the defining of absolute zero, the lowest possible temperature in the universe. Lord Kelvin also holds the record for being both the youngest and the oldest matriculated student at the University of Glasgow, having first matriculated at the age of ten and then again after he retired at the age of seventy-five. What is less well known is that Thomson was also an early champion of electric lighting, and in 1881, he made his house on Professors' Square one of the first in the world to be lit entirely by electricity. It took a total of 106 individual arc lamps to achieve this feat.

44. From Lord Kelvin's House, head south between it and the Principal's Lodge, and turn right. As you walk west down the hill, you will pass the Zoology Building (now known as the Graham Kerr Building), which was also designed by John James Burnet and was built in the 1920s. This building marks a transition in the style of buildings created by Burnet and his architectural practice, from a more ornate style inspired by the baroque and Renaissance periods to a more stripped-back and modern style. However, it is not entirely without decoration, and its front doors feature a rather beautiful pair of brass door handles, each adorned with a small snake. This building is also home to the university's Zoology Museum, which has a small, but interesting collection, created primarily as a teaching resource for students, filled with all sorts of weird and wonderful specimens. Immediately to the north of the Zoology Building is the brick-built Joseph Black Building. Named after the chemist Joseph Black, the discoverer of both carbon dioxide and magnesium, who served as Professor of Anatomy and Chemistry at the university between 1756 and 1766, this is a classic example of a mid-twentieth century, art moderne, higher education building. However, despite being home to the Chemistry Department, its southern walls are decorated with some rather well-hidden, but well-executed animal murals. To find these, walk down the small lane between the Zoology Building and the Joseph Black Building, and on the side facing the Zoology Building, you will find depictions of dinosaurs, sharks, sunfish and other animals.

Snake door handle on John James Burnet's 1920s Zoology Building.

45. Walk back past the Zoology Building and continue south down the hill until you reach a gateway in a metal fence on your left. This fence separates the University of Glasgow Campus from the neighbouring Kelvingrove Park. Pass through the gateway, turn left and walk east up the hill. This will take you past the West Medical Building. A monumental structure dating from 1903, it was designed by James Miller in a stripped-back Scottish Renaissance style.

46. A short distance further east, almost in the shadow of the West Medical Building, are two small cottages which seem rather out of keeping with the grand baronial style used for much of the older parts of the neighbouring university campus. These are the Sunlight Cottages, modelled on those in the Port Sunlight Model Village on Merseyside. This village was built in 1888 in an arts and crafts style for the workers in the nearby Lever Brothers' soap factory (which is now part of Unilever), and was named after Sunlight, their most popular product. The Sunlight Cottages were built for the 1901 Glasgow International Exhibition and are the only surviving buildings specifically constructed for it. Rather surprisingly, they were designed by James Miller, the same architect who also designed the West Medical Building which they stand opposite, and they demonstrate the ability of this much underrated and overlooked architect to work in a wide variety of very different styles.

47. Return west down the hill which you just walked up, and at the bottom, turn left onto a stone bridge lined with metal railings. This bridge provides great views up the River Kelvin, with the main buildings and tower of the University of Glasgow visible above its tree-lined banks, making it a very popular spot for taking photographs. This bridge, known as the Snow Bridge, was built around 1800, and used to form the main transport link over the River Kelvin in this part of the city. However, when trams were introduced to the streets of Glasgow in the 1870s, it was found that the angle created by this bridge as it emerged onto Dumbarton Road was too sharp for this new mode of transport to negotiate, and in 1876, it was replaced with the nearby cast-iron Partick Bridge, which still carries Dumbarton Road over the River Kelvin to this day. The Snow Bridge derives its rather unusual name from the gates in the railings on its downstream side. In winter, these would be opened to allow snow cleared from the surrounding roads to be deposited into the river below. Before you leave the bridge, look over the railing on the upstream side at its southern end. Here, passing underneath the final arch of the bridge, you can still make out the remains of the lade (a man-made channel taking water from the main river) for the former Bunhouse Flour Mills, which lay just downstream from this point on the river.

48. From Snow Bridge, carry on south to Dumbarton Road. Cross this road at the traffic lights and then turn right onto the Partick Bridge. On the west side of the river, you will see an ornate, castle-like red sandstone building. Rather surprisingly, this is the Partick Sewage Pumping Station. Built in 1904 and designed by the city engineer and architect, Alexander B. McDonald, it shows how even the most mundane of public buildings were, at one point, designed to blend in with the grand buildings which surrounded them.

49. Further to the west, and on the other side of Dumbarton Road, is a large blonde sandstone building – the former Anderson College of Medicine. Built in 1888, this was the last work of the renowned architect James Sellars. During its construction, Sellars also worked on the site of the main building for the 1888 International Exhibition of Science, Art and Industry (which he had also designed) in nearby Kelvingrove Park, where he stood on a nail. This simple injury developed into blood poisoning, and he died on 9 October 1888, aged just forty-four. The college building was completed by his friend and fellow architect John Keppie, who would later go on to become the mentor of Charles Rennie Mackintosh.

Castle-like 1904 Partick Sewage Pumping Station

50. Turn around and head east. Ahead of you, you will see two very grand buildings. The closest one on the southern side of Dumbarton Road is the Kelvin Hall. Designed in a baroque style by Thomas P.M. Somers, it was built in 1926 as an exhibition hall. It is now used as a museum and sports hall, but over the years it has played host to

a wide variety of different events. The most famous of these are probably the annual Christmas Carnival and Circus, and the city's Transport Museum, both of which sit fondly in the memories of many Glaswegians. The Carnival is now hosted in the Scottish Events Campus, while the transport collection is now housed in the Riverside Museum, both on the banks of the Clyde.

51. On the opposite side of Dumbarton Road from the Kelvin Hall stands one of the jewels in both Glasgow's architectural and cultural crowns: The Kelvingrove Art Gallery and Museum. Completed in 1901, just in time for the Great Exhibition of that year, for which the Sunlight Cottages were built, it was part-funded with money raised by the earlier 1888 exhibition, which inadvertently led to the death of James Sellars. Its design was chosen after a competition, which was won by John W. Simpson and Edmund J. Milner Allen. Featuring sculptures by a range of famous sculptors of the late Victorian Era, the elevation facing Dumbarton Road is actually the rear facade, with the main entrance designed to face towards the equally impressive buildings of the University of Glasgow. If you have time, it is well worth crossing the road at the traffic lights near the front of the art gallery to take a closer look at it, both from the outside and the inside. There is also a cafe at the rear where you can have a well-earned rest and treat yourself to some refreshments.

Edwardian baroque Kelvingrove Art Gallery and Museum.

10. Forth and Clyde Canal and Maryhill

Start Point: The Cleveden Road Canal Bridge, Kelvindale, Glasgow (**Location:** Lat/Lon: 55.89305, -4.30897; What3Words: ///circle.rated.dimes; Plus Code: VMVR+6C6 Glasgow). **Nearest Public Transport:** Subway: None; Train: Kelvindale Station: 1 min); Bus: Cleveden Road (2 mins).

End Point: Canal House, Speirs Wharf, Glasgow (**Location:** Lat/Lon: 55.87173, -4.25753; What3Words: ///prime.mull.after; Plus Code: VPCR+MXW Glasgow). **Nearest Public Transport:** Subway: Cowcaddens Station (10 mins); Train: Queen Street Station: 20 mins); Bus: Cowcaddens Road (15 mins).

Distance: 5.1 kilometres/4.2 miles. **Time:** Allow 3 to 4 hours for this walk.
Level of Difficulty: Moderate. Although this walk is primarily along a relatively flat towpath, there are some sections with steps. In addition, it is a relatively long walk.

Facilities: There are few facilities along the route of this walk. As a result, you will need to make sure that you bring water and snacks with you. Publicly accessible toilets are available in the Maryhill Burgh Halls, about a third of the way along this walk, and in the Maryhill Shopping Centre, which is on the opposite side of Maryhill Road from the Ruchill Parish Church which you will visit close to its midpoint.

Introduction

The Forth and Clyde Canal is not only Scotland's oldest canal, it was also the first sea-to-sea canal constructed anywhere in the world to provide a shortcut for maritime vessels. This makes it the forerunner of the world's two greatest sea-to-sea waterways, the Panama Canal and the Suez Canal. The Forth and Clyde Canal was first proposed in the 1760s, primarily to provide a way for east-coast fishing vessels to reach west-coast fishing grounds without having to sail through the notorious waters of the Pentland Firth and around Cape Wrath, on the north coast of Scotland. Its construction began in 1768, but it did not open until 1790. In total, the canal stretches 56 kilometres (35 miles) across the Central Belt of Scotland from the Firth of Forth to the Firth of Clyde. Although built initially as a maritime shortcut, it also became widely used to move raw materials, such as coal and iron, as well as finished products, such as textiles and ceramics, to and from the many industrial towns and villages that grew up along its route. One such settlement was Maryhill, which was then to the northwest of Glasgow. Built on lands that once formed part of the Gairbraid Estate, it was created in the 1790s, and by 1830, had a population of around 3,000. It was raised to the status of a burgh in 1856, and by 1878, it had its own Burgh Hall. In 1891, it was finally absorbed into the neighbouring city. The origin of its name is rather interesting, as it is not named after the hill on which it is built, but after a woman called Mary Hill. She inherited the Gairbraid Estate from her father, Hew Hill, who died with no male heirs, and she feued the land on which the town was built on the condition it was named after her, and always would be. This was because she was the last of her line and it ensured the name of the Hills of Gairbraid would carry on after her death. With the advent of larger ships, the Forth and Clyde Canal lost much of its business. It finally closed in the 1960s and quickly fell into dereliction. There were proposals to fill it in and build on it in the 1960s, but thankfully this never happened, and since 2000, a lot of work has been put in to revive and reopen it, and it is once more being used as a navigation way, although primarily by recreational vessels.

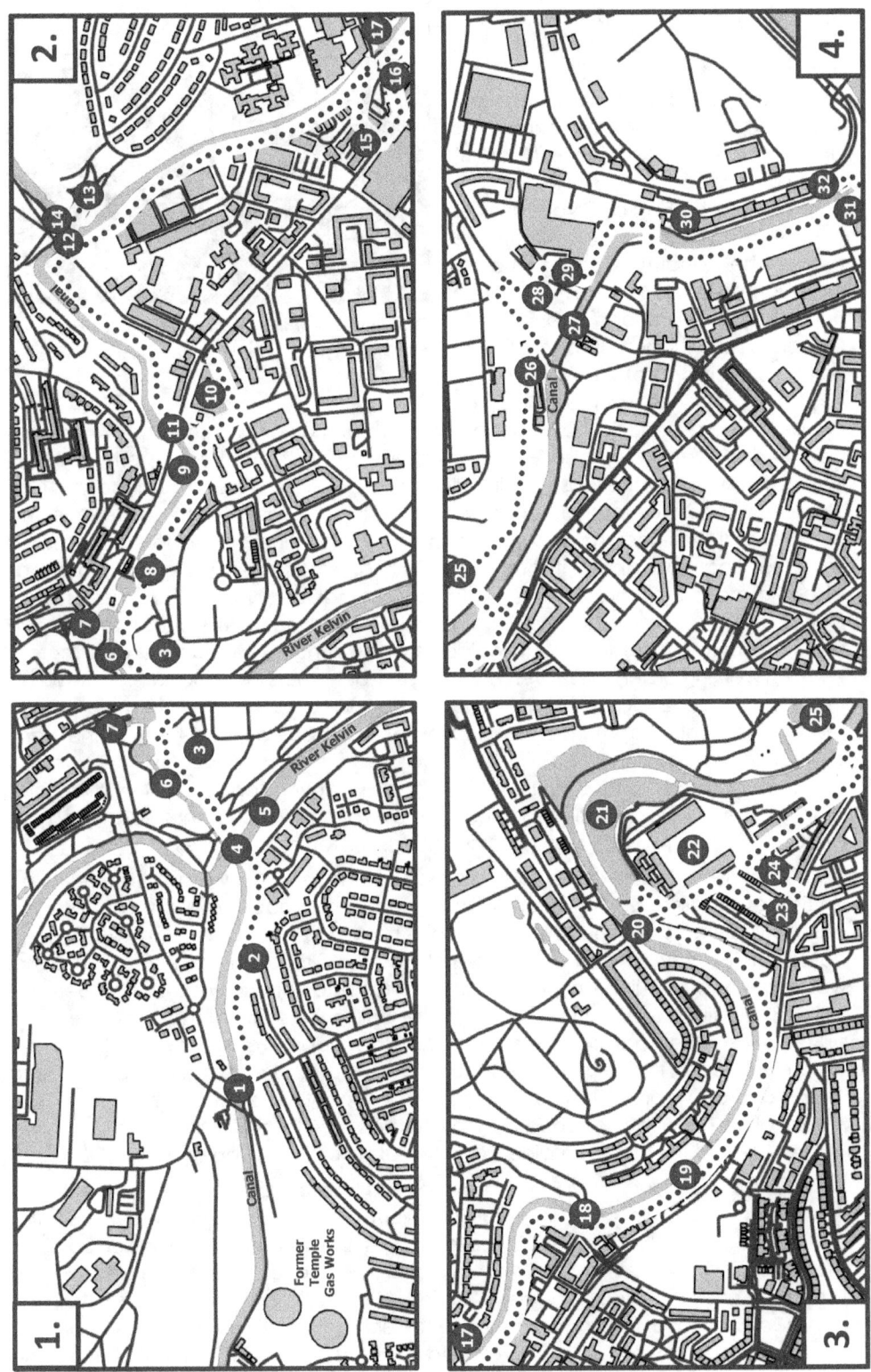

1. The starting point for this walk is the bridge which carries Cleveden Road across the Forth and Clyde Canal close to Kelvindale Railway Station. West from this bridge, the canal runs approximately 14 kilometres (9 miles) through Clydebank to Bowling where it opens into the Firth of Clyde, an arm of the North Atlantic. East of the bridge, the canal runs approximately 42 kilometres (26 miles) through Bishopbriggs, Kirkintilloch and Falkirk to Carron, where it opens into the Firth of Forth, which is part of the North Sea. If you look over the west side of the

   Looking west along Forth and Clyde Canal from Cleveden Road Bridge to former Temple Gasworks

   bridge, in the distance, you can see a large industrial-looking structure which was part of the former Temple Gasworks at Anniesland, on the western edge of Glasgow. This gasworks was built in 1871 for the Partick, Hillhead and Maryhill Gas Company, and was later purchased by the City of Glasgow. It was designed to create what was known as town gas (made by heating coal and so it was also known as coal gas), and at its peak, it was capable of producing tens of thousands of cubic metres (several million cubic feet) of gas per day, which was used to power, among other things, many of the city's street lights. The structure you can see is one of its two remaining gasholders, often wrongly referred to as gasometers. When in working order, these were the largest gas holders in Scotland and between them they were capable of holding up to 280,000 cubic metres (10 million cubic feet) of gas. The commercial production of town gas ceased here in the early 1900s, but the gasholders continued to be used for gas storage, first for town gas and then North Sea gas, until the 1980s. The site is now abandoned, but still retains many of the original structures, including the two remaining gasholders, which are becoming an increasingly rare sight in Scotland's towns and cities.

2. From Cleveden Road Bridge, take the path which leads down onto the towpath on its western side, and then circle back under the bridge to allow you to head eastward towards Maryhill (this route avoids having to cross Cleveden Road, which can be quite busy). The land immediately to the south of this section of the canal was once part of a line constructed by the Caledonian Railway which operated from 1896 until 1920, and if you look over the wall to the south of the canal, you can still see where the track beds used to be. This boundary wall stops a short distance before you reach the Kelvin Aqueduct, and if you are careful, you can climb round its end and down on to the old track bed at the point where it enters a tunnel. This is one of the few abandoned railway tunnels in Glasgow which remain easily accessible, but it is not maintained and for safety reasons, you should not enter it.

3. Staying on the canal towpath, follow it as it curves round towards the Kelvin Aqueduct. As you do so, a single large tower block will come into view. This is the Collina Street Flats. Constructed in the late 1960s, this 19-storey tower block contains 113 flats and was built using the Tracoba technique, which involves slotting together prefabricated concrete slabs. This technique was used for the construction of a large proportion of the tower blocks built across Glasgow around this time, many of which later developed serious problems with damp. The Collina

Street Flats are probably best known as the fictional Osprey Heights, where the characters Jack and Victor lived in the Glasgow-based sitcom *Still Game*.

4. The Kelvin Aqueduct, and the associated Maryhill Locks, are one of the most impressive pieces of Georgian engineering not only along the Forth and Clyde Canal, but in the whole of Britain. Designed by Robert Whitworth and John Smeaton to carry the canal over the valley of the River Kelvin, which presented a potentially insurmountable problem for the canal's construction, its 136-metre (445-foot) length is supported by four arches, each of which is 15 metres (50 feet) wide and 19 metres (62 feet) high. This made it the largest aqueduct in the UK at the time it opened in 1790. At this point, the canal is 2.4 metres (8 feet) deep, deeper than many other canals. This was due to the need to allow sea-going vessels to travel between the east and west coast of Scotland without having to pass through the dangerous waters of the Pentland Firth and around Cape Wrath.

5. If you stop on the first curved bay of the aqueduct's eastern parapet and look over it, far below you will see the River Kelvin as it flows towards the Clyde. A short distance downstream of the aqueduct are a number of tall stone piers which once carried the railway that used to run alongside the canal over the river. Further downstream still you can just make out an unusual V-shaped weir which was built to help provide water for the Kelvindale Paper Mill, one of the largest and longest-lasting local industries. It was founded in the early eighteenth century as the Balgray Snuff Mill, but was acquired around 1840 by the papermaker Edward Collins and Sons. The mill finally closed in the 1970s, ending over 200 years of industry on this part of the Kelvin. There is an optional detour at the point, where you can take the small path leading off to the east at the northern end of the aqueduct and follow it as it snakes down the hill to the river. From here, you can look up at the underside of the aqueduct, giving you a better idea of how it was constructed. When it was first opened, it was common for people to come down to this point on the Kelvin so they could look up and marvel at the boats passing high above their heads. If you take this detour, return back up the same path to the northern end of the aqueduct before carrying on to the next part of the walk.

Looking up at 1790 Kelvin Aqueduct which carries Forth and Clyde Canal across River Kelvin.

6. North of the Kelvin Aqueduct are the Maryhill Locks. This is a series of five locks (Numbers 25 to 21), representing more than 10 per cent of all the locks on the entire 53-kilometre (35-mile) length of the Forth and Clyde Canal. These locks allow the canal to descend part of the way into the Kelvin Valley before crossing the Kelvin via the aqueduct. The top of these locks marks the start of the summit pound, which is the highest point of the canal, some 48 metres (156 feet) above sea level. The summit pound provides all the water for the canal, and from there the water flows west down to the Clyde and east down to the Forth. To prevent this continuous outflow of water from draining the canal, it is continually topped up using water from Banton Loch, a man-made reservoir near Kilsyth to the north of Glasgow. In the 2010s and early 2020s, these locks were the site of the Red Bull Neptune Steps Race, one of the UK's toughest swimming events. The competitors in this race had

to complete a 420-metre-long course (1,377 feet), which involved swimming to the first lock before climbing over the closed lock gates and then carrying on in a similar manner up the remaining four locks. To make matters worse, the event was carried out in March, when the water in the canal was close to its near-freezing winter temperatures.

7. Between Locks 23 and 22 is a small basin which leads off to the north of the canal. This unassuming pool of water is the Kelvin Dock. Constructed in 1789 to build and repair canal boats, it is the oldest boatyard on the canal. By the 1850s, it was owned by Swan and Company, and it was here in 1857 that the first of the legendary Clyde puffers was built. Unique to the west coast of Scotland, these shallow-draft vessels plied their trade up and down the west coast of Scotland, transporting goods to and from remote communities. Fondly remembered, they became known across the world thanks to Neil Munro's *Para Handy* books, which told the adventures of the crew of a Clyde puffer called the *Vital Spark*. In the 1940s, landing craft for the D-Day Normandy landings were built here. The yard finally closed in the 1960s after almost 200 years of boatbuilding.

Former Kelvin Dock, Forth and Clyde Canal, birthplace of legendary Clyde puffers.

8. At the top of the Maryhill Locks, attached to a wall close to Lock 21 is a rather amusing plaque which claims that elephants were used to help excavate these locks, and that as a reward, they were each given a barrel of whisky, resulting in them running amok through the city in search of cream buns. This is part of a long tradition in Glasgow of creating fictional alternative histories and putting up unofficial plaques, often with humorous elements, which adds to the colour of the city as a whole.

9. Since it was cleaned up and reopened in the early 2000s, the Forth and Clyde Canal has become a haven for wildlife, with birds such as kingfishers, swans, cormorants, ducks and coots regularly being seen on it, as well as the occasional otter. However, some of the most colourful birds which you can see along its banks are Glasgow's ring-necked parakeets. Native to the foothills of the Himalayas rather than to Scotland, they are thought to have originated with escaped pets and have grown in number over the last decade or so to a population of several hundred individuals. One spot which is particularly favoured by them is an area on northern side of the canal to the east of the Maryhill Locks, where as many as a hundred of them can be seen at dawn and dusk in the winter months when they come in to roost in the tall trees, safe from predators and human disturbance.

10. At this point, the canal turns sharply to continue its journey eastward, but rather than following it, take the small path which leads off to the right and down to Burnhouse Street. From Burnhouse Street, turn left on to Gairbraid Avenue, which was named after the Gairbraid Estate on whose land the original village of Maryhill was built. This will take you to Maryhill Burgh Halls. This complex of former municipal buildings, designed by Duncan McNaughtan in a French Renaissance style, was opened in 1878 and consisted of a police station, a court room, a fire station with

a tenement to house the firemen, and a public hall capable of seating 900 people. In 1891, Maryhill was absorbed into Glasgow and the buildings lost their civic functions. The police station and fire station remained in use until the 1970s, but after they were moved to newer buildings, the halls fell into disrepair. However, in 2004, the Maryhill Burgh Halls Trust was established and the halls were refurbished so they could be used as a community hub. Among other things, the refurbished burgh halls contain a cafe and a small community museum, as well as some excellent examples of stained glass featuring trades associated with Maryhill. At the entrance to the halls are some metal gates featuring firemen in period clothing, designed by Andy Scott as part of the 2004 renovations. In 1898, a public baths and washhouse was added to the western end of the Maryhill Burgh Halls. Greatly altered behind the remaining facade, these are still in use to this day as Maryhill Leisure Centre. However the original sculpted signs for the bathhouse and the washhouse can still be seen on its western facade facing Burnhouse Street.

Fireman in period clothing, gates of former Maryhill Civic Buildings.

11. Return to the Forth and Clyde Canal by Burnhouse Street, and turn right once you reach it. This will take you over a short aqueduct which carries the canal over Maryhill Road. If you look west along Maryhill Road from this point, you can see a series of traditional buildings. On the right is Gairbraid Church and the Maryhill Burgh Halls, while on the left is a series of red sandstone tenements. Nestled between these tenements is a more ornate classical style building made of grey sandstone. This is Maryhill Library. Designed by James R. Rhind and opened in 1905, it was one of the first built in Glasgow using funds donated by the philanthropist Andrew Carnegie.

12. From the Maryhill Road Aqueduct, follow the towpath eastward until it turns to the right. Here, you will see a modern pedestrian bridge crossing the canal. This is Stockingfield Bridge, completed in 2022 to connect the communities of Maryhill, Ruchill and Gilshochill. This section of the canal is known as Stockingfield Junction, and marks the point at which the canal divides into two parts. The left-hand branch forms the main canal leading east to the Firth of Forth and the Noth Sea, while the right-hand branch is a spur which leads south to Port Dundas in Glasgow, and at one point connected to the Monkland Canal at Pinkston near the centre of Glasgow.

13. Cross over the pedestrian bridge and head up towards the viewing platform on the hill above it. As you do so, you will pass *Bella the Beithir*, a large serpent-like mythical creature designed by Nichol Wheatley as the focus of the Stockingfield Bridge Art Park. Her head is the most spectacular part and looks down onto the canal below, while the rest of her body snakes in and out of the hillside. If you look between her teeth and into her mouth, you will see a world egg hidden within. The head is covered in a mosaic of tiles which, among other things, features the Glasgow coat

of arms on her snout. *Bella the Beithir* is just one of a number of sculptures sited around the Art Park, several of which have been created with the help of local people.

Remains of World War II safety gates, installed to prevent Forth and Clyde Canal flooding north of Glasgow if breached by bomb.

14. Once you reach the viewing platform itself, you will be rewarded with extensive views across Glasgow. However, from this view point you can also see a potential issue created by the positioning of the canal. It is set high above the main body of Glasgow to the south, and if its banks were ever to break, the contents of the canal's summit pound would cascade down across the city, causing death and destruction. This became a real possibility during World War II, when the canal was considered a key target for German bombers. As a result, a series of safety gates were installed which could be closed in the event of a breach, to limit the amount of water which would be released onto the city below. As it turned out, they were never needed, but the remains of one of these gates can still be seen at the start of the section of canal which leads away to the east from Stockingfield Junction. In the event of a direct hit on the canal by a German bomb, these safety gates would have been closed to prevent 27 kilometres (17 miles) worth of water, the distance between this point and the next lock on the main section of the canal, from wreaking havoc on the city below.

15. From Stockingfield Bridge viewing platform, descend back to the towpath and head south along the section of the canal which eventually leads to Port Dundas. After about 700 metres (760 yards), you will come to a road bridge which passes over the canal. Turn right at this bridge and head alongside Ruchill Road to its junction with Maryhill Road. Here, you will find a large red sandstone building which was constructed in the 1890s and designed by Malcolm Stark. At this time, the area directly opposite it on the southern side of Maryhill Road was home to the Wyndford Barracks, and this building served as a respite house for soldiers and their wives. For a small fee, soldiers would rent a quiet room in this building and newlywed ones could spend their honeymoon night there.

16. Cross Ruchill Street at the traffic lights and then turn left up Shakespeare Street. This will take you to the blonde sandstone Ruchill Parish Church Halls and, next to it, the red sandstone Ruchill Parish Church. The church halls were built in 1899, and designed by Charles Rennie Mackintosh in a style typical of his interpretation of art nouveau. After the Glasgow School of Art burned down, first in 2014 and then again in in 2018, this became the only Mackintosh building in Glasgow which is currently still used for its original purpose. The church itself was built in 1903, several years after the hall, and was designed by Neil C. Duff in a perpendicular Gothic style which contrasts sharply with the art nouveau lines of Mackintosh's neighbouring, earlier hall. It is unclear why Mackintosh was not also asked to design the church, but it is not unusual in Glasgow to have a church and its hall designed by different architects, although not usually in quite such contrasting styles.

17. From Ruchill Parish Church, head east along Shakespeare Street to rejoin the towpath. Here, on the opposite bank you will find a well-proportioned polychromatic brick building. Constructed around 1874, this was built for the Glasgow Lead and Colour Works of Alexander Fergusson & Company, and it is an example of the type of industrial buildings which were once common alongside the canal. However, most of these have since either been demolished or simply left to decay.

18. Turn right and head south once more alongside the canal. After a around 400 metres (430 yards), you will reach Bilsland Drive Aqueduct which carries the canal over the road below. Built in 1879, almost a century after the canal was first opened, it is one of a series of similar massive stone aqueducts which allow traffic to pass under the canal, so allowing the free flow of people and products between the areas on either side of it.

19. While walking along the next section of the towpath, between the Bilsland Drive Aqueduct and the Morano Street pedestrian bridge, keep your eyes open for pieces of broken clay pipe. These are mostly found in the earth among the vegetation on the right-hand side of the path and become increasingly more abundant the closer you get to the bridge. These clay pipes were uncovered during an upgrade to the canal towpath in 2023, and there are thousands, if not tens of thousands of fragments to be found along this section of the canal. Some of these have the name 'Murray' stamped on one side of their stem, and 'Glasgow' on the other. This indicates there were made by William Murray at his Caledonian Pipe Works, on Garngad Hill, between 1833 and 1861. Murray pipes are found all over the world and are commonly used to help date archaeological sites. However, the quantity of the remains here suggests they are not simply ones discarded after use. Instead, they represent a debris field from a wreck. It seems most likely that these were part of a consignment of pipes destined for export which had been loaded on to a boat on the Monkland Canal as it passed through Garngad Hill. From there, the boat made its way to Pinkston, where the Monkland Canal joined the Forth and Clyde Canal, and headed towards the Firth of Clyde, where the consignment of pipes would have been loaded onto a larger, ocean-going ship. However, evidence suggests that at this point on the canal, the boat caught fire (a not uncommon occurrence for canal boats) and was destroyed, causing its cargo to be dumped onto the bottom of the canal. Here, the clay pipes lay for an unknown number of years, gradually being spread out by the currents, before being lifted out, probably when the canal was dredged, and dumped alongside the towpath, where again they lay for an unknown period of time before finally being brought to the surface again during the work on the towpath improvements in 2023.

Fragments of 19th-century clay pipes from sunken canal boat unearthed in 2023.

20. From Murano Street bridge, carry on along the canal path as it curves to the left, and eventually reaches a modern concrete bridge which carries Firhill Road over the canal. Called the Nolly Brig, it features two murals based on two pictures painted by Charles Rennie Mackintosh. These are his well-known *Roses* and his less well-known *Sailing Ships*, which date from 1922. The murals were painted by the Art Pistol Projects in 2019.

21. On the far side of Nolly Brig is the Firhill Basin. Like Maryhill, Firhill developed as an industrial area alongside the development of the canal. In particular, a basin offset from the main canal was created in 1788, with a second added in 1849, to offload timber, and by the end of the nineteenth century, it was home to two sawmills, an ironworks and had also become a centre for stained-glass production. Examples of stained glass produced by Stephen Adam at Firhill can be seen in Maryhill Burgh Hall. The presence of the canal and its reputation for glass-making led to Firhill being known as the Scottish Venice. Indeed, Murano Street, which, at this point, runs alongside the canal to its north, is thought to have been named after the Venetian island of the same name, which is also renowned for its glass manufacture.

22. From Firhill Basin, head south away from the canal and down Firhill Road. This will take you past the ground of Partick Thistle Football Club. The club was founded in the Partick area of Glasgow in 1876, just three years after the establishment of the Scottish Football Association in 1873. Having played at a number of different locations across the city and beyond, in the intervening years, in 1909 Partick Thistle finally established a permanent home here at Firhill. The main stand was built in 1927, and has a hint of art deco on the facade facing on to Firhill Road.

23. From Firhill Stadium, cross the road and head south-west down Springbank Street towards Garscube Road. On Garscube Road, to the left of its junction with Springbank Street is the only completed example of a church created by Charles Rennie Mackintosh. Designed for the Free St Matthew Congregation in the 1890s, when Mackintosh was still an assistant at Honeyman and Keppie, it is a masterful mix of art nouveau and Gothic styles. Now known as the Queen's Cross Church, it has largely maintained its original Mackintosh-designed interior. One of Mackintosh's most famous and best-loved creations, it is now home to the Charles Rennie Mackintosh Society. If it is open at the time you are passing, it is well worth taking the time to check out its stunning interior, but please check the opening times in advance if you wish to do so.

Charles Rennie Mackintosh's 1890s Queen's Cross Church.

24. From Queen's Cross Church, turn off Garscube Road onto Firhill Street. As you walk north-east along Firhill Street, you will pass a number of traditional sandstone tenements with fine relief sculptures of plants under their oriel windows. This type of decoration is not common around Glasgow, and it is unclear why some tenement buildings have it, while most do not.

25. When you reach it, turn right onto Firhill Road and walk south towards its junction with Garscube Road. Before you reach the junction, there is a path on the left which leads back up to the canal. Once you reach the towpath again cross over the bridge to Hamiltonhill Clay Pits Local Nature Reserve. This was once the site of a clay quarry where the puddling clay used to line the canal, thus making it waterproof, was dug out of the ground. Since then, it has also been home to a foundry, a boatbuilding yard and a glassworks. However, it is now a 6.7-hectare oasis in the north of Glasgow where a wide variety of wildlife can be found. It also has some of the best views over the city, particularly from the vantage point at the top of the hill above the bridge.

26. From Hamiltonhill Clay Pits, turn right and head south along the western bank of the canal. This will take you to Applecross Basin, where the Glasgow spur of the canal originally terminated. Here, there is a cluster of old buildings. The industrial-looking ones nearest the canal were originally built in the late eighteenth century as workshops for the Canal Company. Between 1782 and 1786, these buildings were also the base for a coach service which took people from the canal basin into the centre of Glasgow. However, in 1790, the canal was extended eastward to Port Dundas, making this service redundant. Set slightly further back from the canal is a large, two-storey house which dates from around 1790. Now known as Rockvilla House, it originally served as the canal manager's house.

1780s Canal Workshop Buildings, Applecross Basin, Forth and Clyde Canal.

27. Head north away from the canal along Applecross Street until you reach a small flight of stairs leading down to the right. Go down these steps and then cross Possil Road at the traffic lights at their base. Turn right and walk south-west along Possil Road and cross Dawson Road, which leads off to your left. At this point, you can look further down Possil Road to see the Possil Aqueduct which carries the canal over it. The original aqueduct was built in 1790 to help complete the route to Port Dundas and connect the Forth and Clyde Canal to Monkland Canal. In the 1880s, it was replaced by a second aqueduct built alongside the original one. This new aqueduct, which is still standing to this day, consists of a heavy central arch which carries the canal itself, with lighter arches on either side to support the towpaths. This aqueduct was the site of one of the more unusual, and lesser-known, events associated with the Forth and Clyde Canal. In January 1883, a solider on leave from the Royal Artillery found a large tin box on the towpath on top of the aqueduct, close to the water's edge. Out of curiosity, he opened it, causing a small explosion and a blue flame to shoot out. This turned out to be one of three bombs which had been planted around Glasgow on the same night. Luckily none of them seemed to explode as intended and they failed to cause a substantial amount of damage. However, if the Possil Road Aqueduct bomb had gone off properly, the effects of the water cascading across the city would have been devastating. A number of people believed to have links to Irish nationalism were eventually arrested and found guilty of planting both the Possil Aqueduct bomb and the two others.

28. If you now look at the corner between Possil Road and Dawson Road itself, you will see that within the tall retaining wall are two entrances, both closed off with rusted iron gates. One, marked 'Girls', leads to an open stone staircase built into the retaining wall, with the other, marked 'Boys', leads to an enclosed staircase which disappears upwards through a cave-like tunnel. Above this, you can just about make out a sign incised into the stonework which reads 'Rockvilla Public School', and which has a small, delicately sculpted dragon at either end. This is pretty much all that remains of a once-magnificent Gothic style school building designed by John Honeyman and constructed in the 1870s. Its unusual entrances allowed children from the surrounding Rockvilla community to make their way up to the school which was perched alongside the canal, high above the surrounding roads and houses. In the 1990s, the school was badly damaged by fire, and most of it was subsequently demolished, leaving these few fragments of what was clearly a rather interesting and unusual building.

Surviving Boys' entrance to now-demolished 1870s Rockvilla Public School.

29. From the entrances to the former Rockvilla School, head south-east up Dawson Road and at its top, turn right into the car park which lies between it and the canal. This was the location of the original Rockvilla House, after which the district is named. After this house was demolished, it became a sawmill, a cotton mill and a distillery, before the current building was constructed as a bonded warehouse in the 1950s. Since 2012, it has been known as the Whisky Bond when it became home to workshops and offices which are occupied by a diverse community of business and artists. The origins of the name Rockvilla House are unclear, but it could have been due to the presence of a large number of quarries in the local area at the time it was built in the late eighteenth century.

30. Continue through the car park to its south-western end where there is a gate which will take you back on to the canal's towpath (If this gate is locked, retrace your route back to the canal and rejoin it to the south of the former canal manager's house). When you reach the towpath, turn left and walk along it until you reach a bridge which you can use to cross to the other side. To the north of the bridge is another former timber basin which used to serve the City Sawmill (now demolished), while to the south of it was, at one time, a cooperage. Ahead of you at this point, you will see the blonde sandstone buildings of Speirs Wharf stretching out along the canal. The nearest of these, standing on its own, is the 1866 Wheatsheaf Building, which originally served as a warehouse for the Port Dundas Sugar Refinery. Although some of the refinery buildings have since been demolished, another part of it remains in the shape of the seven-storey building just to its south. Further on are the buildings of the former City of Glasgow Grain Mill and Stores, which were constructed between the 1850s and 1860s for John Currie and Company. Between these is a former bonded warehouse built in 1861. While these

buildings have been standing for more than 150 years, their use has changed many times across their life time. For example, the sugar refinery had become disused by the 1890s, but later found a new use as the Wheatsheaf Flour Mill. Most recently, in 1989, it was converted into offices. Around the same time, many of the other remaining buildings on Speirs Wharf were converted into residential flats.

31. At the southern end of Speirs Wharf, there is a viewing point where you can look out across the west of Glasgow. However, recent building developments have obscured the views of a number of historic buildings, including the towers of Trinity College to the east of Kelvingrove Park. This highlights a major issue with Glasgow at the moment. Not only is much of its built heritage under threat, with older buildings being demolished at a worryingly rapid rate, but the views of those that are left are being obscured by modern developments which have little local flavour or, indeed, architectural merit. Glasgow has always been an eclectic mix of different architectural styles, but architects previously seemed to have worked hard to maintain a local flavour to the buildings they designed, making it an architecturally unique and distinct city, and one of the best-preserved Victorian and Edwardian cities in the world. However, much of this is now being lost under a wave of generic-looking buildings which can be found in pretty much any city in the world. Just as it was in the 1960s and 70s, when there was a previous wave of destruction of historic buildings across the city, Glasgow is once again at a major crossroads. However, it seems to have failed to learn anything from the disastrous architectural choices of the past, many of which have now had to be demolished, and it seems destined to repeat the same mistakes all over again, and in the process, lose another swath of Glasgow's unique built heritage.

32. Turn back to the canal, and look across to the other side, where you will see Canal House, the final stop on this walk. Built in a classical style around 1800, it was possibly designed by David Hamilton, and originally served as the office buildings for the Forth and Clyde Canal Company. However, with the decline and closure of the canal, the building fell into disrepair. In 1989, it was restored to its former glory and it is once again being used for offices. This just goes to show that after the orgy of destruction in the 1960s and 1970s, Glasgow did return to a period where it renovated and converted its historic buildings rather than abandoning and demolishing them. Hopefully this will happen once again before too much more of Glasgow's heritage is lost.

Classical style Canal House, thought to have been designed by David Hamilton around 1800.

East
of Glasgow

11. High Street, Townhead and Old Glasgow

Start Point: Glasgow Cross, Glasgow (**Location:** Lat/Lon: 55.85655, -4.24363; What3Words: ///farm.pest.crisis; Plus Code: VQ44+JG9 Glasgow). **Nearest Public Transport:** Subway: St Enoch Subway Station (15 mins); Train: Argyle Street Station or High Street Station: 5 mins); Bus: High Street (5 mins).

End Point: Cathedral Precinct, Glasgow (**Location:** Lat/Lon: 55.86282, -4.23544; What3Words: ///piles.curving.groom; Plus Code: VQ77+4RF Glasgow). **Nearest Public Transport:** Subway: Buchanan Street (20 mins); Train: High Street Station: 5 mins); Bus: High Street (5 mins).

Distance: 3.8 kilometres/2.4 miles. **Time:** Allow 2 to 3 hours for this walk.
Level of Difficulty: Moderate. This walk contains a number of steep hills, especially in and around the Necropolis. While there are some steps on the main route, in all cases, there are alternative options without steps nearby.

Facilities: There are a number of shops, cafes, restaurants and bars along High Street where you can stop for refreshments along this route. Publicly accessible toilets are available at the Saint Mungo Museum of Religious Life and Art on Castle Street, which is passed on several occasions during this walk.

Introduction

The areas around High Street are the oldest parts of Glasgow, and High Street can be considered to be the first road established in the city. It originally connected the religious community, founded on the banks of the Molendinar Burn by Saint Mungo in the sixth century, with a small salmon-fishing village on the banks of the River Clyde. From this street, seven others evolved in the Medieval Era to create the seed which would eventually grow into the city of Glasgow as it exists today. These were Rottenrow, Trongate, Stockwell Street and Bridgegate leading west, Drygate and Gallowgate, leading east, and Saltmarket, leading south. By the end of the eighteenth century, five further streets had been added to create the area now known as the Merchant City to the west of High Street. These were Bell Street, Candleriggs, Canon Street (now part of the eastern end of Ingram Street), King Street and Princes Street (now called Parnie Street), From these original thirteen streets, Glasgow expanded throughout the nineteenth and twentieth centuries, first westward, to form the Blythswood New Town and the West End, eastward, engulfing former weaving villages such as Bridgeton and Calton, to create the city's East End, and northward into areas like Sighthill, Royston, Garngad and Springburn. Finally, it expanded southward across the Clyde to create what is now known as the Southside of the city. Given that High Street is the heart of old Glasgow, it is unsurprising that the area surrounding it is home to a number of Glassgow's oldest buildings and institutions, including Glasgow Cathedral, which dates from the end of the twelfth century (although its origins go back much further to the end of the sixth century), the Provand's Lordship, which was built in 1471, making it the city's oldest house, and the Tolbooth, constructed in the 1620s and 1630s as the city's original municipal buildings (of which only the 1660s Tolbooth Steeple remains standing). The High Street area was also the original site of the University of Glasgow, which was founded in 1451, making it the fourth-oldest university in the English-speaking world (behind the universities of Oxford, Cambridge and St Andrews) and Glasgow Royal Infirmary, which was founded by a royal charter in 1792, making it the city's first major hospital. Unlike the university, which moved to the West End in the late 1800s, the Royal Infirmary remains in this area to this day.

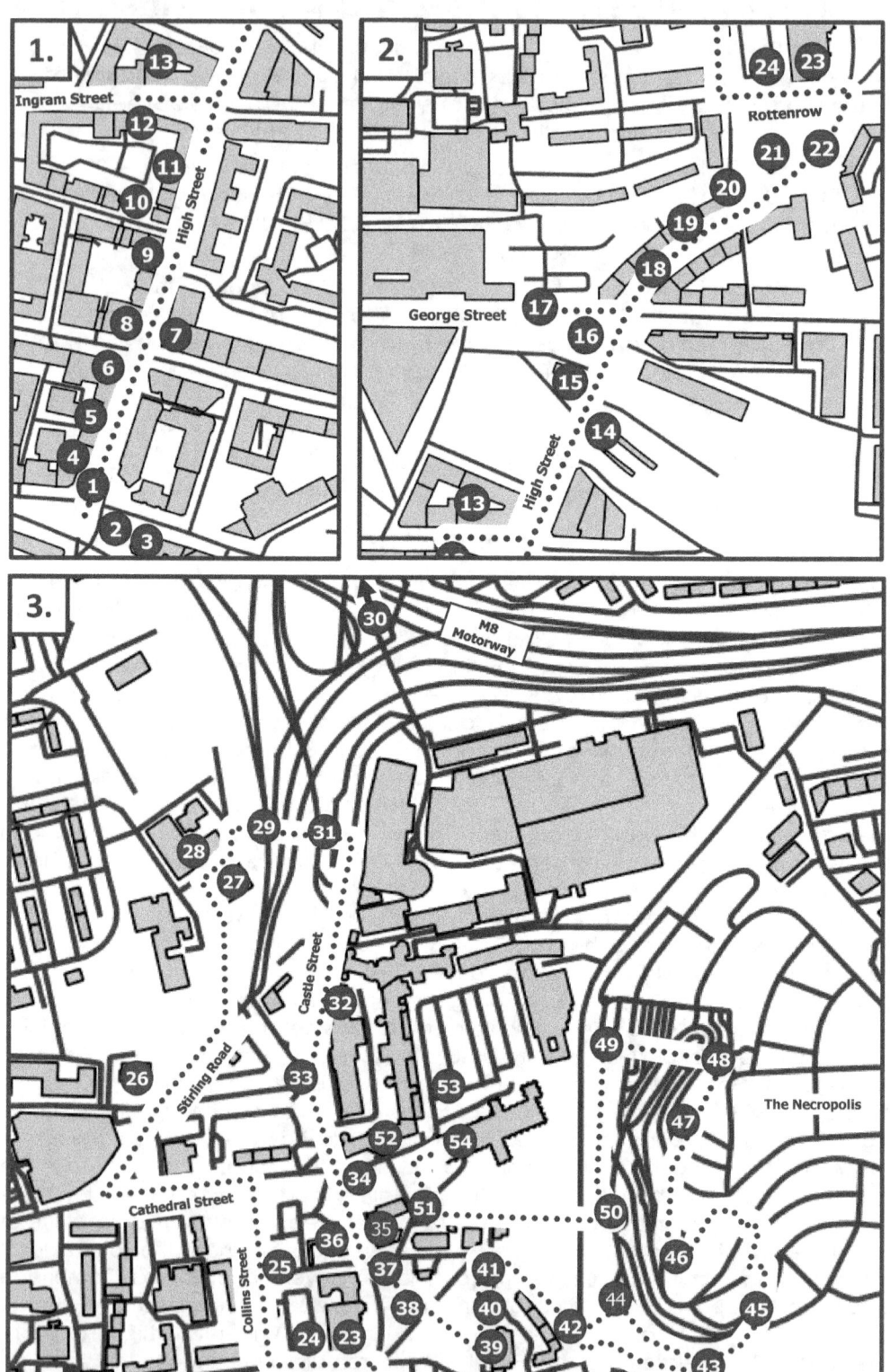

1. This walk starts at Glasgow Cross in the East End of the city, which marks the points where five streets meet. This includes four of the original thirteen streets of the medieval settlement which became the Bishop's Burgh (meaning it was controlled by a bishop) of Glasgow, in 1175. These are Trongate, Saltmarket, London Road, Gallowgate and High Street. At the centre of Glasgow Cross is the Tolbooth Steeple. Designed by John Boyd and completed in 1634, it is all that remains of Glasgow's seventeenth-century Tolbooth. These buildings also became the meeting place for the Royal Burgh of Glasgow, which was officially created by James VI in 1611. Over the years, they also served as a prison, courthouse and site for public executions, but this all changed when new public offices were constructed further south on the Saltmarket in 1814. By the early twentieth century, the Tolbooth had

17th-century Tolbooth Steeple, Glasgow Cross.

become extremely dilapidated and most of it was demolished in 1921, leaving just the steeple. This is not the only ancient steeple visible from Glasgow Cross. To the west is the Tron Steeple, while the Merchants' Steeple is to the south-west, and the steeple of St Andrews in the Square can be seen to the south-east. With the exception of Glasgow Cathedral, these are the oldest remaining steeples in Glasgow. In common with older clocks in other British cities, the faces of their clocks are blue with gold details. This originated with a decree from Henry VIII of England based on a verse from the Old Testament, which stated that Aaron the Priest's garments should be blue with gold bells (Exodus 39). The fashion soon spread beyond England and into Scotland, and set the standard coloration of clocks in Glasgow for several centuries to come.

2. On the eastern side of Glasgow Cross is a low, octagonal tower, topped with a tall shaft supporting a unicorn, Scotland's national animal. This is the Mercat (or Market) Cross. A Mercat Cross was the symbolic centre of a Scottish town or city, and marked the location where markets and other special events took places. Although the design of Glasgow's Mercat Cross is based on similar buildings dating from the seventeenth century found in other Scottish towns and cities, this example was not actually built until 1930. It was designed by Edith Burnet Hughes, the niece of renowned Glasgow architect John James Burnet. After studying at the Sorbonne in Paris, and at Gray's School of Art in Aberdeen, Hughes established her own architectural firm in Glasgow in 1920, making her Britain's first practising female architect.

3. Directly behind the Mercat Cross is the imposing Mercat Building constructed on the narrow strip of land between the Gallowgate and London Road. In Scotland, such strips of land are known as gushets, from the French 'gouchet' or 'gousset', which was a piece of armour for protecting the armpit. The buildings constructed on them are known as gushet buildings, of which Glasgow has many. The Mercat Building is a particularly fine example of the Glaswegian tradition of creating

distinctive gushet buildings, but it is also relatively recent, having only been constructed in 1928 from a design by A. Graham Henderson.

4. Turn your attention back to the Tolbooth Steeple and to its left you will see a large curved building which forms a quarter-circle or quadrant. This was also designed by A. Graham Henderson, and while it was originally designed in 1913, it was not built until 1922, after much of the tolbooth building was demolished. Originally, it was meant to be one of a pair of identical buildings to mark the start of High Street leading up to the north, but the second one on the eastern side of the Tolbooth Steeple was, for some reason, never built.

5. Walk north along the pavement in front of the completed quadrant to the west of the Tolbooth Steeple. This area forms the southern end of High Street. Just past this building is a covered lane leading off to the east. This is Tontine Lane. A tontine is a type of investment plan, devised in 1653 in France by an Italian called Lorenzo de Tonti, whereby the last surviving investor owns the resulting investment outright. In 1782, the Tontine Society of Glasgow was created by various prominent merchants as a forerunner of Glasgow's Royal Exchange (which was based further west in Royal Exchange Square). This society ran the Tontine Hotel, as well as coffee rooms and an assembly hall, all built around this lane behind the existing frontage of the town hall buildings of the Tolbooth. Collectively, these buildings became the social and commercial headquarters of Glasgow and were a favourite meeting place for the city's tobacco and textile merchants, many of whom had made their fortunes from enterprises linked to the slave trade in the British colonies in the Americas. One of the key features of the Tontine buildings was a series of arches featuring keystones decorated with sculpted heads. These became known as the Tontine Heads, and although the Tontine buildings have long since been demolished, the heads were saved and are now housed in St Nicholas Gardens on Castle Street, which will be visited later on this walk.

6. Carry on up High Street to its junction with Bell Street. On the south-west corner of this junction is a large and imposing red sandstone tenement, with space for shops at street level and flats on the floors above. This was built around 1900 by the City Improvement Trust, which was established to help clean up the squalid living conditions that existed in Glasgow in the second half of the 1800s. It was responsible for many of the tenement buildings which you will pass as you walk north along High Street.

1900 City Improvement Trust, red sandstone tenement, retail space on ground floor.

7. On the opposing north-east corner of the junction between High Street and Bell Street is a colossal six-storey former commercial building which disappears off to the east along Bell Street. Built in 1882, this was constructed by the Glasgow and South Western Railway to serve as a warehouse for their College Goods Station and is one of the earliest examples of the use of mass concrete for a Glasgow building. In its time, it was the largest warehouse in the city, and rather than being abandoned or demolished like so many of Glasgow's older buildings were once they have outlived their original purpose, it has been successfully converted into

flats. As such, it serves as a template for how old buildings can be successfully repurposed rather than being left to fall into decay, dereliction and eventual destruction.

8. On the north-west corner of the High Street–Bell Street junction stands the former Bow's Emporium, one of the many family owned department stores which used to exist across Glasgow. Bow's Emporium was started by William Bow in a premises further north on High Street in 1873, and moved to this location in the 1880s. When it opened, it was fitted with all the latest time-saving gadgets, including speaking tubes for communicating between different areas within the building, and what was described as a cash railway. It sold everything from cutlery and china to prams, kids' toys and beds. Paraffin lamps were a particular speciality and they had their own department at the very top of the building. Bow's Emporium ceased to exist in 1947 when it was bought over by E. Wylie Hill & Co. Ltd, which had its own store on Buchanan Street, and which was, in turn, bought over by John Menzies, the newsagents, in 1973.

Former Bow's Department Store, High Street.

9. Further up High Street on its corner with Blackfriars Street is a rather elegant classical style, blonde sandstone tenement. This was built in 1891 for the City Improvement Trust and was designed by Alexander B. McDonald, who worked as the architect for Glasgow's Office of Public Works. McDonald is one of the unsung heroes of the city's architecture. He had a major influence on Glasgow's development around the turn of the twentieth century, and so on how it looks today. He designed a large number and variety of buildings, including several of the City Improvement Trust tenements along High Street. However, probably his most famous building is the magnificent Renaissance style People's Palace on Glasgow Green, which was built in the 1890s as a museum, with a huge winter garden attached to its rear elevation.

10. Blackfriars Street gets its name from a community of Dominican monks, the Black Friars (named after the black robes they wore), who set up a religious community on High Street in 1246. The church they established survived until the 1870s when it was demolished to make way for a railway station. If you now turn left into Blackfriars Street and walk a short distance along it, you will find a small pub housed in a building which looks rather out of place in comparison to the Victorian buildings which surround it. This is because it was built as a villa around 1790, meaning it predates its neighbours by a considerable period of time. It is thought to have been designed by Robert and John Adam.

11. Return to High Street and carry on northwards again to No. 125. This is another of the High Street tenements designed by Alexander B. McDonald, but this time it was built for the Central Fire Station, which was round the corner on Ingram Street, and was linked to it. It is designed in a sixteenth-century Dutch style with distinctive gables and provided housing for the firemen and their families. As with many of Glasgow's older fire stations, it has a large and ornate version of the city's coat of arms on its central gable.

12. To the north of No. 125 is the junction between High Street and Ingram Street. Turn left at this junction and walk a short distance east to 23–33 Ingram Street. This building is the old Central Fire Station. Also designed by Alexander B. McDonald in a similar Dutch style to the tenement at 125 High Street, it was built in 1898. The engines and horses were kept on the ground floor, while the first floor contained the duty room. Above these were the officers' flats. This fire station closed in 1985 when a new station was opened in Cowcaddens to the north of the city centre.

13. On the other side of Ingram Street, at No. 30, is another red sandstone building. Built in an art deco style, this opened in 1936 as the Bell Telephone Exchange to serve the eastern part of central Glasgow, although the building itself is dated 1938. Like many telephone exchanges built at this time, it has the monogram of the sitting monarch on a keystone above its entrance (in this case, that of King George VI). This is a practice which only seems to have begun in the 1930s and older exchanges do not feature these monograms. Until the 1960s, when numerical codes replaced alphabetical codes, its telephone numbers all had the BEL prefix. This building still serves as a telephone exchange to this day.

14. Return to High Street, and look across the road. The area around what is now High Street Station was the original site of the University of Glasgow before it moved to the West End in the 1870s. The university was founded by a charter from Pope Nicholas V in 1451, making it the fourth oldest in Britain (after those in Oxford, Cambridge and St Andrews). To its south was Blackfriars Church, which became part of the university in 1573, and where many of its professors and their families were buried. After the university moved to the West End, both the Old College, as it was known, and Blackfriars Church were demolished to make way for the College Goods Station and Railway Yard, built by the Glasgow and South Western Railway. The original gateway to the Old College was moved to the West End and incorporated into Pearce Lodge on the new Gilmorehill Campus, as was the 1690 Lion and Unicorn Staircase. The remains of the professors and their families were exhumed from Blackfriars Church Yard and re-interred under a new memorial in the nearby Necropolis. Beyond that, little trace remains in the city of the Old College campus.

15. Head north along High Street until you come to a small red sandstone building at No. 215, which currently stands on an otherwise empty lot. This is the former Linen Bank building. A beautiful, if rather neglected, building, it was designed by William Forrest Salmon (the son of the classical architect James Salmon Snr and the father of the art nouveau/Glasgow style architect James Salmon Jnr) and it is dated 1895. Among other architectural features, it has some beautifully carved cherubs or putti surrounding its arched ground-floor window, and another rather cheeky one on the keystone over its entrance. It is also topped by a distinctive ogee-domed tempietto (or little temple) accompanied by a female figure. On the northern side of 215 High Street is a bronze plaque

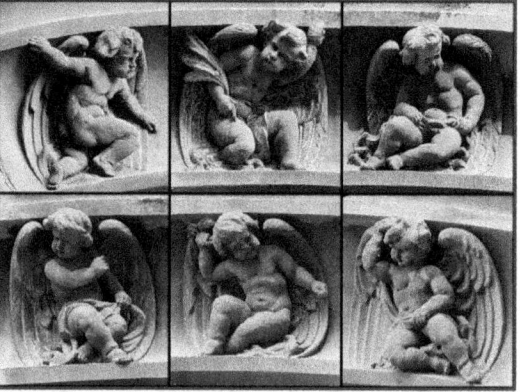

Sculpted putti surrounding arched ground-floor window, 215 High Street.

commemorating the poet Thomas Campbell, who was born here in 1777. Among other things, he served as Rector of the University of Glasgow in the 1820s and was involved in founding University College London. Highly regarded in his own time by the likes of Byron, he published his first major poem, titled 'Pleasures of Hope', when he was just twenty-one. However, he has largely fallen out of favour in the years since his death in 1844, in part due to shifts in social and political fashion. In particular, his poems 'Ye Mariners of England' and 'The Soldier's Dream', regarded as his greatest works, are now viewed as being too fiercely patriotic and linked to imperial expansion. However, he was well enough regarded in his day to be buried in Poets' Corner in Westminster Abbey, in London, alongside the likes of Geoffrey Chaucer, Charles Dickens, Robert Browning, Thomas Hardy, Alfred, Lord Tennyson and Rudyard Kipling.

16. Between 215 High Street and the junction with George Street is a small iron box marked with the Glasgow coat of arms and the letters GCT. This is a Lucy Box for the Glasgow Corporation Tramways. As such, it is a remnant of Glasgow's Tram and Trolleybus networks, which were, at one time, among the largest in the Europe. Opened in 1872, by 1922 the Glasgow tram network had over 1,000 trams and over 160 kilometres (100 miles) of routes. However, the system was gradually phased out starting in 1949, to be replaced first by trolleybuses (which were powered by the same overhead electrical wires as trams, but did not require tracks) and then diesel-powered buses. The last tram route, the No. 9 from Achenshuggle to Dalmuir, finally closed in 1962, bringing to an end almost a century of tram travel in the city.

Glasgow Corporation Tramways Lucy Box, close to 215 High Street.

17. At the junction between High Street and George Street, turn left and walk a short distance west. From this spot, you can see a number of Glasgow's famous murals. To the left is a space-themed mural marking the internationally important role that Glasgow-based engineers play in the space industry. It may seem surprising, but more satellites are built in Glasgow than in any other European city, and the city produces more satellites than anywhere else in the world outside of California. In the middle is a mural the featuring the land ship, a mock ship's navigation bridge fitted with a Kelvin Compass. It was built as a teaching aide and was mounted on a revolving platform on top of the School of Navigation in the Royal College. Finally, on the right, on an exposed gable end of the tenement on the corner of George Street and High Street, is a mural which harks back to the very birth of Glasgow itself. It shows Saint Thenue (also known as Saint Enoch) holding her child, who would go on to become Saint Kentigern. Born in Culross, in Fife, in AD 518, and more commonly known as Saint Mungo, Saint Kentigern founded the city of Glasgow as a religious community later in the sixth century.

18. Return to High Street and follow it up the hill as it curves towards the north-east. This section of High Street is lined by some very attractive red sandstone Scottish baronial style tenements which feature a variety of relief sculptures. Of particular note is the owl with outstretched wings which can be found on one of the

tenements at the north-east end of the block. These buildings, known as the Bell o' the Brae tenements, were designed by William Boston and built between 1901 and 1903 for the City Improvement Trust. They get their name from an old name for this section of High Street, and it refers to what was known as a deid (or dead) bell installed on a turret at the top of the hill. Since medieval times, this bell had been rung during funerals. This hill was also the site of the Battle of the Bell o' the Brae in 1297, when William Wallace, accompanied by 300 horsemen, defeated a 1,000-strong English army lead by Earl Percy in the run-up to the more famous, and larger, Battle of Stirling Bridge.

19. As you walk up High Street, it is worth stopping at Nos. 267 and 275. Fixed to the tiles at the entrance to both of these tenement closes is a small metal ghost sign providing the contact information for the Glasgow Corporation Lighting Department in case there are any complaints about the lighting of the communal stairway in the tenement, or in the street. The phone number given is BEL 976, which is connected to the Bell Telephone Exchange which you visited earlier on Ingram Street. This allows the age of these signs to be estimated at between sixty and ninety years old; that is, between the date the exchange opened in 1936 and 1962, when the letter codes for exchanges were replaced with numerical codes.

Ghost sign, Glasgow Corporation Lighting Department, entrance to tenement close.

20. At the north-western end of this block of tenements is another of Glasgow's gable-end murals. This one features Saint Mungo depicted as a homeless person, with a robin perched on his finger. The association between Saint Mungo and the robin can be traced back to an incident in his youth. Saint Mungo grew up in a monastery run by Saint Serf, who had tamed a wild robin. Legend has it that some of Saint Serf's disciples accidentally killed this robin and then blamed its death on Saint Mungo. Saint Mungo took the bird in his hand and prayed over it, where upon it was restored to life and flew off back to its master. So strong is the association of this story with Saint Mungo that the bird was one of the symbols associated with miracles attributed to the saint which were later incorporated into the coat of arms of Glasgow. Beside the bottom-right corner of this mural, is a small silver plaque telling the story of the St Mungo Mile. This was supposedly a drunken, naked race along High Street originating in the 1450s, based on these symbols along High Street, and run by the students of the University of Glasgow each year on New Year's Day. As amusing as this story is, there's no evidence that it is remotely true.

21. Just to the north of the Bell o' the Brae tenements is an area which is now used as urban allotments. However, in 1895, this was the location of Glasgow's Hydraulic Power Station, which was housed in a rather magnificent castle-like building and used steam engines to pump high-pressure water around Glasgow through more than 48 kilometres (30 miles) of 17-centimetre (7-inch) diameter cast-iron pipes with 2.5-centimetre-thick (1 inch) walls. This provided hydraulic power to various kinds of machinery in workshops and factories throughout the city. Such hydraulic power systems were one of the first attempts to create a centralised power source in

urban areas, rather than requiring each site to generate its own power. At its peak in 1908–1909, it supplied over 750,000 litres (200,000 gallons) of high-pressure water to its subscribers. Hydraulic power was soon superseded by electricity as a centralised power source. However, the system was not closed down until 1964 and you can still find access covers for it, labelled with the letters H.P. embedded in streets across the city. In addition, you can still see some of the walls and one of the original heavy-duty pipes as you walk past this site.

Remains of castle-like Hydraulic Power Station, High Street.

22. On the opposite side of High Street to the former hydraulic power station is an old grey sandstone wall. This is one of the few remnants of Glasgow's notorious Duke Street Prison, which was built in 1798 and finally closed in 1957, shortly before it was demolished. For the first seventy-six years of its existence, it held both men and women, but in 1882 a new male prison was constructed at Barlinnie, and Duke Street became exclusively a women's prison. After the cessation of public executions in Glasgow in 1865, the city's gallows were moved to Duke Street Prison, and twelve executions were carried out there. This included the execution of Susan Newell, the last woman to be hanged in Scotland, in 1923.

23. Further north, where High Street becomes Castle Street at its junction with Rottenrow, is the former Barony Church. It was designed by the architectural firm Burnet, Son and Campbell in an imposing Gothic style and was built in the 1880s. No longer a church, it is now part of the University of Strathclyde.

24. Immediately to the west of the former Barony Church on Rottenrow is a blonde sandstone wall, with a gateway inscribed with the word 'Infants'. This is all that remains of the 1884 Townhead Public School, and the land where it once stood is now used as a carpark. Rottenrow is another of Glasgow's thirteen original medieval streets. The origins of its rather unusual name are unclear, but it may be a corruption of the French words 'routine' and 'route', meaning 'usual way'. In 1805, the Glasgow Lock Hospital was established on this street. The term 'lock' originates from an old English term for a leper house, and the hospital, which operated on a charitable basis, specialised in providing shelter and treatment for impoverished and destitute working-class women and girls suffering from venereal diseases. In the early days, it was little more than a prison where the female patients faced a long and lingering death, but in the early twentieth century, this changed, with a greater emphasis on treatment and better conditions. The hospital finally closed in the 1950s. One of the most notable doctors who served there was James McCune Smith, a former slave and the first African American to obtain a medical degree, which he obtained from the University of Glasgow in the 1830s. During his time at the Lock Hospital, Smith fought strongly for the rights of his vulnerable, working-class, female patients. In particular, despite the potential damage this could have done to his nascent career, Smith worked hard to expose how women were subjected to painful and harmful drug trials using highly concentrated silver nitrate applied to their internal reproductive organs by the hospital's senior doctor,

Alexander Hannay. This involved collating and analysing records of Hannay's patients, a process now known as medical statistics, to show that the trials were both ineffective and risky, something Hannay had himself sought to cover up. In addition, Smith interviewed the female patients (which was unusual for the time) and took seriously their claims of the extreme pain Hanney's experimental treatment inflicted on them. His work was published in the *London Medical Gazette*, one of the leading medical journals of its age.

25. From Rottenrow, turn north onto Collins Street. About halfway along this street on the right-hand side, you will see a sundial. Designed with multiple gnomons (the official name for the bit which casts a shadow onto the dial), it is part of a long tradition of Scottish sundials, dating back as far as the sixteenth century. This includes obelisk sundials, like this one, which are unique to Scotland.

26. Carry on north up Collins Street until you reach Cathedral Street. At this point, turn left and walk along to junction between Cathedral Street and Stirling Road. Cross this junction using the traffic lights and head north along Stirling Road towards the Howgait pub. Outside this pub is a drinking fountain which has a sign inscribed in a rather beautiful art nouveau font stating that it was donated to the citizens of Glasgow by the publican William Annan of Port Dundas, in 1908.

Obelisk sundial, Collins Street.

27. From the William Annan drinking fountain, continue north on Stirling Road, until you see a small pedestrian path leading off to the left which is sign-posted to Martyrs' School. Follow this path until you reach a large red sandstone building. This is Martyrs' Public School, built in 1895 and designed by the great Glasgow architect Charles Rennie Mackintosh. Although Mackintosh was working to the strict requirements of both the site and the School Board of Glasgow, it nonetheless has a number of distinctive Mackintosh-style features. The school seems to take its name from two men who were burned at the stake for Protestant heresy in the 1530s, and after whom the nearby Martyrs' Street (which is no longer in existence) was named. However, these were not the only martyrs associated with this part of Glasgow and in 1684, the Covenanters, James Lawson, James Nisbet and Alexander Wood, were executed at Howgait in 1684 (close to the current location of the William Annan drinking fountain you just visited), leading to confusion over which set of martyrs the school is named after. To the south of Martyrs' School is a pedestal supporting a plaque commemorating the birth of Charles Rennie Mackintosh on 7 June 1868 in a nearby tenement at 70 Parson Street (the street which runs past the west side of the school).

28. Opposite Martyrs' Public School on Parson Street is St Mungo's Church, built in 1841, and its neighbouring retreat, built in the 1890s. St Mungo's Church was designed by George Goldie in a rather beautiful Italianate Gothic style, while the retreat was designed by Osmund Cooke in a more Victorian High Gothic style. Together with Martyrs' Public School, these buildings make up a cluster of architectural gems which are rarely visited by tourists, or even many Glaswegians, but they are a reminder of what the Townhead area of the city formerly looked like before so much of it was demolished (including the tenement where Mackintosh was born) in the mid-twentieth century.

Saint Mungo's Retreat.

29. At the north-east end of Parson Street, just behind the retreat, there is a narrow path. Almost as soon as you start along it, you will see a narrow concrete bridge leading off to the right which will take you over a busy dual carriageway. This is an example of the types of poorly thought through roads constructed in the 1960s and 1970s across Glasgow. Although these roads allowed those living in the surrounding suburbs to reach the city centre rapidly, they decimated communities like Townhead and Springburn, through which they passed, by effectively slicing them in two. As a result, while not necessarily a bad idea in themselves, the way these roads were implemented has turned out to be rather disastrous in the long term.

30. From this bridge, there is the option for taking a detour from the main route of this walk to visit a remnant of the old Monkland Canal, which adds about 800 metres (0.5 miles) to the walk. Completed in 1794, the Monkland Canal was one of Scotland's first canals, and it designed by James Watt to bring coal into Glasgow from the coalfields of North Lanarkshire. It also joined the Forth and Clyde Canal at Pinkston Basin, allowing goods from the East End of Glasgow to be transported out to the Firth of Clyde, and from there to the rest of the world. Most of the Monkland Canal was filled in when the M8 motorway was built in the 1970s. However, one small fragment of the section which once ran through the East End of Glasgow somehow survived under the mass of roads and concrete built on top of it. For this detour, take the branch of the bridge which leads off to the left and follow the walkways underneath the concrete flyovers of the M8. Eventually, you will find a small narrow underpass leading off to your left. If you look closely at this underpass, you will see it is, in fact, a small section of canal (minus the water), complete with stone-built banks. The edges of the stone supports for the road bridge which passes over it still have their iron protectors in place, and these have many deep grooves worn into them by the ropes used to haul barges along the canal. Once you have visited this section of canal, return the way you came, back to the pedestrian bridge at Townhead.

31. As you carry on eastward across the pedestrian bridge, ahead you will see the buildings of Glasgow Royal Infirmary. Further off, you will see the spire of Glasgow Cathedral and above it the graves and memorials of the city's Necropolis. If you look back, you will also see the Martyrs' School perched on a hill above the surrounding roads. At the eastern end of the bridge, you can also look across Castle

Street to an ornate building with a clock tower rising above it. Constructed in a mix of Scottish baronial, European and Gothic styles, this building was designed by William Landless in the 1870s as the Glasgow Blind Asylum. Among other things, at the base of the clock tower, it features a sculpture by Charles B. Grassby, of Christ restoring the sight of a blind child. The Glasgow Blind Asylum was founded in 1804, and provided education to blind people so they could earn an independent living. This included teaching them to be musicians and providing training in different trades. One of the early supporters of this institution was John Alston who, among other things, invented a method to allow blind people to read, first using knots in chords and then using raised letters. He published his alphabet in 1836 and even created an entire bible in it in 1840, using the asylum's own printing press. This system was used beyond Glasgow, including in the School for the Blind in Paris before it was replaced by Braille. In the 1930s, this building was incorporated into the neighbouring Glasgow Royal Infirmary.

Former Glasgow Blind Asylum Building designed by William Landless, built in 1870s.

32. Descend onto Castle Street and cross it at the traffic lights in front of the former Glasow Blind Asylum Building. From here, turn right and head south past the buildings of Glasgow Royal Infirmary. As you do so, keep an eye out for a large plaque commemorating the initiation of antiseptic surgery in the 1860s by Joseph Lister, when he was working as a surgeon at this institution. This was a major advancement in medical science, and in many ways it marks the birth of one of the most important aspects of modern medicine.

33. From the Lister plaque, carry on south down Castle Street before crossing it at the traffic lights directly in front of the main building of Glasgow Royal Infirmary. Once you reach the opposite side of the road, turn and look back at this building as it is only from this position that you can really take in its immense size and grandeur. Glasgow Royal Infirmary received its royal charter in 1791, and opened a few years later in 1794, with the original buildings designed by Robert Adam. Most of the current buildings, however, date from the late 1890s and early 1900s, when the hospital underwent a major redevelopment. They were designed by James Miller in a neo-baroque style with Scottish baronial details and, at the time, they were at the forefront of hospital design. This included an emphasis on cleanliness (reflecting, no doubt, the hospital's links with Lister) and minimising noise, as well as technological developments, such as the use of X-rays. Over the years, Glasgow Royal Infirmary has been deeply involved in the advancement of medicine. This includes Lister's development of antiseptic surgery in the 1860s, the introduction of sterilisable white coats for doctors by William Macewen in 1875, John Macintyre's creation of the world's first Radiography (X-ray) Department in 1896, and the development of diagnostic ultrasound by Ian Donald in the 1950s. It was also where

Rebecca Strong developed and introduced modern training for nurses when she was matron from 1879 to 1884.

34. From Glasgow Royal Infirmary, walk south down the west side of Castle Street. As you do so, on your left, to the south of the hospital, you will see the Cathedral Precinct, with Glasgow Cathedral at its far end, and the city's Necropolis on the hill behind it. These will both be visited later in this walk. On Castle Street, at the entrance to the precinct, you will see a statue of David Livingstone. Born in Blantyre, to the south of Glasgow, in 1813, Livingstone is most well known as an explorer and missionary in Africa. While he was strongly anti-slavery, his explorations also opened up much of central Africa to European colonial expansion and colonisation. He died in what is now modern-day Zambia in 1873, and while his heart was buried under a tree near the spot where he died, his body was returned to Britain and he was eventually buried in Westminster Abbey.

35. To the south of the David Livingstone statue is the Saint Mungo Museum of Religious Life and Art. Despite its appearance, it is a rather modern building which first opened in 1993. Its design, by Ian Begg, pays homage to the medieval Bishop's Castle which formerly occupied the same site. This museum explores the importance of religion in the lives of people across the world and at different times in history, and is free to visit.

36. Opposite the Saint Mungo Museum, on the west side of Castle Street, is the Provand's Lordship. Built in 1471, this is the oldest house in Glasgow. As with many other historic buildings and museums run by the City of Glasgow, it is free to visit. It was originally built as part of the St Nicholas Hospital by Andrew Muirhead, who, at the time, was the Bishop of Glasgow. Behind it, is Saint Nicholas Garden which was established in 1995 and features, among other things, herbs and plants commonly used in medieval medicine. The garden is also home to the Tontine Heads, a collection of thirteen heads carved onto keystones, which were part of Glasgow's original town hall at Glasgow Cross (and to which the Tolbooth Steeple was once attached). They are called the Tontine Heads after the Glasgow Tontine Society which took over this building in 1781. The heads come from a range of time periods, but the oldest were sculpted by David Carlton between 1737 and 1742, and are thought to represent theatrical masks. The meaning of the other, later ones, is less clear and they may represent subjects such the Green Man (an image which is a surprisingly common motif on Glasgow's buildings), caricatures of specific people or advertising for American tobacco through the depiction of an individual wearing a native American headdress. Originally, there were ten of these heads, but in 1869, they were removed from the old town hall and were later reused on a new warehouse on Buchanan Street. At this time a further four were created in a similar style to the original ones by William James Maxwell. In 1888, this new building was destroyed in a fire, and although most of the masks were saved, one

Four oldest Tontine Heads, created between 1737 and 1742.

of the original ones was lost. It was not until the 1970s that all the remaining heads were brought together once more and they were finally moved to their current location in 1994.

37. From the Provand's Lordship, cross Castle Street at the nearby traffic lights and head towards Cathedral Square, the open area to the south of the Saint Mungo Museum. At the entrance to this square is one of Glasgow's remaining police boxes, and it is one of only four still in their original locations. These police boxes were designed by Gilbert Mackenzie Trench in 1928, and provided a way for both patrolling policemen and members of the public to contact the local police station. This particular box dates from the 1930s.

38. Around Cathedral Square are a number of statues. This includes the 1893 statue of the merchant James Arthur, which is situated just behind the Saint Mungo Museum, the 1881 statue of the Reverand Norman MacLeod, to the north of the police box, and a statue of King William III mounted on horseback, which was presented to Glasgow by James Macrae. This last statue was originally sited in front of the Tontine Hotel, close to the start of this walk, but it was moved first in 1897, to a location outside the new Glasgow Cross Railway Station, and then again in 1926, to its current location. At the time Macrae donated the King William III statue to Glasgow, he was the Governor of Madras in India and was famous for his naval exploits against the Irishman Edward England, whose flag, featuring a skull and crossed bones is now synonymous with pirates in popular culture. However, the symbol itself is much older and is an example of one of the many memento mori, or reminders of death, which can often be found on seventeenth- and eighteenth-century Scottish gravestones. Indeed, you can find examples of it on gravestones in the graveyards surrounding Glasgow Cathedral, which you will visit near the end of this walk.

39. Walk diagonally across Cathedral Square in a south-eastern direction. On the far side, you will find the former Barony North Church. This impressive building was designed in an Italianate style by John Honeyman in 1878, and features sculptures of Saint Paul (holding a sword) and Saint Peter (holding keys) in niches at either end, with sculptures of Saints Mathew (with the head of a man at his feet), Mark (above the head of a lion), Luke (above the head of a calf) and John (above the head of an eagle) along the balustrade connecting the two towers.

40. Head north along the eastern edge of Cathedral Square, and set into the wall surrounding the church, you will find a large memorial to Townhead martyrs James Nisbet, James Lawson and Alexander Wood. They were three of twelve Covenanters executed by the Government of the day at Howgate in 1684. The Covenantors were members of a seventeenth-century Scottish political and religious movement, with its origins in a dispute between James VI and his son Charles I, over the structure of the Church and its doctrine. Following the Bishops' Wars

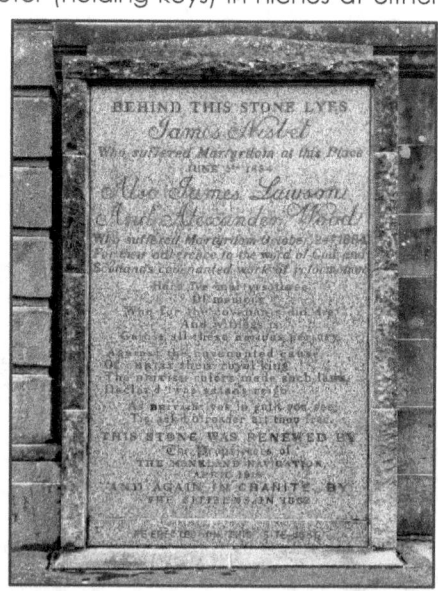

Memoral to Townhead martyrs of 1864.

of 1639 and 1640, the Covenantors took control of Scotland. After Charles I's execution in England in 1649, the Covenanter Government in Scotland restored his son, Charles II, to the throne of Scotland, bringing them into conflict with the forces of Oliver Cromwell. Charles II was restored to the throne of England in 1660, which, in turn, led to the persecution of his one-time Covenanter supporters. The Covenanter Movement eventually came to an end in 1688 following the Glorious Revolution in Scotland, where James VII was replaced by his daughter Mary II and her husband William III (whose statue now stands on the western side of Cathedral Square) as joint monarchs of Scotland and England. This was marked by the re-establishment of the Church of Scotland as Presbyterian, rather than as a branch of the Anglican Church.

41. To the north of the Covenanters' Memorial, on the corner of Cathedral Square and John Knox Street, is a large and rather beautiful Scottish baronial style building. While it looks like a seventeenth-century Tower House (a type of small Scottish castle which could easily be defended by a limited number of people), it was not constructed until 1896, when it was designed by Campbell Douglas for the Discharged Prisoners' Aid Society. This society was established in 1856 with the aim of helping former prisoners to reintegrate successfully into wider society through 'a kindly, helpful, Christian influence'. However, help was only offered to those the society deemed respectable and excluded anyone imprisoned for theft or those with alcohol problems. The location for this building was almost certainly chosen due to its proximity to Duke Street Prison, which was the only prison in Glasgow at the time. Now a boutique hotel, it is reputed to be one of the most haunted buildings in Scotland.

42. Turn right and walk south down John Knox Street. This will take you to the gates of the Necropolis, Glasgow's main Victorian cemetery. Beside this entrance, is the James Crum Memorial Drinking Fountain, one of many such memorial fountains often linked to the Temperance Movement across Glasgow. James Crum was the owner of the Busby Cotton Mill between 1843 and 1874. The fountain was donated to the city in 1860 and was originally erected in George Square, but it was moved to this location in the early 2000s.

43. Before entering the Necropolis, walk down Ladywell Street, which branches off to the east of John Knox Street. At the end of this street is the Lady Well, referring to the Virgin Mary. Based on a natural spring, this is one of Glasgow's ancient Holy Wells. Although almost all the others have been covered up and lost, this one has survived and is now marked by a stone and cast-iron structure which has been restored several times over the years. The well itself was closed when the area to its north was converted into the Necropolis due to fears of contamination from the interred bodies.

44. Return up Ladywell Street and enter the Necropolis through the gates at its corner with John Knox Street by the Crum Memorial Fountain. The Necropolis, literally the city of the dead, was first created in 1832 to accommodate the growing population of

Lady Well, one of Glasgow's ancient Holy Wells.

Glasgow. While it contains approximately 3,500 grave monuments, it is estimated that up to 50,000 people have been buried within its boundaries. Built on the remains of an extinct volcano, it towers above much of the city, with its most prominent citizens buried in lairs (or burial plots) marked with grand monuments on its summit. Those with less money or a lower social standing were buried further down the hill, with the poorest being buried in unmarked graves at its base. While the route for this walk passes through the Necropolis on the way to its end at Glasgow Cathedral, it only visits a small portion of it and If you have the time, the site is worthy of more detailed exploration.

45. Once in the Necropolis, turn right, and walk along the curving path leading east along the base of the hill, The path curves gradually towards the north-east, and then forks. The right-hand fork is paved, whereas the left-hand fork is covered with grass. Take the grassy, left-hand fork and search the slope to your left for a tall, Celtic style cross nestled among the trees, just beyond the end of the low retaining wall. This is the grave of Alexander McCall, the Chief Constable of Glasgow, who died in 1888. McCall's chief clerk was William Mackintosh, the father of the renowned Glasgow architect Charles Rennie Mackintosh, and the design of this gravestone was one of the first professional commissions which the younger Mackintosh undertook when he was just twenty years old.

46. Follow the grassy path up towards the north-east. At the next junction, turn left, and then right onto the path which runs east along the base of the hill. As you walk along this new path, keep your eye out on the left for a small path leading up to a set of steps which will take you to the top of the hill. As you climb these steps, you can see blocks of exposed basalt which make up the extinct volcano on which the Necropolis is built. At the top of these steps, turn left and head towards the mausoleum perched on the edge of the hill. This mausoleum is one of the largest, most prominent and most ornate in the whole of the Necropolis. Designed by David Cousin, it was built for Archibald Douglas Monteath, who was buried here in 1842. Its design is based on the Knights Templar Church of the Holy Sepulchre and is one of the few non-classical monuments within the cemetery. Monteath served in the military in India, and it is rumoured that much of the fortune with which he returned to Scotland was obtained by relieving a maharajah's elephant of its cargo of precious gems, although whether there is any truth in this story is unknown.

Monteath Mausoleum, on top of extinct volcano, Glasgow's Necropolis.

47. From the Monteath Mausoleum, follow the path as it curves around to the north. When you reach the next junction, take the set of steps which leads up the hill to the right. Above you, you will see the Knox Monument. Designed by Thomas Hamilton and featuring a statue by William Warren, it was built in the 1820s, before the Necropolis was opened and it was the first public statue of John Knox, the sixteenth-century Scottish religious reformer, to be erected in Scotland. From the

base of the statue, there are panoramic views across much of Glasgow, with the East End stretching off to your left, while the central and western parts of the city stretch off to the right. In the distance stand the Kilpatrick Hills, which line the northern side of the upper Clyde Estuary.

48. Head north-east along the grassy path which leads away from the Knox Memorial and you will come to a small cluster of ornate, and mostly classically inspired, monuments and mausoleums. Take the steps to the left of these monuments and start working your way down the hill. As you do so, in the far distance, you can see Dumgoyne, a rounded hump at the western end of the Campsie Fells which lie to the north to Glasgow. This is the remains of another extinct volcano, and is one of a string of similar hills across central Scotland. Many of these were used as the sites of forts and castles dating back hundreds and even thousands of years, including some you can still see to this day, such as Dumbarton Castle, Stirling Castle and Edinburgh Castle. Closer to you are the imposing buildings of Glasgow Royal Infirmary. At this point, it is worth considering that these hospital buildings look out directly onto one of the city's largest cemeteries, which might not have been the most comforting sight for those seeking treatment within it.

49. At the base of the first set of steps, turn to the right and then at the next junction turn left down the path which will take you down to the bottom of the hill. When you reach it, turn left and walk along the path which runs parallel to the fence between the Necropolis and Wishart Street. Along this path, you will find the William Wallace Memorial. This memorial was erect in 2016 to mark Wallace's 1297 victory in the Battle o' the Bell o' the Brae, which took place near the area now occupied by the Bell o' the Brae tenements on High Street.

50. From the William Wallace Memorial, carry on south along the path and follow it up the hill to the main entrance of the Necropolis. At this point, turn right and cross the Bridge of Sighs, which forms part of the grand processional way designed by David and James Hamilton, and built in the 1830s to link the Cathedral to the new cemetery. As such, it formed a key part of the final journey from the city of the living to the city of the dead. The Bridge of Sighs crosses Molendinar Ravine, where the Molendinar Burn, Glasgow's third river (after the Clyde and the Kelvin) once flowed. It was

David and James Hamilton's 1830s Grand Processional, linking Necropolis and Glasgow Cathedral via Bridge of Sighs over Molendinar Ravine.

beside this stream that Saint Mungo established his original religious settlement in the sixth century, which would eventually grow into the city of Glasgow many centuries later.

51. After you have crossed the Bridge of Sighs, carry on up the Hamiltons' Grand Processional towards the gates at the entrance to the Cathedral Precinct. These ornate gates were created by Thomas Eddington and feature, as a centrepiece, the coat of arms of the Merchants' House of Glasgow and the text 'William Brown of Kilmardinny, Dean of Guild MDCCCXXXVII'. The Dean of Guild was an ancient organisation consisting of a group of burgh magistrates which, by the nineteenth century, was concerned primarily with building controls within Glasgow. Born in 1792, William Brown was a Scottish merchant and philanthropist who inherited his father's oil and paint company in 1813. He greatly expanded the company and extended its reach into new oil-based products, such as lubricants and fuel. Unfortunately, he became embroiled in the railway boom of the 1840s and lost a great deal of money when this speculative bubble burst in the 1850s. As well as through hard work, Brown owed a significant portion of his wealth to the part-ownership of a slave plantation in the West Indies. When slavery was finally abolished in the British colonies in 1838, as a slave-owner, Brown received compensation and used this money to purchase Kilmardinny House, a grand Georgian mansion to the west of the city.

52. To the north, on the far side of the Cathedral Precinct as you enter it through the William Brown gates, is the imposing edifice of the Jubilee Building of Glasgow Royal Infirmary. Designed in a beaux-arts style by James Miller, it was intended to commemorate the diamond jubilee of Queen Victoria in 1897, and over its entrance, it features a statue of the queen herself created by Albert Hemstock Hodge. Despite all this, the foundation stone was not laid until 1907, and it was only officially opened in 1914, by George V, some seventeen years after the jubilee it was intended to mark, and thirteen years after the queen had died. This was also three years after the death of her successor, Edward VII. Among other things, the Jubilee Building houses a small museum dedicated to the history of Glasgow Royal Infirmary, which is well worth visiting.

53. To the east of the Jubilee Building, and to the north of the cathedral is the cathedral's St Mungo Old Burial Ground, with burials dating back to the 1500s. Sandwiched between the cathedral and the Glasgow Royal Infirmary, some of its graves feature iron cages designed to thwart the actions of body snatchers who tried to dig up the recently interred and sell the bodies to anatomists in nearby medical schools for dissection. One example of this can be seen along the wall just to the east of the entrance to the Old Burial Ground. Further east along this same wall, and incorporated into it, you can also find an example of a skull and crossbones memento mori of the type which formed the basis for Edward England's pirate flag. Further east again, is a rather unusual grave memorial, consisting not of stone, but of ceramic tiles fixed to the cemetery wall, This marks the burial site of a slater by the name of Alexander Smith.

Skull and crossbones memento mori on old gravestone.

54. Finally, turn your attention to Glasgow's magnificent Gothic cathedral. Built in 1197, it is not only the oldest building in Glasgow and the birthplace of the city itself, it is also the oldest cathedral in mainland Scotland. The current building was constructed on the site of the first stone cathedral which was built in 1136 and was centred on the tomb of Saint Mungo, the founder and patron saint of the city. While it was 'cleansed' of most of its alters and sculptures during the Scottish Reformation in the sixteenth century, and its roof stripped of lead, the building itself was retained for Protestant worship, and towards the end of the 1500s, the town council stepped

in to repair and modify it. As a result, Glasgow Cathedral survived the Reformation relatively unscathed in comparison to many other ancient cathedrals in Scotland. As well as marking the foundation of the city, the cathedral itself is also the last resting place for many of those who would have considered themselves the highest echelons of the city, including archbishops and Lord Provosts. It also includes memorials to a number of Glasgow's now infamous Tobacco Lords of the eighteenth century, whose fortunes, built primarily on slave-produced tobacco, helped transform Glasgow into the grand city of trade and industry it became by the end of the nineteenth century.

12. Alexandra Parade and Dennistoun

Start Point: St Andrew's East Parish Church at the junction between Cumbernauld Road and Alexandra Parade, Glasgow (**Location:** Lat/Lon: 55.86280, -4.20837; What3Words: ///flats.chief.tune; Plus Code: VQ7R+4M6 Glasgow). **Nearest Public Transport:** Subway: None; Train: Alexandra Parade Station (5 mins); Bus: Alexandra Parade (2 mins).

End Point: The junction between Duke Street and High Street in central Glasgow (**Location:** Lat/Lon: 55.86030, -4.23980; What3Words: ///assist.tame.flank; Plus Code: VQ66+438 Glasgow). **Nearest Public Transport:** Subway: None; Train: High Street Station (5 mins); Bus: High Street (1 min).

Distance: 4.0 kilometres/2.5 miles. **Time:** Allow 2.5 to 3.5 hours for this walk.
Level of Difficulty: Easy. While relatively long, this walk is entirely on paved surfaces. Although there are some steep hills, the route is primarily downhill rather than up.

Facilities: There are plenty of shops, cafes, bars and restaurants where you can stop for refreshments along this route, particularly on the Alexandra Parade and Duke Street sections. Publicly accessible toilets are available in Dennistoun Public Library around two-thirds of the way along the route.

Introduction

Dennistoun is a relatively large area in the East End of Glasgow which borders High Street and Castle street in the city centre on its western edge, and spreads eastwards along Duke Street. This street was established in the 1790s as the result of a proposal from the Carron Company to provide a more direct route between their iron foundry in Falkirk and the city of Glasgow. Originally called Carntyne Road, it was later renamed Duke Street after the Duke of Montrose. It is officially considered both Glasgow's and Scotland's longest street, although it is debatable whether this title should go to Duke Street or to Argyle Street in the West End, which is slightly longer, but which some do not consider a single, continuous street. Dennistoun itself was established by the merchant and banker Alexander Dennistoun who owned a property on Golf Hill to the east of the city centre. He gradually bought up the neighbouring estates, including Craig Park, Whitehill, Meadow Park and Wester Craigs (names which are now more commonly associated with streets in Dennistoun). Then in 1854, less than a decade after the area was finally incorporated into the City of Glasgow, Dennistoun employed the architect James Salmon Snr to develop the lands he now owned as a garden suburb, laid out with a grid of streets, terraces and drives, and populated by large villas. These plans were never fully enacted and Dennistoun was never able to attract the rich merchants and professionals it was originally intended to attract. This may have been because, being east of the city, the prevailing winds would have carried the pollution produced by the growing city across it rather than away from it, as was the case for the more successful suburbs such as Pollokshields to the south and the Park District to the west. Despite this, Dennistoun still thrived, and found its own niche as a respectable area for working-class families, and this may have saved its many Victorian buildings from the destructive urban redevelopment plans of the post-war years, which decimated the architecture of many other working-class areas of the city.

1.
Alexandra Parade
1
2
3
4
5
6
7
8
9
10
11
12
13
14
15
16
17
18
19

2.
Alexandra Parade
The Necropolis
Duke Street
7
8
9
10
11
12
13
14
15
16
17
18
19
20
21
22
23
24
25
26
27
28
29
30
31
32
33
34
35
36
37
38
39
40

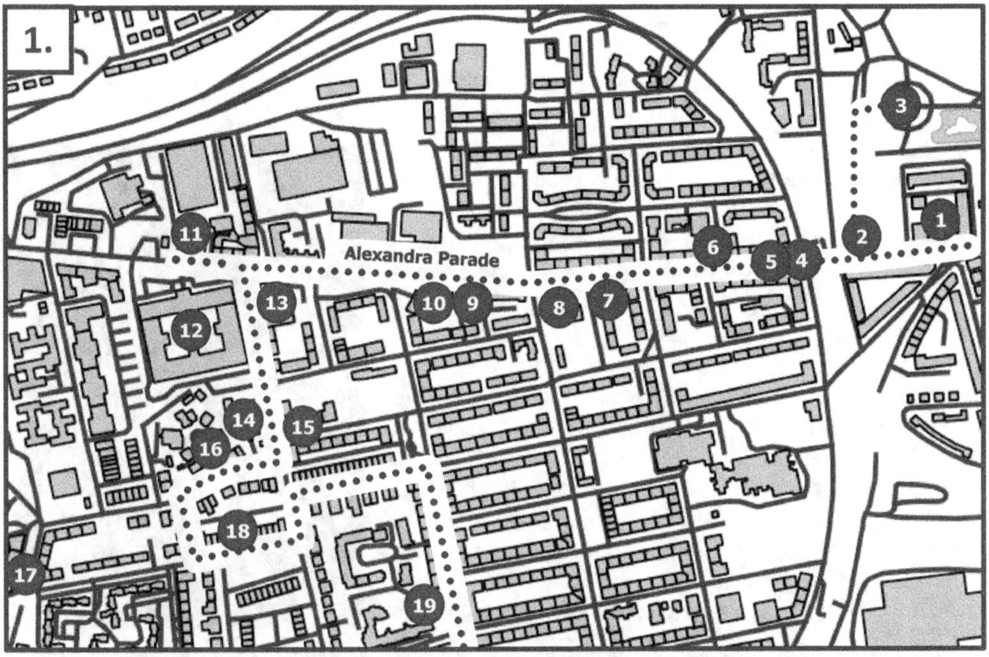

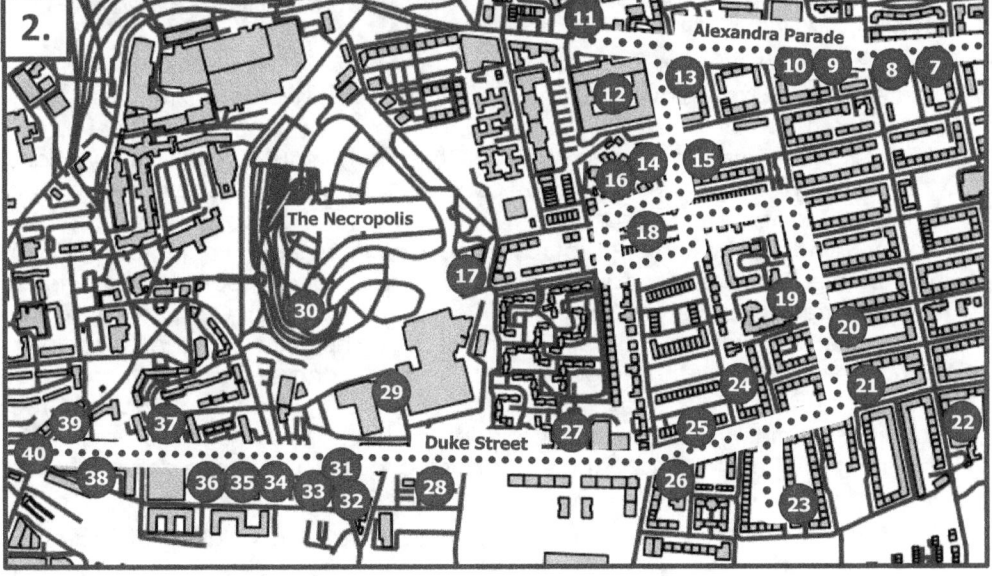

1. This walk starts at St Andrew's East Parish Church at the junction between Cumbernauld Road and Alexandra Parade, which is best viewed from the southern side of Alexandra Parade. The church was designed by James Miller in a mix of Gothic and arts and crafts stye, and was built in 1903. Its neighbouring hall, which is in the Glasgow style, was designed by James Salmon Jnr and John Gaff Gillespie, and was built a few years earlier in 1899. This hall features a rather wonderful art nouveau style sculpture above its left-hand door consisting of a set of three angels labelled Faith, Hope and Love. Between them is an inscription which states 'Greatest of these is love'.

2. From St Andrew's Parish Church, cross Alexandra Parade at the traffic lights and walk west along it to the entrance of Alexandra Park. Named after the wife of the future King Edward VII, it was opened in 1870. Outside the gates is an ornate cast-iron drinking fountain, complete with a central putto, which is identical to the putti on a number of other fountains around Glasgow, including at Govan Cross and in Kelvingrove Park. Hidden within the canopy are a series of rather cute crocodiles, which may be a reference to the seventeenth-century fashion for having a crocodile hanging from the ceiling of cabinets of curiosity. This, in turn, seems to have been inspired by a tradition going back as far as Ancient Egypt of hanging a dead crocodile over the entrance of a building to ward off evil. The cast-iron benches beside the fountain are worth examining as they feature some rather beautiful lion's head armrests.

Crocodile hidden in canopy of drinking fountain outside Alexandra Park.

3. Enter Alexandra Park through the main gates. A short distance into the park, to the east of the main avenue, is the Saracen Fountain. This is a much grander fountain which was designed by David Watson Stevenson, and was made by Walter MacFarlane & Co. at their Saracen Foundry for the 1901 Glasgow International Exhibition. The Saracen Foundry was world-famous for the quality of its decorative ironwork, and while it is in need of restoration, you can see from this fountain why this was the case. At the bottom are four seated figures, representing Science (holding a retort), Literature (with an open book on her lap), Commerce (seated on a model ship) and Art (with a theatrical mask by her right foot and a lyre on her left-hand side). Below these figures are with shell arches surrounding lion heads. Above this, is a model of the Choragic Monument of Lysicrates, an ancient Greek monument dating from 335 BCE, surrounded by the signs of the zodiac at its base and a ring of putti at the top. At the apex of the fountain are three dolphinfish with intertwined tails supporting a quatrefoil bowl.

4. From the Saracen Fountain, return to Alexandra Parade, turn right and head west to its junction with Alexandra Park Street. On the opposite side of Alexandra Park Street are two quite different, but equally fine, buildings. On the northern side is a blonde sandstone tenement with bay windows topped by French Renaissance style roofs with ironwork crests, a feature known as 'brattishing', while on the southern side is a red sandstone tenement with a rather wonderful corner turret

topped by a Glasgow style ogee dome. This is very much in keeping with the Glasgow tradition of having domed towers on buildings at important crossroads throughout the city.

5. Using the traffic lights, cross Alexandra Park Street to the south-western corner of this junction so you can walk west along the south side of Alexandra Parade. This will give you a better view of the blonde sandstone tenement on the north side of the street. If you look between the first-floor windows at the right-hand end of this building, you can see a set of metal rosettes fixed to the wall. These once held the supports for the electric wires which ran down the middle of the street to power trams running along tracks set into the road. As you pass the No. 656, on the south side, it is worth pausing to examine the decorative art nouveau style tiles at its entrance (but please do not go into the close itself as this is a private building). These are just one of many different designs of rather beautiful tenement tiles which can be found in the communal stairwells of tenements throughout Dennistoun.

Imposing French style blonde sandstone tenement, corner of Alexandra Parade and Alexandra Park Street.

6. Carry on along Alexandra Parade until you are opposite the junction with Wood Street. On either side of Wood Street are traditional sandstone tenements. On the right, the tenements date from 1874 and are built from blonde sandstone, while those on the left, built a few years later in 1891, are made from red sandstone. This reflects the major shift in the construction materials used for Glasgow buildings which took place around 1890. Before this, most were constructed with blonde sandstone from local quarries in Giffnock and Bishopbriggs. However, as these quarries became exhausted, builders started looking further afield for alternatives. This coincided with the expansion of the railways, allowing red sandstone to be transported longer distances from Ayrshire and Dumfriesshire in a cost-effective manner. Within a very short space of time, this new sandstone became the construction material of choice, especially for the many tenements built across the city in the 1890s, 1900s and 1910s, changing the dominant colour of Glasgow's buildings from blonde to red. However, due to industrial pollution and smoke from domestic fires, many of these buildings soon became caked in soot and dirt, and this new colour disappeared beneath a layer of blackness. It was only in the 1980s that a campaign to clean Glasgow's buildings was initiated, thus revealing the beautifully coloured stonework which lay hidden beneath nearly a century's worth of grime. This cleaning also revealed many decorative features on tenements, including decorative carvings on lintels above windows, an example of which can be seen on the blonde sandstone tenement to the east of Wood Street, and decorative date plaques, such as the one on the red sandstone building to its west, which features a crown with a phoenix rising out of it (which can be seen above the entrance to No. 599).

7. Continue to 576 Alexandra Parade, where you will find a metal grate filled with small squares of glass set into the pavement at the base of the building. This is an example of a prismatic cellar light. They are so named because the glass squares are actually semi-prisms designed to bend light into the darkest recesses of the cellars beneath the buildings, allowing them to be illuminated without the need for an artificial lights. Also known as 'pavement lights', these were developed in the nineteenth century and were once a common feature on Glasgow's streets. However, their usage declined after cheap electric lighting started to become widely available at the start of the twentieth century and many have now been lost.

8. Further west on the south side of Alexandra Parade is the former Alexandra Parade Public School (now home to the Alexandra Parade Primary School). Designed by the wonderfully named MacWhannel and Rogerson in a restrained art nouveau style, it was built in the 1890s. Of particular note is the beautiful art nouveau/Glasgow style font used to inscribe the school's name on its facade. This is just one example of the large variety of unique and interesting fonts used for Glasgow's public schools between the 1880s and the 1920s. It is always worth keeping an eye out for these as you travel around the city.

Nameplate of Alexandra Parade Public School, in art nouveau style font.

9. A short distance beyond the school is the exposed gable wall of a red sandstone tenement. These are a common site across Glasgow and often mark the site where the tenement building which once stood there has been demolished. Although some were lost as a result of bombing during the Clydebank Blitz in 1941 (when Glasgow was also heavily targeted), many are the result of the widespread destruction of tenements in the 1960s, '70s and '80s. In an attempt to improve the quality of housing in Glasgow, swaths of tenements were demolished and residents were moved to new high-rise developments and housing schemes in other parts of the city, as well as to new towns, such as East Kilbride, constructed beyond the city's limits. While well-intentioned, in retrospect, this is generally seen as a major urban planning failure. Many of the high-rise developments suffered from poor maintenance, and most have now been demolished, whereas the tenements they were meant to replace remain standing. Similarly, the suburban housing schemes and new towns were designed primarily with cars rather than people in mind, and the lack of public transport led to the creation of urban 'traps', where people were isolated from access to services and jobs, resulting in high levels of unemployment and social deprivation which, in some instances, persists to this day. However, there are other, perhaps more interesting, reasons why some gap sites exist in Glasgow. For example, in October 1878, the City of Glasgow Bank

collapsed, owing a sum worth over half a billion pounds in today's money. At the time, the bank's 1,200 shareholders faced unlimited liability, and so were liable for this debt, leading to the financial ruin of almost all of them. In addition, many Glasgow businesses that held accounts with the bank also failed. This included a number of construction companies, leaving long-standing gaps in the city's streets where planned buildings were never erected. Another major shock to tenement building in Glasgow was Lloyd George's 1909-1910 budget. This introduced a land value tax which, pretty much overnight, made tenements uneconomic to build, causing projects to be abandoned mid-construction and resulting in long-standing gaps in the city's streetscapes. This was the case for this particular gap site, and the tenement planned for it prior to this 1909-1910 budget, which would have completed the previously constructed block to its east, remains unbuilt to this day.

10. Carry on further west to No. 504. Here you will find one of the finest examples of an art nouveau style tile design anywhere in Glasgow. The communal entrances and stairwells of tenements, known locally as 'closes', were often lined with tiles, both on the floor and on the walls, in order to make them easy to keep clean. Colloquially known as 'wally closes' ('wally' is the Scots word referring to anything made from china), these often featured highly decorative and colourful

Art nouveau style decorative tiles, entrance to tenement close, 504 Alexandra Parade.

tiles, many of which were art nouveau in origin. Although relatively few wally closes still exist in their original form, they are always worth keeping an eye out for as they are beautiful examples of late-Victorian design. However, please do not venture into the closes themselves as these are private areas of people's homes.

11. At 389 Alexandra Parade is a rather unusual-looking brick building. Constructed in a simple art deco style, this was once an electrical substation and at the time it was constructed, a lot of effort was put into ensuring that such buildings blended in with their surroundings as much as possible. As a result, across Glasgow, you will find substations housed in buildings made from red sandstone, in art deco style brick buildings and even in mock-tenements.

12. Opposite the former substation, on the south side of Alexandra Parade, is a much grander art deco style building. This is the former Wills Tobacco Factory. Designed and built by the Engineers' Office of Imperial Tobacco Company in the 1940s, it was one of the last major art deco buildings constructed in Glasgow. The factory closed in the early 1990s, and it lay unused for many years, apart from a brief stint as the production office for the movie *Trainspotting*, which although set in Edinburgh was filmed primarily in Glasgow. However, it was now been given a new lease of life as office space.

13. From the former Wills Tobacco Factory, head south down Craigpark. On the left as you turn down this street, is a blonde sandstone building with a rather impressive relief sculpture on its facade which features a pair of mermaids. This is the former Dennistoun Baths Club, which opened in 1884 as a private members swimming and

bathing club. It finally closed in 1993 and was turned into a snooker club, where the professional snooker player Alan McManus used to practise.

14. Further south along Craigpark is Our Lady of Good Counsel Church, which was built in 1974 from a designed by Gillespie, Kidd & Coia. Gillespie, Kidd & Coia was founded in 1927 and went on to become one of the most famous Scottish architectural firms of the mid-twentieth century. They were particularly well-known for their application of modernism to churches and other religious buildings, such as St Peter's Seminary in Cardross. Despite their preference for modernist architecture, the roots of Gillespie, Kidd & Coia can be traced back to the 1830s through a series of well-known and well-respected Glasgow architects, all of whom have left their mark on the city. It started with James Salmon Snr who established a practice in Glasgow in 1830 and was instrumental in the planning of a series of ornamental villas and terraced townhouses for what would become the new suburb of Dennistoun, although very few of his plans ever came to fruition. He was joined in this firm by his son, William Forrest Salmon, to become Salmon and Son, and then by his grandson, James Salmon. In 1891, John Gaff Gillespie, who, along with James Salmon Jnr, designed a number of notable Glasgow style buildings in the city (including the hall of the St Andrew's East Parish Church at the start of this walk), joined the firm, and in 1903, it changed its name to Salmon & Son & Gillespie. By the time William Alexander Kidd became a partner in 1918, James Salmon Jnr had left and it had become Gillespie & Kidd. On Gillespie's death, a young architect by the name of Giacomo Antonio, better known as Jack, Coia joined the firm and when Kidd died in 1928, he inherited the practice which was by then known as Gillespie, Kidd & Coia. The firm was gradually wound down after Coia died in 1981, and it was finally dissolved in 1987, ending over a 150 years of influence on the city of Glasgow and elsewhere, which saw architectural tastes shift from classical, through Scottish baronial, art nouveau and the Glasgow style, Edwardian baroque, art deco and into the modernist era of the mid-twentieth century.

15. Opposite Our Lady of Good Counsel, and contrasting sharply with its modernist style, is a more traditional red sandstone tenement, with a corner tower topped by a crenellated parapet. Such corner towers, consisting of a column of circular or near-circular bay windows, topped by battlements, domes or cone-shaped roofs, are a key part of Glasgow's architecture and seem to have grown out of the Scottish baronial style of the Victorian Era. When this Scottish baronial style was mixed with sinuous lines of the Art Nouveau Movement from continental Europe, it gave birth to the very distinctive and beautiful Glasgow style espoused by the likes of Charles Rennie Mackintosh, James Salmon Jnr, John Gaff Gillespie and other graduates from the Glasgow School of Art.

16. From Craigpark, turn right onto Circus Drive and head west to the corner with Broompark Circus. Here, you will find a large Franco-Gothic style villa, which was originally called Highfield, and which may have been one of the large villas

Franco-Gothic style Highfield, possibly original villa designed for planned garden suburb of Dennistoun.

designed by James Salmon Snr for the new suburb of Dennistoun in the 1850s. However, this attribution is far from certain, and it has also been attributed to John Gordon. Dennistoun was just one of a number of similar garden suburbs planned for the rapidly expanding Glasgow of the mid-nineteenth century, but unlike others, such as Pollokshields on the south of the city, it was only partially realised and Circus Drive and Broompark Circus are the only survivors of this original plan.

17. From Broompark Circus, the main walk turns left off Circus Drive and heads south down Broompark Street. However, if you wish, there is an optional detour to head further west to the end of Circus Drive and turn left onto Firpark Terrace (which is set on the small hill above of Ark Lane and runs parallel to it). Here, in a tenement at 2 Firpark Terrace and marked by a metal plaque, was the home of Charles Rennie Mackintosh from the ages of seven to twenty-four (between 1875 and 1892). Mackintosh would go on to become Glasgow's most famous and influential architect, and a major proponent of the Glasgow style of architecture and design. If you take this optional detour, return east along Broompark Drive to its junction with Broompark Street.

18. From Broompark Street, turn east on to Broompark Drive, where you will find a series of unusual and distinctive townhouses constructed towards the end of the 1800s. Once you reach Craigpark, turn left, cross it and then head east along Onslow Drive, past another series of grand townhouses, until you reach Whitehill Street. Turn south and head down Whitehill Street. As you do so, you will notice a change in the surrounding building types from townhouses to tenements. Thus, between Broompark Circus and Whitehill Street, you have seen examples of the three main phases in the typical development cycle of many areas of Victorian Glasgow, starting with the construction of individual villas on the edge of the city, before shifting to the construction of grand townhouses and finally, tenements as the growing city expanded and engulfed them.

19. About halfway down Whitehill Street on the right is a small park which contains a statue of the famous American Wild West showman William Frederick Cody, better known as Buffalo Bill. This may seem an odd statue to have been erected in Glasgow, but it is a reminder of the visit of Buffalo Bill's Wild West Show to the city between November 1891 and February 1892, much to the delight of many Glaswegians. The statue was erected in 2006 and was unveiled on the 115th anniversary of Buffalo Bill's first Scottish show. The park containing the statue is surrounded by an old red sandstone wall, with inscriptions on a number of its piers. This is all that is left of the former Whitehill Public School (later to became Whitehill Secondary School), which was founded in 1891. The original building was demolished in 1977 after a new school was opened on nearby Onslow Drive. This school produced a number of famous Glaswegians, including the artist

Buffalo Bill statue on site of former Whitehill Public School.

Alasdair Gray, the writer Jack House (author of the *Square Mile of Murder* about a number of notorious nineteenth-century murder cases in Glasgow), the actors Ricky Fulton and Dorothy Paul, and folk singer Adam McNaughtan. McNaughtan is perhaps best known for the 'Jeely Piece' song, which was written in the 1960s about life in the new high-rise tower blocks that were springing up around Glasgow to replace the traditional low-rise sandstone tenements. In particular, it focuses on the death of the tradition of mothers throwing snacks, such as sandwiches (known as a 'piece' in Glasgow), from tenement windows to their kids playing in the street below, something that was not possible from the upper floors of a twenty-storey tower block.

20. Opposite the Buffalo Bill statue, on the corner between Whitehill Street and Findlay Drive, is a rather grand tenement building, with a particularly prominent chimney feature rising up through its floors. Dated 1887, this is not only an example of an early use of red sandstone for tenement construction, but also of the change in attitude towards the positioning of chimney flues. In earlier tenements, built in a classical style, there was a particular emphasis on symmetry and chimney flues were typically hidden behind fake windows (often mistaken for a window sealed up due to the introduction of a window tax). However, as there was a shift towards art nouveau and Glasgow style buildings, rather than being hidden, chimney flues were often made into distinctive and prominent features of the building's facade, as is the case with this particular tenement.

Prominent feature chimney, 1887 red sandstone tenement.

21. At the bottom of Whitehill Street is the former Dennistoun United Presbyterian Church. This relatively simple, but attractive, church with a tall, slender tower was originally built in 1869.

22. From Whitehill Street turn right onto Duke Street and head west along it. If you wish, before you do this, you can take an optional detour east along Duke Street to Whitevale Street, where you will find St Anne's Roman Catholic Church. This was one of the earliest buildings designed by Jack Coia, of Gillespie, Kidd & Coia, for the Catholic Church. Its brick-built Italianate style contrasts markedly with the modernist style of Our Lady of Good Counsel, visited earlier on this walk and which was created by the same practice in the 1970s. If you take this detour, return the way you came back to the junction between Duke Street and Whitehill Street before continuing west along the main route.

23. Once you reach the junction between Thomson Street and Duke Street, cross Duke Street at the traffic lights and head south down Thomas Street. Here, you will find the former Thomson Street Public School. Designed by James Thomson and built in the 1870s, this was a relatively prestigious school which charged fees around four times the level of other neighbouring schools. However, the school clearly did a good job and, in 1885, its pupils won twenty-six bursaries towards the cost of secondary education. This led to it providing its pupils with secondary, as well as

primary, education, and it was one of only thirteen public schools in Glasgow to be allowed to do so.

24. Return north to Duke Street, cross it again at the same traffic lights and the head a short distance up Craigpark to Dennistoun Public Library. This was one of a number of public libraries across Glasgow designed in an Edwardian baroque style at the start of the 1900s by James R. Rhind. It is also one of fourteen libraries across Glasgow funded, in part or in full, by philanthropic donations from the Scottish-American industrialist Andrew Carnegie, one of the richest men in the world at the start of the twentieth century. It is topped by a winged figure, designed by the sculptor William Kellock Brown, dressed in classical robes and holding an open book from which she appears to be reading. The same figure, cast from the same mould, appears on two other Glasgow libraries designed by Rhind: Hutchesontown District Library, built in 1905; and Parkhead Library, built in 1906.

Identical winged figures, top of Parkhead Library (left) and Dennistoun Library (right).

25. From Denniston Library, return to Duke Street and continue westward. A short distance further west on the north side of the road is the *Dennistoun Milestone*. Consisting of a semi-representational version of a traditional Glasgow tenement, this distinctive sculpture was designed by Jim Buckley and was created in 1991. It was commissioned by Dennistoun Community Council for Glasgow's Year of Culture in 1990.

26. Just across the road from the *Denniston Milestone*, on the corner with Annbank Street, is the distinctive Visit Dennistoun mural, which was painted in 2020. This was possibly the first in a growing trend across Glasgow of local communities using murals to highlight and promote their local areas. Similar murals can now be found in Battlefield, Govanhill, Mount Florida and Partick, and bring a much-needed splash of colour to the city's streets.

27. Cross to the southern side of Duke Street at the traffic lights at its junction with Westercraigs and Bellgrove Street, and then continue west to the former Duke Street Hospital. Originally called the Eastern District Hospital, this grand and elaborately detailed French Renaissance style building was designed by Alfred Hessel Tiltman and was constructed in 1904. It was originally commissioned as a Poor Law hospital, which provided accommodation for the infirm and the chronically sick who could not pay for their own treatment. The Eastern District Hospital was one of three similar Poor Law hospitals opened in Glasgow on the same day, the others being the Western District Hospital in Maryhill and Stobhill Hospital in Springburn, in the north of the city.

28. Further west along Duke Street is the former Sydney Place United Presbyterian Church. Built in 1857, and designed by Peddie and Kinnear, it is one of the surprising number of churches in Glasgow constructed to resemble an Ancient Greek Temple. The first of these was St Andrew's Parish Church, close to Glasgow Cross, which was built in the 1740s, while the last was Langside Hill Church, built in 1894. A

short distance down Sydney Street, which runs alongside the church, and almost immediately behind the church itself, is the former Wellpark Institute, which was originally constructed as a Free Church School. Designed in an Italianate style, complete with a campanile or bell tower, it was built in 1867.

1857 Former Sydney Place United Presbyterian Church.

29. Return to Duke Street, turn left and head west along it once more. As you do so, you will pass the Tennent Caledonian Wellpark Brewery. Brewing on the Wellpark site can be traced back to one Robert Tennent in 1556, who believed that, thanks to the pure clean water of the Molendinar Burn, it was the perfect place for brewing beer. This makes Tennent's among the oldest businesses still in existence in Scotland. However, it was not until the 1740s that two brothers, Hugh and Robert Tennent, started brewing on a commercial basis. Shortly after this in 1745, Bonnie Prince Charlie and his army are said to have stayed at the brewery following their retreat from England, and on their way to their eventual defeat at Culloden the following year. In 1885, another member of the Tennent family, also named Hugh, discovered pilsner-style beer when on a trip to Bavaria, and on his return to Scotland, launched Britain's first ever lager, the eponymous Tennent's Lager, for which the brewery is now world-famous.

30. On the hill behind the Wellpark Brewery, you can see some of the grander monuments of the Necropolis, Glasgow's Victorian cemetery, where Hugh Tennent was buried after his death in 1890. To the west of the cemetery are the buildings of Glasgow's Royal Infirmary and the medieval Glasgow Cathedral, the city's oldest surviving building. It is likely no coincidence that Glasgow's oldest brewery and its first church lie in quite such close proximity to each other as brewing in the East End of Glasgow may well have begun as far back as the twelfth century with the monks who lived and worshipped in or near the cathedral.

31. To the south of the western end of the Wellpark Brewery is Hunter Street and on its corner with Duke Street is a particularly fine example of a Glasgow gushet tenement. Gushet tenements are ones built on a narrow strip of land between two roads and which have an angle of less than 90 degrees to at least one corner of their facade. This one was designed by John Cunningham and was built in 1897. The ground floor was once occupied by a pub, and it was likely that this was always its intended use. Such ground-floor pubs are a common feature in Glasgow tenements and they likely found such corner locations beneficial for attracting passing trade.

32. Further south on Hunter Street, next to Cunningham's gushet tenement, is another red sandstone building. It was designed by John Gordon and was built in 1901 for the potato and grain merchant J. and A. Arthur. It is particularly notable for the large, vertical sculptured panel featuring emblems and implements associated with the growing and harvesting of potatoes and grain. This is said to be the largest such decorative panel on any tenement in Glasgow.

33. On the opposite side of Hunter Street are two large metal sculptures. Called *The Tree That Never Grew*, these were created in 2010 by Jennifer Grant based on the words of a poem written by Ingrid Lees in 2004, which tells the story of Glasgow and features references to the bird, the bell, the fish and the tree from Glasgow's coat of arms.

34. Return north along Hunter Street to Duke Street and turn left onto it. A short distance west stands a very large stone building. Designed by Charles Wilson, who is probably better known for the grand townhouses he created in the West End of the city, it was opened in 1848 as the R.F. and J. Alexander's Cotton Spinning Mill. However, by 1909 it had been converted to the Great Eastern, a hotel for working men which included a 61-metre (200 foot) long roller-skating rink on its top floor. However, over time, it became a refuge for homeless people. With the original rooms subdivided by low partitions, it frequently housed over 300 men, and sometimes as many as 500. The hotel was finally closed in 2001, and in 2009, it was converted into residential flats.

35. Between the former Cotton Spinning Mill and the next road leading off Duke Street to the south runs the Molendinar Burn. Heavily overgrown, it is just visible if you peer through the iron fence which sits on top of the low wall attached to the former mill building. The Molendinar is Glasgow's third river, after the Clyde and the Kelvin, and was the centre of the original religious settlement from which Glasgow eventually evolved. Once an important source of water for people and industry, over time, it became heavily polluted as the city grew, and much of it was covered over. To the north of this point, it now runs through a tunnel beneath John Knox Street and Wishart Street, which were built at the bottom of Molendinar Ravine, while to the south it travels beneath the city's streets and buildings through a series of culverts before emerging into the Clyde at a point between the tidal weir and the Albert Bridge at Glasgow Green.

36. Just west of the Molendinar is the former Alexander's Public School. Designed by John Burnet in an early Italian Renaissance style with Greek revival detailing, it was built in 1858. Along the facade are a series of busts by the sculptor John Crawford. From left to right these are: Homer, Aristotle, an unidentified man, Shakespeare, Michelangelo and Milton. The unidentified man is believed to be James Alexander, one of the founders of the R.F. and J. Alexander's Cotton Spinning Milll on the opposite side of the Molendinar, who funded the construction of this school. Rather unusually for a Glasgow school, the name of the school is not carved into the facade, but instead is painted on.

Busts on facade of former Alexander's Public School, Duke Street.

37. On the opposite side of Duke Street from the Alexander's Public School is the Ladywell Housing Scheme, which was built in the 1960s. However, for over 150 years, this area was the site of Duke Street Prison. At the time it opened in 1798, Duke Street Prison was one of eight prisons in Glasgow, but within a relatively short space

of time, it was the only one left. While it originally housed both men and women, after a new male prison was built at Barlinnie in 1882, Duke Street became a women-only prison. This meant it was to Duke Street Prison that many Scottish Suffragettes were sent during their campaign for equal voting rights. When the prison was demolished, a cast-iron umbrella stand painted in the Suffragette colours (or as close to them as was likely to be available within a prison) was rescued from the rubble and is now housed in the Glasgow Women's

Wall of former Duke Street Prison visible within 1960s Ladywell Housing Scheme.

Library in Bridgeton. If you look along the opposite side of Duke Street at this point, you will see a low grey sandstone wall. Now much reduced in height, this was formerly part of the prison boundary wall. Another higher section of wall, which formed part of the prison itself, remains visible within the Ladywell Housing Scheme.

38. Head west again along Duke Street, and on its southern side you will come to a low brick facade with tall arched windows in it. This is one of the last remnants of the College Goods Railway Yard, which was built on the site of the original buildings of the University of Glasgow. The university was founded in 1451, and between 1460 and 1870, when it moved to its current location in the West End of the city, it was a major feature of the High Street area of Glasgow. Once the university moved out, the land was sold to the City of Glasgow Union Railway, which demolished the buildings to make way for a goods yard. This, in turn, was closed in 1968 and has now been replaced with the Collegelands Development of offices, student accommodation and a hotel.

39. Opposite the former site of the College Goods Yard is a series of tenements constructed by the Glasgow City Improvement Trust. Along with the neighbouring tenements on High Street, these are known as the Bell o' the Brae tenements (after an old name for the northern section of High Street) and were built in 1905. Constructed in a seventeenth-century Scottish style, they were probably designed by Burnet, Boston & Carruthers. If you look up at the Duke Street facade of these buildings, you can see the Improvement Trust logo which has been incorporated into the overall design.

40. Just beyond the Bell o' the Brae tenements is the junction between Duke Street and High Street, marking the western limit of Dennistoun and the location where this walk ends. This junction features buildings from many different phases of Glasgow's development, including the Bell o' the Brae City Improvement Trust tenements from the turn of the twentieth century, the modern developments of Collegelands, and the 1960s and 1970s buildings of the University of Strathclyde further west along George Street. Of particular note is the large space-themed mural on the university buildings, which celebrates the role that the University of Strathclyde now plays in the development and construction of satellites. In addition, to the south of this junction, the former Linen Bank, a beautiful little building built in 1895, now stands alone at 215 High Street as the sole survivor on its entire city block. This building was designed by William Forrest Salmon, the son of James Salmon Snr, who was engaged by Alexander Dennistoun to draw up the plans for his new eastern garden

suburb in the 1850s, and who founded the architectural firm which would, almost a century later, evolve into the legendary Gillespie, Kidd & Coia. He was also the father of James Salmon Jnr, who along with John Gaff Gillespie, designed some of the most impressive Glasgow style buildings in the city.

13. Bridgeton, the Calton and Glasgow Green

Start Point: Bridgeton Cross, Glasgow (**Location:** Lat/Lon: 55.84911, -4.22650; What3Words: ///handle.suffice.laying; Plus Code: RQXF+JCR Glasgow). **Nearest Public Transport:** Subway: None; Train: Bridgeton Station: 2 mins); Bus: London Road (2 mins).

End Point: The former Templeton Carpet Factory, Glasgow Green, Glasgow (**Location:** Lat/Lon: 55.85063, -4.23505; What3Words: ///boring.castle.ruby; Plus Code: VQ27+7X4 Glasgow). **Nearest Public Transport:** Subway: None; Train: Bridgeton Station: 10 mins); Bus: London Road (1 min).

Distance: 5.1 kilometres/4.2 miles. **Time:** Allow 2.5 to 4 hours for this walk.
Level of Difficulty: Moderate. Although this walk is entirely on relatively flat, paved surfaces, it is also quite long.

Facilities Available Along The Route: There are shops, cafes, restaurants and bars available in the area around Bridgeton Cross at the start of this walk, and along the Gallowgate section about halfway along it. There is also a cafe in the People's Palace on Glasgow Green close to the end of the walk, and a brewery with a beer garden in the former Templeton Carpet Factory at the very end. Publicly accessible toilets are available in Bridgeton Public Library in the Olympia Building near the start of the walk, and in the People's Palace near the end.

Introduction

This walk will take you through the section of the East End of Glasgow which is located between Dennistoun and the Clyde. It is centred around two streets, the Gallowgate and London Road, which meet at Glasgow Cross, the original centre of Glasgow. This area is divided into two main parts, Bridgeton and the Calton. Bridgeton started out as a small weaving village in the early 1700s that remained relatively unimportant until the Rutherglen Bridge, designed by the engineer James Watt, was built over the Clyde in the 1776, earning it the name Bridge Town (or Brig Toun in Scots). By 1846, it had grown substantially and was formally incorporated into the City of Glasgow. Like Bridgeton, the Calton started life as a weaving settlement, but unlike Bridgeton, it developed into its own burgh, with its own provost, in 1817. It too was incorporated into Glasgow in 1846. Despite these areas being close neighbours and having been incorporated into the city of Glasgow for more than 150 years, they each retain their own personality, particularly when it comes to football, Glasgow's most popular spectator sport. Specifically, Bridgeton is generally associated with Rangers, which was traditionally a Protestant team, while the Calton is more commonly associated with its bitter rivals, Celtic, which was traditionally a Catholic team. In the past, this has led to local tensions, especially when the two teams, collectively known as the Old Firm, play each other. However, despite their differences, there are similarities too. In particular, both areas are associated with high levels of social deprivation which comes with a substantial human cost. Although the average life expectancy in the most affluent areas of Scotland can be as high as eighty-two, in the Calton it is as low as fifty-four. Similarly, like many areas of the city, in the past there were also issues associated with gangs and gang violence. In particular, in the 1960s the Calton was known as 'Tongland', after the area's dominant gang, the Calton Tongs, which featured heavily in *Small Faces*, a 1995 film about life in Glasgow at this time. However, gang culture has declined substantially across the city since the 1970s, meaning the traditional Glasgow gangs are no longer the major social influence they once were.

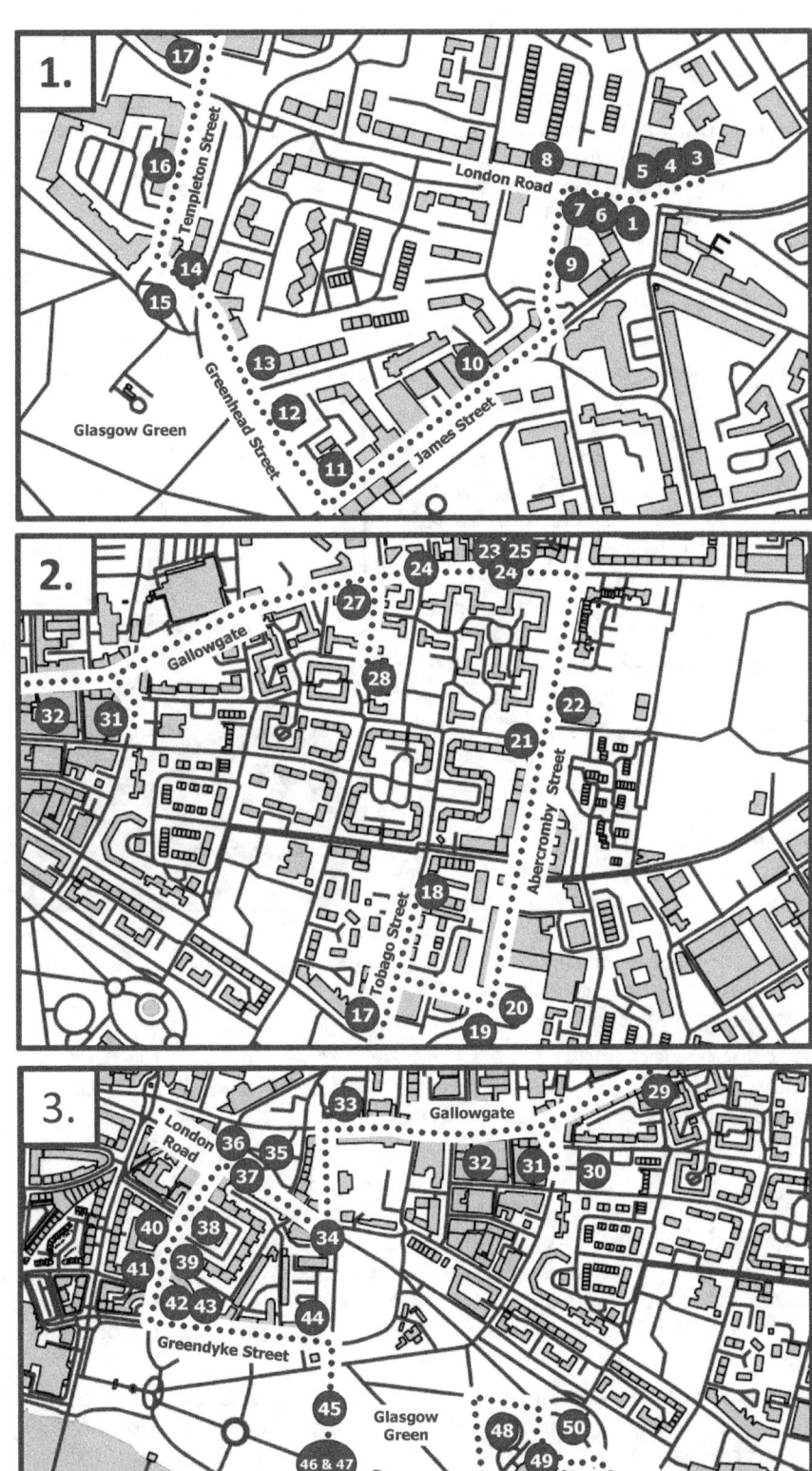

1. This walk starts at the Bridgeton Cross Shelter, a large and recently restored, decagonal cast-iron structure. Nicknamed 'the Umbrella', it was gifted to the city of Glasgow in 1874 by George Smith and Company's Sun Foundry on Port Dundas Road. While perhaps not as well-known nowadays as Walter MacFarlane's Saracen Foundry, the Sun Foundry's decorative ironwork certainly rivalled them, and in some cases surpassed them. Other examples of their work include the drinking fountain at the entrance to the nearby Alexandra Park, the cherubs surrounding the Stewart Memorial Fountain in Kelvingrove Park, and perhaps most spectacularly, the ornamental fountain in Fountain Gardens in Paisley, which includes cherubs, crocodiles and, rather unexpectedly, water-spouting walruses.

2. From the Bridgeton Cross Shelter, look to the south, where you will see Bridgeton Mansions, an impressive gushet tenement topped with a distinctive finial squeezed into the junction between Main Street and Dalmarnock Road. Designed by John Cunningham and constructed in 1896, the corner of this building bears more than a passing resemblance to the bow of a great ship, which may be a reference to the importance of shipbuilding to the economy of Glasgow. The term 'mansions' when applied to tenement buildings often creates confusion for those not from the city. Here the term does not denote a large individual dwelling, but instead refers to a building where the flats are much larger and grander than the typical Glasgow tenement, and which were aimed at more wealthy middle-class occupants. This can also be seen in other buildings across the city such as Charing Cross Mansions and Anniesland Mansions.

Distinctive finial, top of 1896 Bridgeton Mansions.

3. Cross London Road and head east along Olympia Street. At No. 13 is the former Salvation Army Hall, with its distinctive stepped roofline which resembles a fractal. It was designed by John Mailton and built in 1927.

4. Next door to the former Salvation Army Hall is the Miller's Linoleum Store, which retains its ghost sign proclaiming it as 'Scotlands [sic] Leading Linoleum House'. Invented in 1855, linoleum is a floor covering consisting of solidified linseed oil, pine resin, ground cork dust, sawdust and mineral fillers on a canvas or burlap backing. Miller's Linoleum Store was established in Glasgow 1893 by William Millard, a travelling linoleum salesman from London, and this shop opened in 1913. Now called Miller's 1893, it is currently run by Millard's great-grandsons, David and Stephen.

5. On the corner of Olympia Street, London Road and Orr Street, immediately to the west of Miller's 1893, is an imposing red sandstone building called the Olympia. Designed by George Arthur and Son in a restrained Edwardian baroque style, it has followed a fairly typical cycle for a Glaswegian entertainment venue. It started life in 1911 as the Olympia Theatre of Varieties before becoming a cinema in the 1920s.

In the 1970s, the cinema closed and it was turned into a bingo hall. After that, it served time as a furniture warehouse before lying empty for a while. In 2004, like so many empty historic buildings in Glasgow, it was hit by a serious fire in which one person was killed, and as a result, much of the building was demolished in 2011. Luckily, the facade was retained and the new building constructed behind it now serves as Bridgeton Public Library.

6. Almost immediately opposite the Olympia, at 34 London Road, is an unusual French Renaissance style tenement building. Designed by John Burnet, it was built in the 1870s to house a branch of the Glasgow Savings Bank. At the top of the ground floor at its western end are a pair of corbels decorated with some very unusual, and rather stern-looking sculpted heads, which are most likely griffins.

7. In the 1890s, the Glasgow Savings Bank moved out of 34 London Road and into a newly constructed building next door at No. 42. This distinctive red sandstone building, with classical detailing was designed by John Gordon, and is particularly notable for its tall chimneys, which give it a distinctly castle-like appearance, and the heraldic lion perched high above its main entrance. Somewhat unusually, it also features the original royal coat of arms of Scotland adopted in the twelfth century (containing the Lion Rampant on the central shield supported by a pair of unicorns, Scotland's national animal) rather than the Scottish version of the royal coat of arms of the United Kingdom, which was adopted in 1837, and which features more commonly on Victorian and Edwardian banking buildings in Glasgow.

French Renaissance style former Glasgow Savings Bank, 34 London Road, near Bridgeton Cross.

8. Further west on the opposite side of London Road is the former Bridgeton Cross Railway Station. Opened in 1872, it consists of a series of keystone arches flanked by tenement buildings and is thought to have been designed by Thomas R. Peacock. Constructed for the North British Railway, it acted as the terminus for rail services between Glasgow and Helensburgh, Dumbarton and Balloch to the west of the city. It was nationalised in 1948 and its name was changed to Bridgeton Central Station in 1954, before finally closing in 1979. However, many of the lines and tunnels which served this station still exist beneath the East End of Glasgow and it is not uncommon to peak over a low wall and find yourself staring down disused track beds. You will get the opportunity to do this later in this walk.

9. Cross to the southern side of London Road at the traffic lights at Bridgeton Cross, and then head south-east along Landrassey Street, which is to the west of the former Glasgow Savings Bank building at No. 42. A short distance along this street, is the former Bridgeton Public Library. Designed by James R. Rhind in an Edwardian baroque style, it was built in 1903, although unusually for this time it is made from blonde sandstone, rather than the red sandstone which had become more

fashionable and readily available since the 1890s. It also features some wonderful relief sculptures on its facade. It has separate entrances for adults and children, but while girls and boys were routinely segregated in schools at this time, each with their own separate entrances and playground, in libraries such as this one, they were allowed to mix. This buildings is now home to the Glasgow Women's Library, the only accredited museum in the UK dedicated to women's lives, histories and achievements, and it includes an archive and lending library. Displayed within it is the Suffragette Umbrella Stand, a cast-iron umbrella stand painted in the colours of the Suffragette movement which was recovered from Duke Street Prison when it was demolished in the 1950s, and where many Suffragette campaigners were held during their struggle for equal voting rights. At the southern end of this building is a sculpture designed by Collective Architecture to clad a lift tower and which features selected titles from the library's collection.

10. From the Glasgow Women's Library, turn right onto James Street and walk south to No. 89. This is a four-storey structure made from polychromatic bricks, typical of Glasgow's older industrial building. Designed by the wonderfully named Ninian MacWhannel, it was built in 1888 as the Greenhead Weaving Factory, which was founded by Thomas Thomson. By then, weaving had long been a staple of the economy of Glasgow's East End, with Bridgeton starting life as a weaving village called Barrowfield in 1705. Between 1906 and 1908, part of this factory was also home to the All British Car Company founded by George Johnston. However, due to design complexities, only twelve vehicles were ever completed. The Glasgow weaving industry was badly hit by the depression following World War I, and few of the firms survived this period. Subsequently many of the former weaving factories were demolished, making this a rare survivor from an important period in Bridgeton's development. In the early 2000s, it was converted into residential flats.

11. At the southern end of James Street, on its junction with Greenhead Street, is the former Logan and Johnston School for Domestic Economy. Dated 1893, the building was designed in a Scottish Renaissance style by James Thomson, and its Greenhead Street facade features a relief sculpture of a beehive, a common symbol of industriousness in the Victorian Era. One of a number of similar charitable institutions across the city, this school was founded in the 1890s by William Logan and his wife Jean Johnston, to provide assistance, education and upbringing for poor or destitute stepchildren and orphans of Scottish extraction. In particular, it focussed both on giving girls an education in elementary subjects and teaching skills, such as cooking, knitting sewing and laundry duties, required to gain employment as a domestic servant. While this may seem very outdated by today's standards, at the time it was founded, this education gave the girls who attended it the opportunity to earn an independent and respectable living, and so gain a step up in society they would

Scottish Renaissance style former Logan and Johnston School for Domestic Economy.

otherwise have been unlikely to achieve. The school closed in 1936, coinciding with the decline in the domestic service industry in Glasgow and in Scotland as a whole.

12. From the former Logan and Johnston School head west along Greenhead Street to No. 47. Designed in a classical style by Charles Wilson, it was originally known as Greenhead House and was built in 1846 for the cotton mill owner Dugald McPhail, who owned the nearby McPhail's Mill, and after whom the neighbouring McPhail Street was named. However, in 1859 it was converted into the Buchanan Institute for Destitute Children using a bequest from James Buchanan, a Glasgow merchant and philanthropist, making it another of Glasgow's charitable educational establishments which aimed to give impoverished children a better start in life. It features a prominent and beautifully crafted sculpture of a studious young scholar, which was created in 1873 by William Brodie, who is probably most famous for his statue of Greyfriars Bobby in Edinburgh.

Sculpture of young scholar by William Brodie on former Buchanan Insititue for Destitute Children.

13. Just to the west of former Buchanan Institute is the Greenhead Works, which extends north along McPhail Street as well as west along Greenhead Street. This is a collection of buildings constructed in markedly different styles between the 1840s and the 1880s. The oldest part is the polychromatic brick building on McPhail Street, which was originally known as McPhail's Mill. It was purchased in 1859 by R. and J. Dick, who were Gutta-percha merchants. Gutta-percha is a rubber-like material derived from the Gutta-percha tree which was used for many domestic and industrial purposes. The Dick brothers used it primarily to create hard-wearing waterproof soles for shoes, and to this day in Glasgow gym shoes are sometimes referred to as 'gutties'. The original building was expanded south to Greenhead Street, and then west along it by the architect George Fyfe Boyd. These ranges are designed to look like classically inspired domestic tenements, presumably to allow them to blend in with similar surrounding buildings on Greenhead Street. Much of this part of the former Greenhead Works is now abandoned with exposed gables where linking sections of the buildings have been demolished.

14. On the other side of Arcadia Street from the former Greenhead Works is a rather wonderful red sandstone tenement. Built in 1900, it has a nice example of the column of curved corner bay windows which was a common feature of Glasgow tenements from this period.

15. Between this tenement and Glasgow Green, which lies to its south, is the James Martin Memorial Fountain. Created by the MacFarlane Foundry, this elaborate fountain and canopy was erected in 1894 as a memorial to Baillie James Martin, a town councillor who also served as the Master of Works, a member of the Clyde Navigation Trust and a Justice of the Peace. The canopy features a number of animals, including griffins, an eagle, and, on the inside, a series of owls.

16. From the James Martin Memorial Fountain, head north along Templeton Street. As you do so, on your left, you will pass the former Templeton Carpet Factory. Although not as impressive as the western facade (which you will visit at the end of this walk), this is nonetheless an impressive building with an ornate bronze monogram above the entrance. The Templeton Carpet Factory was founded by James Templeton in 1839. When the original factory on King Street burned down in 1856, a new factory was constructed on this site which specialised in producing high-quality picture carpets. During work to extend the factory in November 1889, high winds caused a large section of a new wall to collapse onto the weaving shed, burying many of the workers in the rubble. While a number were rescued, twenty-nine of the women and girls, all from the East End of the city, were killed.

17. At the northern end of Templeton Street, cross London Road at the traffic lights at the junction with Arcadia Street and then head west along London Road to its junction with Tobago Street. Here, outside the Calton Heritage and Learning Centre, is a memorial with the name and age of each of the twenty-nine people killed in the 1889 Templeton Carpet Factory disaster. The youngest was only fourteen years old.

18. From this memorial, turn north and head along Tobago Street to the old police and fire station on its right-hand side. These buildings were designed in a classical style by John Carrick and were built in 1869. The police station finally closed in the early 1980s, and since then it has pretty much lain abandoned and has fallen into a very poor state of repair. However, if you examine the areas around its main entrance, you can see the ghosts of hand-painted signs which once adorned it.

Ghost signs beside main door, former Tobago Street Police and Fire Station.

19. Return south along Tobago Street and turn left at Drake Street, which will take you through to Abercromby Street. On reaching Abercromby Street, look to your right and you will see a large mural painted on the gable of a tenement building. Created by Mark Worst, it features Saint Thenue, also known as Saint Enoch, the mother of Glasgow's patron saint, being guided across the Firth of Forth by a shoal of trout. On her shawl are twenty-nine star-shaped motifs, one for each of the twenty-nine women and girls killed in the 1889 Templeton Factory Disaster.

20. Directly across from the point where you emerged on to Abercromby Street is the Calton Burial Ground, which was established in 1787, making it one of the oldest burial grounds still in existence in Glasgow. It was created by the Calton Incorporation of Weavers, and among the graves are monuments to the martyrs of the 1787 weavers' strike, which protested against the price paid to local weavers for muslin. Three of the strikers, John Page, Alexander Miller and James Ainsley, were shot and killed by soldiers acting under orders from the civic leaders of Glasgow, and they were subsequently interred within this burial ground. A further three died later of their injuries. These weavers are viewed as the first working-class martyrs in Scotland. Another memorial to these weavers is inscribed into flagstones set into

the pavement at the southern entrance to the burial ground, along with other details of its history and the different professions of the people who were buried within it.

21. From the Calton Burial Ground, head north up Abercromby Street to its junction with Millroad Street. Here, on an exposed gable end, you will find a mural welcoming you to the Calton area of Glasgow, which incorporates a number of buildings and place which will be visited later in this walk, including St Mary's Church, the entrance to the former meat and cattle market, the Barras Market and the Daulton Fountain at Glasgow Green. At this same junction is also a Edward VIII post box. Of twenty-seven erected in Glasgow during King Edward's short 326-day reign – more than any other city on Britain – at least thirteen survive to this day. However, this is the only one known to still be standing in the East End of Glasgow.

22. Almost directly opposite Abercromby Street's junction with Millroad Street is St Mary of the Assumption Church and Presbytery. Designed by Goldie and Child, it was built in 1841, making it the second-oldest Catholic Church in Glasgow and at that time, it was one of the largest Catholic churches in Scotland. Outside this church is a sculpture erected in 2021 called *The Tower of Silence*. It was designed by John McCarron, and is a monument to the memory of those who had to flee their homes or who starved to death during to the period of the Great Hunger or An Gorta Mór in Ireland (commonly referred to in Britain as the Irish Potato Famine) between 1845 and 1852. Around one million people died

1841 Saint Mary of the Assumption Church, Abercromby Street.

and about the same number fled, with many heading to Scotland, and more specifically to Glasgow. St Mary's is famous for being the birthplace of Celtic Football Club, one of the two main clubs in Scottish football. This club was founded in the hall of this church (which has since been demolished) by the Irishman Andrew Kerins. More widely known by his religious name of Brother Walfrid, he created it as a social outlet for men in the East End of Glasgow and to raise money to help the poor of the local areas. Their first match was played in 1888 against Glasgow Rangers, setting up a rivalry which persists to this day.

23. Carry on north up Abercromby Street to its junction with Gallowgate. Cross to the north side of Gallowgate, before turning left and walking west to the next road leading off to the north. This is Graham Square, and it leads to Glasgow's former meat and cattle market which was opened in the 1810s. While most of it has been demolished, the classical style entrance facades designed by John Carrick in the 1860s and 1870s have been retained and they feature some wonderful sculpted animal heads. In front of these is a modern sculpture of a yearling calf with a garland around its neck created by Kenny Hunter and installed in 2000 as a reminder of the former use of the site.

24. Set into the pavement at the junction between Graham Square and Gallowgate is one of the memorials of the Glasgow Firefighters' Heritage Trail. These are carved flagstones which mark locations where significant fires, often involving the death of firefighters, have occurred in Glasgow. This one marks the site where four firemen died when a floor of a warehouse collapsed while they were fighting a fire in it on 24 December 1927.

25. Retrace your route back east along Gallowgate and cross to its southern side using the traffic lights at its junction with Abercromby Street. Once you are on the southern side, head west along Gallowgate once more. When you reach a point opposite the junction with Graham Square, stop and look across at the tenement this corner. Designed by Frank Burnet and Boston in 1912, it contains a rather unusual feature. Most tenements were built with a shared drying green to their rear where clothes could be hung out to dry. This was important in the days before tumble dryers and central heating, when hanging clothes outside was the only real option for drying them. However, as space became less freely available within the city, some tenements started having their drying greens situated on their flats roofs rather than at ground level. This particular tenement went one better. Not only did it have a rooftop drying green, but it was also designed to have its own washhouse in its distinctive corner turret.

Burnet and Boston's 1912 tenement on Gallowgate, with rooftop drying green and washhouse in corner turret.

26. Further west at 480 Gallowgate is an unusual art deco style building. Designed by James McCallum, it was built in 1938 as a branch of the National Commercial Bank of Scotland. Above its entrance are two metal emblems, one featuring the coat of arms of this bank, and a second featuring the skull of an ox with a garland draped across its horns. This is known as a Bucranium and it was a common feature of the classical architecture of Ancient Greece. It originated from the practice of displaying the heads of sacrificial oxen on temples, which itself dates back to the Neolithic period. Its use on this building is presumably related to the fact this branch primarily served the businesses in the nearby meat and cattle market.

27. A short distance to the west of the former bank building, turn south down Millroad Drive (which is a narrow pedestrian lane at this point). This will lead you to a small concrete bridge. If you are tall enough you can peek over the parapet of this bridge and look down onto one of Glasgow's many abandoned and disused railway tracks. This particular one was part of the line which led from the city centre to the former Bridgeton Railway Station, which you viewed near the beginning of this walk.

28. Carry on south over this bridge, and on your left you will see the former Tureen Street School. The northern block was designed by John Honeyman and was built in 1875, whereas the central block was designed by James J. Craig and built a decade later in 1885. The final block, at the southern end, was designed by James L. Cowan and built in 1902. This was one of many traditional Glasgow schools which were replaced by new schools between the 1990s and 2010s. However, while some found new uses, many, like Tureen Street School, have been left to decay, resulting in the loss of a number of architecturally and socially important buildings. There is now a concerted effort to save those which are still standing. A good example of this is the former St James Primary School to the south of the Tureen Street School which is currently being refurbished to be reopened as a dedicated Gaelic school. It may seem odd to that two such large schools once existed on the same street. However, at the time they were built, the population density in the East End of Glasgow was much higher, with whole families sometimes crammed into a single-roomed tenement flat (traditionally known as a single-end). In addition, just as Glasgow's two main football clubs were traditionally divided along religious lines, so was – and to a large extent still is – the education system, with Catholic and nominally non-denominational (but still primarily Protestant) schools existing side by side in most areas of the city.

29. Return to Gallowgate, turn left and head west to its junction with Claythorn Street. Here, there are a pair of brick-built residential buildings, one on either side of the junction, dating from the 1770s. The one on its western side has a pub on the ground floor, which was originally called the Old Barracks Vaults as it sat across from the barracks of the 17th Highland Regiment (on the site now occupied by a small shopping centre). The pub's current name, the Hielan Jessie, comes from Jessie Brown, the wife of a sergeant with the regiment. During the Sepoy Mutiny in India in 1857, Jessie's husband was killed after the soldiers from the regiment became trapped in a fort. Encouraged by the sound of bagpipes from another Scottish regiment, Jessie urged the soldiers to

Rear elevation of 1770s tenement building housing Hielan Jessie Pub, which bears striking resemblance to Charle Rennie Mackintosh's Hill House, Helensburgh..

keep fighting until they were rescued. For this act of bravery, Jessie was rewarded with having this pub named after her, although in the intervening years, it has had a number of different names. If you look round the back of this pub, you will see a rounded tower containing a staircase and other features which are almost identical in form to those included by the architect Charles Rennie Mackintosh in a number of his most celebrated buildings, including Hill House in Helensburgh. Mackintosh is most famous for his use of the Glasgow style which blended elements of traditional Scottish architecture with the sweeping curves of the continental art nouveau style, and when viewing eighteenth-century Glasgow buildings such as this one, it is easy to see where he got his inspiration from. In fact, as a resident of Dennistoun between 1875 and 1892, Mackintosh may well have passed this very pub in the 1880s, on his way and from to his apprenticeship with John Honeyman, or his evening classes at the Glasgow School of Art, and could even have stopped in for a drink.

30. From the junction with Claythorn Street, continue west along Gallowgate and then turn south into Bain Street. Just beyond this junction on your left is St Luke's Church, which was designed in a classical style by James Wilson and was built in 1836. Like many former churches in Glasgow, it is now used as a music and arts venue, as well as a bar and restaurant.

31. Almost directly opposite St Luke's on Bain Street is the former Tobacco Pipe Works. This is one of best examples of Glasgow's industrial polychromatic architecture. It was designed by Matthew Forsyth and was built in 1877. The two halves of this building were originally joined by a linking building constructed in a similar style, but this has since been demolished. It was originally home to the William White and Son's Clay Pipes Works, which had been based in the neighbouring Gibson Street since 1824. Until they were largely replaced by cigarettes towards the end of the of nineteenth century, clay pipes were one of the most common ways of smoking tobacco, and White and Son was just one of a number of pipe makers in Glasgow who made pipes not only for the local market, but also for export all over the world.

1877 former White and Son's Pipe Works, Bain Street, East End.

32. Return to Gallowgate and head further west, where you will find the iconic Glasgow Barrowland Market and Ballroom. The market, more commonly known as 'the Barras', was created by Maggie and James McIver on land they purchased in 1921 and it quickly grew into one of the largest markets in Britain. Legend had it that no matter what you were looking for, you could find it for sale somewhere within the Barras. After James died in 1930, Maggie continued to expand the Barras, including building a function hall above the original market which, in 1939, became the Barrowland Ballroom. Maggie died in 1958, but both the ballroom and the market carried on. In recent years, the ballroom has become a music venue which has played host to many of the greatest names in popular music. It still contains a sprung dance floor, and together with its legendary atmosphere and wild audiences, this makes it one of Glasgow's most famous music venues. When it was still a ballroom, the Barrowlands became forever linked to one of the darkest elements of Glasgow's history. Between February 1968 and October 1969, three young women were found murdered, each one of whom had been dancing at the Barrowlands the night before their death. All three were believed to have been killed by the same man, who was nicknamed Bible John as he was heard quoting Old Testament verses to one of his victims. Although there has been a great deal of speculation over the years as to the identity of Bible John, and why he apparently stopped killing almost as suddenly as he started, the murders still officially remain unsolved.

33. A short distance further west along Gallowgate from the Barrowlands is No. 161. This small, unassuming building was home to a Quaker grocer by the name of William Smeal, and through his work, and that of others, Glasgow became one of the key centres of the campaign to end slavery worldwide in the 1820s and 1830s. In particular, in 1846, this building was the base for the US anti-slavery campaigner Frederick Douglass as he toured Scotland. It is also likely that James McCune Smith, the first African American to obtain a medical degree, stayed here on his arrival in Glasgow in the 1830s, to study medicine at the University of Glasgow.

Former shop of William Smeal, 161 Gallowgate.

34. From Gallowgate, turn south onto Charlotte Street and walk down to its junction with London Road. On the far side of this junction, at 52 Charlotte Street, is one of Glasgow's few remaining Georgian villas. Built around 1790 in a classical style similar to Robert Adam, this is the only survivor of a street once lined with grand houses. The grandest of these was built for David Dale, the Scottish industrialist and founder of the cotton mills of New Lanark, where housing, education and social support was provided for the workers and their families. This was considered rather revolutionary for the 1780s. However, Dale's house, which stood at the junction between Charlotte Street and Greendyke Street was demolished in 1954.

35. From Charlotte Street, head west along London Road to Barrowland Park. Here, in this small patch of green in the centre of the city, you will find the Barrowland Park Album Pathway. Created by the artist Jim Lambie, it lists the dates and names of many of the bands and artists who have played at the nearby Barrowland Ballroom since it reopened as a music venue in 1983. Despite being commissioned as a temporary installation as part of the cultural programme for the Glasgow Commonwealth Games in 2014, it has become a much-loved feature of a city which was granted UNESCO City of Music status in 2008.

36. At the south-western end of Barrowland Park, is a metal grate set into a stone wall. This is pretty much the only trace left of St Andrew's Lane, which was more widely known by its nickname 'Schipka Pass' (after the 1877 Battle of the Schipka Pass between Russian and Ottoman forces). Lined by overcrowded and poorly maintained tenements with little or no sanitation beyond the road itself, in the 1800s this narrow lane was frequently described as the worst street in Scotland. The last remnants of Schipka Pass was a small market area, viewed by some, especially in the local council, as an embarrassment to the city. It was finally razed to the ground by a fire in 2011, and the area was later turned into the park which stands on the site to this day.

37. Return to London Road at the eastern end of Barrowland Park, and head further west along it. Here, you will pass one of Glasgow's remaining police boxes. While not in its original location, it is nonetheless a reminder of the role this Glasgow invention played in communication before the widespread availability of home phones and, nowadays, their mobile replacements.

38. From London Road, turn south down James Morrison Street. A short distance from this junction in St Andrew's Square is the magnificent St Andrew's Parish Church. Designed by Alan Dreghorn and built in the mid-1700s, this is one of the oldest churches in Glasgow. Its design is based largely on James Gibb's 1722 St Martin-in-the-Fields, in London, and it was the first of around a dozen imposing churches inspired by classical temples built across the city in the Georgian and Victorian Eras. The central pediment features a rather wonderful version of the Glasgow coat of arms, which has two somewhat peculiar features. The first is that the fish which lies across the trunk of the tree is the correct way up, whereas on most versions of the city's coat of arms it is inverted, to signify that it is dead. In addition, it lacks the usual ring in its mouth. The second is that at its base is a grotesque face, which while not unusual on church buildings, is not usually associated with this coat of arms. These differences may be due to the age of the building, which was well before the standard version of the coat of arms came into use in 1866.

39. On the south-western corner of St Andrew's Square is a former tannery and leather warehouse which was built in 1876. It has the words 'Tannery Building' inscribed over its door, and a rather beautiful sculpted bull's head over one of its arched windows, presumably as an indicator of the industry for which it was built. While this is a wonderful piece of architecture, it is worth considering the smell which would most likely have emanated from it when it was in operation, and which would have drifted over much of the local area. Even though traditional tanning methods, which used, among other things, urine, lime and dog faeces, had been replaced by chrome-based ones by the time this tannery was built, the odour generated by processing animal skins would still not have been pleasant, especially during the warmer summer months.

Sculpted bull's head above arch of old tannery building.

40. Opposite St Andrew's Square, and running down the western side of Turnbull Street (which is a southern continuation of James Morrison Street), is the former Central Police Headquarters. Designed by Alexander B. McDonald in a Renaissance style with art nouveau/Glasgow style features, it was built in 1903 and consisted of offices, cells, a court hall and a recreation area in a large internal courtyard. The entrance to the court hall is flanked by allegorical figures representing Law (on the left) and Justice (on the right), which are attributed to Richard Ferris. After twenty-six years, the Central Police Headquarters moved elsewhere, but the building remained in use, first as the headquarters of the Criminal Investigation Department,

then as a District Court and the Police Museum, before finally closing in 2008. It is currently abandoned and in a very poor state of repair, but there are plans to bring it back into use as residential housing. For the moment, its facade still features a number of interesting ghost signs associated with its former use, and hopefully these will be retained during any future renovations.

41. Next to the former police building is Tent Hall. Built in a late Gothic style in 1876 for the United Evangelical Association, which had previously met in a mission tent on Glasgow Green, it served as a large meeting hall, where the association offered alternative entertainment to bingeing on alcohol. This included lantern slide shows illustrating the evils of the 'demon drink' and extolling the virtues of total abstinence.

42. At the southern end of Turnbull Street, on its corner with Greendyke Street, is another of Glasgow's older churches. Originally called the Church of St Andrew's-by-the-Green, it was designed by Andrew Hunter and William Paull in a classical style. Built in 1750, it was the first Episcopal church constructed in Glasgow. It was also one of the first churches in the city to have a pipe organ installed in it. This was because, at the time, the playing of musical instruments was not permitted in Presbyterian places of worship, including all those operated by the Church of Scotland. The presence of this organ earned this church the nickname of 'the Whistlin' Kirk' (with 'kirk' being the Scots word for a church). While it is no longer serves as a place of worship, it is still surrounded by its small churchyard containing old gravestones decorated with a variety of memento mori. However, please be aware that this is now a private property and you should not enter the graveyard.

St Andrew's-by-the-Green, Glasgow's oldest Episcopal Church.

43. From St Andrew's-by-the-Green, head east along Greendyke Street to No. 35. This large red sandstone building, designed by Honeyman and Keppie in 1890, started life as a hide, skin and tallow market, and like the nearby tannery, when it was fully operational, is likely to have cast a malodorous pall across much of the surrounding neighbourhood. This former market has been converted into flats, and provides a good example of how older buildings can be maintained and adapted for different uses rather than simply being demolished when they have outlived their original purpose.

44. Further east along Greendyke Street, on the corner with Charlotte Street, is the former Lady and Saint Francis Secondary School. Designed by the architectural firm Gillespie, Kidd & Coia in a Modern Movement style, it was inspired by the work of the Swiss-French Architect Charles-Édouard Jeanneret (who was also known as Le Corbusier) and was built in 1963. While not to everyone's taste, it is nonetheless an important illustration of the development of architecture both in Glasgow and across the world. This building was constructed on the site of the Georgian villa designed by Robert Adam for David Dale, which was demolished in 1954. Lady and Saint Francis was founded as a girl's school by Franciscan nuns in 1847, and finally

closed in 1988, when it was merged with Saint Mungo's, the local all-boys school. Locally, Lady and Saint Francis was also known as Charlotte Street, or more colloquially 'Chocolate Street', due to its brown uniform.

45. From Greendyke Street head south into Glasgow Green, the large park which runs along the banks of the River Clyde in the East End of Glasgow. Glasgow Green was established in the fifteenth century, when King James II granted the land to Bishop William Turnbull (after whom the nearby Turnbull Street is named), making it the oldest public park in the city. At that time, it was a swampy area, fed by the Camlachie and Moledinar Burns, with a series of low hills, or 'greens', which were used for grazing, washing linen and drying fishing nets, as well as for recreation. Glasgow Green has always been one of the main focal points of the city, and, as a result, it has played a role in many events of local, national and even international importance. Between December 1745 and January 1746, the green played host to the army of Bonnie Prince Charlie after his retreat from England and before the Battle of Culloden, which would see the end to almost a century of Jacobite uprisings and the suppression of much of Scottish Highland culture. Glasgow Green was also the place where, in 1765, James Watt came up with the idea of using a separate condenser for a steam engine, an invention which would help kickstart the Industrial Revolution. In 1816, around 40,000 people gathered on Glasgow Green as part of the Radical Movement to demand more representative government and an end to the Corn Laws. This was followed in 1820 by meetings and military drills by strikers in the Radical Wars, a brief rebellion which was soon crushed by the Government. This was not the last time the park became the focus for political meetings and demonstrations, and between the 1870s and the 1910s there were regular meetings of the Women's Suffrage Movement on Glasgow Green, as well as anti-war protests in 1914 led by John Maclean, and rent protests in 1920.

46. Glasgow Green is dominated by two major structures, the People's Palace, which you will visit shortly, and the Nelson Monument. This towering obelisk was designed by David Hamilton and erected in 1806, making it the first public monument to be erected in the UK to commemorate Nelson's victory, and death at the Battle of Trafalgar in 1805. Given all the political protests in Glasgow over the years, it may seem odd that Glasgow Green would be the first place where such a monument was erected. However, Scots made up a significant proportion of the sailors in Nelson's navy, and this may have provided the impetus for the monument's erection. As such a tall structure, the monument quickly became a major landmark within the local vicinity, including the nearby Jail Square to the west of the Green. It was here that public executions took place between 1814 and 1865, leading to the local expression 'You'll die facing the monument', meaning that someone was likely to meet their end on the hangman's gallows.

James Watt Commemorative Stone, base of Nelson Monument, Glasgow Green.

47. At the base of the Nelson Monument is a large boulder with an inscription commemorating the fact that James Watt had his revolutionary idea for improving the efficiency of steam engines while strolling on Glasgow Green in 1765. This makes it one of the few scientific advancements which can be pinned to a particular place and time, although like the apple falling on Newton's head (another scientific discovery tied to a specific time and place), it may have been substantially embellished over the years.

48. From the Nelson Monument, head north-east towards the People's Palace. To the west of this building is a small enclosed garden area which contains two major monuments. The first is a black marble sculpture, consisting of a stylised head on a tomb-shaped plinth. This sculpture was commissioned by the Scottish Trades Union Congress to mark International Workers' Memorial Day, which takes place each year on 28 April. The second monument is the upturned hull of a small boat. This is the Irish and Highlands Famine Memorial, which was unveiled in 2018. It marks Europe's great famine of the 1840s and its impact on the people of Ireland and the Scottish Islands, many of whom were forced to flee their native lands. Some chose to settle in Glasgow, while others continued on to begin again in the New World. Those who stayed helped shape the city into the industrial powerhouse it became over the following century.

49. To the east of the Famine Memorial is the People's Palace. Designed by Alexander B. McDonald in a grand Renaissance style, it was built in the 1890s as a museum and winter gardens. The main facade is decorated with a series of allegorical figures by William Kellock Brown representing shipbuilding (holding a model boat), mathematics (holding dividers and an open book), sculpture (holding a figurine), painting (holding a palette and brush), engineering

People's Palace and Doulton Fountain, with Nelson Monument in background.

(holding a crown wheel and pulley), the textile industry (holding a distaff), science (holding a globe and compass), the arts (holding books) and finally at the very top, progress (holding a bronze torch in her right hand, a laurel wreath in her left, and a cornucopia at her feet). Inscribed into a flagstone just in front of the entrance is a mid-twentieth-century poem about the People's Palace. The People's Palace is also home to a plaque to Sister Smudge, the only cat to be a full member of the GMB Union. Smudge was bought into the museum in 1979 to help deal with a rodent problem and quickly became an important fixture within it. She became a full member of the General, Municipal and Boilermakers Trade Union in the 1980s after she was refused admission to the National and Local Government Officers' Association. Smudge left the museum in 1990, and died at her home in 2000. If you have time, the People's Palace is well worth visiting for its exhibits about life in Glasgow, and how it was in the past. In particular, it contains a replica of a single-end, a one-roomed tenement flat with no indoor toilet or washing facilities (these were provided as communal facilities elsewhere in the building or even outside it), where a whole family might live. This is worth viewing to get a sense of the conditions in which many people in the East End of Glasgow would have once lived, especially prior to World War II.

50. Directly to the north of the entrance to the People's Palace is the stunning Doulton Fountain. The largest terracotta fountain in the world, it was designed by Arthur E. Pearce of the Doulton Ceramics Company for the 1888 Glasgow Empire Exhibition, which was held in Kelvingrove Park in the West End. One of the most popular attractions at the exhibition, the fountain is a tribute to the British Empire, and features tableaux representing Canada (modelled by Wiliam Silver Frith), South Africa (modelled by Herbert Ellis), Australia (modelled by Frederick Pomeroy) and India (modelled by John Broad). Above these tableaux are four servicemen, a Black Watch Highlander, a Grenadier Guardsman (now incomplete), a Royal Navy Sailor (now incomplete) and a Royal Irish Fusilier. Finally, at the top, presiding over all those below her, is Queen Victoria (modelled by John Baird). After the exhibition closed, there was much debate as to where the fountain should end up. Options which were considered were leaving it in Kelvingrove Park, moving it to Queen's Park in the Southside part of the city, and erecting it in Cathedral Square in the city centre. However, Glasgow Green was finally selected as its permanent home and it was moved to its current location, where it was inaugurated on 27 August 1890, which was designated as Fountain Day in the city.

51. From the Doulton Fountain, head east towards the western facade of the Templeton Carpet Factory. Designed by William Leiper and built in 1889, this is one of Glasgow's most unique and iconic industrial buildings. Composed of terracotta and multicoloured bricks, as well as faïence tiles, it is built in a Venetian Gothic style (a surprisingly popular style in late Victorian Glasgow), and decorated with extravagant detailing. In keeping with its stunning facade, this factory produced carpets for two British coronations, the White House in Washington DC, and for luxury liners. However, they also produced more mundane items, such as army blankets during World War I. The factory closed in 1982, and while the facade was retained, the interior ranges were demolished to create a courtyard when it was converted into a business centre in 1985.

Part of facade of Venetian Gothic style Templeton Carpet Factory.

Southside
of Glasgow

14. Hutchesontown, the Gorbals and Laurieston

Start Point: St Andrew's Suspension Bridge, Glasgow Green, Glasgow (**Location:** Lat/Lon: 55.84906, -4.23807; What3Words: ///woods.desk.image; Plus Code: RQX6+JQF Glasgow). **Nearest Public Transport:** Subway: None; Train: Bridgeton Railway Station (20 mins); Bus: London Road (10 mins).

End Point: South End of the Jamaica Street Bridge, Glasgow (**Location:** Lat/Lon: 55.85474, -4.25811; What3Words: ///focal.outer.jazz; Plus Code: VP3R+VPQ Glasgow). **Nearest Public Transport:** Subway: Bridge Street Subway Station (5 mins); Train: Central Station (10 mins); Bus: Bridge Street (2 mins).

Distance: 4.5 kilometres/2.9 miles. **Time:** Allow 2 to 3 hours for this walk.
Level of Difficulty: Easy. This walk is entirely on paved surfaces.

Facilities: As it is a primarily residential area, there are only a small number of shops available along this route. However, there are a number of cafes, restaurants and bars on Bridge Street, where this walk ends. Publicly accessible toilets are available at the Gorbals Leisure Centre on Ballater Street, which is near the Blessed John Duns Scotus Church approximately halfway through this walk. There are also publicly accessible toilets at Glasgow Central Station, which is about ten minutes from the end of this walk.

Introduction

Hutchesontown, the Gorbals and Laurieston cover an area stretching along the southern bank of the Clyde as it passes through the East End and the city centre. While they are often collectively referred to as 'the Gorbals', each has its own distinct identity and history. The Gorbals is the oldest of the three and dates back to the medieval period, when, among other things, it was the home of a leper hospital. One possible origin of its name may be from 'gory bells', after the bells lepers used to alert others to their presence. However, more prosaically, it may, instead, come from the old Scots term 'garbales', which originally meant the town's lands. In contrast to the Gorbals, Hutchesontown and Laurieston are newer creations. Hutchesontown was developed as a new suburb of Glasgow to the east of the original Gorbals village in 1794, and is named after Hutchesons' Hospital, which was created with bequests from Thomas and Georgie Hutcheson, and built in the 1640s in central Glasgow. The hospital generated its revenue from the rent of land in the Gorbals and other parts of Glasgow. Laurieston was developed a short time later by James Laurie, after whom the area is named, with the intention of creating a high-class residential neighbourhood. During the 1800s, the Gorbals and its surrounding areas grew dramatically from a small village with a population of around 5,000 people in 1811, to neighbourhood of over 90,000 people by the 1930s. This resulted in an incredibly high population density of around 40,000 people per square kilometre (just over 100,000 per square mile). By comparison, the current population density of Glasgow as a whole is just 3,635 per square kilometre (under 10,000 per square mile). Not surprisingly, this extremely high population density resulted in very poor living conditions, especially given that, at the time, many people were living in Victorian tenements which still lacked indoor plumbing. As a result, the Gorbals became a name synonymous with social deprivation and slums. While Hutchesontown and the Gorbals have been heavily rebuilt several times over the years, Laurieston still retains not only a significant number of its Edwardian and Victorian buildings, but even some of its original Georgian ones.

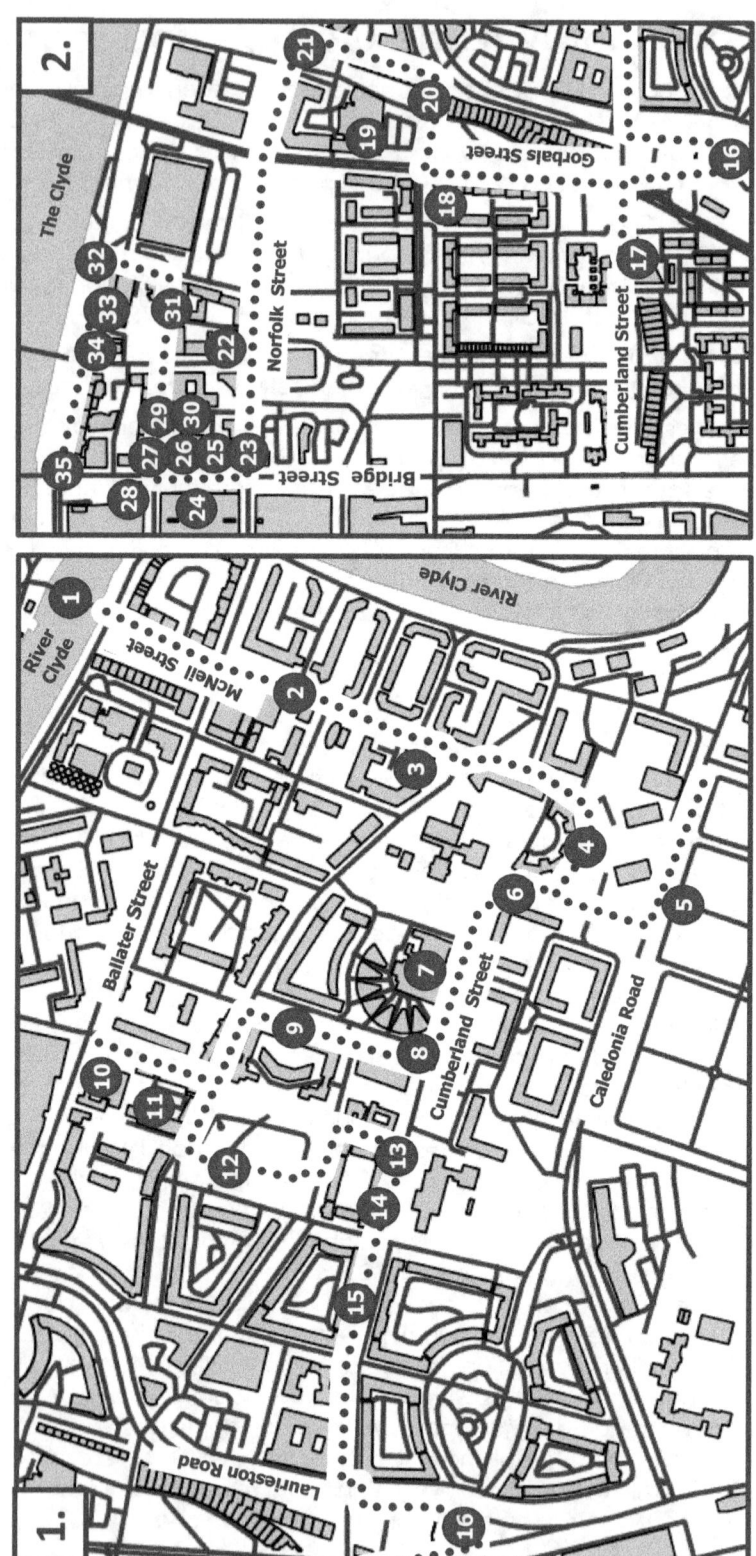

1. This walk starts at the St Andrew's Suspension Bridge which links Glasgow Green to Hutchesontown and the Gorbals on the south side of the River Clyde. This pedestrian suspension bridge, with its cast-iron pylons decorated with Corinthian columns, was designed by the engineer Neil Robson and the architect Charles O'Neill. It was built in the 1850s to enable workers from areas like Bridgeton and Calton in the East End of Glasgow to reach the factories in Hutchesontown easily, and in doing so, it replaced an earlier ferry service at the same location. Primarily built using wrought iron, its single span measures 67 metres (220 feet) in length.

Saint Andrew's Suspension Bridge linking Glasgow Green to Hutchesontown on south bank of the Clyde.

2. From the southern end of St Andrew's Suspension Bridge, head south along McNeil Street. Just after you cross Ballater Street, you will see a series of bronze bollards designed to look like giant pine cones. These were created by Liz Peden and Cath Keay, and were installed in 1998 to help with traffic-calming measures while providing some visual interest to the street.

3. Just beyond the last of the giant pine cones on McNeil Street is the former Hutchesontown District Library. Built in 1904, it was one of the first libraries established in Glasgow using money provided by the steel magnet and philanthropist Andrew Carnegie. Like a number of other libraries constructed in the city around this time, it was designed by James R. Rhind. While most of his libraries are in an Edwardian baroque style, this one was designed in a distinctive French Renaissance style. However, as with Rhind's other Glasgow libraries, it is adorned with sculptures by William Kellock Brown, including a winged figure at the top of its dome, which is identical to the figures on top of Parkhead and Dennistoun Public Libraries. The Hutchesontown District Library also features winged griffins surrounding its dome, and relief sculptures featuring Saint Mungo and the emblems from the Glasgow coat of arts (a tree, a bird, a bell and a fish with a ring in its mouth), both held by female figures flanking Saint Mungo, in their own separate panels. On the southern end of the library is a much newer sculpture titled *Three Dancing Muses*. This was created by members of the Gorbals Arts Project and was installed in 1997. The three muses symbolise Technology (featuring cutouts of microchips), History (featuring cutouts of books) and Architecture (featuring cutouts of the library itself).

4. From Hutchesontown District Library, follow McNeil Street further south to where it becomes Oregon Street. Continue along Oregon Street as it curves to the right to eventually join Cumberland Road. In the 1960s and 1970s, many of the area's traditional sandstone tenements were demolished in an effort to improve the quality of local housing, and were replaced by high-rise flats, such as the ones on the corner of McNeil Street and Oregon Street. While the motive behind these redevelopments may have been well-intentioned, the outcomes were not

particularly successful. This was because many of the high-rise flats suffered from their own set of problems, and the local Hutchesontown flats soon became known as 'the Dampies' due to problems with damp created by the techniques used to construct them. In addition, poor maintenance of lifts often left people stranded on the upper floors high above the streets. Similar situations occurred with other high-rise developments across Glasgow, leading the folk singer Adam McNaughtan to pen the 'Jeely Piece' Song in 1966. This song highlights the issues associated with living in high-rise flats, and particularly the loss of the tradition of parents throwing sandwiches out of their tenement windows to children as they played in the street below. Many of Glasgow's high-rise flats have now been demolished, including in the Gorbals, with the last few in Hutchesontown scheduled for demolition in the near future. Largely, these have been replaced by low-rise modern versions of the traditional tenements which were demolished to make way for them half a century before.

5. When you reach Cumberland Street, turn left and head along it to Caledonia Road. On the opposite side of this road is the Southern Necropolis, one of Glasgow's impressive Victorian-Era cemeteries. However, to reach it, you need to walk east along Caledonia Road to the traffic lights at the junction with Caledonia Street and cross the road at this point. You can then walk back along to the entrance to the graveyard, which is marked by an imposing castellated Romanesque style lodge designed by Charles Wilson and built in 1848. The cemetery itself opened in 1840 to replace the Old Gorbals Burial Ground (which will be visited later in this walk), with the aim of providing an affordable and respectable place of burial for the people of the Gorbals and the surrounding areas.

Entrance to Southern Necropolis, Caledonia Road.

Since it was created, over 250,000 individuals have been interred within it (five times the number buried in the better known, and smaller, Glasgow Necropolis to the east of Glasgow Cathedral). This includes the tea merchant Thomas Lipton, the philanthropist Allan Glen and the architects Charles Wilson (who designed the cemetery's lodge) and Alexander 'Greek' Thomson. The Southern Necropolis is also home to the White Lady, a veiled figure standing beside a broken pillar, which marks the final resting place of John Smith, his wife Magdalene and their housekeeper Mary McNaughton. The statue is said to turn her head to watch you pass, and if you catch her eye, you will be turned to stone. The origin of this legend is unknown, but the statue is often decorated with small offerings of coins and flowers, suggesting that some believe in the power of the White Lady. The other story which is very much associated with the Southern Necropolis is that of the Gorbals Vampire. In 1954, unfounded rumours started spreading that a vampire had killed two local children. This led to hordes of kids, some as young as seven or eight, armed to the teeth with stakes, knives and dogs, descending on the Southern Necropolis for several nights in a row to hunt the vampire, who was said to be '7-foot tall with iron teeth'. So disturbed were adults by these events, that a moral panic ensued. Imported American horror comics were blamed for creating the mass hysteria and this led to the introduction of the Children and Young Persons (Harmful Publications) Act of 1955, which still stands to this day. However, it could just as easily have been inspire by a passage from the Bible (Daniel 7:7), which refers to a beast with great iron teeth.

6. Once you have finished exploring the Southern Necropolis, cross back over Caledonia Road at the traffic lights beside its junction with Caledonia Street, and head north along Cumberland Street. A major thoroughfare through the Southside of Glasgow, it was the origin of the local Gorbals gang name 'the Cumbie'. This was one of many gangs which once dominated life for young working-class men across Glasgow. Some, like the Cumbie, took their names from local streets, while others took their names from their local neighbourhood, like the Bridgeton Derry Gang. However, the names of other gangs had more obscure origins. For example, the Bundy, in Pollokshields, took their name from a street clock, called a 'bundy', used to help keep trams running on time, while the origins of the name for one of Glasgow's most infamous gangs, the Tongs, remains unclear, but it may have come from a 1961 film about a Chinese secret society called *The Terror of the Tongs*. The Tongs were famous for marking their territory in the Calton area of the city with the graffiti saying 'Tongs Ya Bass'. Often taken as slang for 'you bastard', it may have actually originated with the Gaelic battle cry 'aigh bas', meaning 'battle or die'.

7. Just after the corner where Cumberland Street curves to the west, stands St Francis Church. Designed by Gilbert Blout in 1868, and rebuilt by Pugin and Pugin in 1878, this large Gothic style church is one of the few buildings from the pre-1960s Gorbals which remains standing to this day, with most others having been swept away in the post-war slum clearances. With the buildings went the social histories of entire families, along with the streets where they lived in, the schools they attended, the churches they were married in and the cemeteries where they were buried. When you realise quite how much of local communities have vanished, in comparison to the better-off areas of the city like the West End and Pollokshields, you realise that the past is something only the rich seem to have the power, and the money, to be able to afford to preserve. This process is now being repeated once more in areas like the Gorbals as the 1960s tower blocks are being demolished and working-class areas are again the focus of intensive redevelopment plans, although this time round there does seem to be at least some level of community consultation and involvement in the whole process.

Examples of 1960s tower blocks built to replace tenements demolished during post-war regeneration of the Gorbals.

8. A short distance further west along Cumberland Street is its junction with Queen Elizabeth Gardens, which is lined with examples of the modern low-rise housing which has come to dominate Hutchesontown and the Gorbals in recent years. At one time, this junction was home to a sculpture called *The Gorbals Boys*. Designed by Liz Peden and installed in 2008, it was based on a famous picture of three young boys playing in the street in their mothers' high-heeled shoes, taken in 1963 by the Italian-born Scottish photographer Oscar Marzaroli. However, in 2023, the statues were stolen, and while they were eventually recovered, they have yet to be replaced at their original location. Marzaroli's extensive collection of photographs taken on the streets of post-war Glasgow, and particularly in the 1960s, provide an almost unparalleled record of life in the city at a time of great change, and his photographs include images of the Gorbals as the bulldozers cleared away entire streets of traditional sandstone tenements.

9. Other sculptures remain in place throughout the Gorbals, including the giant bird-like creatures above the entrances to the block of flats at the north-western corner of Queen Elizabeth Gardens. These are the distinctive *Birdcatcher* sculptures by David Ralston, and they add a touch of uniqueness to the otherwise rather generic-looking buildings. They can also be seen as modern versions of the architectural sculptures which decorate the facades of older buildings throughout Glasgow, and which form a key part of the city's architectural tradition.

David Ralston's Birdcatcher *sculptures on modern tenements, Elizabeth Gardens*

10. At the northern end of Queen Elizabeth Gardens, turn left onto Old Rutherglen Road and walk west along it until you reach its junction with Commercial Road. Walk north up Commercial Road until you reach Ballater Street. Here, you will find the Blessed John Duns Scotus Church. Built in the modern style it was completed in 1975, when there were still four Roman Catholic churches in the Gorbals, including Saint Francis, which you visited earlier in this walk. However, John Duns is now the only one remaining. It is notable for containing a reliquary containing the forearm of Saint Valentine. This was originally donated by a French Catholic family to Saint Francis when it was built in the 1860s, but it was moved to Blessed John Duns Scotus Church in 1993, where it spent the next six years in a cardboard box on top of a wardrobe. In 1999, the reliquary was rediscovered and the arm is now located in the church in a box marked 'Corpus Valentini Martyris'. The presence of this relic has, at times, led to Glasgow being referred to as the City of Love. However, there are relics of Saint Valentine in a number of other churches around the world, including in Birmingham, Dublin, Poland, Slovakia and the Czech Republic, meaning that Glasgow does not necessarily have a unique claim to this title.

11. Return south along Commercial Street, back towards the Old Rutherglen Road, and as you do so, look to your right. Here, above the newer buildings, you can see the former Main Mill. Built as a cotton mill for Robert Humphries in 1816, it has a cast-iron frame and is the oldest surviving fireproof mill in Glasgow. It later became the

Twomax Knitwear Factory for the hosiery manufacturers McClure and McIntosh (the two Mcs in the factory's name), but by 1988, it had been converted into offices. Its chimney is topped by a rotating sculpture of a cloud of smoke called *Smokestack*, which was created by Rita McGurn and Adrian Russell Lamb in 1994.

12. When you reach Old Rutherglen Road once more, turn right onto it, and then a short distance further west, turn left into the Gorbals Rose Garden. As you walk through this garden, you will see its walls are lined with old headstones, some of which date back to the early eighteenth century. This is because this garden lies on the site of the Old Gorbals Burial Ground, which was established in 1715, and which was replaced by the Southern Necropolis in the late 1800s. As well as the gravestones, it also features a large sculpture of a rose with a fallen petal which is dedicated to the people from the local area who served their country in the armed forces. Its inscription includes the lines 'Stop and look, really look. Tomorrow may be too late'.

Gravestones along wall of former Gorbals Burial Ground, now Gorbals Rose Garden.

13. Exit the Gorbals Rose Garden onto Errol Gardens, to its south, and head east to Jane Place, which you can walk along to return to Cumberland Street. At the junction between these two streets is a sculpture called *Untitled Girl With Rucksack*, which was created by Kenny Hunter in 2004. It depicts a young girl, standing with a rucksack on her back and another between her legs, looking round as if trying to decide where to go. It was designed as a metaphor for the many people who have come to Glasgow and settled in the Gorbals since the Industrial Revolution, only to be later displaced by the successive waves of construction, demolition and regeneration which have swept across the area over the last 200 years.

14. From the *Girl With Rucksack* statue, head west along Cumberland Street, which, at this point, is lined with modern low-rise tenement style buildings that have recently replaced the high-rises of the 1960s. These, in turn, were built to replace the sandstone tenements constructed between 1860 and 1900, which were largely cleared in the 1950s as part of the Gorbals Comprehensive Development Area. However, these tenements were themselves constructed to replace an earlier generation of tenements built between the 1820s and the 1840s, as the Gorbals was starting its growth from a village of a few thousand people in 1811 to its population high of around 90,000 people in the 1930s. At this time, this meant that almost a tenth of the entire population of Glasgow was crammed into this relatively small space, with families of eight or more sharing a single room in a tenement and up to thirty residents sharing a single outdoor toilet. This number of people living in such close proximity made the spread of disease almost inevitable, a situation brought into sharp focus by events which began in 1900 in a tenement at 71 Rose Street, just a short distance to the north of the Cumberland Street. In August of that year, a flat in this tenement became ground zero for the last outbreak of bubonic plague in Scotland. This was part of the third plague pandemic (after earlier ones in the medieval period and in the 1600s), which officially lasted from 1855 until 1960. While it killed millions in India and China, Europe was largely spared until the plague

unexpectedly reached Glasgow. In total, thirty-six cases were identified and sixteen of those infected died. In the densely packed tenements of the early twentieth-century Gorbals, it could so easily have been far worse, and while they were initially slow to realise what was going on, it was probably only the decisive actions of the local health officials which prevented it from being so. However, even with all their efforts, it was not until November 1900 that Glasgow was once again declared plague-free.

15. As well as providing much more generous accommodation, many of these modern buildings also feature small and quirky works of art, such as the metal relief sculptures of fish from the nearby River Clyde on the fence starting in front of No. 215. From east to west, these fish are a stickleback, a grayling, a salmon or trout, and a pike. As with the *Birdcatcher* sculptures on Queen Elizabeth Gardens, visited earlier on this walk, they help give an air of uniqueness to otherwise rather generic-looking buildings.

16. Continue west along Cumberland Street until you reach its junction with Laurieston Road. Cross Laurieston Road using the traffic lights at this junction and then turn left and walk along to its junction with Cathcart Road. Here, you will find the remains of Alexander 'Greek' Thomson's once beautiful and impressive Caledonia Road Church. Occupying the triangular strip of land between these two major roads. it has a design based on that of a classical Greek temple and was built in 1856. However, just over a century later in 1965, it was gutted by fire, and has remained a ruin ever since.

Alexander 'Greek' Thomson's now ruined 1865 Caledonia Road Church.

17. Turn north onto Cathcart Road and walk down to the junction with Cumberland Street. Cross Cathcart Road at the traffic lights at this junction, and walk a short distance further west along Cumberland Street. This will take you to the old Cumberland Street Station. Built around 1900, it has a classical style street-level entrance which would, at one point, have led up to platforms on the raised viaduct which carries the old Glasgow and South Western Railway line across this part of the city. Trains on this line would originally have travelled from St Enoch Station in central Glasgow out to the suburbs of Pollokshields, Strathbungo and beyond. The station closed when services to St Enoch's ended in 1966. There have been proposals to reopen it as part of the Glasgow Crossrail Project, which would help to connect trains serving the south of Glasgow from Central Station to those running to the north and west from Queen Street. However, despite more than twenty years of discussions, nothing so far has happened to make it a reality and while they continue, the station remains closed, falling further into disrepair and dereliction.

18. From the former Cumberland Street Station, return to the junction between Cumberland Street and Cathcart Road. Turn left here and head north along Gorbals Street (which is a continuation of Cathcart Road) to its junction with Cleland Street. The red sandstone building on the west side of this junction is one of the last remaining traditional tenements in the Gorbals. Designed in the Glasgow style by James Salmon Jnr, it was built in 1900 as a branch of the British Linen Bank. While not widely known, James Salmon Jnr (who was nicknamed Wee Troot; the Glaswegian pronunciation of trout) played an important role in Glasgow's architectural history, providing a link between the old classical style typified by his grandfather, James Salmon Snr, the Glasgow style and art nouveau period at the end of the nineteenth century, to which he contributed with his partner John Gaff Gillespie, and the modernist architecture of the mid-twentieth century, typified by Gillespie, Kidd & Coia, which was a continuation of the architectural practice founded by Wee Troot's grandfather in the 1830s. At the northern end of this tenement is a gable sculpture designed by the Gorbals Art Project that celebrates Salmon and his views on architecture and regeneration, which are of particular relevance to the Gorbals. In addition, there is a metal box, which is part of the roof drainage system, at the top of the Gorbals Street facade with the year of construction (1900) and the year of its recent refurbishment (2019). Below these two dates is a relief sculpture of a what looks like a salmon, but could equally be a picture of a wee troot.

James Salmon Junior's 1900 Glasgow style British Linen Bank, one of last traditional tenements in the Gorbals.

19. Just north of the opposite corner of this junction is the Citizens Theatre. With an auditorium originally designed by Campbell Douglas, and a classical exterior created by James Sellars, topped by a row of statues made by the legendary sculptor John Mossman, this theatre originally opened in 1878. While James Sellars' exterior was destroyed by fire in the 1970s, the statues were saved and have recently been re-erected on its new facade. The statues depict four ancient Greek muses (Melpomene, Thalia, Euterpe and Terpsichore), as well as Robert Burns and William Shakespeare. Citizens Theatre, especially with the formation of the Citizens Theatre Company in 1943, rose to become one of the UK's leading repertory theatre in the 1960s, and remains an important cultural institution to this day.

20. Cross Gorbals Street at the traffic lights and head east along Cleland Street. This will take you under the viaduct which carries the still-active railway line from the old Cumberland Street Station towards the city centre. In alcoves under this viaduct are information panels honouring three of the local area's famous former residents: Benny Lynch (1913–1946), Scotland's first World Boxing Champion, the artist and sculptor Anna Frank (1908–2008), and Allan Pinkerton (1819–1884), the founder of the US-based Pinkerton National Detective Agency. This last one is rather an odd choice, given the working-class history of the local area and the role that Glasgow has played in national and international labour movements. This is because, after the US Civil War of the 1860s, the Pinkerton Agency was heavily involved in operations against organised labour and, in particular, was involved in a range of

strike-breaking activities, including during the Homestead Strike of 1892, when nine people were killed.

21. Once you have passed under the railway line, turn left onto St Luke's Place. This will take you parallel to the brick-built railway viaduct which eventually leads to the City of Union Bridge, the first railway bridge constructed over the River Clyde. At the southern end of St Luke's Place, beside its junction with Ballater Street, is a mural dedicated to the story of the Gorbals Vampire created by Ella Bryson and the Artpistol Projects to coincide with a play hosted at the nearby Citizens Theatre in 2016.

The Gorbals Vampire mural, St Luke's Place.

22. From the Gorbals Vampire mural, turn left onto Ballater Street and head west, passing once more under the raised railway line. After a short distance, Ballater Street turns into Norfolk Street, and at the junction between Norfolk Street and South Portland Street, you will find the former Gorbals Public Library. Built by the Office of Public Works in the 1930s, it has a classical appearance reminiscent of a stripped-back art deco design. Again, this is one of the few surviving pre-1960s Gorbals buildings, but it ceased being a library in 1986.

23. Carry on west along Norfolk Street to its junction with Bridge Street, and as you do so, you will notice a sudden and dramatic change in the architecture. No longer are you surrounded by the modern buildings of the most-recent regeneration of the Gorbals. Instead, you are surrounded by much older architecture dating back as far as the early 1800s. This area is known as Laurieston, named after John Laurie, who sought to develop a refined residential area on the south bank of the Clyde. At one time, Laurieston would have been a hive of activity, but in recent years it has very much fallen on hard times, and although it has retained much of its older architecture, most of it is in very poor condition and at risk of being lost. The first of these buildings is a particularly impressive Glasgow style tenement featuring a corbelled octagonal corner turret, built in 1898 and designed by James Miller, situated on the corner of Norfolk Street and Bridge Street.

24. Turn right on to Bridge Street and head north along it. On the opposite site of the road is the former Bridge Street Railway Station, which was also designed by James Miller and opened in 1890. Built for the Caledonian Railways (and featuring their Lion Rampant insignia carved into its facade), it replaced the first Bridge Street Station, which was opened in 1840 on a site closer to the Clyde. Originally, Bridgeton was the main terminus for trains travelling between Glasgow, and the south and south-west of Scotland, with passengers and freight disembarking here before crossing the Clyde on foot, by carriage or by cart. As such an important terminus, the station was surrounded by fine buildings occupied by businesses offering services such as banking. However, when Glasgow Central Station was constructed in the 1870s, and then extended in the 1890s and early 1900s, trains were able to travel across the Clyde into the very centre of the city, and Laurieston lost its role as an important rail terminus. The second Bridge Street Station, which is the one still standing to this day, closed in 1905, and this can be seen as marking the start of the decline of the local area.

25. Opposite the former Bridge Street Station, at 63–67 Bridge Street is a mid-nineteenth-century blonde sandstone tenement, into which a ground-floor red sandstone bank has later been inserted. Designed by John James Burnet, this work was carried out in 1888. It originally served as the South Branch of the Savings Bank of Glasgow.

Blonde sandstone mid-19th-century tenement, with later red sandstone bank building inserted into it, art deco style building to its left, and Glasgow style tenement to its right.

26. Next to the former Savings Bank of Glasgow is a four-storey art deco building constructed in 1935 as a drapery warehouse for the Scottish Cooperative Wholesale Society. It was built as an extension to older the Kinning Park Cooperative Drapery Warehouse on Coburg Street, which you will visit later in this walk. Together with the surrounding buildings, these formed Glasgow's garment district, an industry which came to dominate the area after it lost its status as a railway terminus. This former garment district is important from an architectural point of view as it is one of the few blocks in Glasgow which has pretty much retained its original footprint.

27. Until recently, to the north of the Cooperative Building stood the Renaissance style India Building. Constructed for the wholesale stationery, account book and paper bag manufacturer Robert McGregor and Company, it was built in 1876. However, in recent years it had remained empty and unmaintained, with large amounts of buddleia growing out of its facade and into its roof. In the spring of 2024, it was deemed to be in such a poor state that it was at risk of imminent collapse and, as a result, work to demolish it began. This is an example of a major issue with preserving Glasgow's built heritage. It has a wealth of important older buildings, but many of these have now been poorly maintained for several decades. This can be for a number of reasons, but all too often it is because they are owned by absentee landlords, who either lack the money or the interest to maintain them. If Glasgow is to keep its unique and diverse architectural heritage, this is a problem which needs to be addressed or it risks losing many of its older buildings in the next few years at a rate not seen since the ill-advised wholesale destruction of the post-war period.

28. On the opposite side of Bridge Street, at the junction with Oxford Street to the north of where the India Building once stood, stands another of Laurieston's former grand bank buildings. Thought to have been designed by Bruce & Hay, it was constructed in 1884 as a branch of the Commercial Bank of Scotland, with tenements above it.

29. Turn right into Oxford Street and head east along it. Here, at No. 143, is another art deco style warehouse which once connected to the India Building. Designed by Charles J. McNair, it was built in 1928, with an extra upper storey added by Whyte, Galloway and Nicol in 1937. Originally built for Sloan and Company, who also owned the India Building at this time, in the early 2000s it became known as 'the Chateau' and was home to various art projects. It was also used as a rehearsal space for the then up-and-coming Glasgow band Franz Ferdinand. However, if action is not taken soon, it seems likely it will suffer a similar fate to the nearby India Building.

30. Further east along Oxford Street is its junction with Coburg Street. A short distance south along this street is a red sandstone building dating from 1910. Designed by Bruce & Hay, it was built for the Kinning Park Cooperative Society as a drapery warehouse and connected to the newer art deco style Cooperative Building on Bridge Street, which you viewed earlier on this walk. Again, it lies empty and is slowly decaying, and like its neighbouring buildings, is at risk of being lost.

31. Continue heading east along Oxford Street to its junction with Nicholson Street. Here, you will find a large pink building decorated with classical details. Designed by Alexander B. McDonald, it was completed in 1895 and served as a police station and barracks. It has a number of interesting relief sculptures on it, including a mask of the blindfolded Justice, and the crest of the Glasgow Police, with its motto 'Semper Vigilo' (which is Latin for 'always vigilant').

Fasces carved into facade of former police station and barracks, Oxford Street.

However, it also features a pair of fasces. Representing a bundle of rods with a projecting axe blade, in the middle of the twentieth century this became an emblem of Fascism, particularly in Italy, and indeed the term 'fascist' derives from it. However, it is a much older symbol, dating back at least to Ancient Rome, where it was used to represent the power of law and government, thus explaining its presence on a Victorian police station.

32. From Oxford Street, turn left onto Nicholson Street and head north. At its northern end, turn left into Carlton Place. While the buildings are in a rather poor state, this cobbled street, lined with classical style townhouses, is one of the finest remaining examples of Glasgow's Georgian architecture. Designed by Peter Nicholson and built at the start of the 1800s, these townhouses were originally intended as the centre piece for John Laurie's planned upmarket housing development on the south bank of the Clyde. They are divided into two terraces, with the eastern terrace being the grander of the pair.

33. The most impressive house on Carlton Place is Laurieston House, which at one point was home to John Laurie himself, and whose internal plasterwork makes it one of the most ornate Georgian townhouses left in the UK. This plasterwork, possibly inspired by the excavations at Pompeii and Herculaneum, is in the Greek revival style, and is believed to be the work of Francisco Bernasconi who was brought to Britain to decorate Windsor Castle by King George III. Despite its impressive internal decoration and its importance as a rare surviving representative of the Georgian period in Glasgow, like the rest of Carlton Place, Laurieston House is a very poor state and remains largely boarded up. While there are currently plans to turn it into private residential flats, this work does not seem to be progressing in any consistent manner, and the longer it remains in its current state, the greater the chances are that it will be lost forever. In addition, the current plans raise the question as to why such an architecturally important building has been allowed to remain into private hands in the first place, and why permission has been given to subdivide it, which will potentially risk damaging its unique interior and will certainly result in it being permanently lost from public view. As such, this is a prime example of the types of problems and issues currently facing heritage conservation in Glasgow.

34. Although most of the buildings in Carlton Place are part of Nicholson's two terraces of townhouses, there is one building which is markedly different – the red sandstone building at No. 63. It was built in 1908 as the office and warehouse for the wholesale ironmongers Finnie and Company, with offices presumably in the two-storey section facing on to Carlton Place and the warehouse in the taller building behind it on South Portland Street.

35. The final building on this walk is the third former bank in the Laurieston area. Constructed on the corner of Bridge Street and Carlton Place in 1857, it was designed in a Renaissance style by John Burnet Snr (whose son, John James Burnet designed the South Branch of the Savings Bank of Glasgow a short distance further south on Bridge Street). It was originally built for the Bank of Scotland, and you can still see its crest supported by two figures in classical dress at the very top of the building above the corner door. The fact that there were branches of three major banks along such a short stretch of Bridge Street, all housed in relatively grand, purpose-built premises, demonstrates how much money once flowed through Laurieston in general, and Bridge Street in particular, before its status as a railway terminus was removed. There is a lesson to be learned here by current and future town planners in Glasgow and elsewhere. If the accessibility of a local area is decreased, by removing or disrupting its transport links, whether by walking or by public transport, it can decimate its local economy and its desirability as a place to live and work. This is something which has happened repeatedly across Glasgow over the years, but especially with the construction of the M8 motorway through the city in the 1960s. A prime example of this is Anderston, which was essentially split in two by the construction of the Kingston Bridge (a short distance west down the Clyde from Bridge Street), and which has only recently started starting to recover from the negative impacts inflicted upon it by this, and other poorly thought through planning decisions.

Former Bank of Scotland, corner of Carlton Place and Bridge Street.

15. Tradeston and Kingston

Start Point: O2 Academy, Eglinton Street, Glasgow (**Location:** Lat/Lon: 55.85060, -4.25957; What3Words: ///lifted.kicked.asserts; Plus Code: VP2R+65V Glasgow).
Nearest Public Transport: Subway: Bridge Street Station (3 mins); Train: Central Station (15 mins); Bus: Eglinton Street (2 mins).

End Point: Kingston House, Clyde Place Quay, Glasgow (**Location:** Lat/Lon: 55.85522, -4.26121; What3Words: ///rings.wink.spark; Plus Code: VP4Q+3GM Glasgow). **Nearest Public Transport:** Subway: Bridge Street Station (15 mins); Train: Central Station (20 mins); Bus: Broomielaw (3 mins).

Distance: 4.5 kilometres/2.7 miles. **Time:** Allow 2.5 to 3.5 hours for this walk.
Level of Difficulty: Easy. This walk is entirely on paved surfaces.

Facilities: This is an area which is dominated by businesses. As a result, there are relatively few facilities available within it. There are some shops, cafes and restaurants are available around Paisley Road Toll, about two-thirds of the way into the walk. However, there are no publicly accessible toilets along the route of this walk.

Introduction

This walk covers the neighbouring areas of Tradeston and Kingston on the south side of the Clyde to the west of the Gorbals. The larger of the pair is Kingston, which was established on lands purchased by the city magistrates from Robert Douglas in 1647. However, it does not appear on any maps until around 1800. Although the origins of its name are unclear, it appears to be named after King George III. It was established at a time when the work to make the Clyde navigable as far east as Glasgow was starting to see results, increasing the need for docks within the city itself (rather than further west in the naturally deeper parts of the Clyde Estuary). This led to the establishment of Kingston Dock, the first enclosed dock on the upper Clyde, which finally opened in 1867. Tradeston, which sits between Kingston and the Gorbals, was created by the Trades House of Glasgow on land they purchased in 1790. Over the next thirty years, they created a gridiron of terraced houses, in part to exploit the era's cotton boom. Throughout the rest of the nineteenth century, Tradeston developed into a commercial hub, featuring a range of industries, most of which were associated in some way with shipbuilding and engineering. Unlike the neighbouring areas of the Gorbals to the east and Anderston on the northern side of the Clyde, which were subjected to comprehensive development plans that swept away most of their traditional buildings, both Tradeston and Kingston were left largely to decline as Glasgow's role as the workshop of the British Empire faded as the twentieth century wore on, alongside the Empire itself. This decline was accelerated with the construction of the M8 and M74 motorways, and in particular, the construction of the Kingston Bridge in the 1960s. The result was that by the 1990s, these two areas had many abandoned and derelict former industrial buildings. Since then, efforts have been made to repopulate the area through the conversion of older buildings into residential apartments, and bringing new commercial businesses, such as banks, to the area. However, much of it still retains the feel of a semi-abandoned post-industrial landscape, where newer developments are interspersed with decaying remnants from a long-gone, and much grander, industrial past.

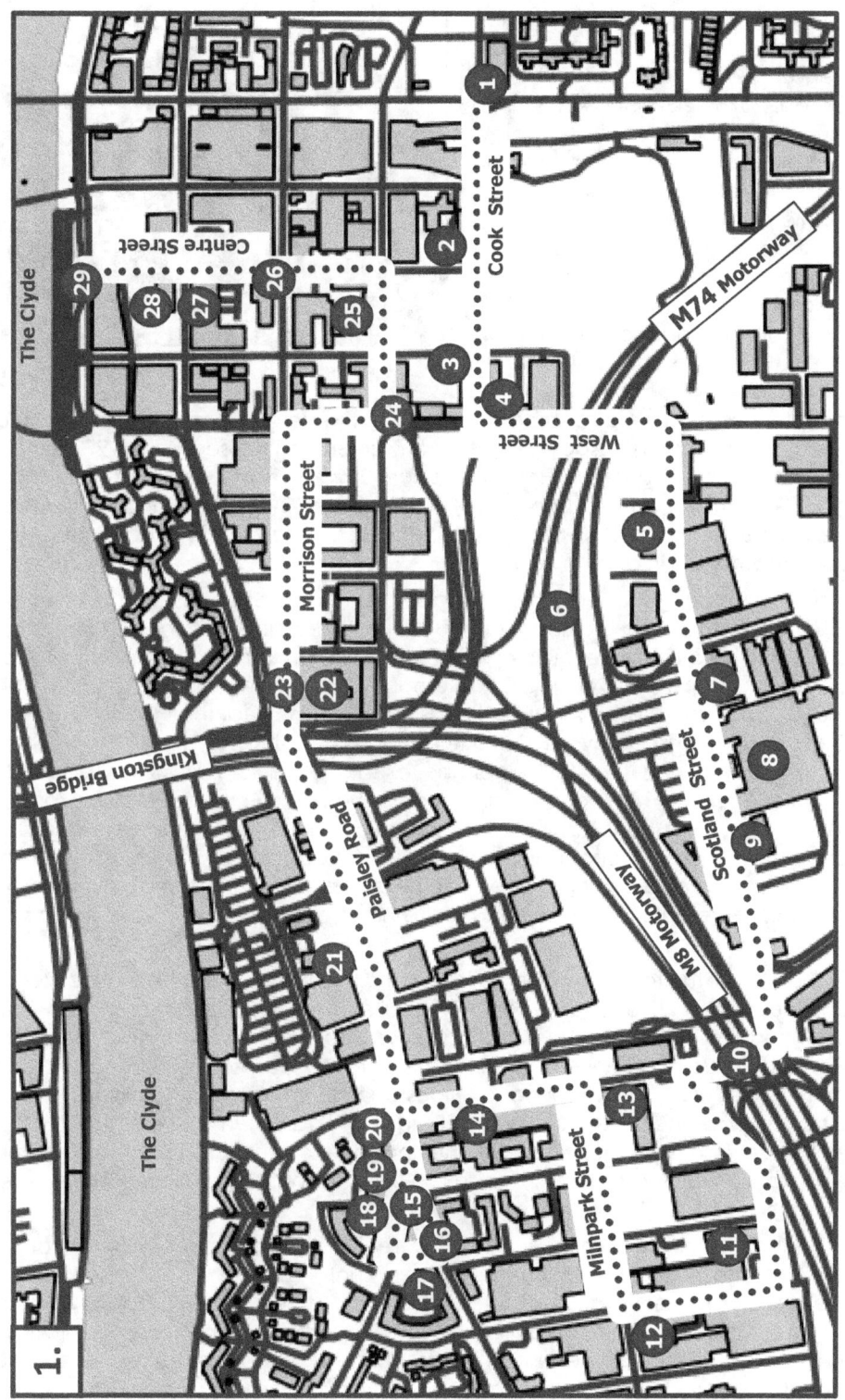

1. This walk starts at an impressive art deco former cinema on Eglinton Street, which forms the boundary between Laurieston and the Gorbals to the east, and Kingston to the west. Originally called the New Bedford Picture House, this cinema was designed by Lennox and McMath, and was built in 1932. It was constructed to replace the first Bedford Cinema, which was created in a converted church in 1920, and burned down in 1932. When it opened, the New Bedford Cinema could hold up to 2,300 people, and it is one of a surprising number of large art deco cinemas which can still be found across Glasgow. As with many cinemas, it closed in the 1970s and was turned into a bingo hall, However, since 2003, it has been home to the O2 Academy music venue. It previously had a sister 02 venue in another former art deco cinema, the ABC on Sauchiehall Street in central Glasgow. However, this was badly damaged in a fire in 2018.

   Art deco style New Bradford Cinema, Eglinton Street.

2. From the former New Bedford Cinema, cross Eglinton Street using the traffic lights and head west along the north side of Cook Street. At its junction with Centre Street is a large neo-baroque building constructed from red brick. This is the former Tradeston Telephone Exchange. Built around 1935, when the telephone network in the UK was rapidly expanding, it has been estimated that when it opened. Glasgow already had over 100,000 telephone lines. This was a great improvement on the time when the first telephone exchange in Glasgow was opened on Douglas Street in 1879, around fifty years before. However, due to advances in technology, and specifically the introduction of all-figure numbers and direct dialling, such large exchanges soon fell out of favour, and by the 1970s, the building had become vacant. While there have been a number of attempts over the years to breathe new life into it, none of these have been successful and it has simply been left to decay.

3. To the west of the former Tradeston Telephone Exchange is another distinctive brick-built building. This Venetian Gothic style building, complete with a tall, tower, was designed by William F. McGibbon and was constructed in 1900 as part of the Clydesdale Paint, Colour and Oil Works. On the corner of the building at the junction between Cook Street and Tradeston Street is a terracotta plaque featuring a stag's head. This is the trademark of Stag Brand paints which were formerly made on this site, and were marketed with the slogan 'Ask for the Stag Brand'. While much of this paint works was demolished in 2002, this distinctive building remains, at least for the time being, but it is at risk of being lost.

4. From the former paintworks, cross Cook Street at the lights directly in front of it. On the opposite side of the road is the former Eglinton Engine Works, which occupies the corner site between Cook Street and West Street. Built in 1855 for A. and W. Smith, it originally specialised in producing machinery for the sugar-processing industry and later became Smith Mirrlees. During its time of operation, this company would have produced sugar machinery that was exported to places like Cuba and Puerto Rico, where the use of slaves on sugar plantations was still legal until later in

the nineteenth century, as well as to other Caribbean islands. By the end of the 1860s, they were also producing railway wagons, weighbridges and even steam locomotives. In the 1950s, the company was taken over by the London-based sugar refiners Tate and Lyle, and manufacturing finally ceased on this site in 1988. In the early 2000s, it was converted into residential housing. This has been done in a relatively sympathetic manner, and you can still recognise the different structures of the original works.

5. From the entrance to the former Eglinton Engine Works, follow its outer wall along Cook Street and then turn south onto West Street. A short distance along West Street, after you have passed under the M74 motorway, the road curves to the right and merges into Scotland Street. Follow this curve and walk along the south side of Scotland Street. On the opposite side of the road you will see a large blonde sandstone building. Designed in a classical style, it was constructed in two parts: the larger western industrial section, featuring an arched cartway, in 1864; and the smaller eastern office section in 1870. At one time, this was home to Blair, Campbell and McLean's Scotland Street Copper Works, which specialised in producing domes for locomotives and copper vessels for the brewing and distilling industry. While much reduced in size today, between 1891 and 1903 this was the largest copperworks in Scotland. The office section also served as part of Howden's Marine Engineering Works, more of which can be found further west along Scotland Street.

6. As you carry on west along Scotland Street, you can see the M74 motorway and its interchange with the M8 running along a raised embankment to the north. Consisting of up to thirteen parallel lanes, between them these motorways create a major barrier to the free movement of people between the south and the north of Glasgow, cutting this area off from the rest of the city. This is likely to have contributed to the decline of an area already affected by the changing industrial activities, and may still be contributing to its current state and lack of regeneration even now, some fifty years later.

7. At 173 Scotland Street is a rather dilapidated brick building with a very interesting history. Designed by the architect John Gordon, and the engineers Simpson and Wilson, it was built in 1895 to house the power station for new Glasgow's Subway system. The third-oldest subway system in the world (after the London Underground and Budapest Metro), it consists of two continuous tunnels forming a rough oval beneath the city's streets.

Former power station for Glasgow Subway system.

As it was entirely underground and its tunnels were much narrower than most other underground systems, this meant its trains could not be pulled by traditional steam locomotives. Instead, two massive steam engines were installed in this building which powered two loops of continuously moving cable, one running the length of each of the two tunnels. The trains were equipped with grippers which would grab onto these cables, allowing them to be pulled through the tunnel to the next station, where the grippers would be released and the train would come to a halt. This unique solution meant that the Glasgow Subway system was not just the only cable-hauled underground passenger system in the world, but it was also substantially cleaner than those that relied on the use of steam locomotives (which generated large amounts of steam, smoke and soot within their tunnels). This may also explain while the Glasgow Subway was still powered by steam engines and cables until 1935, some forty-five years after the first electric trains were introduced on the London Underground. When the Glasgow Subway was converted to electricity in that year, the power station was finally closed. Shortly after this, it became part of the neighbouring Howden Engineering Works. However, by the 1990s, that too had closed and this building has been sliding into dereliction ever since.

8. Next to the old subway power station is the original part of the former Howden's Works. Designed by Nisbet Sinclair, it was built in 1897, with additional buildings added in 1907 and 1908. Howden's was founded by the Scottish engineer James Howden in the 1850s to design and build boilers and steam engines for ships, and he opened his first factory on Scotland Street in 1862. Howden is probably best remembered for his invention of the forced-draught system, which improved boiler efficiency and greatly reduced the amount of coal used by ship's engines. Howden's boiler system was used on more than 1,000 boilers in the 1880s and by the early 1900s, they were fitted to the *Lusitania* and the *Mauritania*, the fastest passenger liners at the time they were built. Howden died in 1913, but his company continued until the 1980s, and its work included building some of the tunnel-boring machines used to construct the Channel Tunnel (work which was carried out on this site). The last of Glasgow's great Victorian engineering works, the Scotland Street site closed in 1988, and has pretty much been left to decay ever since.

9. To the west of the former Howden's Works is the former Scotland Street School, designed by Charles Rennie Mackintosh and built in 1903. While it is viewed as one of his most important commissions, it was not an easy one, with Mackintosh frequently clashing with the school board over its design and the cost of realising it. However, the resulting building remains impressive to this day and it is now viewed as one of Glasgow's architectural gems. One of its most distinctive features is a pair of Scottish baronial style tower staircases with expansive windows to bring light into the building, particularly the ground-floor exercise hall. Originally designed to hold

Former janitor's house, Charles Rennie Mackintosh's Scotland Street School.

1,250 pupils, by the time the school closed in 1979 the surrounding area had experienced a substantial decline, due both to a loss of traditional industries, and the impacts of city-wide urban redevelopment projects, such as the construction of the M8 motorway, and its enrolment had dropped to less than 100. In 1990, the school reopened as the Scotland Street School Museum, where children could, among other things, learn about life in a Victorian school through interactive experiences, including one where actors were employed to play the role of strict disciplinarian teachers. At the time of writing, the museum is closed as it, and the Mackintosh building it occupies, undergoes an extensive programme of refurbishment.

10. From Scotland Street School, head west to the junction between Scotland Street and Shields Road. Cross Scotland Street at these lights and walk a short distance further west before turning right onto Seaward Street. Follow Seaward Street under the M8 and out onto its northern side. As you pass under the M8, you can appreciate its scale and how much of a scar its construction inflicted across the city, with many homes, businesses, streets, and in some cases entire communities, being demolished to make way for it.

11. Once you have reached the north side of the M8, cross Seaward Street at the pedestrian traffic lights, and return south along its western side. Here, you will find a small path leading off to your right which will take you parallel to the M8. This will eventually emerge at the southern end of Stanley Street, one of many roads truncated by the construction of the motorway. Directly ahead of you on Stanley Street, is a large red sandstone building. This is the former Our Lady and St Margaret's Primary School, which was designed by Bruce and Hay, and was built in 1910. At five storeys high, this large palazzo style school gives you an idea of the size of the community which once lived in this area before much of it was bulldozed to make way for the M8. One of the most remarkable features of this school was its playgrounds, which, in order to save on space, were located on its upper storeys, and would have provided impressive views across Glasgow and out to the countryside beyond. Immediately to the north of the school is the former Our Lady and St Margaret's Presbytery. Designed by the noted ecclesiastical architects Pugin & Pugin in 1882, it was once a fine building which is now derelict and in great danger of being completely lost. The associated church, also by Pugin & Pugin, has already been demolished, and the stained glass from its windows can now be found further down the Clyde coast in Ayr's Cathedral of the Good Shepherd.

12. Return to the south end of Stanley Street and walk west between the school and the motorway to reach Portman Steet. This street is lined with polychromatic brick buildings, a style which was widely used on Glasgow's mid-nineteenth-century industrial structures. With the industries which they once housed long-gone, these buildings are now home to a variety of entertainment enterprises, including indoor soft-play arenas and escape rooms. Among the buildings themselves, one of the most important is the former Kingston Engine Works, on the corner between Portman Street and Milnpark Street. The Kingston Engine Works was founded in 1866 and was owned by the Smith brothers (who also owned the Eglinton Engine Works which you passed earlier on this walk). This works specialised in making machinery for Glasgow's many shipbuilders and boilermakers. Beside it, on Milnpark Street, is the former home of the Kinning Park Colour Works. Built in 1892, its cart entrance is a particularly beautiful example of polychromatic brickwork.

Cart entrance to Kinning Park Colour Works, decorated with polychromatic brickwork.

13. From its junction with Portman Street, head east along Milnpark Street to its junction with Seaward Street. Here, you will find the Kinning Park Pumping Station. Designed by the engineers D. and A. Home Morton, it was built at the start of the twentieth century and was the pumping station for the Shieldhall sewage works. Originally, it housed two massive marine steam engines, but these have since been replaced by electrical pumps. With its distinctive curvilinear parapet, this is a nice example of the care put into the design of functional municipal buildings, such as sewage-pumping stations, in the Victorian and Edwardian Eras, something it would be difficult to imagine ever happening today.

14. Turn left onto Seaward Street and head north along it. As you do so, at No. 58 you will pass a distinctive building with tall, arched windows. This is Seaward House and if you touch its facade, you may be surprised to find much of it is made of metal rather than brick or stone. This is because it is one of the few cast-iron buildings left in Glasgow. Its exact history is not well documented, but it may have started life as a smithy or an ironworks.

15. Walk to the north end of Seaward Steet, and turn left on to Paisley Road. When you do, you will find yourself facing one of Southside's best-loved buildings. Situated on a narrow strip of land at the junction between Govan Road and Paisley Road West, it is commonly referred to as the Angel Building, due to the distinctive statue on its summit, but it was originally the built as the Ogg Brothers Department Store. Designed by Bruce & Hay in a beautiful French Renaissance style, it was built in around 1885. The winged figure, which was created by James A. Ewing in 1889, is officially called the *Spirit of Commerce and Industry*. However, it is more frequently referred to as the *Kinning Park Angel*, the *Angel of the South* or simply *Mrs Ogg* (after the former department store on which she stands). At either end of eastern facade of this building are inscriptions which indicate that, in 1949, the ground-floor shop was converted

1889 former Ogg Brothers Department Store, Paisley Road Toll.

into a branch of the clothing shop Burtons. These foundation stones, inscribed with the names of members of the Burton family who installed them, were placed on all branches of Burtons opened in the 1920s and 1930s. However, these are some of the very few examples from the post-war period.

16. Cross the road at the traffic lights in front of the former Ogg Brothers Department Store and walk down the pavement on its left-hand side. On the opposite side of the road, you will find a beautiful, if rather faded, coat of arms on a building at the corner between Paisley Road West and Stanley Street. This is the royal coat of arms of Scotland of James VI (which differs from the United Kingdom's version in having the Scottish unicorn on its left-hand side, rather than on its right, and is topped by a lion holding a sword rather than one standing on all fours). It marks the location of a former branch of the British Linen Bank. This bank was originally formed by royal charter in Edinburgh in 1746 as the British Linen Company, and it commonly used the royal coat of arms of Scotland on its branches and even on its banknotes.

17. At the western end of the former Ogg Brothers Store, turn right and head south along the small lane between it and the Viceroy pub. As you do so, on the back of the pub you will see a number of distinctive murals, including a girl trapping something under a glass. This is designed to be interactive, and if you position yourself correctly, you can take a photograph where it looks like it is you who is being caught in the glass. However, you need to access the pub's beer garden to be able to do this. It was painted in 2021 by Rogue One, an artist who has created some of Glasgow's most distinctive murals.

18. At the northern end of the lane, turn right on to Govan Road and head east, back towards its junction with Paisley Road West. Cross to the northern side of Govan Road at the lights by the front of the Ogg Brothers building and look for a large black metal post set into a small open area in front of a modern housing development. Dating from the early nineteenth century, this is an cast-iron tollgate post that once formed part of Parkhouse Toll, which operated turnpike roads from Glasgow to Greenock via Govan, and to Paisley, between 1780 and 1883. While it might not seem like much, this is a reminder from an important period in the development of Glasgow, and indeed of Scotland as a whole. As the country became more industrialised in the late eighteenth century, both people and goods became increasingly mobile, and with that came the need for a better road network. This came in the form of turnpikes, new roads which charged tolls for their use. There are still many reminders of what is known as the Turnpike era across Glasgow, mostly in the names of major road junctions (such as this one, which is still called Paisley Road Toll), but also in the form of old toll buildings and other related structures, such as this gatepost. This post was moved to its current location in 1988, but a plaque at the edge of the road by the traffic lights marks where it originally stood.

Early 19th-century tollgate post, Paisley Road Toll.

19. To the east of the old tollgate post is Glasgow's Grand Ole Opry, one of largest country and western clubs in the UK, and indeed in Europe. However, the building started out around 1900 as a post office, with a carriage-hirers and stables and a funeral undertakers in the basement. It was then converted into a 1,100-seater cinema called the Imperial in 1921. It was renamed the Ritz after a fire in 1952, and finally closed in 1959, After this, it first became the Marquee Club and then the Grand Ole Opry, which opened in 1974. Much of the building's architecture, both inside and out, is largely unchanged from its days as a cinema, and, apparently, there are still the remains of the retaining walls of a mortuary in the basement, dating back the period when it was home to an undertakers.

20. From the Grand Ole Opry, head east along Paisley Road until you reach its junction with Mavisbank Gardens. Turn left here, and walk along Mavisbank Gardens to its junction with Marine Crescent. To the north of this junction you will find an inscribed commemorative stone marking the commissioning and construction of Cessnock Dock, which once stood on this site. Later renamed the Prince's Dock, it had 35 acres of water, making it the largest dock on the upper Clyde. Costing almost £1 million to build and equip, it was officially opened in 1895. However, it closed in the 1970s and it was largely filled in in the 1980s. In 1988, this reclaimed land formed the site of the Glasgow Garden Festival, an event which is fondly remembered by many Glaswegians, and is often credited with kickstarting the city's post-industrial rebirth. After the Garden Festival closed, almost all of it was dismantled, and housing and leisure facilities were built in its place. However, if you walk a short distance west along Marine Crescent, and look back towards Paisley Road, you will see the emblem of the Garden Festival picked out in contrasting bricks on the exposed gable of the corner tenement.

Emblem of 1988 Glasgow Garden Festival on exposed gable of tenement building.

21. Return to Paisley Road, and turn left. A short distance further east, you will find a large Edwardian baroque red sandstone building. Designed by Robert W. Horne and opened in 1904 (although it is dated as 1903), this was an unusual combination of a public halls, library and police station. It also gives an idea of the previous status of the Kingston area of Glasgow, which became home to the first enclosed dock in the city in 1867, just as Glasgow was rapidly developing into a global mercantile and industrial powerhouse. Kingston Dock was closed in 1966 when work began on the construction of the Kingston Bridge to carry the planned M8 motorway across the Clyde. It was later filled in and the area used for housing.

22. If you look east along Paisley Road from the former Kingston Halls, you will see not only the Kingston Bridge, but also the dome of a large stone building topped by a golden statue. This is the *Spirit of Light and Life*, created in the 1890s by James A. Ewing (who also created the statue on the top of the former Ogg Brothers Department Store) for the headquarters of the Scottish Cooperative Wholesale Society. After a century of being a major landmark in the Southside area of Glasgow, the original sculpture crumbled as it was being removed during work to convert the building into residential housing in the 1990s. However, in 2015, a local engineer by the name of Bill Ritchie realised that as the building was then encased in scaffolding to allow repairs to be carried out, there was a golden opportunity to finally replace the statue. Working with the artist Kenny Mackay, and to a very tight deadline, a replica of the original statue was hastily created and installed in the brief window before the scaffolding came down in June 2016, and once again *Light and Life* can be seen watching over the Glasgow from her vantage point high above the south bank of the Clyde.

23. Walk east along Paisley Road and under the Kingston Bridge. Where the road forks, cross it at the traffic lights so that you can take the right-hand fork (called Morrison Street) to get a closer look at the former Scottish Cooperative Wholesale Society headquarters buildings. Known as Cooperative House, it was designed in a grand Louis XIV French Renaissance style by Bruce & Hay, and was constructed in 1893. An imposing building, it is a reminder of the days when cooperative societies played a major role in the economics of Glasgow. Cooperative societies provided everything from grocery shopping and milk to life insurance and funeral care, and even went as far as producing their own light bulbs to allow them to be sold at a reduced cost. Any profits made by such societies were either re-invested back into their own development, or were paid out to its members as dividends. It is estimated that, at times, as much one pound in every eight spent in Glasgow was spent within the city's various cooperative societies, creating a powerful circular economy which kept the money made in Glasgow within the city. This contrasts sharply with the current situation where much of what is earned in Glasgow now goes into the coffers of multinational corporations based elsewhere, meaning that it is removed from the local economy. At this point, it is worth reflecting on the fact that much of Glasgow was not built, as might be assumed, on unrestrained capitalism, but rather on the principles of municipal socialism and cooperation. In this respect, it is interesting to note that this building's design is thought to be an adaption of Bruce & Hay's submission to the 1880 design competition for the new Glasgow City Chambers, suggesting that the Cooperative Society may have seen itself as a rival to the Glasgow Corporation (as the City Council was then known) in terms of the role it played in the city's economy.

Statue of Light and Life, *top of Scottish Cooperative Wholesale Society headquarters, Morrison Street.*

24. From Cooperative House, head east along Morrison Street before crossing it at the lights at its junction with West Street and heading south to the junction between West Street and Wallace Street. This junction is dominated by a red-brick building which is reminiscent of the former Clydesdale Paint Works Building on Cook Street, which you visited earlier on this walk. This is because it not only stands on the same city block, but it was also designed by the same architect, William F. McGibbon. Designed in a Flemish style, it was built in the 1890s as a grain mill for the millers Hamilton and Manson.

25. On the next block east along Wallace Street, and continuing round onto the neighbouring Centre Street, is the former Southern Fire Station. Designed by Alexander B. McDonald in a free Renaissance style and built in 1914, it was one of the first fire stations in the city to be constructed specifically to accommodate motorised fire engines rather than horse-drawn ones. The building not only housed the fire engines, but provided accommodation for the firemen and their families in thirty-six identical apartments. Its facade features a number of rather beautiful relief

sculptures, all related in some way to fire. Of particular note is the sculpture at the northern end of the Centre Street Facade which features Poseidon, the Greek god of the sea, wrestling with a fire-breathing dragon, and presumably represents the battle between firemen and the fires which they were charged with extinguishing.

26. Head north along Centre Street to its junction with Nelson Street. While it may seem that there is little of note at this junction, it was the site of one of the worst civilian tragedies in the UK during World War II. At 12.01 a.m. on 14 March 1941, a German parachute mine exploded close to this junction, devastating much of the local area. In total, 110 people were killed in the blast, including 11 people on a passing tram and 3 French sailors on the Broomielaw on the far side of the Clyde. This represented almost 10 per cent of all the people killed in what became known as the Clydebank Blitz. However, there remains no memorial to mark the spot, nor indeed to any of the 650 people killed across Glasgow during this bombing campaign.

Junction between Centre Street and Nelson Street where 110 people were killed by German parachute mine on 14 March 1941.

27. Cross Nelson Street using the pedestrian lights and carry on north along Centre Street to its junction with Kingston Street. Turn left onto it and head west to No. 73. This is the Cooperative Memorial Building which was constructed in memory of all the members of cooperative societies who fought in World War I between 1914 and 1919 (which is stated on a plaque above its main entrance). However, despite being a memorial building, it seems to be largely unloved and is in rather poor condition.

28. On the opposite side of Kingston Street is the former warehouse of the draper Robert Kerr. Built in 1878, it is a classical style commercial building with the unusual feature that the shape of the windows on each floor follows a different, but complimentary, design. This building was also, at one time, the home of the Kingston Brass Company, and is now home to Barclays Bank, part of Glasgow's large and growing international financial services sector.

29. Return to Centre Street, cross it using the pedestrian lights and head north to the southern bank of the Clyde. To the left of the northern end of Centre Street is Kingston House, where this walk ends. Built in 1878 as a commercial building, between 1883 and 1927 it served as the Clyde Place Model Lodging House. During this time, it contained over 300 bunks, and only 6 bathrooms, on its 3 upper floors. The lower floors were occupied by a variety of businesses, which over the years included McGregor and Company (which made chronometers for the Admiralty), William Bartons and Company (a ship's chandlers), Russel and Paton (an outfitters) and Hetherington and Company (a file manufacturers). Of course, with Glasgow being Glasgow, there was also a public house on the corner of the ground floor.

16. Govan

Start Point: Cessnock Subway Station, Glasgow (**Location:** Lat/Lon: 55.85201, -4.29410; What3Words: ///always.twice.latter; Plus Code: VP24+R92 Glasgow).
Nearest Public Transport: Subway: Cessnock Subway Station (1 min); Train: None; Bus: Paisley Road West Road (1 min).

End Point: Govan Old Parish Church Glasgow (**Location:** Lat/Lon: 55.86433, -4.31307; What3Words: ///force.alive.goes; Plus Code: VM7P+PQM Glasgow). **Nearest Public Transport:** Subway: Govan Subway Station (10 mins); Train: None; Bus: Govan Road (2 mins).

Distance: 5.3 kilometres/4.2 miles. **Time:** Allow 3 to 4.5 hours for this walk.
Level of Difficulty: Moderate. While this walk is entirely on paved surfaces, it is relatively long.

Facilities: There are shops, cafes, restaurants and bars available at fairly regular intervals along this walk. Publicly accessible toilets are available in Govan Cross Shopping Centre, which is passed about a third of the way along it and again close to its end. Toilets are also available at Elderpark Library which is visited about halfway through the walk.

Introduction

Although many areas of visited during the walks in this book primarily came into existence as Glasgow grew rapidly in the 1700s and 1800s, Govan has a much longer history, and one which can rival that of Glasgow itself. Like Glasgow, Govan owes its origins to being a crossing point for the Clyde, and before it was deepened to allow ships to travel as far east as the city centre, there was a ford at Govan which allowed people to cross the Clyde at low tide. Govan itself may have started out as an early Christian settlement in the fifth and sixth centuries when it was part of the Celtic kingdom of Strathclyde, and it quickly grew to become one of its major centres of power. Govan was also at the forefront of the conflict between the Vikings and the Celtic tribes of the west coast of Scotland, with both Viking and early Christian grave markers having been found within the graveyard of Govan Old Parish Church. This includes an intricately carved sarcophagus which is believed to have once held the body of Saint Constantine, a Pictish king thought to have been killed by Vikings around 876, and which is now on display in this church. The church itself was at the heart of medieval Govan, and first appears in the historic records in the early 1100s. Like many other parts of Glasgow, its early industries included milling and weaving, but by the end of the 1700s it was starting to become more industrialised. In particular, efforts by the River Improvement Trust to make the Clyde navigable as far east as the centre of Glasgow also proved highly beneficial for Govan, allowing it to develop the shipbuilding industry with which it would become synonymous by the start of the twentieth century. This industrialisation led to a massive increase in its population, which rose from just under 10,000 in 1864 to almost 100,000 by 1907, making it the seventh-largest town in Scotland. However, its existence as an independent entity came to an end in 1912 when it was annexed by its larger neighbour and became part of Glasgow. By the end of the twentieth century, much of the shipbuilding on which modern Govan was built had disappeared, resulting in high levels of unemployment and social deprivation. However, despite this, Govan has retained its own unique identity within the larger city and unlike many other working class areas of the city, it has also retained many of its older buildings.

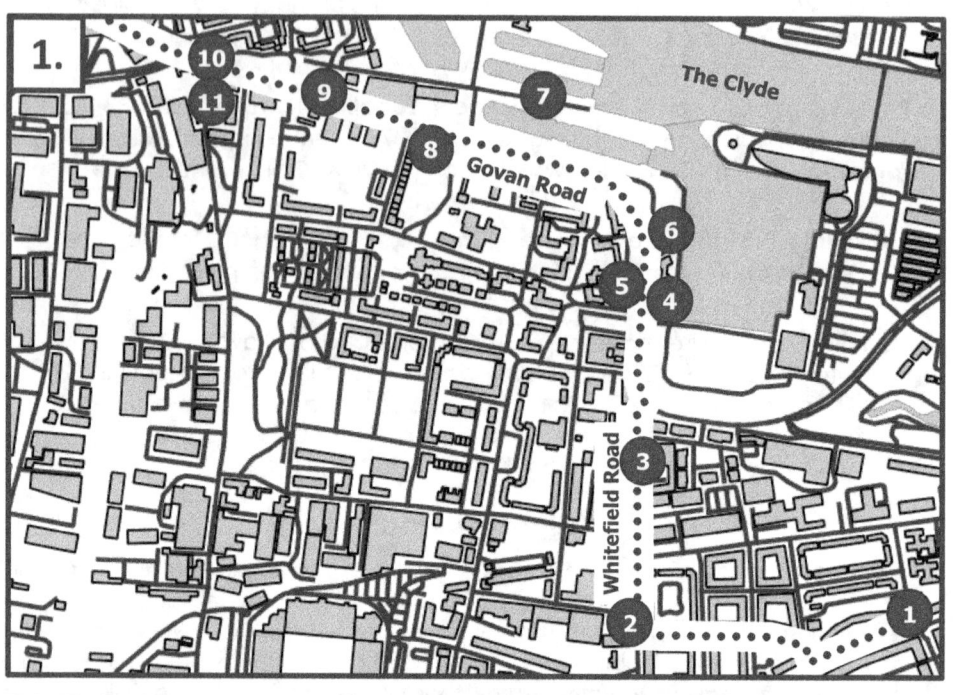

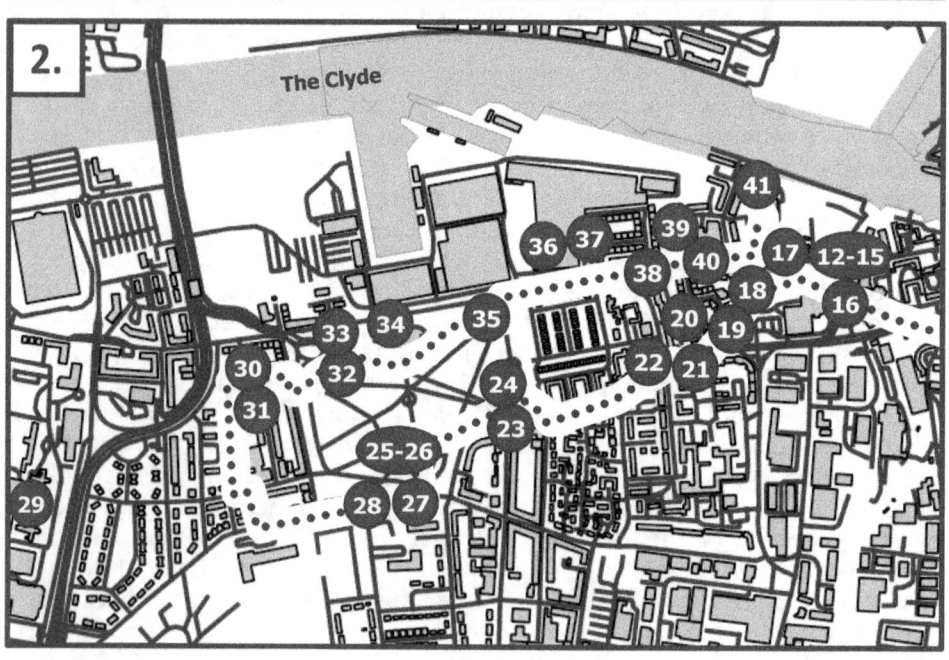

1. This walk starts outside Cessnock Subway Station just to the south-east of Govan. To the west of the entrance of the subway station is Walmer Crescent. Built between 1857 and 1862, it was one of the first and most impressive tenements designed by Alexander 'Greek' Thomson, an architect who, in many ways, set the framework for Glasgow's architectural style for much of the following century. While it is hard to admire most of this building due to the presence of a row of mature trees between it and Paisley Road West, its eastern terminal, with an impressive column of recessed bay windows (which are a characteristic of Greek Thomson's architectural style), is easy to view and appreciate. Below this eastern end is Cessnock Subway Station. Built in 1896, it would have been a substantial engineering challenge to construct this station beneath such an imposing building without damaging it. However, it does mean that Cessnock is the only subway station in Glasgow which is entered through a listed Victorian building.

Terminal pavilion, Alexander 'Greek' Thomson's Walmer Crescent, Cessnock.

2. Walk west along Walmer Crescent, allowing time to admire the rest of Greek Thomson's tenement building, before turning right onto Harley Street and then immediately left onto Ibrox Street. At the western end of Ibrox Street, turn north onto Whitefield Street. Opposite this junction, at 35 Whitefield Street, is a distinctive two-storey classical style building which seems at odds with many of the surrounding buildings. While it might not look like it now, this was once St Michael's Episcopal Church, which was built around 1890 on the site of the former Bellahouston Baths. It was used as a church until the late 1940s when it became an industrial premises. It was presumably around this time that the original entrance in the centre of the building was blocked up and a new one created to its right.

3. From its junction with Ibrox Street, head north along Whitefield Street to No. 140. Here, you will find Graham House, a large building with a design vaguely reminiscent of a castle. Constructed in 1905, it was built as HMS Graham, a military drill hall and headquarters for the Clyde Division of the Royal Navy Volunteer Reserves. It continued its naval role until 1993, but is now home to the 205 (Scottish) Field Hospital, the only Army Reserve Field Hospital in Scotland.

4. Carry on up Whitefield Street to its junction with Govan Road. On the north-east corner of this junction, you will see a Romanesque style brick tower. Built in 1912, this served as an auxiliary hydraulic tower for Prince's Dock, once the largest dock in Glasgow. The purpose of this tower was to act as an accumulator tank for the water used to power a hydraulic coal hoist. The main hydraulic powerhouse for this dock, with its distinctive chimney based on the ancient Tower of the Winds in Athens, can be found further east, on Pacific Quay, close to the Squinty Bridge. This building is visited as part of the Clyde Waterfront walk.

5. Directly to the north of the junction between Whitefield Street and Govan Road is the former Govan Town Hall. Designed by Thomson & Sandilands (the Thomson of which was the eldest surviving son of Alexander 'Greek' Thomson) in a beaux-arts Renaissance style, it was built between 1897 and 1904. Constructed as Govan's answer to the ornate and extravagant City Chambers Glasgow had built on George Square on the 1880s, it shows the extensive resources which the burgh of Govan could draw upon at this time. However, by 1912, Govan had lost its independent status and had been incorporated into the nearby city. As well as its ornate domes, this building features a range of well-executed sculptures by Archibald McFarlane Shannan and James Charles Young. This includes sculptures on the spandrels above the arched windows representing the Textile Industries, Science, Commerce, Architecture, Drama and Music. There is also a rather unique procession of putti playing musical instruments and carrying shipbuilding tools, as well as the Govan coat of arms, on its southern facade. This coat of arms can also be found in the ironwork above the main entrance, where it is flanked by sculpted portraits of James Kirkwood (on the left) and John Marr (right), who were the Provosts of Govan at the time of its construction.

6. Cross to the eastern side of Govan Road at the traffic lights in front of the former Govan Town Hall, and then follow the road northwards until you reach the entrance to Canting Way on your right. From Canting Way, you can look out across a small inlet from the Clyde to an area now known as Pacific Quay. Today, it is dominated by a series of modern buildings, including Glasgow Tower, the Glasgow Science Centre, the IMAX Cinema and the BBC Building. However, this was once the location of the Clyde Navigation Trust's 35-acre Prince's Dock. It closed in the 1970s and was filled in in the 1980s. This then became the site of the Glasgow Garden Festival in 1988, which is seen by many as the event which help kickstart Glasgow's rebirth as a post-industrial city. Little remains of this festival, and one of the few permanent structures associated with it is Bell's Bridge, which allowed pedestrians to cross from the Scottish Events Campus (built on the north side of the Clyde on the site of the former Queen's Dock) to the Garden Festival, and now to the buildings of Pacific Quay. The houses on Canting Way are some of the few buildings left standing from the Garden Festival, and were constructed as model homes to show the type of housing which would be built on the site once the festival itself was over.

7. Return to Govan Road and follow it as it curves to the west. At the junction where Stag Street leads north towards the Clyde, turn right and walk a short distance along it. Through the fence to the east lies the former Govan Graving Docks. Built for the Clyde Navigation Trust (who also constructed Prince's Dock) between 1869 and 1898, it consisted of three dry docks where ships could be built and fixed. At this time, Docks 1 and 3 were the deepest dry docks in Britain and could take the largest ships which then existed. They finally closed in

Dry dock, Govan Graving Docks shipyard.

1987, and have been abandoned ever since. However, they are of historical importance and have a huge amount of potential as a public amenity. Yet, it seems most likely they will eventually be converted into private residential housing.

8. Again, return to Govan Road and head west along its northern side. A short distance beyond the junction with Stag Street, and on the other side of the road, is a four-storey red sandstone building decorated with a series of sculpted portraits. Designed by Frank Stirrat and built in 1890, this is the former Govan Press Building. The portraits are all linked to printing and writing, and represent Johannes Gutenberg (who introduced the moveable type printing to Europe), Robert Burns (Scotland's national poet), Sir Walter Scott (arguably Scotland's most famous and influential writer) and William Caxton (who introduced the printing press to Britain). Between them are

Portraits, Govan Press Building, Govan Road.

portraits of Mr and Mrs Cossar. John Cossar and his wife, Jane White Brown, founded the Govan Press in 1878, but John died shortly after this building was opened in 1890. Jane then ran the business successfully until her own death in 1926. The company they founded (John Cossar Limited) finally closed in 1983.

9. Continue further west along Govan Road to its junction with Napier Street. Here, you will find a gap site where Napier House once stood. This was an ornate Glasgow style building constructed in 1898 using experimental non-reinforced concrete, which served as a lodging house for former seamen. Unfortunately, it was demolished in 2009, and the site is now used as a community garden. Overlooking this site, on the exposed gable of the neighbouring tenement, is a mural of a young girl picking daffodils which was created in 2022 by the street artist Smug.

10. Further west, and on the opposite side of the street at its junction with Broomloan Road, is 705 Govan Road, the former Govan branch of the Glasgow Savings Bank. Designed by Eric A. Sutherland and built in 1906, the ground floor is faced with hard-wearing pink granite, while the upper floors are made of red sandstone. These upper floors are tenement flats, which may have originally been occupied by bank employees. To save on space, the traditional back court drying green for these flats was placed on a flat roof at the top of the building, whereas the corner turret was designed to contain the washhouse, a feature found in few other Glasgow tenements. The shape of his turret presumably gave rise to the building's local nickname of the Potted Heid (i.e. head) Bank.

11. At this point in the walk, there is an optional detour a short distance south along Broomloan Road where you will find the rear elevation of the former Govan Police Station and courtrooms (built in 1866 with its main entrance on the neighbouring Orkney Street). Part of this rear elevation consists of a three-storey polychromatic brick prison block. Built in 1898, it contained forty cells, and still retains the bars on its tiny cell windows. If you take this detour, please cross the road at the nearby traffic lights rather than attempting to cross it at this junction, as at times it can be a surprisingly fast and busy road. If you take this detour, return to Govan Road afterwards and cross to its north side, again using the same traffic lights.

12. From the former Glasgow Savings Bank building, carry on west along Govan Road to Govan Cross, which is marked by a small pedestrianised square centred on an ornamental drinking fountain. The first building of interest for this walk at Govan Cross is Govan New Parish Church, which faces onto its eastern side. Designed in a Gothic style by Robert Baldie, it was built in 1873. To the right of this church is a row of shops, with accommodation above, which was originally used as the church hall and offices. These were also the original home of Fairfield School. Between the church and the hall stands a square tower with a large wooden belfry, which was originally this topped by a 50-metre (150 foot) tall spire.

13. At the centre of the pedestrianised area at Govan Cross is a decorative cast-iron drinking fountain designed by Cruikshanks and Company, and made at the Denny Ironworks in 1884. Dedicated to John Aitkin, the first Medical Officer of Health for the burgh of Govan, who died aged forty-four in 1880, it features a putto holding a paddle, which can also be found on a number of other drinking fountains around Glasgow, as well as some rather wonderful miniature crocodiles on the inside corners of the hexagonal canopy. Surrounding the fountain is a series of inscribed flagstones. These are part of a set of thirty-four engravings positioned around this fountain, outside the nearby subway station and near the Govan Shopping Centre. Created by Kate Robinson, they portray the geographic, religious, industrial and social history of Govan.

14. On the north-western corner of Govan Cross, at 7 Water Row, is a simple but elegant red sandstone building designed by William Tennant. Built in 1897, it was constructed for the Young Men's Christian Institute, which may explain its rather reserved style in comparison to other buildings in Govan and across Glasgow from the same era.

15. Next to the former Young Men's Christian Institute, and facing on to Govan Road itself, is a much more ornate building constructed just two years later. Designed by Salmon, Son and Gillespie, and built in 1899, it is one of the best surviving examples of a Glasgow style commercial building. In this case, it was built as a branch of the British Linen Bank, with flats above. Over its entrance, it features an impressive sculpture by Francis Derwent Wood of the prow of a trireme surrounded by winged allegorical figures representing two winds. The sail of the vessel features the initials 'B.L.Co.', which stand for the British Linen Company, the forerunner of the British Linen Bank. It also features some wonderful sculpted capitals on its Govan Road and Water Row facades containing small figures representing different forms of labour, including beekeeping, fishing and navigation. Finally, while not easily visible from the Govan Cross side of the road, it is topped by a very elaborate lead-covered crown unlike almost anything else in Glasgow.

Sculptures above entrance to British Linen Bank, Govan Cross.

16. Cross to the south side of Govan Road at the traffic lights near the front of the former bank building, and turn left towards the entrance of the Govan Subway Station. In the small open area in front of it is the Mary Barbour statue. Designed by

Andrew Brown, it was unveiled on International Women's Day in 2018, and shows her leading a line of protestors, known as Mrs Barbour's Army, during the Glasgow Rent Strike of 1915. Mary Barbour was a political activist and social policy pioneer who was part of the Red Clydeside Movement of the early twentieth century. Perhaps her most famous moment was the campaign she led against rent increases and evictions in 1915. Such was the effectiveness of this movement that the government of the day soon capitulated and introduced the Rent Restriction Act. She also became one of Glasgow's first female councillors in 1920, and led campaigns for school milk, children's playparks, municipal washhouses and Glasgow's first family planning clinic. The daughter of a carpet weaver, she was born in Kilbarchan in 1875 and died in Glasgow in 1958, aged eighty-three. This is one of only two statues of a Scottish woman which can be found in Glasgow, both of which are in Govan.

17. From the Mary Barbour statue, turn and head back west along Govan Road. As you do so, you will get a much better view of the ornate crown at the top of the British Linen Bank Building which you viewed earlier on this walk. Further along Govan Road, is the Pearce Institute. An impressive building, it was designed by Rowand Anderson in an early seventeenth-century Scottish Renaissance style and was built in 1902. Of particular note is the sailing ship finial on the very top of the western gable, a reference to Govan's links to shipbuilding and other maritime industries. The Institute was given to the people of Govan by the widow of William Pearce, who died in 1888. Pearce was the manager of the Fairfield Shipbuilding and Engineering Company and oversaw its rise to become the leading and most technically advanced shipbuilding company in the world. The Pearce Institute was intended as a social centre for the workers of Govan, many of whom were employed by Fairfields, and it offered men's and women's reading rooms and clubs, a gymnasium, a library, a retiring room and a cooking and laundry department. It also contained a large hall, making it a popular venue for dances and other social gatherings. On the wall inside its entrance is the inscription: 'This is a house of service. For Families, for lonely folk. For the People of Govan. For strangers of the world. Welcome'.

18. Opposite the Pearce Institute, situated at the junction of Govan Road and Burleigh Street, is a bronze statue of William Pearce, which was created by Onslow Ford and erected in 1894. To the west of this statue at the same junction is former Cardell Halls. Built in a Scottish baronial style in 1894, and named after John Cardell, it consisted of a pub on the ground floor with meeting halls above it. Despite the presence of this pub, the meeting halls were originally the headquarters of the Rechabites, a temperance and friendly society. The building itself features a number of interesting sculptures, including a small dragon beside its eastern-most entrance, and a cat set high up on the wall on the Burleigh Road side. This is a monument to the legendary Govan Cat, which is said to have saved a local community from an infestation of rats.

Cardell Halls. Sculpture of Govan Cat below candle-snuffer roof of corner tower.

19. From the former Cardell Halls, head west along Burleigh Road. Turn left onto Harmony Row and follow it until it becomes Langlands Road. At the junction between Langlands Road and Shaw Street, there is an attractive red sandstone tenement with a sweeping curved facade which closely follows the angle of the corner.

20. A short distance north along Shaw Street on the blonde sandstone tenements on its left-hand side are a series of oriel windows (i.e. windows which project beyond the ground-floor facade), underneath which there is a set of intricate carvings. While not a common feature, such carvings can occasionally be found under oriel windows across Glasgow. However, the ones on Shaw Street are particularly fine examples of this craft. They include an owl (which usually signifies wisdom), a beehive (which usually signifies industriousness), and a water scene (which presumable signifies the nearby Clyde, which was the source of Govan's wealth).

Sculptures under oriel windows of tenement, Shaw Street, Govan.

21. Return south along Shaw Street, and then turn right onto Langland Road where it runs parallel to Golspie Street. When you reach the traffic lights at the junction between Golspie Street and Langland Road, cross to the opposite side. Here, you will see a large, Italianate sandstone building with a square tower. Designed by James Thomson (who was no relation to Alexander 'Greek' Thomson), this building was constructed in 1874 as Hill's Trust School. Abraham Hill was a Govanite who became a wealthy Wolverhampton merchant, and on his death in 1757, he endowed a trust with the money to buy land to rent, which would, in turn, create an income to pay for a teacher to provide free education to ten children from the poorest families in Govan. Due to rises in land values, by the 1860s, there was enough money to build this new, larger school. The school itself was managed by the Govan School Board, and was the only private non-denominational school in Govan. It finally closed in 1974 when the pupils were moved to a new school, and the building became a community centre.

22. Set into the pavement just in front of the former Hill's Trust School, is part of a sculpture trail called the Govan Timeline. Created by Kate Robinson, this is a pictorial representation of the history of Govan. Starting at this point, follow the Govan Timeline along Langlands Road (which becomes a small pedestrian and cycle path) as it leads west to its junction with Elderpark Street. It starts with a large picture featuring workers spilling out of the gates of a shipyard at the end of a working day, and also features images based on Pictish sculptures from the Govan Stones, ships reflected in water, weaving, industry, and finally at its end, a Cornucopia, or horn of plenty, signifying the wealth Govan once generated.

23. On the corner between Elderpark Street and Langlands Road is the Elder Park Library. Designed by John James Burnet in an Edwardian baroque style and built in 1902, the library was a gift from Isabella Elder, the wife of John Elder, to the people of Govan. In total, she provided £10,000 to meet the cost of building the library and filling it with books, as well as £17,000 as a fund for its maintenance. One condition of her donation was that the library must open on Sundays, the only day when working-class people would have been free to visit it. The library was opened in 1903 by Andrew Carnegie, the Scottish-American industrialist, who also funded 3,000 public libraries, including more than a dozen in Glasgow.

Elder Park Library, established in 1902 as gift to people of Govan from Isabella Elder.

24. Just behind the Elder park Library is Elder Park itself. Enter it to the right of the library and take the path heading north. Here, you will find a statue of Isabella's husband John Elder, which was created by J.E. Boehm and erected in 1888. Born in Glasgow, John Elder became a marine engineer and shipbuilder, who, in 1860 helped create the shipbuilding firm Randolph, Elder and Company. In 1886, this became the Fairfield Shipbuilding and Engineering Company, one of the most technologically advanced shipyards in the world. The statue features John Elder holding a model of the inverted vertical steam engine which he patented in the 1850s. This engine was so successful that it is said it was largely responsible for setting the Clyde at the forefront of international shipbuilding industry, a position it would occupy for more than 100 years. Elder died in 1869, and his wife Isabella donated Elder Park to the people of Govan in his name in 1885.

25. From the statue of John Elder, return south to the rear of Elder Park Library, and then turn right and follow the path which leads off to the west. Just beyond the point where this path forks is a rose garden, which can be entered by walking along the right-hand fork until you come to a path leading through the hedge to your left. In the middle of this rose garden is a statue of Isabella Elder. Created by Archibald McFarlane Shannan, it was paid for by public subscription and was unveiled in 1906, a year after her death. Born Isabella Ure, she was not only the wife of a wealthy and successful shipbuilder, but also a philanthropist and a champion of working-class welfare and education, particularly of women. As well as building the Elder Park Library, she also set up a School for Domestic Economy, the Elder Cottage Hospital and the Cottage Nurses Training Home, all in Govan. She was instrumental in developing Queen Maragret College, the first college in Scotland to offer higher education to women, and provided funding for the first courses in medicine for women. Such was her popularity with the local people that thousands assembled for the statue's unveiling ceremony. Hers is one of only two public statues of Scottish women to be found in Glasgow, the other being the statue of Mary Barbour which you visited earlier on this walk.

26. In the rose garden area to the south-west of the Isabella Elder statue is one of two identical memorials to those who died in the SS Daphne Disaster (it is rather well hidden, so it may take some searching around to find it). The SS *Daphne* was built in the Alexander Stephen and Sons shipyard in Govan and was launched on 3 July 1883. Around 200 workers were still on board, working to fit her out, when she was launched, a practice which was not unusual at the time. However, there was a problem with the anchors which should have stopped the ship after it had entered the water, and it swung round before flipping over. In all, 124 of the workers died, many of who were little more than boys, and it took more than a fortnight for all the bodies to be recovered. As a result of this disaster, the number of people on board ships during launches became limited to only those needed to moor the ship after it was in the water. The memorials to the SS *Daphne* disaster were created by the former shipyard worker John McArthur in 1996, with one here in Elder Park and the other in Victoria Park on the north side of the Clyde.

Memorial to 124 workers who died when SS Daphne capsized shortly after launch in 1883, Elder Park.

27. From the rose garden surrounding the Isabella Elder statue, take the path leading due south to the gate on Langlands Road. Exit Elder Park by this gate and turn right. A short distance further west along Langlands Road, at its junction with Drumoyne Drive, is the former Elder Cottage Hospital, which was established by Isabella Elder in 1903. Designed by John James Burnet in a late English Renaissance style, it features a relief sculpture of a mother nursing her baby over the main entrance, belying its original intended use as a maternity hospital. However, it ended up specialising in the treatment of industrial injuries. The hospital became part of the new National Health Service in 1948, and finally closed in 1987.

28. On the opposite corner of the same junction is the former nurses' training home, which was also established by Isabella Elder. As with the main hospital building, it was built in 1902 and was designed by John James Burnet in a quite different, but complimentary half-timbered style. The aim of the home was to provide training in the Holt-Ockley system of nursing to allow nurses to give the working-class and poor people of Govan care, particularly maternity care, in their own homes.

29. From the former Elder Hospital and Nurses' Training Home, head west along Langlands Road to its junction with Mambeg Drive (which leads off to the right). Walk north down Mambeg Road until you reach St Kenneth Drive, where you need to turn left and head west to the junction with Kennedar Drive. Ahead of you, beyond the far end of St Kenneth Drive, you will just be able to see the new building of the Queen Elizabeth University Hospital (QEUH) with an older building topped by a clock tower in front of it. Formerly the Southern General, this hospital started life as Govan Poorhouse. The first Govan Poorhouse was established much further east on Tradeston Street in 1845, and in 1852, a larger premises was established in a converted cavalry barracks on Eglinton Street. However, in the 1860s, a new, purpose-built poorhouse was constructed on the Merryflats Estate. Designed by James Thomson, these new buildings, which included the one topped by the clock tower you can see in front of the new QEUH buildings, could house 240 people, with

accommodation for another 180 provided in a separate lunatic asylum, were described at the time as the finest asylum for the poor in Scotland. In 1902, it was expanded to provide an additional 700 beds. This poorhouse became the Southern General Hospital in 1923, but the last poorhouse beds were only taken out of use in June 1936, when it came under the auspices of the Public Health Department. At this point, you have two options. You can either head to the end of St Kenneth Drive, where you can see the imposing former Govan Poorhouse and the associated hospital constructed in the 1860s, and which still forms part of the modern Queen Elizabeth University Hospital complex, or you can take the shorter route which heads north along Kennedar Drive. If you decide to view the former poorhouse, at the end of St Kenneth Drive, turn right onto Skipness Drive and follow it round until you come to the junction with Kennedar Drive. This will add an additional 500 m (300 yards) to the overall length of this walk.

30. At the junction between Kennedar Drive and Skipness Drive, turn right and head east along it. As you do so, on your the right you will pass the beautiful red sandstone former Linthouse Church. Designed by James Miller and constructed in 1899, it features a pair of ogee-domed open cupolas and is one of only a very small number of arts and crafts style churches in Glasgow. It ceased being used as a church in 2008, when its congregation merged with those of Govan Old Parish Church (which you will visit at the end of this walk) and New Govan Church (which you already visited at Govan Cross), where the combined congregation now meets. Such merging of once-separate congregations is a common theme within modern Scotland, resulting in a large number of architecturally important churches becoming empty, with the associated risk to their preservation. Luckily, many have found new uses, allowing them to avoid what has become an all-too-common fate of older Glasgow buildings, which rapidly deteriorate towards dereliction once they are no longer occupied.

31. Just to the east of the former Linthouse Church is Hutton Drive. A short distance south along this road, outside No. 10, is a blue plaque marking the tenement flat where the social campaigner and rent strike organiser Mary Barbour once lived.

32. Return to Skipness Drive and head east to its junction with Drive Road. Cross Drive Road at the traffic lights and re-enter Elder Park at the nearby gate, which is a short distance to the south of these traffic lights. Walk straight ahead for a short distance and at the first junction you come to, take the left-hand pathway. This will take you passed two points of interest on your way through the park. The first of these is the ruins of Mansion House, on the right-hand side of the path. Built in 1791, Mansion House once stood in nearby Linthouse Estate and is thought to have been designed by Robert Adam. The house itself was demolished in 1921 (as part of the expansion of the Alexander Stephen and Son shipyard where the SS Daphne was built), but the portico was saved and reconstructed at its current location in Elder Park.

Remains of portico of Mansion House, Elder Park.

33. On the left-hand side of the path is the original house of Fairfield Farm which, in 1885, became the basis of Elder Park. Now decaying and heavily overgrown (to the point where it is barely visible from the path), the house was thought to have been built in the early 1800s, and was later adapted as a park building, including toilets. Unlike the former Linthouse Church, which has found a new use since its congregation moved out, thus allowing it to be maintained, this building has remained empty after it fell out of use, resulting in it slipping into dereliction. While there have been plans to restore this building, as it currently stands it is little more than a ruin and is at risk of being completely lost.

34. To the east of the original Fairfield Farm building is an old boating pond. Rising out of it is a sculpture called *The Launch*, inspired by the shipbuilding history of Govan. Created by George Wyllie and erected in 1998, it features the stylised bow of a ship, with a champagne bottle standing beside it.

35. Further east still along the same path, close to the Govan Road entrance to Elder Park, is the Submariners' Memorial, which was erected in memory of those killed in the K13 Disaster of 1917. Built at the nearby Fairfield Shipyard, HMS *K13* was a steam-powered World War I submarine, but it sank in Gairloch during sea trials in January 1917. Twenty-six naval personnel and six workers from the Fairfield Shipyard who were on board at the time died. Rather miraculously, forty-eight other people were successfully rescued after some sixty hours trapped at the bottom of the sea. The memorial was paid for by the officials, foremen and employees of the shipyard. Further plaques have been added to this memorial to remember allied submariners who died in World War II.

Memorial to K13 Disaster of 1917, Elder Park.

36. Exit Elder Park by the gate to the north of the Submariners' Memorial, and turn right onto Govan Road. A short distance east along this road is the entrance to the offices of the former Fairfield Shipbuilding and Engineering Company (named after the nearby Fairfield Farm which later became Elder Park). Designed by John Keppie and built in 1890, this classical two-storey building features some magnificent sculptures by James Pittendrigh MacGillivray, and McGilvray & Ferris. The most prominent of these are the two figures which stand on either side of the door. On the right is the Shipwright, with his sleeves rolled up and a large cog and an anvil behind him, while on the left stands the Engineer, who is dressed in collar and buttoned-up waistcoat. This arrangement is very similar to the arrangement of figures on the Govan coat of arms and is most likely a tribute to it. However, it also ties in to the fact that the Fairfield Yard was one of the world's first combined shipbuilding and marine engineering works. Above the door is a pair of mermaids and the mask of a helmeted and bearded Viking sea god. There is also a mask of Neptune in the frieze over the windows of the top storey. The shipyard was established in 1864, and soon became one of the most technologically advanced shipyards in the world. After World War II, production

slowed and despite attempts to modernise it and merge it with other nearby shipyards, including John Browns, it was eventually sold off. However, this was not before the famous work-in of 1971, organised by the legendary shop steward Jimmy Reid. In a reverse of a traditional strike, this saw the employees occupy the shipyard and continue to work to complete contracts despite no longer being paid. The former office buildings are now home to Fairfield Heritage, a small museum dedicated to the history of shipbuilding in Govan.

37. At the eastern end of the former Fairfield Shipyard is the *Govan Milestone*, which features four cormorant-like birds standing at the point where two semicircular arcs meet. Installed in 1993, it was designed by Helen Denerley. It stands at the entrance of the shipyard itself, and set into the cobbles which line the area inside the walls, you can still see the old iron tracks used to move materials around it.

38. From the *Govan Milestone*, head further east along Govan Road, making sure you go straight ahead at the junction with Golspie Street. On the corner with Shaw Street is a fine example of a Glasgow style red sandstone tenement, which was designed by Frank Burnet and Boston, and was built in 1900.

39. Further east still, is the stunning Streamline Moderne style facade of the former Lyceum Cinema. Designed by Charles McNair and Peter Elder, it opened in 1938. It took its name from the earlier Lyceum Theatre, which was built on the same site in 1898. It was converted into a cinema in 1923 before burning down in 1937. With a seating capacity of 2,600, it was classified as a 'suburban supercinema', few of which have survived to this day. After 1981, it was used exclusively as a bingo hall, but it has lain empty since 2006 and is now slowly slipping towards dereliction. This will continue until a new use can be found for it, again demonstrating how quickly buildings can decay if they fall out of use for an extended period of time.

1938 Streamline moderne Lyceum suburban supercinema, Govan Road.

40. On the opposite side of Govan Road from the former Lyceum Cinema is St Anthony's Church. Built in a Byzantine style, it was designed by John Honeyman and was constructed in 1877. It has a particularly attractive polychromatic Roman arch around its main door, made of alternate blocks of red and blonde sandstone, enclosing an inner arch with dogtooth moulding. The square tower at its eastern end is topped with an open-arched belfry below a pyramidal copper roof.

41. The final stop on this walk is Govan Old Parish Church, which stands between Govan Road and the Clyde a short distance further east from St Anthony's Church. Designed by Rowand Anderson, and inspired by both Italian Franciscan basilicas and the Pluscarden Priory in Elgin, the current church building was erected in the 1880s. One of its lesser-known features is the dragon carved into its right-hand side. While this has been somewhat mutilated by a pipe which has been fitted through its face, it is still clearly visible high up around halfway along the eastern-most wall.

A number of smaller dragons can also be found tucked away into the stonework inside the church, particularly on the western side. The current church is the sixth one known to have stood on this site, and its history as a religious site may date back as far as the fifth century, as early Christian burials found beneath the foundations of a later church during excavations in the 1990s have been dated to this time period. The surrounding churchyard is filled with graves dating back at least several centuries, some of which are marked with stones bearing the skull and crossbones symbol which we now associate with pirates. However, this an example of a memento mori, or a reminder of death, which were common on grave markers in the seventeenth and eighteenth centuries. This symbol was only later adopted by pirates, when it featured on the Jolly Roger flag as a message to enemy ships that they should surrender or face death. Other memento mori which can be seen on gravestones on the Govan Old Parish Churchyard include hour glasses, winged skulls, spades and trumpets. A number of even earlier gravestones, both Christian and Viking, some dating from as far back as the ninth century (when the local area was part of the ancient kingdom of Strathclyde) have also been found in the Govan Old Parish Church graveyard. Collectively known as the Govan Stones, these are now housed in the church itself, which has been turned into a museum to display and preserve them. These include an intricately carved stone sarcophagus and a number of Viking hogback stones, and they are well worth viewing (please check the opening hours in advance to avoid disappointment as it is only open at certain times).

Memento mori, 18th-century gravestone, Govan Old Parish Churchyard.

17. Queen's Park, Mount Florida, Crosshill and Govanhill

Start Point: Langside Halls, Langside Avenue, Glasgow (**Location:** Lat/Lon: 55.83139, -4.27799; What3Words: ///pram.paper.nobody; Plus Code: RPJC+HR2 Glasgow).
Nearest Public Transport: Subway: None; Train: Crossmyloof Railway Station (10 mins); Bus: Pollokshaws Road (2 mins).

End Point: Queen's Park Flagpole, Queen's Park, Glasgow (**Location:** Lat/Lon: 55.83104, -4.27013; What3Words: ///sheets.barks.broom; Plus Code: RPJH+CW9 Glasgow). **Nearest Public Transport:** Subway: None; Train: Crossmyloof Railway Station (15 mins); Bus: Pollokshaws Road (5 mins).

Distance: 6.0 kilometres/3.7 miles. **Time:** Allow 3 to 4.5 hours for this walk.
Level of Difficulty: Moderate. This walk is almost entirely on paved surfaces. However, it is relatively long and there are some minor hills and uneven sections towards the end.

Facilities: There are shops, cafes, restaurants and bars available at fairly regular intervals along this walk, but particularly along Langside Avenue, Victoria Road and around Queen's Park. Publicly accessible toilets are available in Queen's Park, which is visited at the start and end of the walk, and at Langside and Govanhill Public Libraries, about a third and halfway through it, respectively.

Introduction

This walk follows a long loop through a number of key areas of the Southside of Glasgow, including Queen's Park, Mount Florida, Crosshill and Govanhill. Most of these areas were formerly independent burghs which were incorporated into Glasgow as it expanded outwards during the latter half of the nineteenth century. Mount Florida was built on the former lands of Mount Floridon, which were sold off in 1814. The area was developed from the 1830s onwards as a suburb of Glasgow, before being incorporated into the city in 1891. Govanhill has a more industrial origin. It started out as a company settlement called Fireworks Village linked to the Dixon Blazes Ironworks. As it developed, it grew into a more substantial settlement, becoming an independent police burgh in 1877, before it too was incorporated into Glasgow in 1891. Crosshill borders Govanhill. However, while Govanhill was in the county of Lanark, Crosshill was in the neighbouring county of Renfrew, meaning it was subject to different local laws overseen by a separate court system. Crosshill was granted the status of an independent police burgh in 1871, but its independence was short-lived as it was absorbed into Glasgow in 1891, alongside Govanhill and Mount Florida. Queen's Park was originally part of the lands of Camphill House, but it was sold to the Glasgow Corporation (as the local council was then known) in 1857 to develop as the city's third public park, after Glasgow Green in the East End and Kelvingrove Park in the west. It was created to provide an open space for recreation for those living in the surrounding tenements of Govanhill, Crosshill, Crossmyloof, Battlefield, Langside, Shawlands and Strathbungo, so placing it at the very heart of the city's Southside. Given the era in which it was developed, it might be assumed the park is named after Queen Victoria. However, it is in fact named in honour of Mary Queen of Scots, who fought and lost the Battle of Langside to the south of the area which is now home to the park in 1568.

1. This walk starts at the magnificent Langside Public Halls. Designed in a classical style by John Gibbon, it was built in the late 1840s. Among other features, it has a series of keystones decorated with masks sculpted by John Thomas, which represent personifications of five major rivers of the Great Britain and Ireland. These are thought to be the Thames, the Severn, the Tweed, the Humber and the Clyde. The one for the Clyde can be found over the main door and features a headdress which includes two fish, each with a ring in its mouth, one of the symbols from the Glasgow coat of arms. It may seem surprising, but Langside Hall has not always only been at this location. Originally, it was situated on Queen Street in central Glasgow, where it served as a branch of the National Bank of Scotland. In 1901, rather than see it demolished, it was deconstructed by the city architect Alexander B. McDonald and rebuilt at its current location, where it served as a public hall for the Langside, Battlefield and Mount Florida areas after they were incorporated into Glasgow in the 1890s. Over the years, it has played host to a variety of political figures, including the Red Clydesider John Maclean, who once taught at the nearby Sir John Maxwell School, and social campaigner and Suffragette Sylvia Pankhurst. At the time of writing, it is lying empty and unused, which is likely to result in a rapid deterioration in its condition if it remains so for much longer.

Keystone mask representing the Clyde, Langside Public Halls.

2. On the opposite side of Langside Avenue is an Edwardian baroque style building which, until recently, was home to The Shed, the largest nightclub in Glasgow's Southside (which closed in 2024). However, when it was built around 1920, it was known as Marlborough House, named after the First Duke of Marlborough, whose family seat is Blenheim Palace in Oxfordshire. Serving as a social venue for events such as wedding receptions, dances and dinners, it featured a series of suites named after the duke's famous victories over the French.

3. To the south-east of Marlborough House, along Langside Avenue, is St Helen's Roman Catholic Church. Designed in a Gothic style by John Bennie Wilson, it was built in 1896 as a United Presbyterian Church. It was originally intended to have a 40-metre (130 foot) tall spire, but this was never completed, a situation which is not unusual for Glasgow churches and usually resulted from financial limitations.

4. Opposite St Helen's Church, to the north-east of Langside Avenue, is the large expanse of Queen's Park, one of the first and largest parks on the Southside of Glasgow. For this walk, enter Queen's Park at the pedestrian gate near the junction with Tantallon Road. A short distance into the park from this point is the Scottish Poetry Rose Garden. It was opened in 2003 to mark Glasgow's hosting of the World Rose Convention, and celebrates the poetry and poets of Scotland written in English, Scots and Gaelic, including Robert Burns, Hugh MacDairmid and Violet Jacobs. The Poetry Garden is laid out in a style reminiscent of Celtic and monastic gardens and at its centre is a rock inscribed with a short poem by MacDairmid called 'The Little White Rose', while the surrounding beds are planted with Scots

briar roses (the type of rose that is the subject of this poem). It is situated on the site of what was once a walled garden for Camphill House, on whose grounds much of the local area was constructed. The walled garden was demolished in the 1930s, but the foundations of a small summerhouse can still be seen to the north of the current rose garden.

5. Carry on south-east through the rose garden. This will take you to a large paved path which leads back to Langside Avenue and its junction with Camphill Avenue. At this junction, there is a large and impressive red sandstone tenement with a wonderfully curved corner frontage which was built in 1903. While such buildings are often referred to just as tenements, their design varies considerably across the city, from relatively basic utilitarian building of the type you will pass in Govanhill, constructed to house working-class residents, to grand and ornate buildings constructed as homes for wealthy professionals, such as the ones which you will see when you reach Queen's Drive towards the end of this walk. These differences reflect four main factors: the socio-economic status of the neighbourhood; the date they were built; the fashions and requirements of the local area; and the architect chosen to design them. The result is an incredible diversity of buildings in a wide variety of sizes and styles, ranging from neoclassical, through French Renaissance to Glasgow style and art nouveau, which are only united by the construction methods that rely solely on stone. This means that while tenement-like buildings were constructed in later years, the traditional tenement era came to an end at the start of the 1910s, when iron frameworks replaced the use of an internal stone structure for the construction of such buildings.

1903 red sandstone tenement, junction of Langside and Camphill Avenues.

6. For this walk, stay in Queen's Park and follow the large paved path which runs south-east parallel to Langside Avenue. This will lead you to the Queen's Park glasshouses. Originally housing subtropical plants and a fishpond, they were built in 1905 and are a typical example of the type of municipal glasshouses constructed in a number of Glasgow's larger public parks, including Glasgow Green, Springburn, Tollcross and Queen's Park. Although many had fallen into disrepair by the end of the twentieth century, there has been a concerted effort to try to save and restore those which remain. While the Queen's Park glasshouses have received some restoration work, they are still lacking their iconic dome, which was temporarily removed for repair some years ago.

7. From the glasshouses, follow the path as it curves to the north-west and then exit Queen's Park by the gate on Langside Road. Directly opposite this gate is the site of the former Victoria Royal Infirmary. This hospital was opened in 1890, with many of its buildings designed by Campbell Douglas and Sellars. The hospital was closed in 2015, with its services either moving to the Queen Elizabeth University Hospital in Govan or to the New Victoria Hospital on a neighbouring site. The site for the original hospital has since been redeveloped for affordable housing. However, this

resulted in accusations of architectural vandalism against the developers after they demolished key parts of the hospital buildings, which many felt should have been retained. Now, one of the few parts which remains standing is its imposing Renaissance style Administration Block, which you will see ahead of you as you leave Queen's Park by this gate. This features a relief sculpture of a big cat, thought to represent a puma, which later became a symbol of the hospital itself. Interestingly, and unusually for a Scottish public building, the royal coat of arms of the United Kingdom featured just below this big cat is the English version (which, among other differences, has the English lion on the left and the Scottish unicorn on the right), rather than the more expected Scottish version, which has the unicorn on the left and the lion on the right.

8. Turn right and head south-west along Langside Road. This will take you to a large roundabout know as Battlefield Place. In the middle of this roundabout is the Battlefield Monument. Designed by Alexander Skirving, a devotee of Alexander 'Greek' Thomson, it was erected in 1887 to commemorate the Battle of Langside where the army of the Regent Moray defeated the forces of Mary Queen of Scots on 13 May 1568. Shortly before this, Queen Mary had escaped from Lochleven Castle, where she had been held prisoner since being force to abdicate earlier in the same year. Following her defeat at Langside, she fled south to England, where she was imprisoned, and eventually executed in 1587, by her cousin Queen Elizabeth I.

9. On the hill to the west of the Battlefield Monument is the magnificent Langside Hill Church. Designed in a Greek temple style and built in the 1890s, it is probably the finest work by Alexander Skirving, the one-time assistant of Alexander 'Greek' Thomson. This was the last of Glasgow's great classical temple style churches, and was constructed at a time when most church architects had come to favour a more Gothic-influenced style, as illustrated by St Helen's Church which you passed earlier on this walk and which was built around the same time.

Alexander Skirving's 1890s Langside Hill Church.

10. From Battlefield Place, turn left and head east down the hill along Battlefield Road. As you do so, on your right, you will pass a polychromatic brick and stone electrical power station featuring classical details. This is an example of how, in the early days of the introduction of electricity, a great deal of effort was expended to ensure that such buildings blended into the surrounding architecture. If you examine this building closely, you will see a very small, and rather amusing, plaque on the right-hand side of its main entrance. This plaque claims to mark the opening of the substation in 1978 (long after it was actually constructed) by a local crimefighting do-gooder called 'the Red Streak'. The creator of the plaque remains unknown, but it has been present since at least 2019, and is part of quite an extensive Glasgow tradition of anonymously erecting tongue-in-cheek and humorous plaques.

11. Further east down Battlefield Road, on the same side as the electrical substation, is Langside Public Library. Designed by George Simpson in an Edwardian baroque style, and opened in 1915, it was the last of the Glasgow libraries paid for with money donated by the Scottish-American Streel magnate Andrew Carnegie. However, it was also the first library in Glasgow to allow public access to its books. This meant that, for the first time, members of the public could freely browse the shelves of the collection rather than having to request a specific book selected from a catalogue and brought to them by a librarian. As a result, it had to be designed with more space around and between the shelves.

12. From Langside Public Library, head east to the junction between Battlefield Road, Grange Road and Prospecthill Road. Here, in the middle of this junction, is the Battlefield Rest. Designed by Frank Burnet and Boston, it is a unique and distinctive piece of Glasgow architecture. Originally designed as a tram shelter, it is the only example of such a large and ornate shelter known to have been built in Scotland. It was constructed in 1914 as the winner of a competition to design tram shelters for Glasgow's extensive tram network, which at the time was the largest in Britain. The outbreak of World War I prevented their rollout across the city and once the war was over, the plan was abandoned, leaving this as the sole example of what could once have been a common sight across the city.

1914 Battlefield Rest Tram Shelter.

13. From the former Battlefield Rest Tram Shelter, head north-east along Prospecthill Road. As you do so, to your right, you will see the rather stunning French Gothic style building set on a hill overlooking the Langside and Battlefield areas of Glasgow. Designed by Salmon, Son and Ritchie, it was built in 1867 for the Glasgow Institute for the Deaf and Dumb, which provided a boarding school for the education of 170 pupils. This Institute was created in 1819, and was originally based on the corner of Glebe Street and Parson Street in central Glasgow. However, demand meant it quickly outgrew these premises and in the 1860s, it moved to this much larger site. During World War II, the school evacuated to Dailly, and when it returned in 1946, the buildings were no longer habitable and accommodation for the school was found elsewhere. In 1947, it became the home of Langside College, but in recent years, it has been converted into residential flats.

14. Further east along Prospecthill Road, on the bridge over the Cathcart Circle railway line, is a pair of relatively new murals. These are examples of a growing number of similar murals across Glasgow highlighting local areas, such as Mount Florida (as in this case), Battlefield and Dennistoun, and in the process adding a great deal of much-needed colour to the streets of Glasgow.

15. On the corner between Prospecthill Road and Cathcart Road are the former Cathcart Parish Council Offices. Designed by Crawford and Veitch, they were built in 1907, prior to Cathcart being absorbed into Glasgow in 1912. This seems to be a relatively common pattern, with surrounding areas constructing their own grand civic buildings a short time before they were annexed by the expanding city. These former council offices are now used as a health clinic.

16. From the former Cathcart Parish Council Offices, turn left onto Cathcart Road and walk north to its junction with Queen's Drive. At this point, turn left onto Queen's Drive and cross the Queen's Drive Railway Bridge. To the north of this point is an area now occupied by the greens of Hampden Bowling Club, but between 1873 and 1884, this was the site of the first Hampden Park football ground, home to Queen's Park Football Club, and the Scottish national football team. Hampden Park was the world's first purpose-built international football ground and the template for all modern football stadiums. It was also the place where a group of players nicknamed the 'Scotch Professors' helped develop the modern style of passing football, leading in March 1882 to Scotland beating England 5–1. Such was the influence of this style of play, that Scottish players also came to dominate English football to the extent that the entire Liverpool team of 1892 consisted of Scottish players. The 1882 Scotland vs. England match was also notable as being the last of three matches when captain Andrew Watson played for Scotland. Born in 1856 in what was then British Guiana (now Guyana) to a Scottish father and a British Guianese mother, Watson was not only the first black player to play at international level, but with a career which started in 1876, he was also the first black professional football player in the world. In 1884, the original Hampden stadium was demolished to make way for a new railway line, which was to pass through the ground's western terrace, and a second one was built at Cathkin Park. However, this only lasted until the early 1900s, when a new stadium was built at the current Hampden Park location. It surprises many people when they find out that Hampden Park, the spiritual home of Scottish national football team, is named after John Hampden, an English Civil War soldier and cousin of Oliver Cromwell, who fought for the Roundheads. The name comes from nearby Hampden Terrace, which leads off from the junction of Cathcart Road and Prospecthill Road.

Location of original Hampden Park, world's first purpose-built international football ground.

17. From Queen's Drive, turn right into Queen's Park Avenue, and head north along it to rejoin Cathcart Road. As you do so, you will pass a fine block of red sandstone tenements on the right-hand side, with a prominent corner tower and some beautifully painted glass plates above their doors. These were common features on Glasgow tenements around the time they were built.

18. Once you reach Cathcart Road again, head north to its junction with Dixon Avenue. Here, there is a beautiful Scottish baronial style building dating from 1879 and designed by Frank Stirrat. Originally built as the Crosshill and Govanhill Burgh Hall, it was paid for by William Smith Dixon, the owner of the Govan Ironworks in the nearby area of Hutchesontown. As Crosshill was then part of Renfrewshire and Govanhill was in neighbouring Lanarkshire, it was sited on Cathcart Road on the border between the two regions. Inside, there were separate courtrooms for each region, each with their own access from opposite sides of the building. However, it was Govanhill which got the rather beautiful and imposing corner tower,

suggesting that the two were not necessarily viewed as equal partners in this arrangement. As with the former Cathcart Council Offices you visited earlier, this ornate municipal building was constructed a few years before both Crosshill and Govanhill were incorporated into Glasgow in 1891. The building was renamed Dixon Halls shortly after it was constructed (presumably as a result of annexing these areas into the neighbouring city), and it is still referred to by this name to this day.

Former Crosshill and Govanhill Burgh Hall.

19. Further north along Cathcart Road, cross Allison Street and then turn right into Bankhall Street. A short distance east along this road is a beautiful green-and-white-tiled Egyptian style building which was originally constructed as the Govanhill Picture House. Dating from 1926, it is one of the few Egyptian-themed cinemas ever built in the UK, and its design by Eric Sutherland was presumably inspired by the mania for ancient Egypt which swept much of the world following the rediscovery of the tomb of Tutankhamun by Howard Carter in 1922. When it opened, it seated 1,200 people, and remained in use as a cinema until 1961, before becoming a bingo hall, and then a warehouse. It is currently used as a shop. The last film shown here was *Song Without End*, the Oscar-winning 1960 biopic of the pianist Franz Liszt starring Dirk Bogarde, who lived in Bishopbriggs on the outskirts of Glasgow during his early teenage years, and for three years went to Allan Glen School in the city.

20. Return west along Bankhall Street, cross Cathcart Road and walk along it to its junction with Daisy Street (named after one of the daughters of William Smith Dixon, who provided the money for the construction of the nearby Dixon Halls). At this junction stands Govanhill Church, which was designed by Robert Baldie and was built in 1878. The view down the tenement-lined Bankhall Street to this church has changed little since it was built, with the exception of the now-ubiquitous presence of parked cars everywhere and a rather intrusive modern building filling a site where a tenement was demolished on its northern side.

21. Turn left onto Daisy Street, and then right onto Allison Street. Here, between Daisy Street and Garturk Street, is one of the last tenements designed by Alexander 'Greek' Thomson. Construction was started in 1875, the year that Thomson died, and it was most likely completed by his partner Robert Turnbull, which might explain why it features a slightly simplified version of Thomson's usual style.

22. Continue along Allison Street and then turn north into Annette Street (named after another of William Dixon's daughters). About halfway along this street is the former Govanhill Public School (now Annette Street Primary School). Built in 1886, it was designed in a palazzo style by brothers David and Hugh Barclay, and was one of a number of such schools the pair designed across Glasgow and the surrounding areas. As was a requirement for schools of its time, there was an almost complete segregation between boys and girls, with each having their own playgrounds and entrances (the boys' was on the left-hand end of the building while the girls' was on its right-hand end). The signs for each of these entrances are still visible, inscribed into the stone posts by their respective gates.

23. At the north end of Annette Street, turn left onto Calder Street. A short distance further west, at the junction between Calder Street and Langside Road, is the Govanhill and Crosshill Public Library (now just called Govanhill Public Library). Built in 1902, it was designed by James R. Rhind in an Edwardian baroque style. Like many of Rhind's other Glasgow libraries, it features prominent sculptures by William Kellock Brown. On the Calder Street facade are two sculptural groups, both consisting of a female figure surrounded by two children. On the Langside Road facade, on top of the dome is a winged female figure (in common with a number of Rhind's other Glasgow libraries) referred to locally as 'Minerva', the Roman goddess of wisdom. Below her, at the base of the dome, are two more female figures. The left-hand one (holding an open book) is thought to represent learning, while the one on the right (holding a globe and a pair of dividers) is thought to represent Geography.

Some of William Kellock Brown's sculptures, top of Govanhill Public Library.

24. A short distance further west on Calder Street is the former Calder Street Public Baths and Washhouse. Designed by Alexander B. McDonald in an Edwardian baroque style, and dating from the 1910s, it was built at a time when few of the surrounding tenements had indoor plumbing, and so was an important public facility. As well as a laundry (known in Glasgow as a 'steamie'), it originally contained a mixed bathing pool, a women's and infants' pool, a private pool, Turkish baths, and a steam room and sauna. Now called Govanhill Baths, it is owned by a local community trust and at the time of writing, is in the process of being refurbished.

25. From the former public baths and washhouse, continue west along Calder Street, cross Victoria Road, and then turn south onto Craigie Street. At the junction between Craigie Street and Allison Street is the Scottish Renaissance style former Queen's Park Fire Station, with an attached police station to the south. As with many of Glasgow's public buildings of the late 1800s and early 1900s, they were designed by the city engineer Alexander B. McDonald. Above the door of the police station on Craigie Street is a particularly fine example of the Glasgow coat of arms.

26. Directly opposite the old police station on Craigie Street is the former Strathbungo Public School (and now home to St Bride's Primary School). Featuring classical detailing, it was designed by John Gordon and Thomas Baird Jnr, and built in 1894. As well as the separate girls' and boys' entrances typical of schools of its time, it also had a rather more unusual feature: a swimming pool in its basement. Unfortunately, this is no longer in use.

27. Return north along Craigie Street to Allison Street, turn right and walk along it until you reach Victoria Road. On the corner between Victoria Road and Allison Street is a mid-1860s classical blonde sandstone tenement, with an early 1900s art-nouveau pub on its ground floor which features fine examples of acid-etched windows and carved timber decorations, particularly over the entrances. It was at a meeting in this block of tenements on 9 July 1867 that Queen's Park Football Club,

the first amateur football club outside of England, was formed. This was also the team which organised the world's first international football match, played between Scotland and England on the West of Scotland Cricket Club in Partick, on Saint Andrew's Day in 1872. It ended in a 0–0 draw.

28. On the opposite side of Victoria Road is the Victoria Cross Building. Constructed in the latter part of the nineteenth century, it features a tower of polygonal corner bay windows with a crested French roof topped by ornate metal brattishing (or decorative ironwork). Written across it in a font which is edging towards the art nouveau, are the words 'Victoria Cross'. Many Glasgow crossroads are marked by statement buildings with corner towers, but this is a particularly fine example of this tradition.

29. Turn left and head north along the east side of Victoria Road for about around 30 metres (100 feet) to No. 385. Here, in the entrance to a tenement close, you will find a wonderful set of decorative art nouveau tiles. While most are not quite as impressive as this particular example, such tiles can be found in tenement closes throughout the local area, and across Glasgow as a whole, and represent another important architectural tradition in the city. Locally, they are known as 'wally' tiles (a nickname for ceramics), and when the communal stairway of a tenement is decorated throughout with such tiles, it is known as a 'wally close', something many people aspired to live in (and still do).

Decorative art nouveau tiling, entrance to 385 Victoria Road.

30. From No. 385, turn around and head south along Victoria Road to No. 498, which is on the corner with Torrisdale Street. This is an unusual Tudor style building that continues as a larger structure down Torrisdale Street itself. Despite its unique appearance, there is little information available to explain its distinctive, yet unusual (for Glasgow) appearance. However, it is situated next to a railway line, and many older Tudoresque buildings in the city have links to the railways.

31. From Victoria Road, turn left onto Albert Road and walk along to its junction with Langside Road. If you look to the left at this junction, a short distance to the north on Langside Road is the Gothic style former Hutchesontown Free Church, which was designed by John Bennie Wilson and was built in 1891. It has a particularly unusual octagonal turret, beside which is a rather nice example of a Glaswegian Gothic gargoyle on one of its drainpipes.

32. On the south-west corner of the junction between Albert Road and Langside Road is a mid-nineteenth-century tenement with a public house on the ground floor. At the time of writing, this is called the Rose Reilly. Born in Scotland, Reilly played football for her native country until the early 1970s. However, in 1973, she moved to A.C.F. Milan and, despite having no formal links to that particular country, she was selected to play for Italy. In 1984, she was part of the Italian national team which won the Mundialito, the unofficial precursor to today's Women's World Cup, and was voted its best player. As such, Rose Reilly can be considered the only Scottish football player, male or female, ever to have won a World Cup.

33. Turn right and head south along Langside Road. At its corner with Queen's Drive is a very distinctive French Renaissance style tenement which was designed by William M. Whyte and built in 1885. While the most impressive facade for this building faces onto Queen's Drive itself, one of its most distinctive features is only visible from Langside Road. This is a large stone Statue of Liberty set high up on the corner with Queen's Drive. Although Glasgow is often said to have at least five versions of the Statue of Liberty, the others are actually personifications of different characteristics, leaving this as the only true Statue of Liberty in the city. However, no one is quite sure exactly why it adorns this building.

William M. Whyte's 1885 French Renaissance style tenement building.

34. The Queen's Drive facade of Whyte's French Renaissance style tenement is quite spectacular, and is probably one of the most well-kept tenement buildings in Glasgow. One of the key features is the steps leading up to a row of three doors. The central door opens into a communal stairway used to access the flats on the upper storeys, while the doors on either side access self-contained ground-floor flats. The corbels between some of these doors are decorated with beautifully sculpted figures which are grouped into a variety of themes, including the crafts, the seasons and the arts. Above the windows on either side of these doorways are pairs of male figures. The two most westerly ones have been identified as portraits of the building's architect William Whyte and its builder Hugh Wilson. The remaining figures are thought to be caricatures of a number of the bailies (local officials) who had initially objected to the construction of the building, but there is no direct evidence to support this claim.

35. The main route for this walk re-enters Queen's Park at this point, via the gate at the southern end of Victoria Road. However, if you wish, before you do this, you can take a short detour further west along Queen's Drive to the sole surviving lamp standard known to have been designed by Alexander 'Greek' Thomson. Despite not being in great condition, if you examine it closely, you can make out intricate geometric designs, similar to those used on many of Thomson's buildings, with which it is decorated.

36. On entering Queen's Park via the Victoria Road gate, turn right, and follow the path which leads west and initially follows the line of Queen's Drive before the two diverge. As you do so, you will pass a small oval area surrounded by an iron fence on your right-hand side. This is all that remains of a pony track, where, in the 1960s, children could take rides on ponies or be pulled around by them in small carriages. It is now used as a dog park.

37. Further west along this path is the Balvicar Drive entrance of the park, which is dominated by the magnificent Queen's Park Church. Originally built as the Camphill United Presbyterian Church in 1875, it was designed in a Normandy Gothic style by William Leiper, and features some wonderful sculptural details by MacCulloch and Company.

38. From the Balvicar Drive gate, take the main path which leads off to the south, past the old boating pond on the right. This will take you to Camphill House, which was built around 1798 for the cotton manufacturer Robert Thomson. Thomson owned the Adelphi Cotton Works in Hutchesontown, which is thought to have been the first factory in Glasgow to manufacture cotton goods. Camphill House was designed in a classical style, possibly by David Hamilton, and was originally built as a country house. However, it was first overtaken by the expanding suburbs of Glasgow and then by the city itself. Be aware that this is now a private residence, and please respect the privacy of the occupants.

39. Continue to follow the same path as it bends to the left (keeping left at the fork which would otherwise take you back to the Poetry Rose Garden you visited earlier). A short distance further on, turn left at the set of stone steps and head up the path to the top of the hill. This will take you to the Queen's Park Earthworks. Consisting of an approximately circular shallow ditch and low mound enclosing a central area, they can be hard to spot. These earthworks are believed to be the remains of an Iron Age structure and may date back several thousand years. However, this has yet to be definitively confirmed.

Queen's Park Earthworks, thought to date back to Iron Age.

40. From the Earthworks, head east along the path to the Queen's Park Flagpole, where this walk ends. Erected in the 1860s, when Queen's Park was first laid out, it sits on one of the highest points on the south side of Glasgow and offers great views over much of the city. On a clear day, you can easily see the distinctive shape of Dumgoyne at the western end of the Campsie Fells and even as far as Ben Lomond, more than 50 kilometres (30 miles) away. You can also see many of the tenements, towers and spires of the south and west of the city (including that of the University of Glasgow), as well as being able to see how much the city centre is now dominated by modern, and rather generic-looking, high-rise buildings which block views of much of its traditional architecture.

18. Pollokshields, Strathbungo and Shawlands

Start Point: Pollokshields Burgh Hall, Glencairn Drive, Glasgow (**Location:** Lat/Lon: 55.83883, -4.28689; What3Words: ///newest.habit.hulk; Plus Code: RPQ7+G6Q Glasgow). **Nearest Public Transport:** Subway: None; Train: Maxwell Park Station (10 mins); Bus: St Andrews Drive (15 mins).

End Point: Shawlands Cross, (**Location:** Lat/Lon: 55.830512, -4.28086; What3Words: ///square.cost.alone; Plus Code: RPJ9+6M2 Glasgow). **Nearest Public Transport:** Subway: None; Train: Crossmyloof Station (15 mins); Bus: Pollokshaws Road (1 min).

Distance: 5.4 kilometres/3.4 miles. **Time:** Allow 3 to 4.5 hours for this walk.
Level of Difficulty: Moderate. This walk is entirely on paved surfaces, but is relatively long.

Facilities: There are shops, cafes, restaurants and bars available at fairly regular intervals along this walk. Publicly accessible toilets are available in the Tramway Arts Venue about halfway through this walk and further south along Pollokshaws Road in Queen's Park, opposite the Camphill Gate Tenement.

Introduction

The neighbouring areas of Pollokshields, Strathbungo and Shawlands lie to the west of Queen's Park on the Southside of Glasgow. Originally countryside, these areas were gradually overtaken as the city expanded outwards in the nineteenth and early twentieth centuries, first by suburbs and then by Glasgow itself. However, among the area's many fine tenements and townhouses there are still remnants of the time before the city over took it, in the form of grand country villas like the Knowe and Camphill House. Pollokshields, in particular, has an interesting history as it was originally developed as a garden suburb in the mid-1800s on lands owned by the Maxwells of Pollok. Between 1876 and 1891, Pollokshields operated as an independent burgh, complete with its own burgh hall, before it was finally incorporated into Glasgow. In contrast to the planned development of Pollokshields, Strathbungo started out as a small village on the road between the settlements of Glasgow and Pollokshaws, centred around the crossroads between what is now Pollokshaws Road, Nithsdale Street and Allison Street. However, just like Pollokshields, it was developed around the 1850s as a suburb of Glasgow, complete with fine townhouses designed by major architects of the day, such as Alexander 'Greek' Thomson, who designed a number of key buildings which will be visited on this walk. As with Pollokshields, it was soon swallowed up by the expanding city and much of what was once considered Strathbungo is now considered parts of the neighbouring areas of Crosshill and Govanhill. Shawlands also started as a small village, but unlike Pollokshields and Strathbungo, it has more of an industrial and commercial past, with the development of businesses such as the Crossmyloof Bakery. Despite their different origins, together Pollokshields, Strathbungo and Shawlands, along with the neighbouring areas of Queen's Park, Govanhill, Crosshill, Mount Florida, Battlefield and Langside make up what many would now consider the heart of Glasgow's Southside.

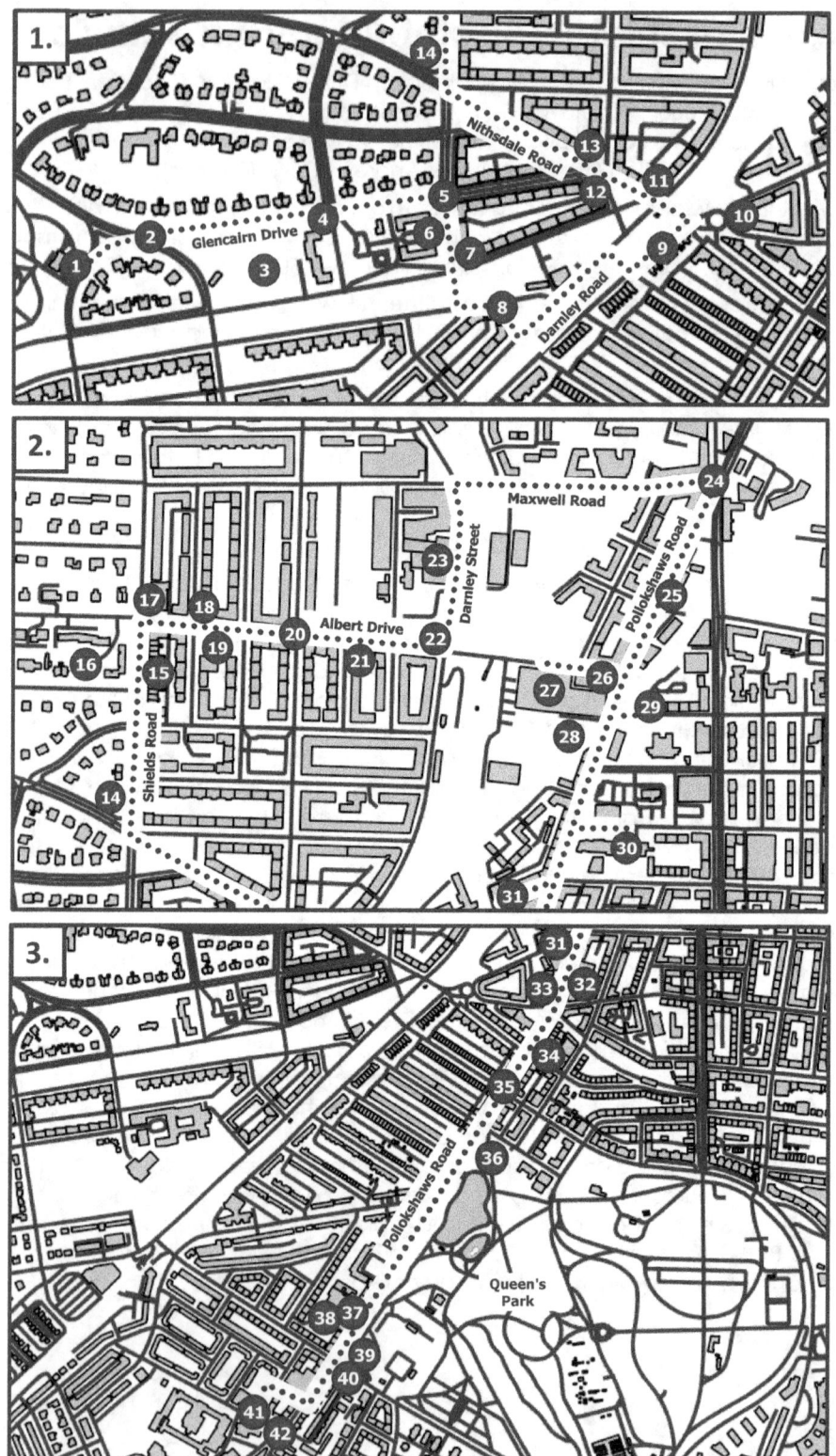

1. This walk starts at the former Pollokshields Burgh Hall on Glencairn Drive in the Pollokshields area of Glasgow. Set in the grounds of Maxwell Park, one of Glasgow's smaller parks, Pollokshields Burgh Hall was designed in a distinctive Scottish Renaissance style by Henry E. Clifford in 1890. This was a year before the area ceased being an independent burgh and was incorporated into the neighbouring City of Glasgow. It has a particularly fine pair of lions above its main entrance, each of which holds a monogrammed shield. Between these two is the coat of arms of the burgh of Pollokshields, as well as the date when the building was constructed. To the left of the main building is a small lodge, part the entrance of Maxwell Park itself, and on a panel at the back of the building is a series of Masonic symbols with the inscription 'No. 772', marking the use of this building as Lodge Pollok, Pollokshields' Masonic lodge. This lodge was established in the same year the building was constructed.

Part of 1890 Scottish Renaissance Pollokshields Burgh Hall.

2. From the former Pollokshields Burgh Hall turn left onto Glencairn Drive and follow it as it curves to the right before heading almost due east. This area is dominated by large late-nineteenth-century villas, which were built for the growing number of well-to-do merchants, professionals and industrialists who owned and operated Glasgow's thriving businesses, as it settled into its role as the workshop and second city of the British Empire.

3. On the south side of Glencairn Drive are the Titwood Lawn Tennis Club and the Titwood Bowling Club. The bowling club's pavilion, which can be seen from Glencairn Drive, is a rather beautiful arts and crafts style building with geometrically patterned half-timber walls and a conical roof which was designed by the architects Clarke & Bell, and was built when the club was established in 1890.

4. Further east along Glencairn Drive, at its junction with Leslie Road, is one of the 26 post boxes erected in Glasgow during the brief 326-day reign of King Edward VIII. Only 161 such boxes were erected in the whole of the UK, and it is unclear exactly why Glasgow ended up with quite so many of them – more than anywhere else in the whole country. At least thirteen of these boxes remain in place, three of which will be passed on this walk.

5. From the junction with Leslie Road, carry on east along Glencairn Drive to its junction with Shields Road. This marks the point where the large villas to the west give way to tenements to the east, although these tenements are still relatively grand in comparison to many other parts of Glasgow. Both tenements at the junction itself have corner towers, topped with conical roofs, something which is common throughout Glasgow and representative of one of its most distinctive architectural features. This is an example of how, at the end of the nineteenth century, features from the Scottish baronial style were incorporated not just into grand villas, municipal buildings, banks and warehouses, but also into more humble residential buildings, even if it was in a much more restrained manner.

6. Turn right onto Shields Road and walk south along it. As you do so, look to your right, where, in among the hedges and trees surrounding a modern housing development, stand the last remaining fragments of Trinity United Presbyterian Church (also known as Pollokshields-Glencairn Church). Designed by William G. Rowan and constructed in 1891, all that remains is the boundary wall and the main doorway. This doorway is surrounded by relief sculptures featuring scenes from the Old Testament on the left and the New Testament on the right, with a figure of the infant Jesus in a tabernacle separating the two. The church itself burned down 1988, but the arch was salvaged and re-erected as an ornamental feature in the new housing development built in its place in 1997. Due to its position, it is best viewed from the eastern side of Shields Road.

Remaining fragments of Trinity United Presbyterian Church, Shields Road.

7. Further south on Shields Road, at its junction with Terregles Avenue, and stretching east along that street, is a rather unusual set of tenements. Designed by Henry E. Clifford in 1895 (who designed the nearby Scots Revival style Pollokshields Burgh Hall a few years earlier), they are relatively streamlined and feature Modern Movement/early art nouveau style details. This contrasts sharply with the more ornate architectural styles, such as neoclassical, Gothic, Scottish baronial and beaux-arts, which came before it.

8. Cross Terregles Avenue, walk over the Shields Road railway bridge, and then turn left on to Fotheringay Road. Here, at the junction with Darnley Place is a much more traditional block of red sandstone tenements, which bear the date 1902. This shows that even as styles such as art nouveau were becoming more common in Glasgow, many tenements were still being built in more traditional styles.

9. From Darnley Place, head east along Darnley Road and cross over the railway line to its south, using the pedestrian bridge, to Moray Place, Here, on your left you will find a rather wonderful terrace of classical-inspired townhouses. Built in 1859, they were designed by Alexander 'Greek' Thomson, one of Glasgow's most celebrated architects. As you will see on the next section of this walk, Thomson's classical style had a major and lasting impact on the architecture of both Pollokshields and Strathbungo, not just through the buildings he designed, but also through the buildings designed by those he mentored and inspired, such as Alexander Skirving. Moray Place itself is a masterpiece of stripped-back classical design with a timeless quality that is just as desirable today as when it was first bult over 160 years ago. Thomson himself lived at 1 Moray Place from 1861 until his death aged fifty-seven in 1875, while a generation later Henry E. Clifford, who designed the Modern Movement tenements on Terregles Place which you viewed earlier, lived at No. 12.

10. At the east end of Moray Place is its junction with Nithsdale Road. If you look to your right at this junction, you will see a monumental curved tenement building called Salisbury Quadrant which has a design which is very much in a Thomson-esque style. Built in 1878, it is credited to Thomson and Turnbull, a partnership created between Alexander 'Greek' Thomson and Robert Turnbull in 1873, just two years before Thomson's death. While Salisbury Quadrant was not designed by Thomson himself (who died three years before it was built), it illustrates his enduring influence on the design of the many new buildings which were constructed in Strathbungo and Pollokshields as they developed into suburbs of the nearby city in the latter half of the nineteenth century.

Thomson-esque Salisbury Quadrant, Pollokshields.

11. From its junction with Moray Place, turn left and head north along Nithsdale Road to its junction with Darnley Street. On the north-east corner of this junction is another tenement building designed by Thomson and Turnbull, and which was built 1873, prior to Thomson's death. The shallow, recessed bow windows, which would have originally been fitted with curved glass, are a particularly fine feature. Their subtlety is markedly different from the Scottish baronial-inspired projecting corner towers which would become a key feature of Glasgow tenements a few decades later. However, these two very different styles are nonetheless united by the Glaswegian architectural tradition of including feature corners on buildings, especially at major road junctions.

12. Cross Darnley Road at the traffic lights and head north-west along Nithsdale Road to Kildrostan Street. Here, you will find a row of red sandstone tenements, with a parade of shops on their ground floor. A number of these shops retain their relatively traditional shopfronts, particularly the one on the left-hand corner. These traditional shopfronts are very different from the rather garish modern shopfronts found in many areas of Glasgow, which can detract significantly from the surrounding traditional architecture.

13. On the opposite side of Nithsdale Road, on the corner with Kenmure Street, is another, slightly older set of tenements which were built around 1870. In 1883, the ground-floor flats were converted into shops, one of which was occupied by a pharmacy owned by G.S. Illingworth, and later G.S. Kitchin. This led to this site becoming a well-known local landmark and for many years it was known by the nickname of 'Kitchin's Corner'.

14. From Kitchin's Corner, carry on north-west along Nithsdale Road until you reach its junction with Shields Road. Once again, you will see the demarcation between the large villas to the west of Shields Road and the tenements to its east. However, to the north of this junction is the former Pollokshields West Church. While it was designed by William G. Rowan and built in the late 1870s, there is once again a strong Thomson-esque influence to it, including the Doric portico to Shields Road with anthemion finials and the tall, square corner tower. This latter feature is almost identical to the tower on 'Greek' Thomson's 1850s Greek revival church on St Vincent Street in central Glasgow.

15. Head north along Shield's Road towards its junction with Albert Drive. As you do so, on your right, you will see a long tenement building known as Knowe Terrace. Built in the mid-1870s in a classical style, again it shows the influence that Alexander 'Greek' Thomson had on the local area. This is particularly noticeable in the shapes of the dormer windows along the roofline which are similar to those on Thomson and Turnbull's nearby Salisbury Quadrant.

16. At Albert Drive, turn left and walk a short distance west along it. Here, you will find an old gateway and gatehouse apparently leading into a relatively new development of flats. Walk though this gateway and follow the road as it leads round to the right. This will take you to the Knowe, one of the few villas designed by Alexander 'Greek' Thomson. With its Romanesque detailing and square tower, it is similar in design to Holmwood House, Thomson's best-known, and best-preserved, villa. The Knowe was built in the 1850s as a country house for the Glasgow merchant John Baird, but it has since been engulfed by the expanding city and now finds itself surrounded by villas, townhouses, tenements and a modern housing development.

The Knowe, 1850s Alexander 'Greek' Thomson country villa.

17. Return to Albert Drive and head east to its junction with Shields Road. Cross this junction carefully to reach the church on its north-east corner. Designed by Robert Baldie in a Gothic style, it was built in 1878 as Pollokshields Established Church. In front of the Shields Road side of the church is a war memorial for the members of the church congregation who died in World War I. Erected in the 1920s, its design is based on that of the Ruthwell Cross, an eighth-century Anglo-Saxon cross from the ancient kingdom of Northumbria, which once occupied an area now covered much of north-east of England and the south-east of Scotland. Follow the church round to its Albert Drive facade, and look above the ground-floor windows. Here you will find a pair of small but beautifully sculpted dragons at the base of the spandrels between the arched windows. Such dragons are a common feature on Glasgow's many neo-Gothic style Victorian churches, and while they are not always obvious, at least one is almost always present somewhere on such buildings.

18. From the church on the corner with Shields Road, head east along Albert Drive. At its junction with Herriet Street, you will find another example of a post box from the brief reign of Edward VIII. If you examine its base, you will see this one was created by the Carron Company, which is based in Stirlingshire and was one of a number of foundries which made post boxes for the Post Office. The Carron Company was founded in Falkirk in 1759, and was a major player in the Industrial Revolution in Scotland and the rest of the UK. At one point, it employed 5,000 people, operated its own steamships and even issued its own currency to enable it to trade globally. Its famous short-barrelled and short-range Carronade cannons were used by Wellington at the Battle of Waterloo and were fitted to Lord Nelson's flagship, HMS *Victory*. More recently its name has become synonymous with Britain's famous red telephone boxes and its iconic post boxes. In Glasgow, it was responsible for the creation of Duke Street in 1790, to give it more direct access to the city's markets,

and when the Clyde Tunnel was dug in the 1960s, it was the Carron Company which produced the cast-iron rings used to line it. The foundry finally closed in 1982, 223 years after it was established, when the company became insolvent. However, its name persists in the Carron Phoenix Company, which is best known today for manufacturing sinks.

19. On the opposite side of Albert Drive is Albert Road Public School (from the original name for the street before it became part of Glasgow in 1891 and was remained Albert Drive). It opened in 1882 and while it initially only offered elementary education, it expanded to include secondary education when it became the Albert Road Academy in 1926. The building itself was designed by Hugh and David Barclay in a palazzo style, and was one of a number of similar school buildings they created across Glasgow for both the Glasgow School Board and the Govan School Board, which was responsible for many of the schools in what is now the west and south of the city. This school almost led to the end of the careers of the Barclay brothers when a play shed collapsed shortly after it was opened, and David was arrested on a charge of culpable homicide. However, he was later acquitted and the reputation their architectural practice had built up over the years was sufficient to see them through not just this disaster, but also the severe recession of the 1880s which hit west of Scotland particularly hard due to the collapse of the City of Glasgow Bank in 1878, an event which left many of its shareholders bankrupt.

20. Further east, at the junction between Kenmure Street and Albert Drive, lies Albert Cross. This was once the commercial centre of the Victorian burgh of East Pollokshields, and like many such important crossroads in Glasgow it was, at one time, marked by fine tenements, three of which featured corner towers of bay windows topped by impressive turreted roofs. However, after two separate fires, the first in 2019 and the second in 2020, only one remains standing. The major impact these fires have had on the local streetscape can be seen by looking at the older images available on Google Streetview. They show how much the unique feel of Glasgow's streets can be lost when key buildings are damaged or removed, whether by accident, as in this case, or by poor planning decisions.

Last surviving feature corner tower, Albert Cross, old Victorian Burgh of East Pollokshields.

21. To the east of Albert Cross, at the junction between Albert Drive and Glenapp Street, is a grand free Italian Renaissance style church designed by John Bennie Wilson and built in 1886. Of particular note is the 43-metre (140 foot) tall campanile with its distinctive open belfry stage, which towers over the surrounding streets. Originally Stockwell Free Church, it is now known as St Albert the Great Roman Catholic Church.

22. At 100 Albert Drive, on the corner with Darnley Street, is a large red sandstone building with a distinctive style which contrasts with the surrounding tenements. Built in 1895, this was once home to the wonderfully named the Glasgow Laundry and Carpet Beating Works. Founded by Thomas Donald in the same year, it provided mechanised cleaning and ironing of flat linen items, like bedding and tablecloths, to the wealthy occupants of the townhouses and villas of the suburb of Pollokshields. The carpet-beating side of the business utilised the newly invented mechanical beaters and is a reminder of a time when, if you could afford carpets, rather than having them cleaned in situ, you sent them out to be cleaned instead.

23. Turn left and head north to 50 Darnley Street. Once home to the Miller & Lang Print Works, it was designed by David B. Dobson and was built in 1902. It is one of the most impressive and distinctive art nouveau commercial buildings in Glasgow and features a range of sculptures, including a statue of a female allegorical figure (possibly Minerva, the Roman goddess of the arts and poetry, which would fit with the subject matter of books which Miller and Lang specialised in publishing) and a rather unusual double-tailed mermaid. Finally, at the northern end of the building is an incredibly detailed piece of decorative ironwork consisting of a dragon inserted into the joint between two sections of pipe.

Decorative cast-iron dragon, former printworks, 50 Darnley Street.

24. Carry on north along Darnley Street, turn east onto Maxwell Road and continue east to its junction with Pollokshaws Road. Originally created in the early 1800s, this junction is known as St Andrew's Cross due to the angles at which the road meet. It is also known as Eglinton Toll as it served as the entry point to the Port Eglinton industrial area which lay between Pollokshields in the south and Tradeston in the north. This junction is home to two particularly distinctive buildings: the 1890s red sandstone YMCA Building designed in late Gothic style by Robert Miller; and the St Andrew's Cross Building, one of Glasgow's best known and best-loved gushet buildings. A gushet building is the name given to unusually shaped buildings constructed on the narrow strips of land between two roads, which meet at an angle of less than 90 degrees, and which are common across the city.

25. From St Andrew's Cross, turn right and head south along Pollokshaws Road. As you do so, on your left-hand side, you will pass a large and imposing Scottish baronial tenement which was built in 1884.

26. Further south on the corner of Pollokshaws Road and Albert Drive is the French Gothic style St Ninian's Episcopal Church. Designed by David Thomson, it was built in the mid-1870s. David Thomson was not related to Alexander' Greek' Thomson, but after 'Greek' Thomson's death in 1875, he formed a partnership with 'Greek' Thomson's former partner Robert Turnbull, and they continued to trade as Thomson and Turnbull. In this role, David Thomson helped not only complete the firm's outstanding contracts, but also to adapt 'Greek' Thomson's unbuilt designs for new clients, including Salisbury Quadrant on Nithsdale Drive which you visited earlier on this walk. This partnership came to an end in 1883.

27. Just to the west of St Ninian's Church on Albert Drive is the former Coplawhill Tram Depot. The first parts of this depot were built 1894, when Glasgow's trams were still horse-drawn. It originally housed trams on the ground floor and had stable for the horses on the first floor (such upper-floor stables were not uncommon in Glasgow at this time). However, in 1897, horse-drawn trams were gradually phased out and by 1901, they were all powered by electricity. This tram depot was gradually expanded in stages between 1899 and 1912, including the construction of an electrical substation and a tram works. As well as serving as a tram depot, it also acted as a recruiting office during World War I, and as a site for manufacturing aircraft wings in World War II. In the 1960s, when the tram network was finally replaced by diesel-powered buses, it became home to the city's Transport Museum. However, this was moved to Kelvin Hall in the West End of the city in the 1980s, and the old tram depot was then converted into its current use as an arts venue called the Tramway, an idea which was first proposed in 1989 to celebrate Glasgow's status as the 1990 City of Culture. This redevelopment was carried out by Zoo Architects.

28. Return to Pollokshaws Road and walk a short distance southwards to the point where a small lane leads west to the rear entrance of the Tramway. In this lane, you can still see examples of iron tram tracks set into the ground among the cobbles. At the end of this lane is the Hidden Gardens, an urban green space filled with a variety of artworks. There is also a cafe, which is a good place to stop for a rest before you complete the last section of this walk.

Iron tram tracks at entrance to Hidden Gardens behind the Tramway.

29. From the entrance to the Hidden Gardens, cross Pollokshaws Road at the traffic lights at its junction with Albert Drive and walk south to its junction with Coplaw Street. A short distance east along this street is a former military drill hall. Designed by John Bennie Wilson in a collegiate Tudor style and built in 1884, it was the headquarters of the 3rd Lanarkshire Rifle Volunteers, part of the Rifle Volunteer Corps created in 1859, and after whom the 3rd Lanark football club was originally named. This was one of many drill halls constructed between 1880 and 1910, when the various volunteer units were consolidated into a single Territorial Force. The construction of drill halls ended after the cessation of World War I, and in 1920, the Territorial Force became the Territorial Army. Of the 344 drill halls built in Scotland, around 182 still survive, although almost all of them are now used for alternative purposes.

30. Return to Pollokshaws Road and continue south again. At its junction with Kingarth Street is Hutchesons' Grammar School. This school was founded in 1641 with an endowment from Glasgow merchants George and Thomas Hutcheson, to provide a home and education for indigent orphans. The original school was built at Trongate in the centre of Glasgow, before moving in 1799 to a new site on Ingram Street (a building which still exists to this day). In the 1870s, the school shifted its emphasis to become the fee-paying school it is today. The building on Kingarth Street was originally designed as the girls' school in 1912, by Thomson & Sandilands,

an architectural firm established in 1886 as a partnership between Robert Sandilands and John Thomson, the oldest surviving son of Alexander 'Greek' Thomson. While initially very successful, the partnership suffered a decline in 1906, and only recovered when Sandilands won the competition to design this school in 1910.

31. Further south along Pollokshaws Road is its junction with Nithsdale Drive and Calder Street. For this walk, turn right into Nithsdale Drive. A short distance along this road, you will find the third and final Edward VIII post box which you will pass on this walk. Just beyond it, on the south side of Nithsdale Drive, is Nithsdale Hall, which was originally constructed as the Mission Hall for Queen's Park United Presbyterian Church in 1887. It is reminiscent of the work of Alexander 'Greek' Thomson, but it was in fact designed by Alexander Skirving, who trained with 'Greek' Thomson and went on to become his chief assistant. Skirving is often described, somewhat unfairly, as a 'Greek' Thomson imitator, but his work stands in its own right, particularly his Langside Hill Free Church. Constructed in 1894, it is seen as marking the end of the widespread use of the classical style in Glasgow.

32. Return to Pollokshaws Road, and look right. Here, you will see the tower of Strathbungo Parish Church. Designed by James McKissack in 1886, it combines Scottish Gothic and Romanesque elements to create a unique structure with a distinctive open crown spire. While the rest of the church has been demolished, the tower remains and has been incorporated into a newer development. Of particular note are the carvings around the Roman-arched entrance, which consist of a bizarre menagerie of intertwined beasts and monsters, including dragons, bats, mermaids, birds with human heads and snake-eating devils. It really needs to be examined in detail to take it all in.

Carving, entrance of former Strathbungo Parish Church.

33. Just south of the tower of Strathbungo Parish Church, but on the opposite side of the road, is No. 674. Here, a small pend leads beneath the red sandstone tenements to an area behind them which is home to a series of small commercial units. This pend is lined with a stone tramway leading off from the street. Older than their metal counterparts on which Glasgow's famous trams ran, stone tramways were lines of smooth, hard-wearing stones set into cobbled streets to make it easier for horses to pull carts along them. While once common on the streets and lanes of Glasgow, such stone tramways are increasingly rare.

34. Continue south along Pollokshaws Road to its junction with Torrisdale Street. The ornate red sandstone building which stands at this junction was built as a branch of the British Linen Bank towards the end of the nineteenth century, and has many features typical of a bank building of this time. This includes the classical style detailing, the monogram of the bank above the door and the selection of a site at a major road junction.

35. To the south of the red sandstone tenements, between Torrisdale Street and Titwood Road, Pollokshaws Road is lined with three-storey, classical Georgian style, mid-nineteenth-century tenements. These would have been among the first tenements built as the area was developed from the 1850s onwards.

36. Further south again, on the right-hand side of Pollokshaws Road, lies Queen's Park, which was designed by Joseph Paxton, the architect of the Crystal Palace in London, and was laid out between 1857 and 1862. It covers some 60 hectares (148 acres), making it one of Glasgow's larger parks, and also a major feature of the Southside area of the city. The lands it was created on were originally owned by Maxwells of Pollok. It later became Camphill Farm in 1799, which was eventually sold to the Glasgow Corporation in 1857. However, its history stretches back much further than this. The name Camphill is believed to originate from the use of the local area as a Roman encampment, and there are the remains of earthworks within the park which may date back as far as the Iron Age. Queen's Park is explored in more detail as part of Walk 17 in this book,

37. Opposite Queen's Park, at Nos. 988–1006 Pollokshaws Road, is Camphill Gate. Built in 1906, this is one of the finest examples of a classic Glasgow red sandstone tenement. Created by John Nisbet, who designed many of the red sandstone tenements built by John McTaggart across Glasgow, it is unusual in having five storeys rather than four, which was more typical of the time it was constructed. This

Nameplate, Camphill Gate, Pollokshaws Road.

made it one of the tallest residential buildings in the city when it was built. In order to accommodate the extra density of residents created by this additional floor, as well as the usual ground-level drying greens, it was also built with an additional rooftop drying green, which is now used as a roof terrace and provides magnificent views across the city and out into the surrounding countryside as far as Ben Lomond. It was also one of the first tenements in Glasgow to be built with fireproof concrete slabs between the floors, to reduce the risk of a fire starting in one flat and spreading throughout the rest of the building. Camphill Gate is also a great case study in the preservation of a listed building by a community group created by the owners of the flats who, over the years, have worked hard to raise the money needed to repair and refurbish this much-loved building.

38. To the right of Camphill Gate, a narrow lane leads to an area behind it which contains a series of small commercial units. This area was once home to the old Crossmyloof Bakery. This bakery was established by Neale Thomson of Camphill House (which can still be see in Queen's Park) in the mid-1800s to ensure his workers at the Adelphi Cotton Works, in nearby Hutchesontown, could purchase good quality bread at a price which was much cheaper than was available elsewhere. Having inherited the business from his father in the 1830s, Neale Thomson became well known for the care he showed for his workforce, and as well as the bakery, he encouraged them to open savings accounts, and matched their contributions with his own money. He also commissioned Alexander 'Greek' Thomson (who was not a relative) to build terraced housing for his workforce. Although the bakery started

as a philanthropic enterprise, it proved rather successful and quite soon shops were opened where large crowds often gathered to meet the delivery vans. Neale Thomson died at Camphill House in 1857, but the bakery business survived until 1880, and parts of its former buildings still exist behind the more recent tenements.

39. From Camphill Gate, head south along Pollokshaws Road to its junction with Langside Avenue. Here, on the left is the magnificent Langside Hall. Designed in a classical style by John Gibbon, it was built in the late 1840s, and among other features, it has a series of keystones decorated with masks sculpted by John Thomas, which represent personifications of five major rivers of Great Britain and Ireland. These are thought to be the Thames, the Severn, the Tweed, the Humber and the Clyde. The one for the Clyde can be found over the main door and features a headdress which includes two fish, each with a ring in its mouth, one of the symbols from the Glasgow coat of arms. It may seem surprising, but Langside Hall has not always only been at this location. Originally, it was situated on Queen Street in central Glasgow, where it served as a branch of the National Bank of Scotland. In 1901, rather than see it demolished, it was deconstructed by the city architect Alexander B. McDonald and rebuilt at its current location.

Langside Hall, junction between Pollokshaws Road and Langside Avenue.

40. On the opposite side of the junction between Langside Avenue and Pollokshaws Road to Langside Hall is an ornate single-storey public house designed by Clarke & Bell, and built in 1912. It is an example of one of the three things traditionally found at most major junctions in Glasgow: a bank, a church or a pub. Above the doors of the Corona Bar and set into the tiled threshold of its entrance on Pollokshaws Road, is a symbol of a hand with a cross on it. This symbol is a play on the local place name Crossmyloof. 'Loof', or 'luif', is an old Scots word for the palm of the hand, and the name is said to have originated with a local fortune-teller who offered to tell Mary Queen of Scots her fate before the Battle of Langside in 1568, as long as the queen crossed her loof (or palm) with silver. This story seems to have inspired Clarke & Bell to include the symbol of a palm with a cross on it (or a crossed palm) in their design for this public house.

41. From its junction with Langside Avenue, head south along Pollokshaws Road before turning right into Abbot Street and then left into Frankfort Street. At the end of Frankfort Street, where it meets Moss-Side Road, is the former Waverley Cinema. Designed by Watson, Salmond and Gray, it was built in 1922. As such, it is an early and important example of a purpose-built cinema. Over the years, the Waverley has followed a typical trajectory for a Glasgow cinema. It closed in 1973 and was turned first into a bingo hall and then a snooker club, before lying empty for a substantial period of time. It was then turned into a bar-restaurant, but at the time of writing is once again lying empty and at risk of being lost.

42. After viewing the former Waverley Cinema, turn left on to Moss-Side Road and walk east along it to Shawlands Cross, where Moss-Side Road, Pollokshaws Road and Kilmarnock Road meet, and where this walk ends. This junction is marked by examples of all three types of buildings typically found at such a major junction in Glasgow: a church (Shawlands Cross Church), a pub (on the ground floor of Crossmyloof Mansions), and at least one bank (a former branch of the Glasgow Savings Bank). Shawlands Cross Church is a fine example of the Late perpendicular Gothic style and was designed by John Hamilton in 1898. Of particular note are the rather cute grotesques on either side of the door and on the octagonal towers which rise above it. To the left of Shawlands Cross Church, on the narrow triangular strip between Pollokshaws Road and Kilmarnock Road, is Crossmyloof Mansions, another of Glasgow's many gushet buildings. Its ground floor was originally home to a bar called Samuel Dow's. Samuel Dow was a wine and whisky merchant established in Glasgow in 1807 by Samuel McCalman, from Lochaber, when he opened a small bar on King Street in central Glasgow. It was Samuel Dow's grandson, also called Samuel Dow, who expanded the business by opening further bars, including the one on the ground floor of Crossmyloof Mansions in 1899. Finally, to the north of Crossmyloof Mansions on the corner between Moss-Side Road and Pollokshaws Road is the former Glasgow Savings Bank building. Designed by Neil C. Duff, and built in 1906, the bank was situated on the ground floor with tenement flats above it. Among other things, this building features the type of ornate corner tower, topped with a dome, typical of many Glasgow junctions. Thus, Shawlands Cross is a great example of a number of key Glasgow architectural traditions which contribute to its distinctive streetscapes. However, many of these traditions are not being continued in modern buildings, and the result is the loss of many of the elements which make Glasgow such an architecturally unique city.

Pub, church and bank, all housed in grand buildings, Shawlands Cross.

Additional Resources

If you wish to learn more about any of the buildings, locations or areas, which you have visited or passed as part of the walks included in this book, you might find the following resources helpful.

Websites

1. **Historic Environment Scotland Listed Buildings Database:** This website provides a database of all the listed building in Scotland, including details about their date, their architects and their original use. It can be searched either by an address or using a map. https://www.historicenvironment.scot/advice-and-support/listing-scheduling-and-designations/listed-builings-search-for-a-listed-building/.
2. **Canmore:** This website provides a national record of the historic environment, often with old pictures which allow you to see how a particular building or street used to look, and includes both listed and unlisted buildings. https://canmore.org.uk.
3. **National Library of Scotland Geo-referenced Online Historic Maps:** This is a portal which allows you to access a range of geo-referenced online maps, some going back to the early nineteenth century, which enable you to compare the existing streetscape to historic ones. It can be searched by place names or by manually zooming in. https://maps.nls.uk/geo/explore/.
4. **Glasgow Sculpture Database:** This website provides information about many of the public sculptures which can be found in Glasgow, both free-standing and on the facades of buildings. http://glasgowsculpture.com.
5. **The Glasgow Story:** This website provides pictures and other useful information about the social history of many of Glasgow's buildings and places. https://www.theglasgowstory.com.
6. **The Dictionary of Scottish Architects:** This website provides biographic information about many of Scotland's architects and architectural firms, including lists of buildings which they created. http://www.scottisharchitects.org.uk/architect_list.php.

Social Media

The following pages/accounts are also a great resource for learning more about Glasgow.

1. **Past Glasgow:** Channel devoted to the history of Glasgow, which features many older pictures of the city. It can be found on Instagram (@past.glasgow) and X (@pastglasgow).
2. **Lost Glasgow:** Channel devoted to the many changes Glasgow has undergone over the years. Again, it provides many older pictures of the city. It can be found on X (@lostglasgow).
3. **Glasgow City Heritage Trust (and Niall Murphy):** An independent charity devoted to conserving Glasgow's built heritage, it can be found on Instagram (@glasgowheritage) and X (@glasgowheritage). Its director, Niall Murphy, also has his own social media account which is well worth following on X (@MurphyNiallGLA)
4. **Tenement Tiles:** Channel devoted to the decorative tiles found in tenement closes across Glasgow. It can be found on Instagram (@tnmnttiles) and X (@tnmnttiles).

5. **South Glasgow Heritage and Environment:** A charity created to champion and explore the history and places of the South of Glasgow. It can be found on Instagram (@sghetter) and X (@SGHETorg).

6. **Dennistoun Style:** Channel which showcases the history, heritage and social history of the East End and other parts of Glasgow, It can be found on Instagram (@dennistounstyle) and X (@dennistounstyle).

7. **This Is My Glasgow:** Channel of Colin M. Drysdale, the author of this book, which features photographs and information about Glasgow and the surrounding areas. It can be found on Instagram (@ThisIsMyGlasgow) and X (@is_glasgow).

Index

ABC Cinema 46, 47, 232
Abercromby Street 202, 203, 204
Adam, Robert 35, 167, 174, 207, 209, 251
Adam, Robert and John 167
Albany Place 47, 49
Albert Drive 272, 273, 274, 275
Alexander Stephen and Son (shipyard) 250, 251
Alexandra Parade 3, 182, 184, 185, 186, 187
Alexandra Park 125, 129, 184, 185, 198
Allison Street 262, 263, 267
Anderson, Rowand 247, 253
Anderston Centre 64, 69, 74
Anderston Comprehensive Development Area 64, 69, 73, 75
Anderston Cross 73, 98
Anderston Pyramid 72, 73
Applecross Basin 155
Argyle Street 3, 7, 17, 19, 20, 21, 29, 38, 51, 66, 69, 71, 72, 73, 74, 75, 76, 77, 78, 83, 84, 85, 86, 87, 88, 103, 114, 128, 130, 163, 182
Argyll Arcade 19, 85
Argyll Chambers 19
Armadillo 100, 102
Baird, John 15, 19, 33, 55, 83, 85, 212
Baird, John Logie 80
Ballater Street 217, 219, 222, 226
Barbour, Mary 94, 246, 247, 249, 251
Barclay, Hugh and David 44, 63, 133, 262, 273
Barrowland Ballroom 206, 207
Barrowland Market 203, 206
Barrowland Park Album Pathway 207
Bath Street 41, 42, 43, 46, 47, 48
Battlefield Monument 259
Battlefield Road 259, 260
Bell and Miller 91, 123
Bell o' the Brae 170, 179, 194
Bell o' the Brae, Battle of 170
Bell Street 31, 32, 163, 166, 167
Beresford Inglis, William 48
Berkeley Street 107, 108, 109
Blackfriars Street 31, 167
Blockade Runners 94, 95
Blythswood Hill 56, 58
Blythswood New Town 51, 57, 58, 163
Blythswood Street 45, 64, 75
Bonnie Prince Charlie 29, 87, 192, 210

Boots Corner (Dizzy Corner) 83
Botanic Gardens Garage 137
Botanic Gardens Railway Station 118, 123
Bothwell Street 62, 63, 64, 79
Boucher, James 21, 27, 119, 126
Bridge Street 77, 94, 95, 217, 226, 227, 228, 229, 230
Bridge(s) to Nowhere 74, 105
Bridgegate 26, 34, 92, 163
Bridgeton Cross 196, 198, 199
Bridgeton Public Library 196, 199
Britannia Panopticon 30
Bromhead, Horatio, K. 84
Broomielaw, The 67, 77, 78, 95, 96, 97, 98, 230, 240
Brown, William Kellock 33, 191, 211, 219, 236
Bruce & Hay 41, 227, 228, 236, 239
Bruce Report 69
Bubonic plague 223
Buchanan Street 7, 9, 10, 11, 12, 13, 15, 16, 17, 18, 19, 20, 21, 22, 24, 27, 38, 40, 51, 57, 84, 103, 109, 163, 167, 175
Buffalo Bill (William F. Cody) 189
Burnet and Boston 59, 60, 137
Burnet, Boston & Carruthers 20, 194
Burnet, Frank 45, 53, 59, 60, 76, 87, 204, 253, 260
Burnet, John 14, 26, 35, 50, 61, 193, 199, 229
Burnet, John James 10, 11, 12, 14, 26, 35, 50, 58, 61, 64, 65, 67, 79, 81, 96, 105, 139, 140, 142, 143, 165, 227, 229, 249, 250
Burnet, Son & Campbell 100
Burnet, Son and Campbell 171
Burnhouse Street 150, 151
Burns, Robert 86, 225, 245, 257
Byres Road 109, 115, 117, 130, 137, 138
Ca' d'Oro Building 82
Calder Street 263, 276
Calder Street Public Baths and Washhouse 263
Caledonia Road Church 224
Caledonian Mansions 53, 123
Caledonian Railway 77, 79, 80, 81, 82, 95, 118, 123, 148, 226
Calton Burial Ground 202, 203
Campbell Douglas and Sellars 258

282

Campbell, John A. 9, 10, 55, 86
Camphill Gate 267, 277, 278
Camphill House 255, 258, 266, 267, 277
Canal House 146, 157
Candleriggs 31, 32, 163
Carlton Place 93, 228, 229
Carnegie, Andrew 151, 191, 219, 249, 260
Carron Company 182, 272
Castle Street 163, 166, 171, 174, 175, 176
Cathcart Road 224, 225, 260, 261, 262
Cathedral Precinct 163, 175, 179, 180
Cathedral Square 176, 177, 212
Cathedral Street 172
Central Fire Station 167, 168
Central Hotel 62, 80
Central Police Headquarters 208
Central Station 7, 51, 53, 62, 69, 77, 78, 79, 80, 81, 82, 83, 95, 199, 217, 224, 226
Centre Street 232, 239, 240
Charing Cross 38, 49, 50, 65, 103, 105, 198
Charing Cross Mansions 38, 50, 65, 105, 198
Charlotte Street 90, 207, 209
Cheapside Street 32, 98
Citizen Building 13, 14
Citizens Theatre 225, 226
City Chambers 24, 33, 36, 68, 101, 239, 244
City Improvement Trust 31, 166, 167, 170, 194
City of Glasgow Bank 31, 186, 273
City of Glasgow Union Bridge 77, 91, 95
Clarke & Bell 33, 92, 105, 269, 278
Clarke, Bell & J.H. Craigie 85
Cleopatra's (Clatty Pats) 122, 123
Clifford, Henry, E. 74, 97, 269, 270
Clyde Navigation Trust 51, 67, 77, 88, 96, 101, 102, 201, 244
Clyde Street 91, 92, 94
Clydebank Blitz 113, 186, 240
Coburg Street 227, 228
Cook Street 232, 233, 239
Coplawhill Tram Depot 275
Covenanters' Memorial 177
Craigpark 187, 188, 189, 191
Cranston, Catherine (Kate) 17, 27, 45, 84, 85
Crosshill and Govanhill Burgh Hall 261

Crossmyloof 255, 267, 277, 278, 279
Culloden 29, 53, 87, 192, 210
Cumberland Street 220, 221, 222, 223, 224, 225
Cunningham, John 192, 198
Daily Record Building 61
Darnley Road 270, 271
Darnley Street 271, 274
Daulton Fountain 203
Dawson, Archibald 57, 58, 64, 142
Dennistoun, Alexander 182, 194
Derwent Wood, Francis 60, 63, 114, 246
Douglas, Campbell 177, 225
Douglass, Frederick 24, 32, 207
Dreghorn, Alan 208
Duff, Neil C. 76, 152, 279
Duke Street Prison 90, 171, 177, 193, 200
Dumbarton Road 130, 144, 145
Eglinton Engine Works 232, 233, 235
Eglinton Street 230, 232, 250
Egyptian Halls 82
Elder Cottage Hospital 249, 250
Elder Park 249, 250, 251, 252
Elder Park Library 249
Elderpark Street 248, 249
Empire Exhibition 48, 141, 212
Ewing, James A. 49, 193, 236, 238
Exhibition of Science Art and Industry 125
Fairfield Shipbuilding and Engineering Company 247, 249, 252
Finnieston Crane (Stobcross Crane) 99, 100, 141
Firhill 154, 155
Forth and Clyde Canal 3, 114, 146, 148, 149, 150, 151, 153, 155, 157, 173
Frampton, George 35, 114
Frank Burnet and Boston 45, 53, 60, 76, 87, 204, 253, 260
Gallery of Modern Art (GoMA) 16, 24, 26
Gallowgate 90, 163, 165, 196, 203, 204, 205, 206, 207
Garscube Road 154, 155
George Square 24, 26, 33, 34, 36, 68, 177, 244
George Street 13, 51, 53, 54, 56, 136, 169, 194
Gibbon, John 257, 278
Gilbert Scott Building 114
Gilbert Scott, George 140, 141
Gillespie, John Gaff 61, 73, 140, 184, 188, 195, 225

Gillespie, Kidd & Coia 18, 188, 190, 195, 209, 225
Gilmorehill Campus 115, 118, 130, 133, 134, 135, 142, 168
Glasgow Botanic Gardens 109, 115, 118
Glasgow Bridge 77, 94
Glasgow Cathedral 34, 90, 98, 163, 165, 173, 175, 176, 178, 181, 192, 220
Glasgow Corporation 68, 88, 117, 118, 128, 169, 170, 239, 255, 277
Glasgow Corporation Tramways 117, 169
Glasgow Cross 30, 90, 110, 163, 165, 175, 176, 191, 196
Glasgow Empire 41, 48, 212
Glasgow Evening News 79
Glasgow Garden Festival 101, 238, 244
Glasgow Green 3, 40, 87, 88, 90, 91, 125, 132, 167, 193, 196, 201, 203, 209, 210, 211, 212, 217, 219, 255, 258
Glasgow Harbour Tunnel 99, 100
Glasgow Herald 18, 19
Glasgow Institute for the Deaf and Dumb 260
Glasgow International Exhibition 125, 143, 184
Glasgow Lock Hospital 171
Glasgow Royal Exchange 26, 166
Glasgow Royal Infirmary 53, 163, 173, 174, 175, 179, 180, 192
Glasgow School of Art 46, 73, 152, 188, 206
Glasgow Science Centre 99, 101, 244
Glasgow Subway 9, 233
Glasgow Tower 101, 102, 103, 141, 244
Glasgow University Union (GUU) 133, 140
Glasgow Weekly Mail 63
Glasgow Women's Library 133, 194, 200
Glassford Street 28, 29, 30, 31, 35
Glassford, John 29, 31, 87
Gorbals Vampire, The 220, 226
Gordon Street 15, 77, 80, 81, 82
Gordon, John 189, 192, 199, 233, 263
Govan Cross 129, 184, 241, 246, 251
Govan Graving Docks 101, 102, 244
Govan Old Parish Church 241, 251, 253
Govan Poorhouse 64, 250
Govan Road 64, 100, 236, 237, 243, 244, 245, 246, 247, 252, 253

Govan Stones 248, 254
Govan Town Hall 101, 244
Govanhill and Crosshill Public Library 263
Govanhill Picture House 262
Graham Square 203, 204
Grahamston 78, 79, 82, 83
Granville Street 40, 84, 107
Grassby, Charles B. 14, 54, 174
Gray, Alisdair 115, 190
Great Western Road 115, 117, 118, 120, 122, 123
Greendyke Street 90, 207, 209, 210
Greenhead Street 200, 201
Grosvenor Terrace 117
Hamilton, David and James 40, 179
Hamiltonhill Clay Pits Local Nature Reserve 155
Hampden Park 261
Hatrack, The 60, 61
Henderson, George 43, 45, 166
High Street 3, 7, 66, 134, 140, 142, 163, 165, 166, 167, 168, 169, 170, 171, 179, 182, 194
Hillhead 115, 124, 130, 133, 135, 136, 137, 148
Hodge, Albert Hemstock 67, 73, 82, 96, 180
Honeyman and Keppie 49, 57, 110, 154, 209
Honeyman, Jack & Robertson 72
Honeyman, John 57, 82, 109, 156, 176, 205, 206, 253
Honeyman, Keppie and Mackintosh 136
Hope Street 43, 55, 60, 61, 62, 79, 80
Howden's Marine Engineering Works 233, 234
Howgate 90, 176
Hunter, Kenny 30, 80, 203, 223
Hutcheson Street 26, 33, 34
Hutcheson, George and Thomas 34, 275
Hutchesons' Grammar School 34, 275
Hutchesons' Hospital 34, 217
Hutchesontown District Library 191, 219
Hydro Arena 100, 102
Ingram Street 11, 17, 27, 31, 33, 34, 35, 36, 90, 103, 163, 167, 168, 170, 275
International Exhibition of Science, Art and Industry 144
Isabella Elder 94, 249, 250
Jail Square 91, 210

Jamaica Street 77, 83, 84, 94, 217
James Watt Street, 75, 76, 96
John Knox Street 177, 193
Justiciary Buildings 90
K13 Disaster 252
Kelvin Aqueduc 148, 149
Kelvin Bridge Station 123, 124
Kelvin Dock 150
Kelvin Hall 103, 130, 141, 144, 145, 275
Kelvin Walkway 119, 120, 121, 122, 123
Kelvin Way 113, 114, 115, 130, 132, 133, 142
Kelvin, Lord 45, 132, 141, 142, 143
Kelvin, River 102, 114, 115, 119, 120, 121, 123, 124, 130, 132, 144, 149
Kelvinbridge Parish Church 122
Kelvingrove Art Gallery and Museum 27, 114, 126, 130, 138, 141, 145
Kelvingrove Park 111, 112, 113, 115, 124, 125, 126, 128, 129, 130, 141, 143, 144, 157, 184, 198, 212, 255
Kennedy, John F. 48, 80
Keppie, John 18, 43, 45, 47, 49, 57, 113, 144, 252
Kibble Palace 46, 119
King Street 163, 202, 279
Kingston Bridge 64, 69, 72, 73, 75, 97, 98, 99, 229, 230, 238, 239
Kingston Dock 98, 230, 238
Kingston Engine Works 235
Kingston House 230, 240
Knox, John 177, 178, 193
La Belle Place 110, 111, 128
La Pasionaria 94
Lady Well 177
Langlands Road 248, 249, 250
Langside Avenue 255, 257, 258, 278
Langside Hill Church 191, 259 276
Langside Public Halls 257, 278
Langside Road 258, 259, 263, 264, 265
Langside, Battle of 255, 259, 278
Laurieston House 93, 228
Leiper, William 28, 54, 212, 265
Lion and Unicorn Staircase 142, 168
Lister, Josseph 106, 132, 174
London Road 165, 196, 198, 199, 202, 207, 208, 217
Lord Roberts Memorial 126, 128
Lyceum Cinema 253
M8 motorway 38, 51, 64, 71, 72, 73, 75, 97, 98, 103, 105, 173, 229, 234, 238
Macdonald, Margaret 45, 135
MacFarlane & Co 43, 184

MacGillivray, James Pittendrigh 252
Mackay, Kenny 9, 238
Mackintosh, Charles Rennie 17, 18, 20, 22, 27, 43, 44, 45, 46, 49, 57, 61, 69, 71, 73, 84, 92, 109, 110, 113, 135, 144, 152, 154, 172, 178, 188, 189, 205, 234
MacWhannel and Rogerson 186
MacWhannel, Ninian 200
Mandela, Nelson 10, 11, 12, 53, 58
Mansion House 251
Mary, Queen of Scots 255, 259, 278
Maryhill Burgh Halls 146, 150, 151
Matcham, Frank 41, 48
McDonald, Alexander B. 33, 91, 92, 113, 118, 144, 167, 168, 208, 211, 228, 239, 257, 263, 278
McGibbon, William F. 232, 239
McIver, Maggie and James 206
McKissack, James 137, 276
McNair, Charles J. 46, 227, 253
McNaughtan, Adam 190, 220
McNaughtan, Duncan 66, 150
Miller, James 13, 22, 53, 59, 61, 62, 77, 80, 82, 123, 143, 174, 180, 184, 226, 251
Moray Place 270, 271
Morrison Street 68, 239
Mossman, John 11, 14, 34, 35, 36, 45, 67, 86, 110, 128, 130, 225
Mossman, William 55, 107
Nagasaki Peace Tree 119
Necropolis 98, 163, 168, 173, 175, 177, 178, 179, 192, 221, 223
Nelson Monument 90, 210, 211
Nelson, Lord 90, 210, 211, 272
New Bedford Picture House 232
Nisbet, James 172, 176
Nithsdale Drive 274, 276
Nithsdale Road 271
Nithsdale Street 267
North Street 71, 73, 103, 105
Ogg Brothers Department Store 236, 238
Old College 134, 142, 168
Old Gorbals Burial Ground 220, 223
Oxford Street 227, 228
Pacific Quay 243, 244
Paisley Road 230, 236, 237, 238, 239, 241, 243
Paisley Road West 236, 237, 241, 243
Park Church 100, 108, 265
Park District 108, 115, 126, 128, 182
Parnie Street 30, 163
Parson Street 172, 173, 260

Partick 74, 88, 103, 115, 130, 144, 148, 154, 191, 264
Patterson, Alexander N. 22
Pavilion Theatre 42
Pearce Institute 247
Pearce Lodge 134, 168
Peden, Liz 219, 222
People's Palace 125, 167, 196, 210, 211, 212
Pollokshaws Road 255, 267, 274, 275, 276, 277, 278, 279
Pollokshields Burgh Hall 267, 269, 270
Pomeroy, Frederick 212
Port Dundas 43, 151, 152, 155, 156, 172, 198
Port Glasgow 88, 94, 95, 103
Prince's Dock 100, 101, 238, 243, 244
Prospecthill Road 260, 261
Provand's Lordship 163, 175, 176
Queen Maragret Drive 119, 120
Queen Margaret Union (QMU) 133, 140
Queen Street 7, 24, 26, 27, 38, 51, 146, 224, 257, 278
Queen's Cross Church 154
Queen's Dock 102, 244
Queen's Drive 258, 261, 265
Queen's Park 3, 212, 255, 257, 258, 261, 263, 265, 266, 267, 276, 277
Queen's Park Football Club 261, 263
Radical Wars, The 210
Ramshorn Cemetery 29, 31
Reilly, Rose 264
Renfield Street 42, 43, 54, 61, 81
Renfrew Street 43, 49, 50
Rhind, James R. 151, 191, 199, 219, 263
Rhind, William Birnie 44, 50, 54, 81, 125
Riverside Museum 88, 102, 145
Robertson Street 51, 66, 67 96
Rochead, John T. 26, 31, 108, 117
Rottenrow 81, 163, 171, 172
Rowan, William G. 270, 271
Royal Crescent 111, 112
Royal Exchange Square 16, 26, 166
Royal Faculty of Procurators 11, 51, 53
Ruchill Parish Church 146, 152, 153
Saint Enoch 21, 169, 202
Saint Mungo 21, 30, 35, 63, 75, 76, 114, 163, 169, 170, 175, 176, 179, 180, 210, 219
Salmon & Son & Gillespie 188
Salmon, James Jnr 60, 61, 63, 73, 168, 184, 188, 195, 225
Salmon, James, Snr 35, 41, 61, 168, 182, 188, 189, 194, 225
Salmon, Son and Gillespie 246
Salmon, Son and Ritchie 260
Salmon, William Forrest 61, 168, 188, 194
Saltmarket 90, 91, 163, 165
Saltoun Street 137, 138
Saracen Foundry 119, 184, 198
Saracen Fountain 125, 184
Sauchiehall Street 3, 11, 38, 40, 41, 42, 43, 44, 45, 46, 47, 48, 49, 50, 51, 103, 105, 106, 107, 109, 110, 111, 112, 115, 128, 130, 232
Scotland Street 233, 234, 235
Scotland Street School 234, 235
Scott, Andy 71, 151
Scottish Cooperative Wholesale Society (SCWC) 68, 227, 238, 239
Scottish Events Campus (SEC) 99, 102, 103, 141, 145, 244
Sellars, James 13, 18, 20, 26, 35, 55, 107, 112, 128, 130, 133, 137, 144, 145, 225
Shannan, Archibald McFarlane 132, 244, 249
Shawlands Cross 267, 27
Shields Road 235, 269, 270, 271, 272
Simpson, John 114, 145
Skirving, Alexander 28, 259, 270, 276
Smeaton, John 149
Smith, James McCune 24, 139, 171, 207
Soddy, Frederick 139
Somers, Thomas 95, 120, 144,
Speirs Wharf 146, 156, 157
Springburn 100, 163, 173, 191, 258
Squiggly Bridge (Tradestone Bridge) 95
Squinty Bridge (The Clyde Arc) 99, 100, 243
SS Daphne Disaster 250
St Andrew's East Parish Church 182, 184, 188
St Andrew's Halls 84, 107, 108
St Andrew's Parish Church 30, 165, 184, 191, 208
St Enoch Square 7, 21, 22
St Enoch Station 7, 10, 21, 51, 69, 75, 77, 85, 88, 91, 102, 224
St Enoch Subway Station 22, 163
St George's Church 7, 11, 12
St Vincent Place 13, 15, 26, 54
St Vincent Street 58, 59, 60, 61, 69, 71, 103, 108, 271

Stanley Street 235, 236
Stark, Malcolm 152
Stark, William 11, 90
Statue of Liberty 14, 36, 265
Stevenson, John James 115, 122
Stewart Memorial Fountain 115, 128, 130, 198
Stockingfield Bridge 151, 152
Stockwell Street 92, 163
Stodart, Archibald 97
Strathbungo Parish Church 276
Submariners' Memorial 252
Sunlight Cottages 125, 143, 145
Sutherland, Eric A. 93, 245
Tall Ship Glenlee 103
Templeton Carpet Factory 196, 202, 212
Tennent Caledonian Wellpark Brewery 192
Thomson & Sandilands 16, 31, 101, 244, 275
Thomson and Turnbull 271, 272, 274
Thomson, Alexander 'Greek' 13, 15, 28, 47, 57, 64, 81, 82, 86, 112, 120, 136, 220, 224, 243, 244, 248, 259, 262, 265, 267, 270, 271, 272, 276, 277
Thomson, James 13, 20, 44, 55, 60, 61, 62, 64, 76, 82, 190, 200, 248, 250
Thomson, Robert 19, 79
Thomson, Sandilands & MacLeod 29
Thomson, William 45, 132, 142
Titan cranes 100, 141
Tolbooth 30, 90, 163, 165, 166, 175
Tolbooth Steeple 30, 163, 165, 166, 175
Tontine Heads 166, 175
Torrisdale Street 264, 276, 277
Townhead 3, 106, 163, 171, 173, 176
Trades House 35, 88, 230
Trams 62, 76, 117, 144, 169, 185, 221, 275, 276
Tramway, The 267, 275
Tramways 62, 276
Trench, Gilbert Mackenzie 118, 176
Trinity College 100, 108, 109, 127, 157, 270
Trongate 24, 29, 30, 31, 69, 87, 88, 90, 163, 165, 275

Turnbull Street 208, 209, 210
Turnbull, Robert 262, 271, 274
Turnbull, William 210
Union Street 78, 81, 82, 83
University Avenue 133, 134, 135, 139, 140
University Gardens 135, 139, 140
University of Glasgow 32, 48, 100, 101, 103, 106, 108, 109, 111, 113, 114, 115, 118, 122, 126, 127, 130, 132, 133, 134, 135, 139, 140, 141, 142, 143, 144, 145, 163, 168, 169, 170, 171, 194, 207, 266
University of Strathclyde 31, 171, 194
upper Clyde 100, 101, 179, 230, 238
Victoria Road 255, 263, 264, 265
Victoria Royal Infirmary 258
Vital Spark, The 79, 114, 150
Wallace, William 170, 179
Washington Street 72, 74, 75, 97, 98
Washington Street School 74, 75, 97
Waterloo Street 14, 64, 65, 66, 74, 79
Watson, Thomas Lennox 13, 134, 136
Watt, James 11, 29, 31, 67, 73, 75, 76, 88, 96, 132, 133, 173, 196, 210, 211
Wellington Church 134, 136
Wellington Street 56, 57, 60, 62, 63, 66
West Campbell Street 57, 58, 63, 64
West George Street 13, 26, 51, 53, 54, 55, 56, 58
West Nile Street 40, 41, 53
West Regent Street 57
West Street 232, 233, 239
Whitefield Street 243, 244
Whitehill Street 189, 190
Wilson Street 28, 29, 32, 33, 34
Wilson, Charles 11, 15, 53, 108, 110, 111, 112, 126, 128, 134, 193, 201, 220
Wilson, John Bennie 257, 264, 273, 275
Wishart Street 179, 193
Woodlands Terrace 126, 127
World War I 80, 81, 124, 142, 200, 212, 240, 252, 260, 272, 275
World War II 69, 77, 97, 101, 113, 127, 152, 211, 240, 252, 260, 275
Wyllie, George 114, 252

www.ingramcontent.com/pod-product-compliance
Lightning Source LLC
Chambersburg PA
CBHW052015070526
44584CB00016B/1755